The Crosscultural, Language, and Academic Development Handbook

Related Titles of Interest

The Crosscultural, Language, and Academic Development Handbook

Lynne T. Díaz-Rico
Kathryn Z. Weed
California State University, San Bernardino

Allyn and Bacon
Boston • London • Toronto • Sydney • Tokyo • Singapore

Copyright © 1995 by Allyn & Bacon
A Simon & Schuster Company
Needham Heights, Massachusetts 02194

Library of Congress Cataloging-in-Publication Data
Díaz-Rico, Lynne T.
    The crosscultural, language, and academic development handbook /
  Lynne T. Díaz-Rico and Kathryn Z. Weed.
        p.   cm.
    Includes bibliographical references (p.   ) and indexes
    ISBN 0-205-15048-9 (pb)
    ISBN 0-205-16555-9 (c)
    1. English language--Study and teaching (Higher)--Foreign
  speakers--Handbooks, manuals, etc.   2. Multicultural education-
  -United States--Handbooks, manuals, etc.   3. Language and education-
  -United States--Handbooks, manuals, etc.   4. Education, Bilingual-
  -United States--Handbooks, manuals, etc.   I. Weed, Kathryn Z.
  II. Title.
  PE1128.A2D45   1995   94-18789
  428´0071´173--dc20   CIP

Printed in the United States of America
10 9 8 7 6 5 4 3 2   98 97 96 95

Dedication

. . . to Phillip, with deepest thanks, for his wisdom, love, and understanding, and to Eva, Daniel, and Voltaire, for their companionship and humor.

LTD-R

. . . to my husband, Steve, for his unfailing support, to my son Timothy and my daughter Diana for their patience at their mother's long working hours, and to our new Norwegian daughter, Marianne Sandnaes, a language minority student in the U.S. school system.

KZW

Contents

Preface

The presence of many linguistic and ethnic minority students in the United States has challenged educators to rethink basic assumptions about schooling. School models and methods based on the notions that students share the same cultural background, speak the same language, and have the same academic preparation are not meeting the needs of today's students.

In the past, schools were designed to educate specialists (those students who were capable of completing graduate study), professionals (those students who completed college study and obtained white-collar employment), and blue-collar workers who may or may not have graduated from high school. Those who could not succeed in school generally could find a place in society, though not always with secure employment. For the most part, those students who found professional or specialist positions in society represented a similar cultural background—that of the white middle class. Schools reflected the values and habits of this class; little wonder then, that students with this background were the most successful.

Today's students come from diverse cultural backgrounds. They, like their traditional predecessors, aspire to economic and social success and view schools as the means to accomplish their dreams. But are schools accommodating them? The cultural patterns of schools and classrooms may not ensure that all students have equal opportunity to succeed. Culture is a part of the educational process that has been invisible but can no longer remain so. Through an understanding of the influence of culture, educators can avoid inadvertently allowing those students who share the dominant culture to be at an advantage over those students whose cultures differ from the mainstream. Culture includes more than the habits and beliefs of students and teachers; the school itself is a culture in which the physical environment, daily routines, and interactions advantage some and alienate others. Educators now need a foundation of cultural awareness in order to adapt schools to the needs of multicultural students.

Similarly, schools in the United States were generally designed to educate students whose native language was English. Students whose home language was other than English were expected to succeed without special language assistance. This sink-or-swim approach functioned in a simple manner: Those with the ability to understand English "swam," and those who could not "sank." Luckily, those with poor English skills could often find adequate employment without advanced schooling. In today's complex society, however, those without schooling often are offered employment barely at minimum wage, and jobs at the high end of the technological scale are well beyond their grasp.

In the sink-or-swim approach, there was general naïveté about the role of language in learning and a lack of understanding about language acquisition processes. The principal belief in the approach was that exposure to English was the means to learning it. More was better (the more exposure to the English language, the more rapid students' advancement). If schools recognized a need for English language instruction, such instruction took on a compensatory air. Students without English language skills were deemed deficient and remediation was prescribed. English as a second-language was considered a remedial curriculum—one that often emphasized grammatical accuracy, correct spelling, and flawless pronunciation. However, many language minority students did not find success in public school despite many years of instruction in English.

Language acquisition research findings now stress the importance of language in providing a cognitive foundation for instruction—a foundation that must be properly laid. Language and academic development are better approached through a respect for, and incorporation of, a student's primary language. Moreover, an emphasis on grammar, spelling, and accurate pronunciation is secondary to the primary purpose of language instruction: to teach students to communicate and to function in society. To help students attain their goals, educators now need a foundation of language acquisition and development principles and knowledge of language development methodology in order to adapt instruction to the needs of multilingual students.

One exciting advance in teaching methodology in classes with English learners is the increased use of Specially Designed Academic Instruction in English (SDAIE). Rather than relying heavily on lectures to transmit information, teachers are using cooperative learning, audiovisual media, multicultural sources, various grouping strategies within and across grades, and other instructional techniques that help motivate students to learn English as they learn academic content. Although schools with large numbers of immigrants from specific language groups are able to schedule classes in academic subjects using the students' home language, schools with a linguistically diverse student body can offer special "sheltered" sections of academic subjects in which English skills and academic content are developed simultaneously. Teachers who use SDAIE techniques find that mainstream students benefit as well.

The *Handbook* brings together theories and resources in promoting crosscultural awareness, language development, and academic progress. Part I offers insights from classic and contemporary research in language acquisition and development (Chapter 1), particularly in the context of the classroom. A focus on psychological factors in language learning encourages the recognition that language learners are individuals; attention to sociocultural factors extends this understanding to acknowledge that individuals sharing similar cultural patterns may learn in similar ways (Chapter 2). Chapter 3 introduces language structure and functions.

Part II examines English language development (ELD) methods (Chapter 4) and models of schooling for language instruction and academic development (Chapters 5 and 6). The key role of assessment in determining academic progress is discussed in the context of curriculum design (Chapter 7).

Part III contains a broad look at culture, exploring how culture influences every aspect of life, including schooling (Chapter 8), and offering a historical background on cultural diversity and its treatment in the United States (Chapter 9). Specific insights for classroom teachers on the use and understanding of culture are available in Chapter 10.

Language policies and specific program models constitute Part IV. Rather than summarizing the policy big picture—at the national or state level—Chapter 11 begins with the role of the classroom teacher in daily policymaking and proceeds from that level to a more comprehensive overview. To encourage educators to think creatively about policies and programs, Chapter 12 contains specific models and issues for elementary and secondary schools.

Care has been taken to use acceptable terminology to denote various racial and ethnic groups. The terms *Hispanic* and *Hispanic-American* denote those whose ancestors originated in Spain or Spanish America. Although some dislike this term, it is probably preferable to any alternative (Hernandez, 1993). *European-American* is used in preference to *White* or *Anglo* to denote those whose ancestral background is European. *African-American* is similarly used to refer to those whose ancestors came from Africa. Other ethnic group labels follow a similar logic. In some cases, data are cited that classify groups according to other labels; in these cases, the labels used in the citation are preserved.

Burgeoning information in the areas of culture and linguistic/academic development has made this *Handbook* a difficult, yet useful synthesis. The result, we believe, is a readable text that brings into focus the challenges and possibilities in educating new Americans. We hope this *Handbook* will be beneficial in the process of teacher preparation and school restructuring. Principles and practices that promote crosscultural understanding are relevant for all. Knowledge about second language acquisition helps not only those working with English learners but also anyone in the teaching field.

Studying language acquisition involves processes and principles that are appropriate across the curriculum. Principles of specially designed academic instruction are, in reality, principles that constitute good teaching.

No handbook about teaching is ever vital enough to reflect the actual experience of the classroom, replete with challenges and triumphs for teachers as well as students. The reward for educators in the skillful use of this *Handbook* will be the success of students, and students' success is the ultimate measure of the worth of this work.

Acknowledgments

A book like this could not have been written without the help and support of numerous individuals. The teachers and students with whom we have worked have given us insights and examples. Our colleagues have shared their experiences and expertise. We would particularly like to thank Dr. Billie Blair, chair of the Department of Elementary and Bilingual Education at California State University, San Bernardino (CSUSB), for her leadership in planning the program for the California Multiple Subject credential with a (Bilingual) Crosscultural, Language, and Academic Development emphasis. Thanks also go to Dr. Jean Ramage, dean of the School of Education, CSUSB. We are grateful also to those who provided helpful reviews of the manuscript: Rosalie Giacchino-Baker, who slaved over early chapters; Nancy Pine, who read an initial draft of the entire document and who made encouraging and insightful comments; and Marilyn Joshua-Shearer at the Claremont Graduate School, Patricia Richard-Amato at California State University, Los Angeles, and Patricia Shoemaker at Radford University, who read the subsequent draft and whose collective suggestions added substantially to the depth and flow of the book. Thank you all for your comments.

We owe a debt of gratitude to both Monica Ford and Rosalie Giacchino-Baker for their contributions in the final chapter of this book. Finally, we thank the editors at Allyn and Bacon for their efforts in producing this *Handbook*.

About the Authors

Lynne T. Díaz-Rico is associate professor of education, California State University, San Bernardino (CSUSB). She joined the faculty of the Department of Elementary and Bilingual Education in 1989 after three years as a fellow in cognitive psychology at Duke University. Dr. Díaz-Rico obtained the doctoral degree in English as a Second Language at InterAmerican University in Puerto Rico. At CSUSB, Dr. Díaz-Rico is coordinator of the M.A. in Education, English as a Second Language Option program. Dr. Díaz-Rico has published numerous articles on computer-based instruction in ESL, innovative teaching techniques, and cultural diversity.

Kathryn Z. Weed received her Ph.D. from Claremont Graduate School in 1992 and is currently assistant professor of Education at California State University, San Bernardino. Her areas of emphasis include discourse analysis, language acquisition theories, and literacy education. The bulk of Dr. Weed's fifteen years of classroom experience was in teaching English as a Second Language (ESL) to children and adults. She currently teaches methods courses to preservice and early service teachers and works with ESL master's students. She is active in developing innovative language development and teacher education programs in elementary schools. Her research explores the role of language in the classroom.

Introduction

The urgent need to provide a high-quality education for students in the United States whose native language is not English calls for increased expertise on the part of classroom teachers, administrators, and community leaders. Much has been written that serves as general and specific information about the effect of culture on schooling, second language acquisition, and ways to help these "language minority" students to achieve access to the core curriculum. In order to synthesize this wealth of information, a means of organizing this knowledge is needed. The central elements that tie together culture, language, and academic achievement in the context of education are the learning that takes place, the instruction that promotes learning, and the policies that govern schooling. Figure I-1 combines these elements to illustrate their influence and interdependence on one another.

In the figure, *learning* occupies the central area. Learning is subdivided into *domains* and *factors*. The three domains are culture, language, and academic content. The factors are the language acquisition processes, psychological and sociolinguistic influences, and the structure of the language being learned. Within the cultural context, all learning is affected by instruction and policies. Understanding the nature and interdependence of the domains and factors helps teachers to meet the needs of individual learners. Learning is discussed in Chapters 1, 2, and 3.

Instruction is the second major area that organizes knowledge about teaching language minority students. This term refers to both the *curriculum* and the *methods* employed in classrooms. Curricular content is determined at various levels (state, district, school, classroom) and is interpreted differently by teachers and students (the "taught" curriculum, the "received" curriculum). This book provides examples of curricular content in the context of second language acquisition but does not attempt an exhaustive presentation. Methods are the manner in which curriculum is taught. Current understanding about language acquisition has revolutionized traditional

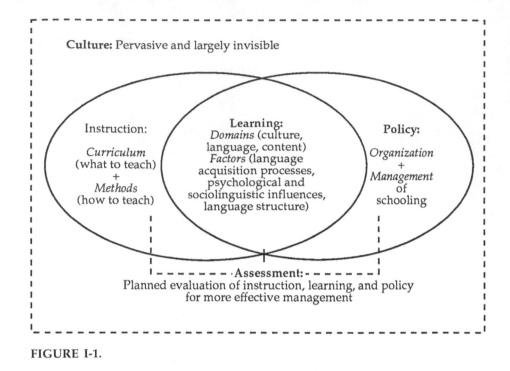

Culture: Pervasive and largely invisible

Instruction:

Curriculum
(what to teach)
+
Methods
(how to teach)

Learning:
Domains (culture,
language, content)
Factors (language
acquisition processes,
psychological and
sociolinguistic influences,
language structure)

Policy:

Organization
+
Management
of
schooling

Assessment:
Planned evaluation of instruction, learning, and policy
for more effective management

FIGURE I-1.

language methodology. Methods for English language learners fall into three
categories: English language instruction, specially designed academic instruction (also known as sheltered instruction), and primary language instruction within bilingual education models. Instruction is discussed in
Chapters 4, 5, and 6.

Assessment practices are influenced by instruction and policymaking,
and assessment, in turn, affects learning. Assessment of students is the way
to determine if curricular content is appropriate and teaching methods are
successful. Through assessment, one can ascertain what learning has taken
place. The placement of students as a function of assessment influences the
organization and management of schooling; thus, assessment involves not
only issues of instruction and learning but policy as well. Assessment will
be discussed in Chapter 7.

The third area, *policy*, denotes the *organization* and *management* of schooling, elements that affect the operation of schools. Policy can be top down,
driven by national or state agendas. Conversely, policy can be bottom up, as
an outgrowth of teachers' daily plans. Because the policies affecting schooling can be better understood with a background on the influence and importance of culture, policy for English language learners is discussed in
Chapter 11 which follows the chapters on culture.

Culture permeates the activities of learning, instruction, and policymaking. Fundamental insights into the nature of culture, cultural influence on schools, and a brief history of cultural and immigration policies in the United States are offered in Chapters 8 and 9. Chapter 10 provides the means for learning about cultures and culturally appropriate pedagogy.

A description of an exemplary program for language minority students and a case study describing issues about policy put into perspective the various components described in Figure I-1 and discussed throughout the book. Chapter 12 provides actual examples and issues of teaching with language minority students.

Teachers can be resources within their schools and districts on matters pertaining to English language and academic development for their multicultural and multilinguistic students. A framework that organizes crosscultural, language, and academic development in terms of learning, instruction, and policy contributes to teachers' ability to describe, communicate, and teach others about this field.

Chapter *1*

Second Language Acquisition and Learning: Theory and Practice

Without communication the world would be so dark. Life would be boring. It is through language that we find a way into people's hearts, their lives, and their culture. Through language we explore into the secrets of other cultures.

I was born in Afghanistan. . . . I came to the United States when I was sixteen years old. This was my new home and yet, because I could not speak any English, I was a stranger to my new home. How I wished to express my gratitude to people who helped my family and me, but all I could do was to give them an empty look and a confused smile. I was living among the people and yet I was not one of them. I thought everybody was cold and unfriendly. Sometimes I got angry and wanted to scream at the whole world.

Slowly the ice broke. I started learning English. New windows started opening. The once cold and unfriendly became warm and caring. My family and I found a way into the hearts of the people. Ahmad Shukoor, grade 12. (Shukoor, 1991, p. 34)

Language is largely responsible for the human ability to form a society. Schools, as an institution within a society, perform an important role in socializing students and helping them gain the knowledge and skills they need for success. Schools help students to acquire the roles and identities within the larger culture and to maintain social relationships. In the majority of schools of the United States, the English language is the dominant vehicle for expression. Students who enter school must develop a high level of English proficiency, and teachers are challenged to develop English skills during the K–12 period of schooling. With the influx of large numbers of students who speak languages other than English, schools are seeking teachers who not only can help students develop literacy, but also can teach the fundamentals of speaking and listening to those students.

The challenge is obvious, the prospect exciting. Teachers have the opportunity to guide and inspire language minority students in new ways; to learn about their students, their lives and cultures, their dreams and expectations; to expand their own teaching repertoire. By knowing about language acquisition and use, teachers (particularly those who are monolingual) can come to recognize and use communication strategies that help break down barriers. Collaboration and cooperation with students, parents, and community members enrich the lives of all. Classrooms become lively and productive places.

The purpose of this book is to help the language development teacher with tools and insights to guide successful language and content learning in their students. But a caution is necessary: Schools are not perfect. They are institutions within a society and, as such, have rules and practices that perpetuate attitudes and beliefs of the larger society. In effect, schools function as filters or gates; some students advance more rapidly than others. In the case of language minority students, those who demonstrate appropriate use of English grammar are judged as more competent, more intelligent, and as potential "winners" in U.S. society. Language is such an important criterion of social judgment in U.S. society that teachers cannot help but be influenced by the tendency to equate language success with academic potential. Teachers are caught up in the societal and school norms that reward and punish, and they are given the role of gatekeeper for academic success in U.S. schools. Try as they might, teachers cannot create success for students if they unwittingly promulgate society's use of schools to differentiate winners from losers.

On the other hand, teachers who have the requisite linguistic, cultural, and pedagogical knowledge and who understand that the school has as much a role in student achievement as do the students themselves can create climates of acceptance and worth. Such teachers are instrumental in students' success. In order for English language development teachers to guide the learning of their language minority students, a knowledge of some general factors about language acquisition is necessary (see Figure I-1). This chapter presents an overview of historical and contemporary theories of teaching and learning that will help the teacher place issues of English language development within an orienting framework.

HISTORICAL THEORIES OF LANGUAGE DEVELOPMENT

Humans have been describing and analyzing language for over 2300 years. As early as the fourth century B.C., Greek philosophers were debating the nature of language. Early theory held that words were the natural and logical representations of ideas and objects, rather than arbitrarily chosen symbols. The early Greeks identified two classes of words, one that identified the action performed in a sentence, and the second, the person or thing that performs the action. In about the second century B.C., Dionysius Thrax identified eight different word classes. His book, *The Art of Grammar*, became a model for both Greek and Latin grammars. Latin was the model for grammar throughout the Middle Ages. When grammarians finally began writing grammars for vernacular languages, they generally copied the Latin grammars, using the same terminology and the same word classes (Kitzhaber et al., 1970).

Prescriptive Grammar

Using Latin grammar as a model, English grammarians not only ignored the syntactic differences between Latin and English but also tried to force English to fit the Latin description. Moreover, in copying from the Latin, they limited themselves to using classical grammar to prescribe how language should be used. No effort was made to describe the nature of language or how people use it (Kitzhaber et al., 1970).

This approach to language led to the grammar-translation method of instruction, in which learners memorized long lists of vocabulary words, verb forms, and noun declensions. The chief activity in class was to translate written texts. Teachers were not expected to speak the language, merely to have a thorough knowledge of grammatical rules.

Descriptive Linguistics

In the eighteenth and nineteenth centuries, scholars began to notice similarities that existed among some ancient languages. Studying written documents of earlier forms of languages, they traced back the origin of words and sounds and attempted to show particular changes languages had undergone over time and the historical relationships among various languages. These linguists analyzed the sound units of a language, showed how these units were organized, and described the structure of sentences. The descriptive linguists developed a method for identifying the speech sounds of languages, for analyzing words into morphemes, and for analyzing the forms of sentences. They did not concern themselves with describing the meaning of sentences or how sentences relate to each other.

Diagramming sentences became an important pedagogical tool based on the language descriptions. Teachers began the analysis of sentences by dividing sentences into two parts, or constituents, each of which could be further subdivided, until the entire sentence had been analyzed. Knowledge of the structure of one language was believed to transfer to a second language. Furthermore, it was believed that a thorough understanding of the phonetic basis of the first language could help to contrast the phonemic constituents of the target language. Knowing about the structure of the first and second language was an important part of the teacher's role, so that the second language could be explained in terms of the first.

Behaviorist Theory

Although behaviorism is not strictly a linguistic theory, its vast influence on learning theory has affected second language teaching. Behaviorists claim that the mind is a "blank slate"; a learner must be filled with content during the course of teaching. Strict principles of timing, repetition, and reward led to classroom methodology that incorporated extensive drill and practice of language components—from sounds to complex sentences.

The audiolingual method of language learning is based on behavioral principles. Oral language practice is believed to be the primary means to language learning. Teachers provide constant oral pattern drills that are based on specific grammatical forms; for example, a complete lesson can be centered around the tag question (It's cold today, *isn't it?*). Meaning is not specifically addressed, only the appropriate form.

CURRENT THEORIES OF LANGUAGE DEVELOPMENT

The prevailing belief that language is learned through constant verbal input shaped by reinforcement was promulgated in B.F. Skinner's book *Verbal Behavior* (1957). Noam Chomsky (1959) wrote an incisive review of this book, asserting that if language were learned solely by reinforcement, native speakers would find it impossible to understand sentences that they had never before heard. Chomsky asserted that language is not learned solely through a process of memorizing and repeating, but that the mind contains an active language processor, the language acquisition device (LAD), that generates rules through the unconscious acquisition of grammar. Hymes (1961) directed attention away from the purely descriptive linguistic approach or structural analysis of language towards the idea of communicative competence: that the *use* of language in the social setting is important in language performance. Halliday (1975) elaborated on the role of social relations in language by stating that the social structure is an essential element in linguistic interaction. Current theories of language have thus moved away from the merely linguistic components of a language to the more inclusive realm of language in use—which includes its social, political, and psychological domains.

Three major ideas are shaping language teaching today. First, the shift toward a cognitive paradigm means that learning has taken precedence over teaching. What the student learns is the important outcome of the teaching/ learning process, not what the teacher does. Second, teaching/learning is maximized when it is compatible with the processes that take place naturally within the brain. Brain-compatible methods of language instruction have been an important outcome of the cognitive revolution. Third, integration of knowledge is an important contemporary theme uniting teaching objectives across content areas (thematic integration), and unifying reading, writing, speaking, listening, thinking, and acting is an overarching principle in today's thinking about language learning. These changes in thinking about language learning began in the late 1950s with the birth of the cognitive perspective and information-processing theories of learning. Chomsky's work on transformational grammar was an important impetus.

Transformational Grammar

Transformational grammarians, following Chomsky's lead, assume that language consists of a set of rules that human beings unconsciously know and use. They believe that human beings have an innate ability to understand and produce sentences they have never before heard because the mind has the capacity to internalize and construct these rules. According to this view, human beings do not need prior experience with a particular sentence in order to produce or understand it. The rules help native speakers to distinguish whether or not a group of words forms a sentence in their language. The goal of transformational grammar is to understand and describe these internalized rules.

In the early 1970s, some grammar texts created for the use of classroom teachers included the use of transformational grammar to explain language structures. Much research has been published about children's acquisition of language using the transformational paradigm. Although this paradigm never became a second language teaching methodology per se, much of Krashen's Monitor model can be traced to Chomsky's influence.

Krashen's Monitor Model

Krashen (1981b, 1982) has proposed a theory of second language acquisition that provides a framework for understanding the processes by which adults learn second languages. Krashen's theory includes five hypotheses: the *acquisition-learning hypothesis,* which distinguishes acquisition (which leads to fluency) from learning (which involves knowledge of language rules); the *natural order hypothesis,* which asserts that language rules are acquired in a predictable order; the *Monitor hypothesis,* which postulates a device for attaining accuracy;

the *input hypothesis*, which claims that languages are acquired in only one way—by comprehending messages; and the *affective filter hypothesis*, which describes the mental and emotional blocks that can prevent language acquirers from fully comprehending input. Although the Monitor model has been extensively criticized, it has nonetheless provided the theoretical base for the Natural Approach, which has had an extensive impact in changing the nature of second language instruction in the United States.

The acquisition-learning hypothesis. This hypothesis defines *acquisition* and *learning* as two separate processes in the mastering of a second language. *Learning* is "knowing about" a language. It is the formal knowledge one has of a second language. Formal teaching promotes learning by providing the learner with explicit knowledge about the rules of a language. *Acquisition,* on the other hand, is an unconscious process that occurs when language is used for real communication. Formal teaching of grammatical rules is not a part of acquisition (Krashen, 1981b, 1982, 1985). Acquirers gain a "feel" for the correctness of their own utterances but cannot state any specific rules as to why such utterances are "correct."

Krashen distinguishes the role each process plays, but considers acquisition more important. He turns to child language acquisition studies to strengthen his point. "Research in child language acquisition suggests quite strongly that teaching [the rules of a language] . . . does not facilitate acquisition. Error correction in particular does not seem to help" (Krashen & Terrell, 1983, p. 27).

Other researchers have criticized Krashen for insisting on the distinction between acquisition and learning. Af Trampe (1994) finds unrealistic Krashen's claim that acquisition and learning represent two totally separate mechanisms; the distinction is vague and difficult to prove. Moreover, Ellis (1986) notes that the distinction between learning and acquisition cannot be tested. McLaughlin (1990) finds that the conscious versus-unconscious distinction is misleading. The acquisition-versus-learning hypothesis is based on the assumption that the processes of first and second language acquisition are the same, a point that Dunlop (1994) does not accept and one that has certainly not been proved. In addition, it is not clear that dividing learning into formal and informal processes leads to useful teaching strategies. Shannon (1994) comments that many language teachers view learning and acquisition as interconnected and impossible to distinguish.

Despite these criticisms, Krashen has drawn attention to the importance of natural processes in learning language. Children learn more language when they chat with one another as they stroke the classroom pet rabbit or recreate meiosis with modeling clay than by sitting and discussing the appropriate use of an apostrophe.

The natural order hypothesis. This hypothesis draws on studies done in first and second language acquisition of children. According to this hypothesis, certain rules of the language tend to be acquired before others. Following first language acquisition work done by Brown (1973), second language researchers have discovered that there appears to be a natural order of acquisition of English morphemes for child second language learners also. The order is slightly different from the first language order, but there are similarities. This natural order is best acquired in normal conversational situations, not by means of direct grammar instruction. Within this natural acquisition order, there is a process that learners go through to achieve full control of a structure. Thus a listener, and specifically a teacher, cannot expect perfect formation of a grammatical structure even after intensive drilling.

Here is an example of the developmental sequence for the structure of negation:

1. negative marker outside the sentence
   No Mom sharpen it.   (child L1 acquisition)
   Not like it now   (child L2 acquisition)
2. negative marker between the subject and verb
   I no like this one.   (L2 acquisition)
   This no have calendar   (L2 acquisition)
3. negative marker in correct position
   I don't like this one. (Krashen, 1982)

This example demonstrates that children acquire correct usage of grammatical structures in their first language gradually, and so do children acquiring a second language.

McLaughlin (1987) argues that there is insufficient evidence for the natural order hypothesis; longitudinal studies indicate that there is much variability in learners' acquisition. Ellis (1994) discusses the variability that learners display across various linguistic and situational contexts, which casts doubt on the hypothesis that structures are acquired in a predictable order.

The Monitor hypothesis. This hypothesis states explicitly the relationship between acquisition and learning. These two processes are used in very specific ways: Acquisition initiates an utterance and is responsible for fluency; learning serves to develop a Monitor, an editor (Krashen, 1981b, 1982). The Monitor is an error-detecting mechanism; it scans utterances for accuracy in order to make corrections. An individual initiates an utterance and that individual's Monitor edits—that is, confirms or repairs—the utterance either prior to or after attempted communication. However, the Monitor cannot always be used. In a situation involving rapid verbal exchange, an individual may have little time to be concerned with grammatical correctness.

By positing the Monitor construct, Krashen has changed the orientation that previously drove language instruction. The notion that language learning, conscious knowledge of rules, leads to language acquisition has been replaced by the realization that a "natural" language-rich environment facilitates acquisition. The Monitor hypothesis, however, is not without flaws. The Monitor is impossible to observe or distinguish during its use (Shannon, 1994). Krashen's claim that children are more successful language learners because they are not burdened by the Monitor is disputed by McLaughlin (1987), who argues that adolescents are more successful learners than are children. Thus, the usefulness of the Monitor as a construct is disputed.

The input hypothesis. The input hypothesis claims that language is acquired in an "amazingly simple way—when we understand messages" (Krashen, 1985, p. vii). Language is acquired, not by focusing on form, but by understanding messages that contain new structures, messages that are a little beyond the acquirer's current level of competence (1981a, 1981b, 1982). As a listener seeks to understand communication, the proper kind of input is crucial for developing understanding. Simply immersing a learner in a second language is not sufficient. Competence increases by listening to what Krashen calls "comprehensible" input.

What makes speech comprehensible? Comprehensible input has generally been assumed to contain elements characteristic of "caretaker" speech, the speech directed to young children by their primary caregivers. This caretaker speech (which includes shorter sentences; more intelligible, well-formed utterances; less subordination, and more restricted vocabulary and range of topics) focuses on communication. It is not meant to teach language. Topics often center about the here and now. Simpler structures roughly tuned to the child's ability are used, and speech is slower.

However, caretaker speech is not a universal phenomenon. Other languages and cultures use context, world knowledge, and extralinguistic information to help in comprehensibility. The African-American children studied by Heath (1983b) received a large amount of exposure to language. The Samoan children in Ochs's study (1982) heard conversations that focused on the immediate past (accusations), the immediate present, and an immediate future (directives). Guatemalan children studied by Harkness (1971) benefited by a variety of input sources. Thus, simplified language may not be the central criterion in making language comprehensible; rather, the focus on the message and its relevance for the language learner within the environment appear to be more critical.

Krashen has introduced an expression to conceptualize the input hypothesis. This expression is $i + 1$, where i stands for the current level of the acquirer's competence and 1 is the next structure due to be acquired in the natural order. Input needs to contain structures at the $i + 1$ level in order for the acquirer to proceed. However, research in first and second language acquisition, including that of caretaker speech, indicates that such speech is not what Krashen calls "finely tuned"—that is, including only structures at the $i + 1$ level. Critics have pointed out that there is in fact no way of measuring what is the $i + 1$ level. Therefore, it is impossible to tell what "comprehensible input" really means. As Marton (1994) points out, Krashen's emphasis on comprehensible input ignores the active role of the learner in communicating and negotiating useful and understandable language. The role of the teacher is to provide opportunities for students to interact and communicate.

The affective filter hypothesis. This hypothesis relates to emotional variables, including anxiety, motivation, and self-confidence. These are crucial because they can block input from reaching the language acquisition device (LAD). If the affective filter blocks some of the comprehensible input, less input enters the learner's LAD. A positive affective context increases the input. These emotional variables are discussed in Chapter 2. Like others of Krashen's hypotheses, the affective filter is virtually impossible to define operationally. Larsen-Freeman and Long (1991) contend that the affective filter is useful only as a metaphor. Most teachers understand that a non-threatening and encouraging environment promotes learning. There is probably no specific agreement on what constitutes an environment that various students find encouraging, nor is a teacher able to measure or raise or lower an affective filter for individual students. Certainly one would like to believe that English language development (ELD) is a positive experience for all students.

Teaching practices consistent with the Monitor model. A brief summary of Krashen's theory is that people acquire second language structures in a predictable order only if they obtain comprehensible input, and if their affective filters are low enough to allow input into the system. A Monitor edits language usage. Each of Krashen's hypotheses can be incorporated into teaching practices.

• *Acquisition versus learning:* The most important facet of acquisition is that language is used to communicate. Conveying meaning is more important than drill and practice. An important part of acquisition is that children be given time to internalize language before they are expected to respond. Partial comprehension and incomplete utterances are acceptable.

• *Natural Order:* Teachers need to recognize that the mind does not assemble from simple sentences to more complex sentences in any structured way. Rather, language learners seem to find order by seeking patterns from the input they see and hear. Therefore, the curriculum need not be organized around grammatical structures. Language generated in inquiry and problem-solving situations will naturally contain structures from which students can acquire rules.

• *Monitor:* Additional mediation can be provided for students in the form of specific suggestions or explicit grammatical hints. On the whole, however, rich input is the appropriate means by which students develop and internalize a sense of structural and communicative models. Students will monitor themselves. The teacher's explicit correction rarely changes students' writing or speaking behavior.

• *Comprehensible input:* Simplified language, such as caretaker speech, probably works better with some students than others. Factors such as the learners' needs, age, socioeconomic status, gender, and first language characteristics need to be considered (Larsen-Freeman, 1985). Teachers can provide comprehensible input in a number of ways: by making instruction relevant and meaningful; by using shorter and less complex sentences with a subject-verb-object word order, fewer contractions and pronouns, frequent comprehension checks, and variety in intonation, volume, and pitch. The teacher can structure cooperative learning activities to ensure that students acquire comprehensible input from their peers.

• *The affective filter:* Teachers can lower the "affective filter" by fostering a spirit of mutual respect, high expectations, and cooperative learning. Moskowitz's (1978) *Caring and Sharing in the Foreign Language Classroom* offers techniques designed to relax students, increase the enjoyment of learning, raise self-esteem, and blend self-awareness with an increase in proficiency in the target language.

The following interaction demonstrates how a teacher is able to accept a student's responses and stretch his resources to produce more complex utterances. The teacher gives feedback by expanding utterances and supplying missing pieces, and also by rewarding successful communication.

Teacher: I want you to tell me what is happening in this picture.

José: (pause) Ta—Taking . . . trees.

Teacher: That's right. They are cutting down the trees. Why are they cutting down the rain forest?

José: Cutting down trees . . . forest . . . for farmers.

Teacher: Yes. They use the land for farming. How does this affect the environment?

José: (pause) People need land for farm . . . for food. And people need trees for air.

Teacher: Why yes! Very good.

Communicative Competence

Since Hymes (1972) introduced the term "communicative competence," the teaching of languages has taken a new direction. Communicative competence is the aspect of language users' competence that enables them to "convey and interpret messages and to negotiate meanings interpersonally within specific contexts" (Brown, 1987). Language is a form of communication that occurs in social interaction. It is used for a purpose, such as persuading, commanding, and establishing social relationships. No longer is the focus on specific knowledge of grammatical forms. Instead, the competent speaker is recognized as one who knows when, where, and how to use language appropriately.

Canale (1983) identifies four components of communicative competence: grammatical competence, sociolinguistic competence, discourse competence, and strategic competence.

Grammatical competence. This component involves knowing the language code: vocabulary, word formation and meaning, sentence formation, pronunciation, and spelling. This type of competence focuses on the skills and knowledge necessary to speak and write accurately.

Sociolinguistic competence. This involves knowing how to produce and understand language in different sociolinguistic contexts, taking into consideration such factors as the status of participants, the purposes of the interaction, and the norms or conventions of interaction. The appropriateness of an utterance refers to both meaning and form. One of the tasks of kindergarten and first-grade teachers is to help children use both appropriate forms and appropriate meanings when interacting in the classroom. Unfortunately, in language classrooms, emphasis has been placed on grammatical competence over sociolinguistic competence. This emphasis gives the mistaken impression that grammatical correctness is more important than sociolinguistic competence.

Discourse competence. This involves the ability to combine and connect utterances (spoken) and sentences (written) into a meaningful whole. Discourse ranges from a simple spoken conversation to long written texts. An example of discourse competence can be seen in the following conversation between two kindergarten boys, one a native-English speaker and the other an English-as-a-second-language speaker.

Andrew: Can I play?

Rolando: No.

Andrew: There're only three people here.

Rolando: Kevin went to the bathroom.

Andrew: Can I take his place 'til he comes back?

Rolando: You're not playing.

Rolando was able to respond appropriately (though not kindly) to Andrew's request and to add information about his decision at the proper moment This conversation shows that Rolando has discourse competence. We have all experienced situations in which a speaker has spoken both grammatically correctly and at the proper time, but the utterance has left us mystified. "Where did that come from?" we ask. Such a disconnected utterance shows a lack of discourse competence.

Strategic competence. Strategic competence involves the manipulation of language in order to meet communicative goals. It involves both verbal and nonverbal behaviors. Canale (1983) notes that speakers employ this competence for two main reasons: to compensate for breakdowns in communication (as when a speaker forgets or does not know a term and is forced to paraphrase or gesture to get the idea across), and to enhance the effectiveness of communication (as when a speaker raises or lowers the voice for effect).

Building on strategies for communicative competence. Chesterfield and Chesterfield (1985) found a natural order of strategies in students' development of a second language. These incorporate sociolinguistic, discourse, and strategic factors. Teachers who are aware of this order can recognize the strategies and use them to build upon students' developing competence. These strategies, in their order of development, include the following:

- *Repetition:* Imitating a word or structure used by another
- *Memorization:* Recalling by rote songs, rhymes, or sequences
- *Formulaic expressions:* Using words or phrases that function as units, such as greetings ("Hi! How are you?")
- *Verbal attention getters:* Using language to initiate interaction ("Hey!" "I think . . .")
- *Answering in unison:* Responding with others
- *Talking to self:* Engaging in subvocal or internal monologue
- *Elaboration:* Providing information beyond that which is necessary
- *Anticipatory answers:* Responding to an anticipated question, or completing another's phrase or statement
- *Monitoring:* Correcting one's own errors in vocabulary, style, or grammar
- *Appeal for assistance:* Asking another for help
- *Request for clarification:* Asking the speaker to explain or repeat
- *Role play:* Interacting with another by taking on roles

Weed (1989) found evidence of almost all of these strategies among language minority kindergarteners. For example, the earliest strategy, repetition, occurred while three kindergarten girls were working puzzles together. Upon noticing that one of the girls had new shoes, the English speaker started chanting, "Pretty shoes, Daniella, pretty shoes." One of the Spanish-speaking girls picked up the chant and repeated "Pretty shoes." A spontaneous role-play, a later strategy, occurred in the same kindergarten class. Ms. Anderson, the teacher, had to use the phone, which was situated by the playhouse area. "Excuse me, children, I have to use the phone," she said. Jimmy, a Vietnamese speaker, picked up the play phone and watched the teacher's actions. After a pause, he said, "Hello, hello, anybody home?" He then left, but another boy picked up the phone and called, "Jimmy, it's your mom."

"Where, where," called Jimmy as he ran to the phone. "Hi, mom," he said as he spoke into the instrument.

Teachers can specifically plan to increase students' skills in discourse, sociolinguistic, and strategic competence by building experiences into the curriculum that involve students in solving problems, exploring areas of interest, and designing projects. Students carry over knowledge of how to communicate from experiences in their first language. This knowledge can be tapped as they develop specific forms and usage in English.

In the high school economics class, Mr. Godfried often demonstrated consumer economics to the students by having them role-play. In the fifth-period class, several students were recent immigrants who had been placed in this class as a graduation requirement despite their limited English. Mr. Godfried's job became more complicated than in the past; he had to teach not only economics, but also basic communication skills in English. The process of opening a checking account was not difficult for Takeo, a Japanese student, who had had a checking account as a student in Japan. But Vasalli, an immigrant from Byelorussia, found the task mystifying. He had had limited experience with consumerism in general and no experience with the concept of a checking account. What he did have, however, was a general knowledge of how to interact with an official. Through the role-plays, Mr. Godfried was able to help the students use their background knowledge to conduct appropriate verbal interactions in the banking situation and use their communication experience to expand their content knowledge.

The Social Context for Language Learning

Examining the social contexts in which learning takes place expands language teaching and learning from a strictly communicative endeavor to one that includes the analysis of social and cultural interaction. The Russian psychologist Lev Vygotsky emphasized the role played by social interaction in the development of language and thought. According to Vygotsky (1978), teaching must be matched in some manner with the student's developmental level, taking into consideration the student's "zone of proximal development." Vygotsky defines this zone as "the distance between the actual developmental level as determined by independent problem solving and the level of potential development . . . under adult guidance or in collaboration with more capable peers" (p. 86).

Second language learners profit most from language that is slightly more complex than they can themselves easily understand. In this way they are challenged to acquire more complex vocabulary and structures. Using peer conversation as a means for enriching a student's exposure to language maximizes the opportunity for a student to hear and enjoy English; mixing more skilled with less skilled speakers supplies more advanced language models to English learners. Thus, the context of instruction plays as critical a role as the actual language exchanged.

The teacher who is aware of the social uses of language provides a classroom environment where students engage in communicative tasks. These can include practicing a Reader's Theater with older students in order to perform for their class or school; writing letters to pen pals, editors, authors, city officials, or even the president of the United States; and talking with the principal concerning rules and procedures.

Discourse Theory

Discourse theorists (Brown & Yule, 1983; Fox, 1987; Hatch, 1992) have expanded the analysis of communicative competence to understand how conversation is used to negotiate meaning. According to discourse theorists, face-to-face interaction is a key to second language acquisition. By holding conversations (discourse), nonnative speakers acquire commonly occurring formulas and grammar as they attend to the various features in the input they obtain. Through their own speech, their *output*, they also affect both the quantity and the quality of the language they receive. The more learners talk, the more other people will talk to them. The more they converse, the more opportunity they have to initiate and expand topics, signal comprehension breakdowns, and try out new formulas and expressions.

In constructing discourse, second language learners use four kinds of knowledge: knowledge about the second language, competence in their native language, ability to use the functions of language, and their general world knowledge. The language they produce is an *interlanguage*, an intermediate system that learners create as they attempt to achieve native-like competence. Selinker's interlanguage hypothesis (1972, 1991) asserts that "non-native speaking students do not learn to produce second languages; what they do is to create and develop interlanguages in particular contexts" (1991, p. 23). Through a variety of discourse opportunities, learners sort out the ways language is used and gradually achieve proficiency.

Teachers need to provide many opportunities for nonnative speakers of English to interact with native speakers in a variety of situations. ESL program models that confine English learners to certain tracks or special classrooms, without incorporating specific opportunities for native/nonnative speaker interaction, do a disservice to English learners. *Bridge to Communication,* an ESL program published by Santillana (1992), encourages native/nonnative speaker interaction by asking students to interview others briefly on topics such as "My favorite sport" (Middle Level B, p. 7) and "Most popular tool" (Middle Level B, p. 21). The responses from the interviews are tallied and form the basis for subsequent class discussion in conjunction with a thematic unit. Teachers can also incorporate opportunities for nonnative English speaking students to interact with native English speakers during school hours through cross-age or peer interactions.

Contributions of Whole Language

Whole language is a theory embedded in practice that supports specific views of learning, language, and language learning. Whole language advocates support the view of language as espoused by Halliday—that language is a complex system for creating meanings through socially shared conventions (Halliday, 1978). Three characteristics of language are integral to instruction based on whole language principles: that language is social, that it is made up of interdependent and inseparable subsystems, and that it is predictable. Language is *social* in that it occurs in social contexts, in which a community of users attaches meaning to their experiences (Edelsky, Altwerger, & Flores, 1991). It is *interdependent* and *inseparable* because learners do not learn one subsystem (phonological, syntactic, semantic, pragmatic) at a time but develop them all simultaneously and use them all as they use language. Language is *predictable* in that there is an organizing structure of each subsystem and for the language system as a whole.

Whole language advocates view the learning of language as the process that occurs when language is used for specific purposes. Language is learned not from drills and worksheets but, rather, from the active process of seeking meaning. It is best achieved through direct engagement and experience when the learners' purposes and intentions are central. Whole language has provided the impetus for approaches that encourage language development and literacy across a wide variety of academic contexts. For further discussion of the whole language theory, see *Whole Language: What's the Difference* (Edelsky et al., 1991), *What's Whole in Whole Language?* (Goodman, 1986), and *Whole Language Theory in Use* (Newman, 1985).

A related part of the whole language philosophy as well as of cognitive theory is schema theory. Schema theory emphasizes the importance of background knowledge in comprehension. *Schemata*—the organized, general pieces of knowledge a person has in order to make sense of an event—are mainly used in two ways: to guide actions in typical situations and to help the individual make inferences and fill in information. Schema theory has important implications for English language development (ELD) teachers as it provides a means to help students understand events and information. A useful text about schema theory is *Reading, Schema Theory and Second Language Learners* (Kitao, 1989).

Contributions of Semiotics

The previous theories have attempted to explain second language acquisition in linguistic, psycholinguistic, or sociolinguistic terms. *Semiotics* is a discipline that studies the ways in which humans use signs to make meaning. Signs are the "codes by which communication occurs" (Eakin, 1985); basically, everything is or can be made into a sign. Some things are obviously signs—stop signs and signs over stores and shops. Other things are recognized as signs once they are pointed out as such—for example, words. Still other things are generally not recognized as signs—the architecture of houses or the style of clothes and hair. Yet all these signs mean something. They are used for thinking, communicating, creating, and organizing experience. Three major channels are used to receive or produce signs—acoustic, visual, and tactile. Semioticians explore the ways people utilize these channels to make meaning and then compare them. They strive to make the implicit explicit—to formalize what we all do that we are not aware of.

Semiotics provides a perspective for examining human development: that humans have the capacity to make meaning from experience. By adopting this perspective, teachers accept that students are learning from the experiences provided to them. They recognize that knowledge is constantly being advanced and that the curriculum can provide students with ways of knowing, not with mere static knowledge. Students learn how to construct meaning, not merely how to receive information. Teachers and students actively create curriculum. Using themselves, students, other teachers, the community, and culturally authentic materials (phone books, voice mail messages, advertising brochures, music videos), teachers along with students examine ways of knowing in a more encompassing context. For further information about a semiotically informed approach to curriculum, see Eisner (1985) and Greene (1986).

Contributions of Research about the Brain

Almost all the foregoing theories have left to speculation the involvement of the brain in learning language. Neurofunctional theories attempt to explain the connection between language function and neuroanatomy—to identify, if possible, which areas of the brain are responsible for language functioning. Functional and clinical studies (Asher & Garcia, 1969; Krashen, Long, & Scarcella, 1979; Lenneberg, 1967) have focused on specific aspects of language acquisition: age differences, neural maturation, and the like. Although previous language learning theories acknowledge the role of the brain in learning, several contemporary educators have specialized in developing learning methods that take into consideration brain processing.

According to current research (Caine & Caine, 1991; Hart, 1975, 1983; Nummela & Rosengren, 1986), learning is the brain's primary function. Many aspects of the brain help to process reality simultaneously, using thoughts, emotions, imagination, and the senses to understand and interact with the environment. This rich reaction can be tapped in heretofore unrealized ways to facilitate language acquisition. Table 1-1 lists principles of brain-based learning (Caine & Caine, 1991) and provides teachers with a way to apply knowledge about the brain to language teaching. For further information about brain-based learning, *Making Connections* by Caine and Caine (1991) is a highly readable and insightful text.

TABLE 1-1 Principles and Implications for Brain-Based Instruction

Principle	Implications for instruction
1. The brain can perform multiple processes simultaneously.	Learning experiences must be "orchestrated" so that many aspects of the brain become involved. Teachers need a vast repertoire of methods and approaches from which to choose.
2. Learning engages the entire physiology.	Stress management, nutrition, exercise, relaxation, and natural rhythms and timing should be taken into consideration during teaching and learning.
3. The search for meaning is innate.	Language learning should provide both stability and familiarity as well as satisfying curiosity and offering an abundance of choices.
4. The brain is designed to perceive and generate patterns.	The ideal teaching process presents information in a way that allows brains to extract patterns and create meaning rather than react passively.
5. Emotions are crucial to memory.	Instruction should support the students' background and language. Interaction should be marked by mutual respect and acceptance.
6. The brain processes parts and wholes simultaneously.	Language skills, such as vocabulary and grammar, are best learned in authentic language environments (solving a problem, debating an issue, exploring).
7. Learning involves both focused attention and peripheral perception.	Music, art, and other rich environmental stimuli can enhance and influence the natural acquisition of language. Subtle signals from the teacher communicate enthusiasm and interest.
8. Learning always involves conscious and unconscious processes.	Students need opportunities to review what they learn so they can reflect, take charge, and develop personal meaning.
9. There are at least two types of memory: spatial memory and rote learning systems.	Teaching techniques that focus on the memorization of language bits—words and grammar points—use the rote learning system. Teaching that actively involves the learner in novel experiences taps into the spatial system.
10. Learning occurs best when facts and skills are embedded in natural, spatial memory.	Discrete language skills can be learned when they are embedded in real-life activities (demonstrations, field trips, performances, stories, drama, visual imagery).
11. Learning is enhanced by	Teachers need to create an atmosphere low in

| challenge and inhibited by threat. | threat and high in challenge. |
| 12. Each brain is unique. | Teaching should be multifaceted. ELD students can express their understanding through visual, tactile, emotional, and auditory means. |

Theories of second language acquisition provide the rationale and framework for the daily activities of instruction. Excellent general background readings to theory and practice in second language acquisition are Hatch's *Second Language Acquisition: A Book of Readings* (1978) and *Studies in Second Language Acquisition* (1979). Teachers who are aware of the basic principles of contemporary language acquisition and learning are better equipped to plan instruction and explain their practices to peers, parents, students, and administrators.

Although the teacher's role is valuable as students learn a second language, the actual language learned is the responsibility of the learner. What we know about cognitive processes is that the learner constructs language using rules internalized during problem solving or authentic communication. The shift from *what the teacher does* to *what the learner does* is a characteristic of contemporary thinking about learning in general and language acquisition specifically, and has wide implications for teaching with language minority students.

Chapter 2

Second Language Acquisition: Psychological and Sociocultural Factors

I believe the single most important strategy for a teacher to practice is to be a good listener. By this I mean genuinely listen to the children. If a child comes to speak, face him, put down the work you are doing and give him your whole attention. . . . In this way children see themselves as valued members of the special community of the classroom. . . .

When they do speak, it is important to listen to the meanings. I remember the following exchange between Jack and a teacher.

"We went to Nagi on Saturday, Sir."

"How far away is Nagi, Jack?"

"Four drums, Sir."

(The journey in a dinghy driven by an outboard motor would take four drums of petrol.)

What it really comes down to is that we must have respect for the children themselves. . . . With respect comes confidence. With confidence comes a willingness to take risks. With risk taking comes learning. (Louise Carothers, teacher of Torres Strait Island children, in Murray, 1989)

Language cannot be learned in a vacuum. It involves interaction with others. Psychological and sociocultural factors play important roles in a learner's success in acquiring and using a second language (see Figure I-1). Each learner is simultaneously an individual and a member of a group. As an individual, a person carries character traits that enable him or her to function in specific ways and deal with situations in a unique style. As a member of a group, a person learns characteristic ways of behaving and, largely unconsciously, adopts rules for interaction and takes on roles appropriate for effective functioning in that group. These individual (psychological) and group (sociocultural) factors influence second language acquisition as much as does the nature of the target language. Both psychological and sociocultural factors are examined in this chapter in light of their implications for language development classrooms.

PSYCHOLOGICAL FACTORS

Traits specific to individuals that enable them to acquire a second language are psychological. Learners use the assets of their personalities to absorb the ambiance of the culture, to process the language heard, and to create meaningful responses. Psychological factors can be divided into two categories: affective/emotional and cognitive (although it is often difficult to separate neatly affective and cognitive processes in language learning). The sense of mastery of a language creates an affective/emotional response: enjoyment, pride, competence. The work of mastering a second language can be considered cognitive. Teachers can help students to be aware of those psychological factors that further their language learning and can work with students to ensure that these factors promote rather than impede their learning.

Affective/Emotional Factors

The affective domain, the emotional side of human behavior, is the means through which individuals become aware of their environment, respond to it with feeling, and act as though their feelings make a difference. This emotional dimension helps determine how language acquisition and communication take place. Some affective factors within this domain pertain specifically to individuals' feelings about themselves, whereas other factors pertain to their ability to interact with others. Those affective factors that are discussed here are self-esteem, motivation, anxiety, attitude, and other related factors.

Self-esteem. A large part of one's feelings revolve around how one feels about oneself, one's self-esteem. According to Schumann (1978b), there are three aspects of self-esteem: *global* (overall assessment of one's worth); *specific* (self-evaluation in various life situations such as work and social interactions and in individual characteristics such as personality and intelligence); and *task* (self-valuation in particular tasks). It is unclear whether high self-esteem *causes* language success or *results from* language success. Research is lacking about the influence of global, specific, or task self-esteem in any particular situation. Many teachers, however, intuitively recognize that self-esteem issues play important roles in their classrooms and encourage students to feel proud of their successes and abilities. Global self-esteem enhancement, such as efforts to empower students with positive images of self, family, and culture, may facilitate language learning. Teachers also strive to ensure that learners feel good about specific aspects of their language learning (speaking, writing) or about their success on a particular task.

Anita Alvarez was a Spanish-speaking first grade student at the beginning stages of English language acquisition. She was shy and retiring, and Mrs. Figueroa noticed that she seldom took advantage of opportunities to chat with her peers. Anita seemed physically well developed for her age and had good sensory motor abilities. She was particularly adept at building three-dimensional models following printed diagrams. When Mrs. Figueroa observed that Mary, another student in the class, had a lot of difficulty in constructing objects, Anita was teamed with Mary, and, with Anita's help, Mary completed her project successfully. Noting this success, Mrs. Figueroa "assigned competence" to Anita by publicly praising her to the class and referring students to her for help. This boosted Anita's feelings of worth—her "task" self-esteem—and the effects transferred to academic areas. Mrs. Figueroa was pleased to see that, subsequently, Anita talked more with other students and seemed to acquire English at a faster rate.

Moskowitz's *Caring and Sharing in the Foreign Language Classroom* (1978) offers many activities that enhance self-esteem. "Me Power" is an activity that asks students to imagine they are going to give a speech before a large group of people. The assignment is to write a brief description of their accomplishments for the person who is to introduce them. Another activity, "Success Story," asks students to describe an incident in which they achieved a victory or reached a goal. A third activity, "Ageless," asks students to think positively about their age and other ages by answering eight questions, such as "What do you like about being your present age?" and "What did you like about being younger?" In these and other activities, a theory of humanistic education is elaborated and many suggestions are given for building a climate of acceptance, trust, and low anxiety to increase language learning.

Related to self-esteem is the concept of *inhibition*, a term that suggests defensiveness against new experiences and feelings. Guiora, Beit-Hallami, Brannon, Dull, and Schovel (1972) refer to a "language ego" that either defends against or facilitates verbal input and expression. Guiora and his colleagues have investigated ways to encourage the language ego to be productive. In one experiment, small quantities of alcohol were used with a group of college students to reduce inhibition. The student "imbibers" outperformed the control group! One recent language teaching methodology in particular (see Suggestopedia, Chapter 4) focuses on a reduction of inhibitions so that students can communicate more freely. Emphasizing fluency over accuracy in the first stages of language learning may help students to feel less inhibited.

A *tolerance for ambiguity* is also related to self-esteem, particularly in the area of task esteem. Such tolerance may help learners react in language situations where the topic and purpose of the conversation, as well as the appropriate response, are unclear. Rather than reacting with avoidance or dislike, a person with a high tolerance for ambiguity may be able to listen more attentively and perform more efficiently.

The ability to *take risks*, to "gamble," may facilitate second language acquisition. Intuitively, educators believe that those who are willing to guess at meaning when it is not clear and to be relatively unconcerned with creating errors will progress in language skills more rapidly than their more inhibited colleagues. As Brown (1987) points out, however, students who make random guesses and blurt out meaningless phrases have not been as successful. It appears that moderate risk takers stand the best chance at language development.

Motivation. Motivation has been defined as the impulse, emotion, or desire that causes one to act in a certain way. Humans need to be active—to acquire knowledge, explore, manipulate, and enhance the ego. They strive to meet their basic needs, to achieve an identity within a group, and to learn about their world. Various individual, sociocultural, and instructional factors impact motivation. Gardner and Lambert (1972) have postulated two types of motivation in learning a second language: *instrumental* motivation, the need to acquire a language for a specific purpose such as reading technical material or getting a job, and *integrative* motivation, the desire to become a member of the culture of the second language group. Research suggests that these differences are not mutually exclusive; most situations involve a mixture of both types.

As with any of the affective factors, motivation is hard to identify and study. Research has demonstrated that motivation is a key to learning, but actually defining and detailing the components of motivation have not been done. Generally, in classrooms, teachers organize their instruction on the basis of one of two subconscious notions about motivation—that it is a trait or a state. As a *trait*, motivation is seen as being relatively consistent and persistent and is attributed to various groups—parents, communities, or cultures. The stereotype of the overachieving Asian student may be one example wherein student success is attributed to a trait of motivation. Students are motivated to learn English by such incentives as the desire to please—or not to shame—their families or by the drive to bring honor to their communities. As a *state*, motivation is viewed as a more temporary condition that can be influenced by the use of highly interesting materials or activities, or by contingencies of reward or punishment (Tharp, 1989b). The belief that motivation is a trait may be a disincentive for teachers to alter the curriculum for those students whose interest or achievement flags. The belief that motivation is a state may be a motivator for teachers to exert themselves to involve learners actively.

Anxiety. Anxiety when learning a second language can be seen as similar to general feelings of tension that students experience in the classroom. Almost everyone feels some anxiety when learning, and having to perform in a new language compounds anxious feelings. Anxiety about learning language resembles communication anxiety—that is, feelings of self-consciousness, desire to be perfect when speaking, and fear of making mistakes. In some ways, however, anxiety in a second language is more than simply communication anxiety; using a foreign language can threaten a person's sense of self because speakers know they cannot represent themselves fully in a new language or understand others readily (Horwitz, Horwitz, & Cope, 1991).

Because anxiety can cause learners to feel defensive and can block effective learning, several language educators have developed methodologies that make the learning environment as comfortable as possible and reduce tension and nervousness (see, e.g., Gattegno's Silent Way and Lozanov's Suggestopedia in Chapter 4). Scovel (1991) comments that these methods have not been proved to reduce anxiety directly, but insofar as they are effective it is probably because "language teachers have known all along that students learn better in a supportive, nonthreatening environment" (p. 23). Crookall and Oxford (1991) suggest that the classroom become a place of warmth and friendliness, where risk taking is rewarded and encouraged, and peer work, small group work, games, and simulations are featured. In such contexts, student-to-student communication is increased.

Classroom techniques can teach students to confront anxiety directly (Crookall & Oxford, 1991). Specific activities explicitly train students to recognize their anxiety. "Agony Column" allows students to write a letter to an imaginary Ann Landers relating a particular difficulty they have in language learning and asking for advice. Students working in groups read and discuss the letters, offer advice, and return the letters to their originators for follow-up discussion. "Mistakes Panel" is an activity in which students collect mistakes over a number of classes and, in groups, assess the errors. They then rate the errors on a scale of 1 to 3 for such qualities as amusement, originality, and intelligibility; and they tally points to reward the "winning" mistake. Again, class discussion follows. "Anxious Photos" features a series of photos of people in a wide range of communicative contexts, such as a restaurant, a post office, a family visit, and a classroom. Student groups arrange the photos in sets according to their own criteria, which reflect their judgments about the anxieties provoked in these situations. Students discuss in pairs their reasons for the photo sets that they created, and why anxiety is aroused in each context.

Koch and Terrell (1991) suggest several types of activities that allow all students to participate with little apprehension. Performing interviews in pairs makes students feel most comfortable because it gives them the opportunity to get to know a classmate. "Preference ranking" enables students to voice their opinions without using complex language. Beginning students tend to feel more comfort in activities that require sensorimotor involvement (see Total Physical Response, Chapter 4) and with hands-on tasks such as working with maps or playing games like Simon Says. These are simple activities that do not require complex production or a verbal response in English.

Woolfolk (1990) offers guidelines for dealing with excessive student anxiety. Teachers should monitor activities to ensure that students are receiving no undue pressure; should ensure that students in competitive tasks have a reasonable chance to succeed; and should avoid situations in which anxious students have to perform in front of large groups. When using a novel format or starting a new type of task, teachers should make sure students are given examples or models of how the task is done. Occasional take-home tests lower unnecessary time pressures for performance. Teaching test-taking skills explicitly and providing study guides give a boost to students who may need extra help to prepare academically. A variety of assignments distribute the opportunity to earn points toward grades over different types of schoolwork. If students are low in energy in class, teachers may wish to increase arousal by giving them a brief chance to be physically active, by introducing stimuli that whet their curiosity or surprise them. In this way, students can be energized without becoming overly anxious.

Attitudes. Attitudes play a critical role in learning English. Attitudes toward self, toward language (one's own and English), toward English-speaking people (particularly peers), and toward the teacher and the classroom environment affect students (Richard-Amato, 1988). One's *attitude toward the self* involves cognition about one's ability in general, ability to learn language, and self-esteem and its related emotions. These cognitions and feelings are seldom explicit and may be slow to change. *Attitude toward language and those who speak it* is largely a result of experience and the influence of people in the immediate environment, such as peers and parents. Negative reactions are often the result of negative stereotypes or the experience of discrimination or racism. Peñalosa (1980) points out that if language minority students are made to feel inferior because of accent or language status, they may have a defensive reaction against English and English speakers. Students may also experience ambivalent feelings about their primary language. In some families, parents use English at the expense of the primary language in the hope of influencing children to learn English more rapidly. This can cause problems within the family and create a backlash against English or English speakers. Other students who acquire English at the expense of their primary language may be considered traitors by their peers or families.

Attitudes toward the teacher and the classroom environment play an important role in school success in general and English acquisition in particular. Families may promote positive attitudes toward school, thus influencing their child's success. However, Ogbu (1978) states that parents who have experienced discrimination and negative experiences at school may sub-consciously mirror these same attitudes, adding to their children's ambiva-lent attitudes toward education. Students may emphasize cultural behav-iors that help them differentiate themselves from the dominant culture and cling to language behavior that characterizes their group as opposed to the language group represented by the school. Some theorists have postulated that students' refusal to learn what schools teach can be seen as a form of political resistance, which promotes misbehavior, vandalism, and poor re-lationships with teachers (Nieto, 1992). Moskowitz (1978) offers techniques that can alter attitudes from hostile or apathetic to positive.

Other affective factors. In addition to those affective factors discussed in this section, other affective factors involve the connection of oneself to oth-ers. *Empathy* is the capacity to be aware of another's feeling and to share it. When learning a second language, listeners must understand the intentions and emotions of a speaker and attempt to comprehend the message. Al-though some research has shown empathy to be predictive of success in language learning, it is difficult to know if empathy can be learned or taught. Using a methodology such as Community Language Learning has provided students with increased opportunities to share with and belong to their group and has led to significant language gains (Curran, 1982). *Extroversion* can be seen as the need to receive ego enhancement from other people. Some stereo-types exist that connect extroverted behavior with a lack of inhibition or an increased communicative ability. However, Brown (1987) points out that the definition of extroversion may vary considerably from one culture to another. Some students are more willing to speak out and to participate in class; this could be a personality factor or a cultural trait. Although the ex-trovert may be perceived as a person who takes more risks with language, an introverted or more reserved person may show more intuitive under-standing or empathy with others.

Cognitive Factors

The cognitive perspective helps educators to understand language learners as people who are active processors of information. Learners seek out infor-mation to solve problems; reorganize what they already know to achieve new learning; and actively choose, pay attention, ignore, and make many other responses as they pursue goals (see Wittrock, 1978). Students enter school knowing how to learn—from those around them and from personal experience. Students' primary languages, for the most part, are well devel-oped before they enter school. For all children, however, not only for lan-guage minority children, the language used in schools is different to some degree from their home language. Language is used in school in expanded ways: to create meaning from print, to encode ideas into print, to analyze and compare information, and to respond to classroom discussion. All of these activities involve cognitive factors. Students learn in many different ways using a variety of strategies and styles. The general cognitive processes that all individuals use to learn language are explored in this section, followed by a brief overview of individual learning styles. Finally, various types of bilingualism and their related cognitive effects are discussed.

Cognitive Academic Language Proficiency. Cummins (1979a, 1980) has posited two different yet related language skills: Basic Interpersonal Communication Skills (BICS) and Cognitive Academic Language Proficiency (CALP). BICS involves those language skills and functions that allow individuals to communicate in everyday contexts. It is language that is *context embedded* because participants can provide feedback to one another, the situation itself provides cues that further understanding, and factors apart from the linguistic code can furnish meaning. CALP, as the name implies, is the language needed to perform school tasks successfully. Such tasks generally are more abstract and decontextualized. Students must rely primarily on language to attain meaning. Cummins (1984) calls this *context-reduced* communication because there are few concrete cues to aid in comprehension. Thus, students need to master much more than everyday English in order to have access to the school curriculum. Successful educators are aware that children need skills in both language domains. Students who may appear to be fluent enough in English to survive in an all-English classroom may in fact have significant gaps in the development of academic aspects of English. Conversational skills have been found to approach native-like levels within two years of exposure to English, but five or more years may be required for minority students to match native speakers in CALP (Collier, 1987; Cummins, 1981a).

> Mrs. Gómez found in her second-grade transitional bilingual class that, although the students were fairly fluent English conversationalists, they were performing poorly in academic tasks. Students seemed to understand English when pictures and other visual clues were present. However, when Mrs. Gómez gave instructions or briefly reviewed concepts, the students appeared lost. She became aware that students needed to be provided with lessons that eased them along the continuum from their interpersonal language usage to the more abstract academic requirements. She noticed that Linda and several of her classmates enjoyed jumping rope during recess. Mrs. Gómez wrote down many of the patterned chants the girls were reciting. She transferred these to wall charts and read and recited them with the children. Next she introduced poems with more extensive vocabulary on wall charts, supplementing the charts with tapes that children could listen to in learning centers. At the same time, the class was studying the ocean. Mrs. Gómez set up other learning centers with shells, dried seaweed, fish fossils, and other ocean objects. The instructions for these centers featured patterned language similar to that already encountered in the rhymes and

poems. Gradually Mrs. Gómez was able to record more complex and abstract instructions in the learning centers. This progression and integration of activities helped the children to move along the continuum from BICS to CALP.

The difficulty that language minority students have in acquiring CALP reinforces the need for maintenance bilingual programs in which students do not transition into English abruptly. Although critics of bilingual education have charged that educating children in the primary language reduces their opportunity to acquire English, this argument assumes that proficiency in English is separate from proficiency in a primary language. The assumption is that content and skills learned through the primary language do not transfer to English. This notion of "no interrelationship between languages" (Cummins, 1981b) has been termed *separate underlying proficiency* (SUP). The contrasting notion, "significant interrelationship between languages," asserts that cognition and language fundamentals, once learned in the primary language, form a basis for subsequent learning in any language. This position assumes a *common underlying proficiency* (CUP) and is characterized by the belief that a second language and the primary language have a shared foundation. For example, children learning to read and write in Korean develop concepts about print and the role of literacy that make learning to read and think in English easier, despite the fact that these languages do not share a similar writing system. The surface differences in the languages are less important than the deeper understandings about the function of reading and its relationship to thought and learning. Cummins (1981b) cites much evidence to support the idea of a common underlying proficiency. Once a student has a strong foundation in the native language, learning a second language—and learning in general—readily builds upon this foundation. Students do not have to relearn in a second language the essentials of schooling: how to communicate, how to think critically, and how to read and write (Association for Supervision and Curriculum Development, 1987).

Age. The age of the learner is an important factor to be considered in the discussion of language. Second language acquisition is a complex process that occurs over a long period of time, and the optimum age for its inception has been widely debated. Although many people believe that children acquire a second language more rapidly than adults, recent research counters this notion. It is true that natural exposure to second languages during childhood can lead to higher second language proficiency than exposure that begins in the adult years, but this generally pertains only to pronunciation (see Point/Counterpoint on page 31). Contrary to popular belief, adults proceed through early stages of syntactic and morphological development faster than children do; older children acquire a second language faster than younger children (Collier, 1987; Krashen et al., 1979). Cummins (1980) suggests that older learners acquire cognitive/academic proficiency more

Point/Counterpoint: What is the best age for second language acquisition?

Most bilingual programs in elementary schools are based on the premise that students who enter kindergarten or first grade with a primary language other than English can become fluent enough in English to move to an all-English program by grade 3 or 4. This premise is based on the belief that, for children, second language acquisition is relatively easy and should take no more than a few months of schooling. Most adults, in contrast, find learning a second language to be relatively difficult. What, then, is the best age for learning a second language?

Point: Children learn second languages easily.

Those who argue that a child can learn a second language more rapidly than an adult usually base this claim on Lenneberg's 1967 book *The Biological Foundations of Language,* in which he postulates that the brain has a language acquisition processor that functions best before puberty. Lenneberg argued that the brain has a "critical period" for learning language. Despite the fact that the critical period hypothesis has not been proved, people continue to use Lenneberg's work to assert that the child's brain is better able to learn language rapidly.

Many people believe that children are more fluent in a second language; however, the language children speak is relatively simple (shorter constructions with fewer vocabulary words than adults') and thus, may appear to be spoken more fluently. People also believe that children are less inhibited than adults when speaking a second language, but this is not so. Children are just as likely to be embarrassed around their peers as are adults, and are more likely to be shy when speaking before adults (McLaughlin, 1992).

One area in which prepubscent youth may have an advantage is in the acquisition of native-speaker-like pronunciation skills. Research (Oyama, 1976) has found that the earlier a learner begins to learn a second language, the closer the accent will become to that of a native speaker. Older learners may not have an advantage in the areas of oral fluency and accent.

Counterpoint: Adults learn languages more skillfully than children.

Research comparing adults to children has consistently demonstrated that adolescents and adults outperform children in controlled language learning studies (e.g., Snow & Hoefnagel-Hoehle, 1978). Adults have access to more memory strategies; are, as a rule, more socially comfortable; and have greater experience with language in general.

(Continued)

> Macnamara (1973) has questioned the critical period hypothesis, point-
> ing out that there is no evidence to show that a language cannot be
> learned just as well after puberty as before. In general, the self-disci-
> pline, strategy use, prior knowledge, and metalinguistic ability of the
> older learner create a distinct advantage for the adult over the child
> in language acquisition.

rapidly than younger learners because the CALP in their first language (L1)
is better developed. Five-, six-, and seven-year-old ESL students need at
least two years of academic achievement in the first language, and most
students take anywhere from four to eight years or more to reach the average attainment of native speakers on standardized tests. If these students
are economically disadvantaged, the process may take even longer
(Cummins, 1981a).

Language acquisition processes. These processes involve mental activities
that people employ to be able to communicate ideas. Two of these processes
are directly related to the general cognitive mechanisms that individuals
use in any type of learning: transfer and generalization. Transfer is applying
old learning to new situations, and generalization involves inferring or drawing conclusions in order to make a response to a situation.

In language learning, transfer is most noticeable when learners use rules
from their first language that are not applicable to the second. This has been
called *negative transfer*. After working with second language learners, most
teachers have numerous examples, often humorous, of sentences, phrases,
or words students have transferred from their first language that have no
direct equivalence in their second. One of the authors (Weed), for example,
once mistakenly referred to a coconut as *"coco-noix"* instead of *"noix de coco."*
She was using English word order—adjective + noun—instead of the French
pattern—noun + attribute. Meaning, however, was not lost. Weed's French
friends knew exactly what she was talking about; she had the correct concept and had used it in the correct situation. The "negative" element was
merely the surface representation. Unfortunately, the emphasis on negative
transfer of surface grammatical or pronunciation errors can hide the more
powerful *positive transfer* that occurs and allows people to respond appropriately and meaningfully in new language situations.

Much research has been carried out and numerous studies have been
made comparing various features (phonological, syntactic, and semantic)
of languages. Contrastive analysis, a tool for analyzing and learning that
emphasizes comparisons between the first and second language, rests heavily
on behaviorist and structuralist tenets. Classroom materials based on this
approach encourage comparisons of those structural elements deemed by
the materials developer to be the most troublesome. Contemporary theory

recognizes the importance of the first language in a global sense and does not encourage learners to compare minute surface forms of the first and second languages as they learn.

The second general cognitive strategy used by all learners is generalization—the act of drawing a conclusion or making an inference. In first language acquisition, this process is seen when young children begin to acquire concepts and put labels to them. "Dada," a child may say to any male, or "ball" about any round object. The child has understood an aspect of the concepts *father* and *ball* and generalized the terms to all objects representative of the understood aspect. In second language acquisition, the term *overgeneralization* is more frequently used and refers to situations in which the learner incorrectly generalizes a rule to cases where it does not apply. English learners may say, for example, "I don't can do that." In this case, the student has overgeneralized the rule "insert *do* in negative clauses." In another example, the student may say, "He asked me that should he go." Here, the student has overgeneralized the question–word order rule.

Point/Counterpoint: How does a person's first language affect learning a second language?

Individuals who have learned more than one foreign language sometimes find that a first foreign language interferes with a second: in trying to say the pronoun *il* ("he") in French, for example, one could mistakenly use the word *el* (Spanish). More difficult to sort out is the influence of the first language on the second. Much was made of error analysis in the 1960s, as teachers sought to document a predictability in the errors made by native Japanese speakers, for example, when learning English. What is the effect of the first language on learning a second language?

Point: Skill in a first language helps second language learning.

Current research has shown that learning the first language and learning a foreign language resemble each other to some extent. The "mistakes" that both children and adults make in the second language are similar to the errors that children make in learning their native language. In many ways, learning the first language accomplishes a rich foundation for learning another tongue. Learning that things have names, that language classifies reality, and that language is a means for sharing experience with others—none of these insights need to be discovered anew in the second language. A learner can immediately begin to transfer concepts from the first language to the second. Knowledge of the world, as well as knowledge of language (metalinguistic awareness) enables a learner to streamline language learning the second time around.

Continued

Cummins (1981b) emphasizes that students who have the opportunity to develop cognitive and academic skills in their first language before being asked to develop these skills in the second language are more successful in school. Moreover, students who receive a high level of academic support from parents in the home are more likely to develop academic language skills in the second language. When children and parents share a common language, such support is more likely.

Counterpoint: The first language interferes with second language learning.

The idea that early learning, such as learning a native language, interferes with later learning (such as a second language) is called *proactive interference.* Such interference has been explained by Schunk (1991) as confusion resulting from the same or similar schema or script being used on different occasions. Many terms in a second language cannot be translated directly into the first language, and attempts to form cognates interfere with understanding rather than facilitate comprehension. For example, who can fully translate the Russian word for *comrade,* with its associated connotations in the world experience of an ex-Soviet?

According to Skuttnabb-Kangas (1981), many bilinguals feel that their second language is somehow impoverished, that it is poorer in emotion and feels colder, more alien, more superficial, and less rich in words than the first language. In some sense, the first language has interfered with learning the second; the native language has taken up the role most central to the heart, leaving little emotional space for the second. No matter how rich the experience of learning the second language, the first dominates the personality. For others, however, the second language represents new learning opportunities and experiences not available in the first language. For these learners, the second language augments, rather than interferes with, the first language.

As parallels between first and second language acquisition have become more evident, a shift has occurred in understanding second language acquisition processes. Learners are no longer seen as second language bumblers whose every mistake needs "fixing." Instead, they are recognized as intelligent, hypothesis-forming individuals who use the knowledge of their first language and a growing awareness of the second to progress toward native-like second language fluency. The precise way in which knowledge of the first language affects second language acquisition is not certain (see the Point/Counterpoint on pages 33–34).

The interlanguage produced by second language learners is an intermediate language, a form that features some combination of constructs carried over from the first language with elements of the second. Corder (1978) calls this "language-learner language" and characterizes it as a different language from that of the native speaker but very similar to that of other language learners. Instead of criticizing language-learner language as error-ridden and deficient, full of overgeneralizations and negatively transferred elements, a teacher can recognize it as a dynamic system that is in constant progression toward increased proficiency. Interlanguage is a continuum stretching from the mother language to the target language. Teachers knowledgeable about this interlanguage help students progress along this continuum, correctly assessing the strengths of the learner and providing additional mediation of elements still unknown and/or unmastered.

Stages of development. Second language learners are individuals, who vary greatly in their acquisition of a second language. However, there are generally accepted stages of development through which learners progress. Krashen and Terrell (1983) have posited three: comprehension, early production, and extending production. In the first, the *comprehension stage*—also called the silent period or preproduction stage—the learner of a new language simply needs to absorb the sounds and rhythms of the new language, becoming attuned to the flow of the speech stream and beginning to isolate specific words. For the most part, learners in the silent period feel anxious when expected to produce speech. Once a learner feels more confident, words and phrases may be attempted. This is called the *early production stage*. Responses can consist of single words ("yes," "no," "O.K.," "you," "come"), two- or three-word combinations ("where book," "no go," "don't go," "teacher help"), and phrases ("Where are you going?" "The boy running."). In the third stage, *extending production* or speech emergence, second language acquisition speeds up considerably. Utterances become longer and more complex, students begin to recognize and correct their own errors, and they become more comfortable at initiating and sustaining conversations.

The American Council for Teachers of Foreign Languages (ACTFL) divides the stages into six numbered levels. A learner's oral proficiency is measured from 0 to 5 on a scale that depicts the progression of language learning from novice to native-like fluency. Krashen and Terrell's stage of speech emergence would correspond to the 1+ or 2 stage on the ACTFL scale. Regardless of the scale, it is now recognized that, in natural situations, learners progress through stages in their acquisition of a second language. These stages are predictable, and learners advance through them at their own pace. Undue pressure to move through the stages rapidly only serves to frustrate and retard language learning.

Learner strategies. Aside from general language acquisition processes that all learners use, there are individual strategies that learners adopt, consciously or unconsciously. Second language acquisition research divides individual learner strategies into two types: communication and learning. *Communication strategies* are employed for transmitting an idea when the learner cannot produce precise linguistic forms, whereas *learning strategies* relate to the individual's processing, storage, and retrieval of language concepts (Brown, 1987). This distinction between *output* and *input* helps distinguish these two types of strategies since research in this area of second language acquisition is still ongoing and sometimes the two terms are confounded.

The work by Chesterfield and Chesterfield (1985) that was summarized in Chapter 1 provides a list of communication strategies that Mexican-American children used to learn English. (Chesterfield and Chesterfield call them learning strategies.) These verbal strategies relate to the actual utterances children were heard to make. Brown (1987) examines four broad categories of communication strategies based on Tarone's work (1981). These strategies make use of both verbal and nonverbal devices.

- *Avoidance:* Evading the use of sounds, structures, or topics that are beyond current proficiency. For example, a student may avoid sharing plans because of an inability to use the future tense.
- *Prefabricated patterns:* Memorizing stock phrases to rely on when all else fails.
- *Appeal to authority:* Asking a native speaker for help or pausing to consult a dictionary.
- *Language switch:* Falling back on the primary language for help in communication.

This last strategy, often called *code switching*, has been studied extensively because it permeates a learner's progression in a second language. Code switching, the alternating use of two languages on the word, phrase, clause, or sentence level (Valdés-Fallis, 1978), now has been found to be used for a variety of purposes, not just as a strategy to help when expressions in the second language are lacking. Baker (1993) lists ten purposes for code switches: (1) to emphasize a point; (2) because a word is unknown in one of the languages; (3) for ease and efficiency of expression; (4) as a repetition to clarify; (5) to express group identity and status and/or to be accepted by a group; (6) to quote someone; (7) to interject in a conversation; (8) to exclude someone; (9) to cross social or ethnic boundaries; and (10) to ease tension in a conversation. Code switching thus serves a variety of intentions beyond the mere linguistic. It has important power and social ramifications.

A recent Spanish-speaking immigrant to the United States might acquire whole phrases or words in English from a fellow student and then intersperse these when speaking Spanish to gain access to his peer group. Children speaking English on the playground have been heard to repeat in Spanish something just said in English, perhaps to clarify what was said or to identify with two groups. The use of target language vocabulary is particularly noticeable in bilingual classrooms in which children are learning concepts in two languages and pick the term in one language as a preferred usage. The content of the course, the interpersonal link between speakers, and the speech community's values are factors in language choice. Very often, one language may be associated with certain activities, situations, or social practices of the speakers. Words or phrases from this language are used when discussing such activities in a second language (Peñalosa, 1980). In many models of bilingual schooling, students are encouraged to use only English or only the primary language in certain contexts. Language purists look down on language mixing. A more fruitful approach might be to let children learn in whatever manner they feel most comfortable so that anxiety about language will not interfere with concept acquisition.

The second category of individual learner strategies is learning strategies. These include the techniques a person uses to think and to act in order to complete a task. Extensive work in identifying learning strategies has been done by O'Malley and Chamot (O'Malley, Chamot, Stewner-Manzanares, Kupper, & Russo, 1985a, 1985b), who have incorporated specific instruction in learning strategies in their Cognitive Academic Language Learning Approach (CALLA). They have organized learning strategies into three major types: metacognitive, cognitive, and social-affective (Chamot & O'Malley, 1987). These will be discussed in Chapter 4.

Cognitive style. This is the last intrapersonal factor to be discussed that bears relevance to one's acquisition of a second language. A cognitive style refers to "consistent and rather enduring tendencies or preferences *within* an individual" (Brown, 1987, p. 79). Long lists of cognitive styles, including such constructs as sensory modality strengths, types of information processing, motivation, attributes, and value judgments, have been assembled by educators and psychologists. For the teacher of language minority students, however, elements that have shown cultural differences are the ones to note. Tharp (1989b) suggests two cognitive styles that have relevance for classrooms: visual/verbal, and holistic/analytic. On a continuum from visual to verbal and from holistic to analytic, it is the latter element in these two styles that schools expect and reward. For students who have a more visual orientation, and whose previous learning consisted of observing and learning by doing rather than through verbal instructions, schools may be mystifying until they catch on to a different cognitive style. Similarly, students with more holistic thought processes understand pieces of a process through knowledge of the pattern as a whole. "Wholistic comprehension proceeds by incorporating phenomena into ever-expanding circles of context, rather than by reducing phenomena to their disassembled parts" (Tharp, 1989b, p. 353).

Another area that has received wide attention among second language educators is the construct known as field dependence/independence.

Ramirez (1991), who prefers the term "field sensitive" to "field dependent," finds that field-sensitive learners like to work with others, are open to others' feelings and opinions, openly express emotions, seek rewards in relationships, and prefer concepts to be contextualized in stories and personal experiences. In contrast, field-independent students prefer to work alone, compete for individual recognition, interact formally with their teachers, seek nonsocial rewards, and deal well with math and science concepts. They are task oriented and inattentive to their working environment. Minority students have been characterized as being more field sensitive (Ramirez & Castañeda, 1974). This can have broad implications for teaching. It should be noted, however, that research in the area of field dependence/independence is conflicting and has not necessarily led to important educational insights (Cazden & Leggett, 1981).

Cazden and Leggett list a variety of cognitive styles drawn from many sources. These styles include cognitive complexity versus simplicity, reflectiveness versus impulsivity, leveling versus sharpening (how memory assimilates information), and constricted versus flexible control (susceptibility to distraction). Many aspects of cognitive style have been demonstrated to show cultural differences (see Cohen, 1969), although other researchers have considered the connection between cognitive styles and cultural styles to be overrated (O'Neil, 1990). Cognitive styles, along with affective behaviors and preferences, form learning styles.

Types of bilingualism and related cognitive effects. Early studies on bilingualism have reported both positive and negative cognitive and academic effects. To account for this inconsistency, Cummins (1979b) analyzed the language characteristics of the children studied and suggested that the level of bilingualism attained is an important factor in educational development. *Limited bilingualism,* or subtractive bilingualism, can occur when children's first language is gradually replaced by a more dominant and prestigious language. This has also been called semilingualism (Díaz, 1983). In this case, children may develop relatively low levels of academic proficiency in both languages. *Partial bilingualism,* in which students have achieved a native-like level in one of their languages, has neither positive nor negative cognitive effects. The most positive cognitive effects are experienced in *proficient bilingualism,* when students attain high levels of proficiency in both languages. This is also called additive bilingualism.

Whether or not bilingualism presents a cognitive advantage has been actively researched (see the Point/Counterpoint on page 39). Cummins (1976) posits a *threshold hypothesis:* Children must attain a critical level, or threshold, of linguistic proficiency in order to avoid cognitive deficit and allow their bilingualism to benefit their cognitive growth. There are actually two thresholds. Attaining the first generally ensures that negative cognitive effects will not occur, and attainment of the second may lead to accelerated cognitive growth. A variety of researchers have found that proficient

Point/Counterpoint: How does being bilingual affect learning?

The Bilingual Education Act of 1968 authorized funds for the education of students who were "educationally disadvantaged because of their inability to speak English." This law was explicitly compensatory in nature; it attempted to remediate the "handicap" of being bilingual. Does being bilingual cause learning problems, or does it involve associated cognitive strengths?

Point: Bilingual children are hampered in school because of cognitive interference.

Early research on bilingualism concluded that speaking two languages was so taxing on the mental development of the child that cognitive abilities suffered. Díaz (1983) summarizes research performed prior to 1962, which built a case for a "language handicap" in bilingual children. Researchers found evidence that bilingual children had "poorer vocabulary," "deficient articulation," "lower standards in written composition," and "more grammatical errors" that nonbilinguals. One interpretation was that bilingualism caused "linguistic confusion" that deeply affected children's intellectual ability and academic performance.

Counterpoint: Being bilingual may have cognitive advantages.

Cummins (1976) found early studies that claimed a "language handicap" were often flawed by the failure to separate the economic status of children from the measure of their academic ability. Moreover, Díaz (1983) found that these studies systematically failed to define *bilingual* in a satisfactory manner, often confusing such factors as parents' birthplaces and family name with bilingual proficiency.

A number of studies have shown that bilingual children perform better than monolinguals on tests that measure various aspects of cognitive and linguistic development. In a study involving ten-year-old French-Canadian children, Peal and Lambert (1962) showed a positive correlation between bilingualism and general intelligence. In this research, however, the students chosen as subjects had equally developed French and English skills; critics have charged that these students were likely to have been gifted and therefore naturally scored highly on a test of general intelligence.

Subsequent research has shown that higher degrees of bilingualism are correlated with increased cognitive abilities in such areas as concept formation, creativity, knowledge of the workings of language, and cognitive flexibility (Díaz, 1983; Galambos & Goldin-Meadow, 1990). Skutnabb-Kangas (1981) sums up other research that shows a positive effect of bilingualism on general intellectual development, including the mixed results of research on bilingualism and divergent thinking.

bilinguals who have high levels of primary and second language outperform monolinguals on a variety of cognitive tasks (Duncan & DeAvila, 1979; Kessler & Quinn, 1980). This research indicates that a strong bilingual program provides an important prerequisite to subsequent academic success. Chapter 6 discusses bilingualism and bilingual education in greater detail.

SOCIOCULTURAL FACTORS

Language learning and language teaching occur within social and cultural contexts. As one masters a language, one is also becoming a member of the community that uses this language to interact, learn, conduct business, love and hate, and participate in a myriad of other social activities. A part of the sense of mastery and enjoyment in a language is acting appropriately and understanding cultural norms. Learners adapt patterns of behavior in a new language and culture based on experiences from their own culture. They carry from their home culture certain patterns of behavior that are used automatically as they learn a new language. These patterns of behavior can be both helpful and limiting in learning the second language community's patterns of interaction.

Culture includes the ideas, customs, skills, arts, and tools that characterize a given group of people in a given period of time (Brown, 1987). One's own culture forms the template of reality; it operates as a lens that allows some information to make sense and other information to remain unperceived. When two cultures come into contact, misunderstandings can be created because members of these cultures have differing perceptions, behaviors, customs, and ideas. Thus, sociocultural factors—how people interact with each other and how they carry out their daily business—play a large role in second language acquisition.

If, as many believe, prolonged exposure to English is sufficient for mastery, why then do so many students fail to achieve the proficiency in English necessary for academic success? Some clues to this perplexity can be found beyond the language itself, in the sociocultural context. Do the students feel that their language and culture are accepted and validated by the school? Does the structure of the school mirror the students' mode of cognition? A well-meaning teacher, with the most up-to-date pedagogy, may still fail to foster achievement if students are socially and culturally uncomfortable with, resistant to, or alienated from schooling.

As students learn a second language, their success is dependent on such extralinguistic factors as the pattern of acculturation for their community; the status of their primary language in relation to English; their own speech community's view of the English language and the English-speaking community; the dialect of English they are hearing and learning and its relationship to standard English; the patterns of social and cultural language usage in the community (see Labov, 1972); and the compatibility between the home culture and the cultural patterns and organization of schools. These issues are explored here with a view toward helping teachers facilitate student learning by bridging the culture and language gap.

Acculturation Variables

Acculturation is the process of adapting to a new culture. Language minority students in the United States, by the mere fact of living in this country and participating in schools, learn a second culture as well as a second language. How the acculturation proceeds depends on factors beyond language itself and beyond the individual learner's motivation, capabilities, and style. Moreover, acculturation may not be a desirable goal for all groups.

In studying students' differential school performance, Ogbu (1978) draws a distinction between various types of immigrant groups. *Caste-like minorities* are those minority groups that were originally incorporated into society against their will and have been systematically exploited and deprecated over generations through slavery or colonization. Caste-like minorities traditionally work at the lowest paying and most undesirable jobs, and they suffer from a job ceiling above which they cannot rise regardless of talent, motivation, or achievement. Thus, academic success is not always seen as helpful or even desirable for members of these groups. *Immigrant minorities* who are relatively free of a history of deprecation, on the other hand, such as immigrants to the United States from El Salvador, Guatemala, and Nicaragua, believe that the United States is a land of opportunity. These immigrants do not view education as irrelevant or exploitative but, rather, as an important investment.

Schumann (1978a) has developed the acculturation model that asserts that "the degree to which a learner acculturates to the target language group will control the degree to which he acquires the second language" (p. 34). He lists the following social variables that he concludes are important factors in acculturation:

- The primary language and English language groups view each other as socially equal, of equal status.
- The primary language and the English language groups both desire that the L1 group assimilate.
- Both the primary language and English language groups expect the primary language group to share social facilities with the English language group.
- The primary language group is small and not very cohesive.

- The primary language group's culture is congruent with that of the English language group.
- Both groups have positive attitudes toward each other.
- The primary language group expects to stay in the area for an extended period.

The positive attitudes between groups of speakers (primary language and English-speaking groups), as well as the small numbers of primary language individuals, help these students to acquire English; if these factors are not present, primary language students can be hindered. Therefore, if a classroom has large groups of primary language speakers whose language is not valued by English speakers, then English language acquisition is not promoted despite the teacher's best intentions.

Differential Status of Languages

In the previous section, reference was made to status and how a group's status may affect members' school performance. A related issue is that of the status of a group's language. In modern U.S. culture, the social value and prestige of speaking a second language varies with socioeconomic position; it also varies as to the second language that is spoken. Many middle-class parents believe that learning a second language benefits their children personally and socially and will later benefit them professionally. In fact, it is characteristic of the elite group in the United States who are involved in scholarly work, diplomacy, foreign trade, or travel to desire to be fully competent in two languages (Porter, 1990). However, the languages that parents wish their children to study are often not those spoken by recently arrived immigrants (Dicker, 1992). This suggests that a certain bias exists in being bilingual—that being competent in a "foreign language" is valuable, whereas knowing an immigrant language is a burden to be overcome.

In the following informal sociolinguistic ranking task, rank from 1 to 4 the following language situations according to the probable socioeconomic status of an individual in that situation (1 = highest socioeconomic status).

_____ A child in a Miami neighborhood speaks Haitian French.

_____ A child in a Washington, D.C. suburban preschool learns French.

_____ A student in an El Paso middle school is placed in a Spanish-for-native-speakers class.

_____ A student in a Minneapolis high school studies Spanish as a second language.

Did you rank the preschool child as representing the highest socioeconomic class? In the United States, members of the upper middle class in the diplomatic communities in New York and Washington place great value on the acquisition of French, to the extent of enrolling young children in preschools that feature French instruction. In contrast, a native speaker of French from Haiti receives very little social status from the knowledge of French because it is not acquired in the context of possible use in the upper classes. In fact, the Haitian immigrant may represent one of the lowest economic classes in the United States (rank = 4 on this 1–4 scale). Middle-class students in U.S. high schools routinely enroll in French, German, or Spanish classes to meet college entrance requirements. Therefore, this middle-class language acquisition probably represents a ranking of 2 on the exercise. Spanish-speaking students in the Southwest do not need Spanish taught as a foreign language, but their social status as Spanish speakers is paradoxically lower than that of mainstream U.S. students who acquire Spanish as a foreign language. This task illustrates the differential social status of second languages in the United States.

Not only are second languages differentially valued, so too are various aspects of languages. Judgments are made about regional and social varieties of languages, "good" and "bad" language, and such seemingly minor elements as voice level and speech patterns. Native Americans may value soft-spoken individuals and interpret European-Americans' loud voice tone as angry. The standard middle-class speech patterns of female teachers may be considered effeminate by lower-class adolescent boys and thus rejected (Saville-Troike, 1976).

There are many ways in which a second-class status is communicated to speakers of other languages. Because language attitudes usually operate at an inconspicuous level, school personnel and teachers are not always aware of the attitudes they hold. It is not possible to completely inventory those factors that influence language attitudes and the practices perpetuated because of those attitudes. The sensitive teacher can, however, learn areas where there may be differences in language use and where those differences might create friction because the minority group's use may be deemed "inferior" by the majority. Furthermore, teachers can be honest with themselves about their own biases, recognizing that they communicate these biases whether or not they are aware of them. Everyone has biases, so being aware of them and being candid about changing injurious biases can go far in affecting the climate of the school and the perception of students regarding their own value. Generally, attitudes toward second languages need to be broadened. If Americans, consciously or unconsciously, are going to maintain certain "foreign" languages as the prestige languages in the coming century, they are cutting themselves off from the social and economic advantages available to those who value a wide range of languages and cultures.

Value Systems

As student populations in U.S. schools become increasingly diversified both linguistically and culturally, teachers and students have come to recognize the important role that attitudes and values play in school success. Values, like attitudes, operate at an intuitive level and unknowingly permeate all interactions.

> Amol is a third-grade student whose parents were born in India. As the only son in a male-dominant culture, he has internalized a strong sense of commitment toward becoming a heart surgeon. His approach to classwork is painstaking. His writing is particularly labored. Although English is the dominant language in the home, Amol's writing in English is slow and careful. Often, he is the last one to be finished with an assignment during class. His teacher places great emphasis on speed in learning and considers time a critical factor in the display of capability. The teacher's main frustration with Amol is that he cannot quickly complete his work. (Do we want the future heart surgeon to be quick?)

In this example, the teacher epitomizes a mainstream U.S. value: speed and efficiency in learning. This value is exemplified in the use of timed standardized testing in the United States. Teachers often describe students of other cultures as being lackadaisical and uncaring about learning, when in fact they may be operating within a different time frame and value system.

Other values held by teachers and embodied in classroom procedures have to do with task orientation. The typical U.S. classroom is a place of work in which children are expected to conform to a schedule, keep busy, maintain order, avoid wasting time, conform to authority, and achieve academically in order to attain personal worth (LeCompte, 1981). Working alone is also valued in school, and children spend a great deal of time in activities that do not allow them to interact verbally with other people or to move physically around the room.

Children need to find within the structure and content of their schooling those behaviors and perspectives that permit them to switch between home and school culture without inner conflict or crises of identity (Pérez & Torres-Guzmán, 1992). Teachers need to feel comfortable in the values and behaviors of their students' cultures in order to develop a flexible cultural repertoire within the context of teaching. In order to begin to understand the values placed on various aspects of interaction, teachers can examine the importance of the following dichotomies in their classrooms—cooperation versus competition, aggression versus compliance, anonymity versus self-assertion, sharing time versus wasting time, and disorder versus order (Saville-Troike, 1976)—and examine their feelings about them in order to understand their personal value system.

Mrs. López teaches in an elementary school that draws students from several neighborhoods in Chicago. About one-third of the students are from Puerto Rican families, another one-third from Mexican-American families, and the last third from African-American families. Rather than lumping the Spanish-speaking children together, Mrs. López is aware that the Puerto Rican and Chicano families have distinct values. In many Puerto Rican families, a young woman cares for one or more children. Often the mother visits the classroom to voice opinions and concerns about education. In contrast, Mexican-American families tend to be male-dominated, and the mothers are seldom vocal about their children's needs. Other differences, such as dialect, mannerisms, and diet, distinguish the Spanish-speaking populations. Mrs. López, herself a Puerto Rican–American, tends to identify with that community but has learned to alter her dialect and interpersonal communication style to be effective with the Mexican-American students. Having been raised in New York City, Mrs. López has had extensive experience in mixed Puerto Rican and African-American neighborhoods and is equally effective with African-American communication styles. This flexible cultural repertoire helps Mrs. López to form a facile rapport in the classroom. Ramirez (1991) calls this a "flexible cognitive style."

For teachers who have not had such rich cultural experiences as Mrs. López, one way to begin developing their own cultural repertoire (and that of their students) is through the following (from Pérez & Torres-Guzmán, 1992, p. 15):

- validate the child's experience
- acknowledge linguistic and cultural differences, and
- integrate the community as a resource in development

Developing a cultural repertoire refers to enabling each individual (students and teachers) to participate in the cultural practices of more than one group, in more than one language, while creating and maintaining his or her identity at multiple levels. In *Learning in Two Worlds,* Pérez and Torres-Guzmán offer a rich source of learning activities to promote cultural flexibility.

The danger of excluding the students' culture(s) from the classroom is that cultural identity, if not included, may become oppositional. Ogbu and Matute-Bianchi (1986) describe how oppositional identity in a distinctly Mexican-American frame of reference influences the performance of Mexican-American children. They attribute achievement difficulties on the part of some Mexican-American children to a distrust of academic effort. When schools were segregated and offered inferior education to this community, a general mistrust of schools caused a difficulty in accepting, internalizing, and following school rules of behavior for achievement. Parents in this community, who may have experienced rejection themselves and who do not view schooling as a source of success, may unknowingly and subtly communicate ambivalence and disillusionment about the value of academic effort to their children. Deviant behavior, in Ogbu and Matute-Bianchi's perspective, is a reflection of the destructive patterns of subordination and social and economic deprivation of the minority group. Doing well in school, for some students, is not a part of the code of conduct that wins them affirmation among their peers in the community. This element of resistance or opposition is not always overt but often takes the form of mental withdrawal, high absenteeism, or reluctance to do classwork.

Schools with high concentrations of minority students often deprive children of using their cultural knowledge and experience, even when staff are well meaning. It is easy to give lip service to the validation of the child's culture and values. However, if teachers consistently use examples drawn from one culture and not another, use literature that displays pictures and photographs of one culture only, and set up classroom procedures that allow some children to feel more comfortable than others, the child will be forced to accept alienation from home, family, and culture. This is unfair and damaging. The concept of a rich and flexible cultural repertoire is the theme that can allow cultures to mix constructively and promote achievement.

> They should have African-American ethnic studies class, a Hispanic class, an Asian class and different ethnic background classes. Because then other ethnics would learn about different ethnic groups and that would help a lot. (African-American male high school student, Institute for Education in Transformation, 1992, p. 25)

Dialects and Standard Languages

All speakers have three or more levels in their language usage—levels of which they may or may not be aware. There is an intimate speech used in home; an informal but slightly restrained speech used in semipublic situations; and the carefully prepared, deliberate, formal speech of public addresses. Some of this speech may belong to the standard dialect, some to other regional or social dialects. The terms *standard* and *dialect* indicate that certain forms are more acceptable than others. It is not the case, however, that certain forms are inadequate for the task demanded of them. All languages and dialects are adequate. It is only that people believe certain forms are "better." "The community's choice of what shall count as the norm and what shall be rated as 'bad' . . . is an arbitrary choice, so that usage is never good or bad but thinking makes it so" (Joos, 1967, p. 14). What, then, is the standard dialect and what characterizes other dialects? And where does the interlanguage used by minority language students as they learn English fit into the standard/dialect mix?

Standard English operates on both a formal and an informal level. The formal standard follows a prescribed code, is relatively homogeneous, and is largely confined to the style used when writing, giving public speeches, or talking on television. It is the form taught in schools for expository or argumentative writing and is characterized by a restrained vocabulary; strict adherence to grammatical elements such as subject–verb agreement, pro-noun–antecedent relationships, and tense sequences; and use of complex sentence structures. The informal standard is more subjective and flexible and is sensitive to the context in which it is used. The language used in a store when asking for assistance, the talk at the office water cooler, and the conversation at parties and receptions are examples of informal standard. It has a written form—personal correspondence and business and social notes (Pooley, 1977).

A dialect is a variety of a language, usually regional or social, that is distinguishable from other varieties by differences in pronunciation, vocabu-lary, and grammar. Everyone speaks a dialect, and, as stated previously, no dialect is good or bad in itself. The difference in the prestige of certain dia-lects comes from the prestige of the speakers of that dialect.

Teachers in general often feel that their role is to enforce the phonology, semantics, and syntax of standard English in the classroom (Roberts, 1985) and not to accept or validate other dialects. Teachers may take one of three philosophical positions on the teaching of Standard English:

- *Replacive or eradicationism:* Standard English supplants the dialect of ver-nacular-speaking students. Following this philosophy, teachers see their role as correcting students' "errors."
- *Additive or bidialectialism:* Maintains both the standard and vernacular variety for use in different social situations. Following this philosophy, teachers may encourage students to use colloquialisms to lend flavor to creative writing or dialog, while reserving standard English for formal classroom contexts.
- *Dialect rights:* Rejects the necessity to learn and practice standard spoken English. Following this philosophy, teachers do not teach stan-dard English. (Wolfram, 1991).

Regardless of teachers' attitudes toward nonstandard dialects, the lan-guage spoken by a child—whether standard or nonstandard—is the best means of direct communication between teacher and child. An understand-ing of the child's language is a necessary first step toward understanding a student (Labov, 1969).

In 1974, the National Council of Teachers of English (NCTE) took a strong position on students' language rights:

We affirm the students' right to their own patterns and varieties of the language—the dialects of their nurture or whatever dialects in which they find their own identity and style. Language scholars long ago denied that the myth of a standard American dialect has any validity. The claim that any one dialect is unacceptable amounts to an attempt of one social group to exert its dominance over another. Such a claim leads to false advice for speakers and writers, and immoral advice for humans. A nation proud of its diverse heritage and its cultural and racial variety will preserve its heritage of dialects. We affirm strongly that teachers must have the experiences and training that will enable them to respect diversity and uphold the right of the students to their own language. *(College Composition and Communication, Students' Rights of Language,* 1974, pp. 2–3)

One issue raised concerning dialects has been their effect on basic educational skills such as reading and writing. An important question for educators has been: Does language variation contribute to educational failure or problems in a significant way? The answer is probably "No." Attitudes appear to play a larger role in student success and failure than do dialectal differences. If teachers use dialect to evaluate students' potential or use proficiency in standard English to predict school achievement, then it is possible that the teacher's own attitude toward the students' dialects—either positive or negative—has more to do with students' cognitive and academic achievement than does the dialect. Speaking a dialect other than standard English may cause miscommunication between the student and teacher. For example, a student may say "wif" and not "with" or read "She didn't pay no attention" when the text has "She didn't pay attention." If the teacher makes a correction, the student may not hear it or even understand why the teacher has interrupted. All the child will remember is that the teacher interrupted. A continuing pattern of such interruptions can serve to silence the child. Transformations such as those cited have not been found to interfere with comprehension. Ultimately, a greater block to comprehension may be a lack of prior knowledge about a topic, a factor that may be attributed to the sociolinguistic aspect of the dialect: Certain speech communities have access to prior knowledge that others do not (Wolfram, 1991).

The interlanguage of English language development students may be considered a dialect of English. If teachers devalue the accent students use as they learn English, English language learners receive the message that their dialect is not accepted. Using the philosophy underlying the Natural Approach (Krashen & Terrell, 1983), an English teacher can model correct usage without overt correction, and the student, in time, will self-correct—*if* the student chooses standard English as the appropriate sociolinguistic choice for that context.

Cultural Patterns and Organization of Schools

Often, minorities in U.S. society experience school failure. Several conflicting hypotheses try to explain this. One is that students of these groups are unmotivated—that the students and/or their parents are uninterested in education and unwilling to comply with teacher-assigned tasks. A second hypothesis is that students who grow up as native speakers of another language are handicapped in learning because they have not acquired sufficient English. A third hypothesis is that there are cultural differences, cultural mismatch, between the ways children learn at home or among their peers and the ways they are expected to learn at school. A fourth hypothesis is that teachers have lower expectations for their non-European-American students and thus provide them with a less rigorous instructional program. A fifth hypothesis is that schools operate in ways that advantage certain children and disadvantage others, and that these distinct outcomes align with social and political forces in the larger cultural context. In this section, organization and patterns within the school are examined to explore the fifth hypothesis and extend the understanding of sociocultural factors that influence schooling for language minority students.

Some social theorists see the culture of the school as maintaining the poor in a permanent underclass and as legitimizing inequality (Giroux, 1983). In other words, schooling is used to reaffirm class boundaries. McDermott and Gospodinoff (1981) postulate that students who come to school without an orientation toward literacy present organizational and behavior problems to teachers who are pressured to produce readers. Both teachers and students use systematic miscommunication to achieve a compromise around this difficulty. This compromise creates an educational class system in which minority students—or any students who are not successful in the classroom—emerge from their schooling to occupy the same social status as their parents.

An incident that demonstrates the way schools use language to perpetuate social class inequality was recorded by Erickson (1977).

> The fourth-grade class was electing student council representatives. Mrs. Lark called for nominations. Mary, a monolingual English-speaking European-American student, nominated herself without bothering to follow the class rules of raising her hand and waiting to be called upon. Mrs. Lark accepted Mary's self-nomination and wrote her name on the board. Rogelio, a Spanish-speaking Mexican-American child with limited English proficiency, nominated Pedro. Mrs. Lark reminded the class that the representative must be "outspoken." Rogelio again said, "Pedro." Mrs. Lark announced to the class again that the representative must be "a good outspoken citizen." Pedro turned red and stared at the floor. Mrs. Lark embarrassed Rogelio into withdrawing the nomination. No other Mexican-American child was nominated, and Mary won the

election. Pedro and Rogelio were unusually quiet for the rest of the school day and avoided making eye contact with the teacher.

Incidents like this one are generally unintentional on the teacher's part. Teachers have specific ideas and guidelines about appropriate conduct, deportment, and language abilities. If students are not aware of the teacher's values and intention, miscommunication can occur. A beginning step in helping all students be an integral part of the class and the learning environment is for teachers to become sensitive to their own cultural and linguistic predispositions.

Nieto (1992) identifies numerous structures within schools that affect student learning: tracking, testing, the curriculum, pedagogy, the school's physical structure and disciplinary policies, the limited roles of both students and teachers, and limited parent and community involvement.

- *Tracking* (placement of students in groups of matched abilities), despite its superficial advantages, in reality often labels and groups children for years and allows them little or no opportunity to change groups. Unfortunately, these placements can be based on tenuous, ad hoc judgments. A study of inner-city primary students showed how teachers classified, segregated, and taught students differently beginning from their first weeks in school (Rist, 1970). Secondary school personnel who place ESL students in low tracks and/or in nonacademic ESL classes preclude those students from any opportunity for higher track, precollege work. Furthermore, tracking systems serve to divide a campus and can increase prejudicial and racist feelings. Gibson (1987) found that non-English-speaking Punjabi students in the ESL track were treated with hostility by the majority students, who believed that ethnic relations would improve if the Punjabis would give up their values and conform to European-American norms. Faculty and staff at the high school gradually became aware that the majority students needed crosscultural understanding in order to help the immigrants adjust to their new environment.

- *Testing* impedes equity in schools by affecting the way teachers present curriculum to various groups. Students who respond poorly on standardized tests are often given "basic skills" in a remedial curriculum that is basically the same as the one in which they were not experiencing success.

- *Curriculum* design is often at odds with the needs of learners. Only a small fraction of knowledge is codified into textbooks and teachers' guides, and this is rarely the knowledge that language minority children bring from their communities. In addition, the curriculum is systematically watered down for the "benefit" of children in language minority communities through the mistaken idea that such students cannot absorb the core curriculum. As a result, students' own experiences are excluded from the classroom, and little of the dominant culture curriculum is provided in any depth.

• *Pedagogy* is often tedious and uninteresting, particularly for students who have been given a basic skills curriculum in a lower track classroom. The pressure to "cover" a curriculum excludes learning in depth and also frustrates teachers of lower track classes.

• The *physical structure* of the school also determines the educational environment. Many inner-city schools are built like fortresses to forestall vandalism and theft. Rich suburban school districts, by contrast, may provide more space, more supplies, and campus-like schools for their educationally advantaged students.

• *Disciplinary policies* often discriminate against certain students, particularly those who wear high-profile clothing, have high physical activity levels, or tend to hold an attitude of resistance toward schooling. Williams (1981) observed that students in urban African-American ghetto schools may skillfully manipulate the behavioral exchanges between peers to test, tease, and sometimes intimidate teachers. By interpreting this as delinquency, teachers leave these interpersonal skills undeveloped, and students may become more disruptive or rebellious. Rather than defining students' predilections as deviant or disruptive, teachers can channel these interactions into cooperative groups that allow children to express themselves and learn at the same time.

• *The limited role of students* excludes them from taking an active part in their own schooling, and alienation and passive frustration may result. In classrooms on the Warm Springs (Oregon) Reservation, teacher-controlled activity dominated. All the social and spatial arrangements were created by the teacher: where and when movement took place; where desks were placed and even what furniture was present in the room; who talked, when, and with whom. For the Warm Springs students, this socialization was difficult. They preferred to wander to various parts of the room, away from the lesson; to talk to other students while the teacher was talking; and to "bid" for each other's attention rather than that of the teacher (Philips, 1972).

A time-honored activity in mainstream classrooms is the small reading group, where participation is usually mandatory, individual, and oral. For Native American children, this structure was particularly ill fitting. They frequently refused to read aloud, did not utter a word when called on, or spoke too softly to be audible. On the other hand, when students controlled and directed interaction in small group projects, they were much more fully involved. They concentrated completely on their work until it was completed and talked a great deal to one another in the group. Very little time was spent disagreeing or arguing about how to go about a task. There was, however, explicit competition with other groups. A look at the daily life of the Warm Springs children revealed several factors that would account for their willingness to work together and their resistance to teacher-directed activity. First, they spend much time in the company of peers, with little disciplinary control from older relatives. They also spend time in silence, observing their elders and listening without verbal participation. Speech seems to be an optional response rather than a typical or mandatory feature of interaction. One last characteristic of community life is the accessibility and openness of community-wide celebrations. No single individual directs and controls all activity, and there is no sharp distinction between audience and performer. Individuals are permitted to choose for themselves the degree of participation in an activity (Philips, 1972). Schooling became more successful for these students when they were able to take a more active part.

• *The limited role of teachers* excludes them from decision making just as students are disenfranchised. This may lead teachers to have negative feelings toward their students.

• *Limited parent and community involvement* may characterize inner-city schools with large language minority populations. Parents may find it difficult to attend meetings, may be only symbolically involved in the governance of the school, or may feel a sense of mismatch with the culture of the school just as their children do. In circumstances like these, it is simplistic to characterize parents as being unconcerned about their children's education. School personnel, in consultation with community and parent representatives, can begin to ameliorate such perceptions by talking to each other and developing means of communication and interaction appropriate for both the parent and school communities.

Teaching and learning in mainstream classrooms is often organized with social structures that deny the ways in which students are most likely to learn. Tharp (1989b) describes the typical North American classroom. Students are seated in ranks and files, and a teacher-leader instructs the whole group. Individual practice and teacher-organized individual assessment are parts of this practice. Many students are not productive and on task in this environment. Instead, they may pay little attention to teachers and classwork and seek attention from peers. Cultures that feature collaboration, cooperation, and assisted performance may find the traditional U.S. classroom a detriment to learning. Other cultures may find the grouping of boys with girls to be contrary to cultural values. In the case of the Punjabis, for example, teenage boys and girls avoid conversation in mixed company, and girls do not speak up in the presence of males. Coeducational physical education classes were particularly torturous for the girls, who have been taught to avoid physical activity and to keep their legs fully covered (Gibson, 1987).

Cooperative learning has positive results in the education of minority students (Kagan, 1986). Positive race relations among students and socialization toward prosocial values and behaviors are potential outcomes of a cooperative learning environment. Classroom structures that emphasize individual performance, the teacher as controlling authority, and little or no student control of participation may be "culturally incongruent" with the background of many groups (Cazden, 1988; Erickson & Mohatt, 1982; Heath, 1983b; Philips, 1972). Cooperative learning may restore a sense of comfort in the school setting to children of a variety of cultures. Students may gain psychological support from each other as they acquire English, and this support can help the students work as a group with the teacher to achieve a workable sociocultural compromise between the home culture and the culture of the school.

Chapter 3

Language Structure and Use

The first time that I saw you.
I was paralized [sic] with emotion
that everything I didn't expected [sic].
I was in love with you
and because of anything
My eyes were telling you beautiful things.
Everything started from the first time
I saw you.
I felt as if I had found
What I was looking for.
I never before had so much happiness in
my life.
I have found in you many reasons to live
maybe because with you I have learn [sic]
what's love.
You have showed me new happiness
having you, I can't ask for more
> *for all of this.*
> *I love you!*

ESL high school student

Language—what it can do for us! It allows us to express deep feelings, as this student has done in her love poem. It takes us beyond the here and now, allowing us to recall past events and to anticipate the future. It is a means of connection between one individual and another. It communicates the heights of joy and depths of despair. Language belongs to everyone, from the preschooler to the professor. There is almost no aspect of our lives that is not touched by language: We all speak and we all listen. We argue about language, sometimes quite passionately and eloquently. Language is universal, and yet each language has evolved to meet the experiences, needs, and desires of that language's community.

It is important for teachers to understand language structure in order to help their students to learn (see Figure I-1). Languages share certain features, such as the ability to label objects and to describe actions and events, and certain functions, such as the facility to obtain favors, to make demands, to express imagination, and to make apologies. This chapter explores the elements that make up languages in general, paying attention to those elements particular to the English language, and the use to which languages are put. Components of nonverbal communication are also discussed in order to highlight the power of the nonverbal system.

LANGUAGE UNIVERSALS

According to Michael Krauss (Stephens, 1993), a professor of linguistics at the University of Alaska, there are 6,000 dialects, give or take 10 percent, that are still spoken in today's world. Although one cannot be absolutely sure that all of these languages exemplify each and every one of the language universals, in general, linguists agree that languages contain many of the same organizing principles. The following list offers an idea of some universal facts about human language.

- Wherever humans exist, language exists.
- There are no "primitive" languages. All languages are equally complex and capable of expressing any idea.
- Every normal child, born anywhere in the world, of any racial, geographical, social, or economic heritage, is capable of learning any language to which he or she is exposed.
- The relationships between the sounds and meanings of spoken languages or gestures and meanings of sign languages are, for the most part, arbitrary.
- All human languages use a finite set of sounds or gestures that are combined to form meaningful elements or words that then combine to form an infinite set of possible sentences.
- Every spoken language uses discrete sound segments and has vowels and consonants.
- Speakers of any language are capable of producing and comprehending an infinite set of sentences.
- All grammars contain rules for the formation of words and sentences.
- Similar grammatical categories are found in all languages.
- Every language has a way of referring to past time; the ability to negate;

the ability to form questions; issue commands; and so on.
- Semantic universals, such as "male" or "female," are found in every language in the world.
- All languages change through time. (Fromkin & Rodman, 1983, pp. 15–16)

THE STRUCTURE OF LANGUAGE

Language has been divided into various subsystems that allow us to study distinct components. These include *phonology,* the study of the sound system of a language; *morphology,* the study of how words are built; *syntax,* the study of the structure of sentences; *semantics,* the study of the meanings of a language; and *pragmatics,* the use of language in social contexts. These components have often been considered to form a hierarchy from the small sound bits to elaborate discourse. However, according to principles of brain-based learning (Caine & Caine, 1991; Hart, 1975), the mind processes wholes and parts simultaneously. This implies that language is learned without regard for any hierarchy. In fact, educators who employ a whole language approach to instruction have specifically opposed the idea that children need to learn separate parts of language out of context and in tightly controlled sequences. Thus, for English language development teachers, a knowledge of the various structural aspects of language is important in order to recognize the richness and variety of students' interlanguage and to provide support and guidance in specific areas when necessary.

Phonology: The Sound Patterns of Language

The phonology of a language is the way in which speech sounds form patterns. Speakers' phonological knowledge enables them to form meaningful utterances and to recognize what is or what is not a sound in their own language. For example, the Russian language features as an initial consonant the sound made by the *g* in the French word *rouge.* Many English speakers find this consonant difficult to pronounce in an initial position, even though it occurs, albeit infrequently, in English. They "know" this is not an English pattern.

Phonemes. Phonemes are the sounds that make up a language. These are distinctive units that "make a difference" when sounds form words. For example, because the only difference between the two Chinese words /ti/[1]

---

[1]A convention of linguistic notation is to use a phonetic alphabet to represent sounds and to place the phonetic symbols between slashes. This avoids confusion between spelling conventions and phonemic representation. This convention is used in this text.

and /di/ is the initial consonant, /t/ and /d/ are phonemes in Chinese. (The first word is used in a compound meaning *tears*, and the second means *earth* or *soil*.) In English, the main difference between the words /stet/ (*state*) and /sted/ (*staid*) is the final consonant (although notice that the spelling conventions appear to indicate a greater difference). Thus /t/ and /d/ are also phonemes in English. The number of phonemes in a language ranges between 20 and 50; Hawaiian is a language with one of the fewest (18), while English has a high average count (from 34 to 45, depending on the dialect).

Each language has permissible ways in which phonemes can be combined. These are called *phonemic sequences*. In English, /spr/ as in *spring*, /nd/ as in *handle*, and /kt/ as in *talked* are phonemic sequences. Languages also have permissible places for these sequences. They may occur initially (at the beginning of a word), medially (between initial and final position), finally (at the end of a word), or in a combination of these positions. Spanish, for example, uses the sequence /sp/ medially—*español*—but never initially. This would explain why, in speaking English, native Spanish speakers may say *"espeak."* English speakers have a similar problem when confronted with African words beginning with sequences such as /ts/ or /ng/. These sequences occur in final position in English—*cats, purring*—but never in an initial position. On the other hand, in English, the sequence /st/ occurs both initially and finally—*stop, forest*. Not all of the permissible sequences can be used in every pattern. For example, English has *cr* and *br* as initial consonant clusters. *Craft* is a word but at present *braft* is not, although it would be phonologically permissible. *Nraft*, on the other hand, is not permissible, because *nr* is not an initial cluster in English.

Phonemes occur in predictable groups called *natural classes*. Speech sounds can be described in terms of their characteristic point of articulation (tip, front, or back of the tongue), whether the vocal cords vibrate or not (voiced and voiceless sounds), and the manner of articulation (the way the airstream is obstructed). Table 3-1 shows the English stops (sounds that are produced by completely blocking the breath stream and then releasing it abruptly). The point placements given in the chart relate to the positions in the mouth from which the sound is produced. Other languages—for example, Spanish—have different qualities to the stop sounds. Not all languages distinguish between voiced and voiceless sounds, which are distinctive to native English speakers. Arabic speakers may say *"barking" lot* instead of *"parking" lot* because, to them, *p* and *b* are not distinguishable.

Pitch. Besides the actual formation of sounds, other sound qualities are important in speech. Speakers of all languages vary the pitch of their voices when they talk. In English, pitch is important in distinguishing meaning within a sentence: "Eva is going," as a statement, is said with a falling pitch, but when it is used as a question the pitch rises at the end. This use of pitch to modify the sentence meaning is called *intonation*. Languages that use the pitch of individual syllables to contrast meanings are called *tone languages*.

TABLE 3-1   Point of Articulation for Voiced and Voiceless English Stops

Point		Labial		Dental			
		Bilabial	Labiodental	Interdental	Alveolar	Palatal	Velar
Manner	*Voicing*						
Stop	voiceless	p			t		k
	voiced	b			d		g

Most of the languages of the world are tone languages: There are more than 1,000 tone languages in Africa alone. Chinese, Thai, and Burmese are tone languages, as are many American Indian languages (Fromkin & Rodman, 1983). Pitch, whether at the word or at the sentence level, is one of the phonological components of a language that plays an important role in determining meaning.

Stress. Stress, another phonological component of languages, can also occur at the word or the sentence level. Within words, specific syllables can be stressed. In the following examples, the stressed syllable is indicated by the accent mark ´:

pérfect	adjective, as in "She handed in a perfect paper."
perféct	verb, as in "It takes so long to perfect a native-like accent."
rébel	noun, as in "James Dean played the role of a rebel."
rebél	verb, as in "Adolescents often rebel against restrictions."

Like pitch, stress modifies the meaning of words. Stress can further be used at the sentence level to vary emphasis. For example, the following sentences all carry different emphases:

Shé did that.
She díd that.
She did thát.

When words are combined into phrases and sentences, one of the syllables receives greater stress than the others. Students who learn a second language sometimes find difficulty in altering the sound of a word in the context of whole sentences. Current language pedagogy, along with the whole language philosophy, discourages the teaching of words isolated from the context of sentences and paragraphs. Not only is the meaning of the word difficult to learn in isolation from context, but the sound of a word can differ when it is pronounced in normal conversation than it is when it occurs in a vocabulary list. For example, in a vocabulary list, *west* is pronounced

/wɛst/, whereas in the phrase "she's flying to the West Coast on Monday," it is pronounced /wɛs/. The final /t/ is deleted.

Native speakers are seldom, if ever, taught explicitly the phonological rules of their language, yet they know them. Phonological knowledge is acquired as a learner listens to and begins to produce speech. The same is true in a second language.

Morphology: The Words of Language

Morphology is the study of the meaning units in a language. Many people believe that individual words constitute these basic meaning units. However, many words can be broken down into smaller segments that still retain meaning.

Morphemes. Morphenes, small, indivisible units, are the basic building blocks of meaning. *Equalizers* is an English word composed of four morphemes: *equal* + *ize* + *er* + *s* (root + verb-forming suffix + noun-forming suffix + plural marker). Morphemes can be represented by a single sound, such as *a*, meaning *without*, in *amoral* or *asexual*; a syllable, such as the noun-forming morpheme *-ment* in *amendment*; or two or more syllables, such as *tiger* or *artichoke*. Two different morphemes may have the same sound, such as the *-er* in *dancer* ("one who dances") and the *-er* in *fancier* (comparative form of *fancy*). A morpheme may also have alternative phonetic forms: The regular plural *-s* can be pronounced either /z/ (*bags*), /s/ (*cats*), or /iz/ (*bushes*).

Different morphemes serve different purposes. Some create new words by either changing the meaning (*clear/unclear*, both adjectives) or the part of speech (*ripe/ripen*, an adjective to a verb). Others add information (*play/played*). *Free morphemes* can stand alone (*envelop*), whereas *bound morphemes* occur only in conjunction with others (*-ing, -est*). Bound morphemes occur as *affixes*. Those at the beginning of words are *prefixes* (*ver-* in the German word *verboten*, "forbidden"); *suffixes* (*-isch* in the German word *kanadisch*, "Canadian"); and *infixes* (*-zu-* in the German word *anzufangen*, "to begin").

Students who learn English as a second language may profit from learning sets of words at one time that share a similar root morpheme or *root word*. Learning the verb *authorize* can lead to the use of the root *author-* to generate the related words *authority, authorization, authoritarian, author, authoritative, unauthorized*, and *authoritatively*. This is a way for students learning English to expand their vocabulary quickly. Compounds can be learned in a similar manner, although in English many compounds no longer connote the original roots—for example, *household, cupboard, breakfast*.

New words are often coined from morphemes that carry intrinsic meanings. Madison Avenue has added many new words to English by using morphemes to invoke specific meanings in the mind of the consumer (Brillo, *brilliant*; Jello, *gel*; Kleenex, *clean*). In some cases, coining the right name for a new product is a marketing challenge. Mercan Company, Inc., a multinational pharmaceutical company, takes an average of two months to find an acceptable name for a new drug. The constraints: The name must be easy to remember, powerful sounding, and not too similar to the name of any drug already on the market. Successful new names? "Nix," a new head lice cream rinse; "ViaSpan," an organ transplant solution; "Nuprin," a shortened version of "new ibuprofen," a pain reliever (Doheny, 1993). Morphemes can be a multimillion-dollar business!

Syntax: The Sentence Patterns of Language

Syntax refers to the structure of sentences and the rules that govern the correctness of a sentence. English, like all languages, has generally accepted patterns for sentences. Sentences are composed of morphemes, but sentence meaning is more than the sum of the meaning of the morphemes. The sentence, "The teacher asked the students to sit down." has the same morphemes as "The student asked the teacher to sit down." but not the same meaning; and the string of morphemes "*asked the the teacher to down students sit"[2] has no linguistic meaning. There are rules in one's grammar that determine how morphemes and words must be combined to express a specific meaning. These are the syntactic rules of the language.

All native speakers of a language can distinguish syntactically correct from incorrect combinations of words. Even very young English-speaking children know that "the paper is on the desk" is meaningful, but "*the is on paper desk the" is not. This syntactic knowledge in the native language is not taught in school but is constructed as native speakers acquire their language as children. Internal knowledge is used to decide whether the sentence is syntactically correct even if the sentence has never been heard before. (We recognize the sentence " 'Twas brillig and the slithy toves did gyre and gimble in the wabes" in Lewis Carroll's "Jabberwocky" as syntactically correct English, yet the words are nonsense.) During the silent period of second language acquisition, learners are building the internal knowledge of what makes an acceptable sentence in the second language. This is a process that is not well understood as yet. What is known is that correcting a learner's grammar is less useful than supplying to that learner a rich language environment so that the brain can use its ability to acquire syntactic knowledge to best advantage. In fact, second language learners seldom produce grossly inaccurate syntax; the mistakes that second language learners

---

[2]In linguistic notation, an asterisk (*) is used before a word or string of items to indicate it is not a possible combination in the language cited.

make are usually fairly minor, considering the tremendous work the brain has done in transferring the syntactic rules of the first language to the second.

Many colloquial usages are acceptable sentence patterns in English even though their usage is not standard. From a purely descriptive standpoint, the sentence "I ain't got no pencil" is acceptable English syntax. It is not, however, standard usage. *Syntax* refers to the rules that make sentences. *Grammar,* on the other hand, looks at whether or not a sentence conforms to a standard. Learning the syntax of a language is a dynamic process in which progress is made toward grammatical accuracy. The learner acquires syntactic knowledge, semantic meanings, and phonological accuracy simultaneously, and good teaching supports this acquisition.

Semantics: The Meanings of Language

Semantics is the study of meanings of individual words and of larger units such as phrases and sentences. Speakers of a language have an inherent knowledge about the words and phrases of their language that allows them to make judgments about those words and phrases when they occur. When speakers use language to make meaning out of events that occur in the world, they must fit together the meaning of language as they know it to the occurrences. Some words carry a high degree of stability and conformity in the ways they are used (*kick* as a verb, for example, must involve the foot—"he kicked me with his hand" is not semantically correct). Other words carry multiple meanings, ambiguous meanings, or debatable meanings (*marriage,* for example, for many people can only refer to heterosexual alliances, and to use it for nonheterosexual contexts is not only unacceptable but inflammatory). Recognizing the meaning of words involves various kinds of knowledge about words. Table 3-2 illustrates the kind of judgments that a language user can make. For second language acquisition, the process of translating already recognized meaning from one language to the next is only part of the challenge. New semantic meanings must be continually acquired if the mind is to develop while second language learning takes place.

Part of the difficulty in learning English as a second language is that the English language is extraordinarily rich in synonyms. The *Oxford English Dictionary* lists about 500,000 words; a further half million technical and scientific terms are not included in this tally (compared with French, with fewer than 100,000 words) (McCrum, Cran & MacNeil, 1986). The challenge when learning this vast vocabulary is to distinguish denotations, connotations, and other shades of meaning. Bolinger and Sears (1981) give the example of a series of terms (*coax, persuade, convince*) that are synonymous but have varying implications. "I was convincing him to go" could be used only if the result was successful. "Persuade," however, puts the result in doubt: "I was persuading him to go" also tells us nothing about the result, but

TABLE 3-2   Semantic Properties of Words

Property	Meaning	Example
ambiguity	having more than one sense	She cannot bear children.
anomaly	incongruous in context	They remodeled the dog.
contradiction	opposite in nature	odorless pine scent
redundancy	using surplus words	return back
related meaning	sharing one or more elements	dazzle, shimmer, sparkle, gleam, shine
specificity	narrowing the meaning	fall—tumble; furniture—chair
entailment	logically related to previous meanings	She is his mother → He is her son
connotation	implying suggested meanings	pig → sloppy, dirty, messy
association	frequently connected meanings	The wealthy are privileged.

emphasizes his reluctance. To go further, "twisting his arm" would imply a more extreme reluctance as well as more extreme persuasion.

Part of the semantic knowledge we receive in a conversation is carried by the intonation used by the speaker: Contrast "*You* went?" with "You *went*?" The meaning of words, therefore, comes partially from the stored meaning and partially from the meaning derived from context. The lexicon is the sum total of the meanings stored, the association of these meanings with the correct context, the ability to pronounce the word correctly, the knowledge of how to use the word grammatically in a sentence, and the knowledge of which morphemes are appropriately connected with the word. This knowledge is acquired as the brain absorbs and interacts with the meaning in context.

Pragmatics: The Influence of Context

The general study of how context affects the user's interpretation of language is called pragmatics. Pragmatics deals with the extralinguistic knowledge a speaker must have to obtain meaning from a situation. One part of this knowledge is situational, the understanding of fundamental patterns of human interaction. A related part of this knowledge is the way in which patterns of interaction vary depending on culture.

Scripts. Every situation carries with it the expectations of the speakers involved and a script that carries out those expectations. In a restaurant, for example, the customers pause at the front counter to see if someone will escort them to their seat. They anticipate being asked two questions: "How many [people in the party]?" and "Smoking or non-[smoking]?" To continue the script, when they are seated, they expect to be approached by a waiter, given a menu, and asked if they would like a drink before ordering. This interchange follows a predictable sequence, and pragmatic knowledge is needed to carry out the parts of the dialogue. Obviously, a fast food restaurant has a very different script. Another typical script is the sequence of language that takes place when callers are confronted on the telephone with an answering device. They must wait for the machine to answer, deliver the prerecorded message, and produce the cueing tone. Then they deliver their own message. Even if this recording is delivered in a foreign language, the "script" contains the same pragmatic elements. When one of the authors called the Netherlands, an answering machine answered the call. Even though Weed did not know Dutch, her pragmatic knowledge allowed her to respond appropriately (in English) after the signaling beep.

Cultural context. Pragmatics implies a cultural context in which the language is embedded. Introductions in Japanese contain a mandatory bowing behavior that varies in depth in relation to the status of the participants. The process of making introductions in Japan, therefore, pragmatically differs from that in the United States. The speech acts performed during introductions are conjoined with the many social conventions controlling what participants expect from one another. To illustrate the pragmatics of a classroom situation, consider the following: A teacher calls out to a child who is sitting at her seat, "Are you finished with your work?" In some cultures, the child might expect praise for having completed the work; but in most classrooms in the United States, this question implies that the student should find something else to do and not "waste time." The pragmatic context of the situation implies that the child should display the cultural values of industriousness and self-direction. Many times, teachers make judgments about students' academic potential on the basis of their ability to respond to pragmatic features of classroom discourse. If this is the case, explicit attention paid to these features will benefit students' classroom success ("When I say, 'it's time for lunch', I mean, put your books away and take out your lunch money"). This will help students gain an awareness of pragmatic features of language.

Discourse: Oral Interaction

Maintaining a conversation in a second language requires the ability to take turns; to initiate relevant topics and to understand and respond appropriately to a topic that has been introduced; to repair misunderstanding; and to tailor the interaction suitably to the gender, status, age, and cultural background of the conversational participants.

Turn-taking. This is a basic element in successful oral interactions, yet it is never explicitly addressed. Speakers of a language have implicitly internalized the rules of when to speak, when to remain silent, how long to speak, how long to remain silent, etc. In European-American English, for example, conversationalists "know" that only one person is to talk at a time. Teachers often try to enforce this pattern in classroom recitation, yet many times the outspoken students who do not wait to take turns tend to dominate the discourse.

Topic focus and relevance. These elements involve the ability of conversationalists to explore and maintain each other's interest in topics that are introduced, the context of the conversation, the genre of the interchange (story-telling, excuse making), and the relationship between the speakers.

Conversational repair. This involves techniques for clearing up misunderstanding and maintaining the conversation. For example, a listener confused by the speaker's use of the pronoun *she* might ask, "Do you mean Sally's aunt or her cousin?"

Appropriateness. In general, this may cover all other aspects of conversational discourse. The gender, status, age, and cultural background of both speakers in a dialogue constitute a wide range of factors that influence the discourse.

The term *speech register* is often used to denote the varieties of language used for specific purposes. Native speakers learn to adopt different styles for different contexts as they mature in language skills. A formal register can be heard when an orator speaks before a large audience. In this setting, intonation is exaggerated and wording is carefully planned in advance. In contrast, casual conversation is more intimate and may feature slang and more spontaneous emotion (Brown, 1987).

Discourse: The Written Genre

Some of the same principles that apply to oral discourse can be seen in written text. In some ways, creating a coherent paragraph or essay is similar to having a conversation with the reader. Some shared knowledge can be assumed, but writing has to be more explicit because there is no pragmatic feedback from the reader, such as scratching the head, wrinkling the nose, or giving a blank look. As in oral discourse, register and cohesion are important elements. The register of a written text must be appropriate for the audience, for the context, and for its function. Cohesion involves five areas: reference, substitution, ellipsis, conjunction, and lexical cohesion (Halliday & Hasan, 1976).

Reference. Reference involves devices in the text that signal the need to retrieve information elsewhere (outside the text, preceding or following text). For example, a student writing a brief summary of a guest speaker's presentation might begin, "She showed us pictures of dolphins." A teacher's reaction might be, "Who showed us? Begin with Mrs. Quiles' name." The student's writing indicated she expected the reader to know who "she" was. The teacher's reaction was an attempt to have the student learn to write for an audience beyond those present for the speaker or, more specifically, to learn that a pronoun must refer to a preceding noun.

Substitution. Substitution allows the writer to avoid repeating elements in a text. For example, one child wrote: "Henry got a Nintendo for Christmas. I did too." By using the cohesive device substitution, the child was able to avoid repeating "got a Nintendo for Christmas."

Ellipsis. Ellipsis allows the writer to assume certain information without making it explicit. The student writes, "For the Homecoming dance, I was on the decorating committee and Julio was on refreshments." The word *committee* is understood after *refreshments* and does not need to be repeated.

Conjunction. Conjunction includes devices that are additive *(and, besides, furthermore)*; expository *(that is, in other words)*; comparison *(similarly, as . . . as)*; contrastive *(however, on the other hand)*; causal *(so, therefore)*; temporal *(next, after that)*; and many others.

Lexical cohesion. Lexical cohesion involves such areas as vocabulary use, incorporating synonyms when repeating the same term would be stylistically boring *(sundown* for *sunset).*

LANGUAGE FUNCTIONS

The various phonemic, morphemic, syntactic, and semantic components of a language are parts of the structure of a language—the building blocks. However, this structure is only part of the language system. A meaning system undergirds the structure. In learning a language, children first learn what language can do for them—what functions it can perform—and then encode this meaning into words and sentences. Halliday (1978) outlines seven categories of language function.

- *Instrumental:* To manipulate the environment to cause certain events to happen.
- *Regulatory:* To enable one to control events or the behavior of others (including approval, disapproval, and setting rules and laws)
- *Representational:* To allow an individual to communicate information to the world, to convey facts and knowledge
- *Interactional:* To get along with others and maintain social communication

- *Personal:* To allow a speaker to express the personality in feelings and emotions
- *Heuristic:* To use language to acquire knowledge, to explore and find out about the world
- *Imaginative:* To allow the individual to create a personal world, freed from the boundaries of the everyday, using language for sheer pleasure

These language functions are not mutually exclusive. A single sentence might incorporate many functions simultaneously. To elaborate these basic functions, a curriculum might encourage students to perform a wide variety of functions such as complimenting, reporting, evaluating, questioning, and critiquing. Many other functions are not necessarily encouraged by schools but take place in schools nonetheless: interrupting, shifting the blame, threatening, accusing, arguing, demanding, and making excuses. Once having learned a language, second language learners do not need to master the functions for language. These they have already discovered and internalized. Their task in acquiring a second language is to match new forms and context to those functions. This process applies to written as well as spoken language.

LANGUAGE CHANGE

One last, sometimes ignored, universal language principle is that of language change. The English language, which in its current form is about five hundred years old, has changed considerably even from Middle English to Modern English. Words for common tools have come and gone. Who knows today what an *adz* is, or a *tang* or the *heft* of a knife? The grandparents of the current teachers in the schools may have never dreamed that a *chip* would be a minuscule bit of computer architecture. These lexical changes are immediately noticeable, but languages change in every system—phonology, morphology, syntax, semantics, and pragmatics.

As English evolved from its roots in the Germanic branch of the Indo-European family of languages, certain sound shifts took place such as the gradual loss of the guttural *ch*. Thus, the Germanic *ich* became the English *I*. Similarly as English absorbed the French influence after the Norman invasion, many words beginning with *p* became *f*: French *poisson* became English *fish*. Morphological change occurred with the gradual elimination of declension ends in English nouns and verbs. Only the change in form of the third person *he goes* remains in the declension of present-tense verbs, and only the plural shift remains in the inflection of nouns. Syntactically, as the inflections dropped off nouns, word order became fixed. Pragmatically, the fusing of the English second person into the single form *you* avoided many of the status distinctions still preserved in European languages. This may have accompanied the loss of other deferential behaviors (bowing, removal of the hat) that occurred with the rise of mercantilism and the decline of feudalism.

NONVERBAL COMMUNICATION

A discussion of language would not be complete without mention of the vast nonverbal system that accompanies, compliments, or takes the place of the verbal. "An elaborate and secret code that is written nowhere, known by none, and understood by all," is Edward Sapir's definition of nonverbal behavior (quoted in Miller, 1985). Teachers cannot communicate verbally with all students in the class simultaneously, but they unconsciously use nonverbal behaviors to maintain interaction. This interaction performs several functions: It helps teachers classify students into those with academic potential and those who may be "behavior problems"; it helps students gain attention from the teacher (positive or negative); it distinguishes students by culture and gender; and it is a primary vehicle for administrators' judgments about whether teachers are "in control" of the group. These unconscious dimensions of behavior are powerful, yet often unexamined.

Body Language

One way in which teachers communicate their authority in the classroom is through their body language. Standing in front of the room, teachers become the focus of attention; standing arms akimbo communicates impatience with students' disorder; passing from desk to desk as students are working communicates individual attention to students' needs. In turn, students' body language communicates that they are paying attention ("eyes up front, hands folded" is the standard way teachers expect attentive students to act). Students who look industrious are often seen as more effective academically, and a student who approaches obsequiously to ask permission to leave the classroom will often receive the permission that was denied a more abrasive interrupter. In a parent conference, cultural differences in body language may impede communication. For example, parents may need to be formally ushered into the classroom and not merely waved in with a flick of the hand. Parents from a culture that offers elaborate respect for the teacher may become uncomfortable if the teacher slouches, moves her chair too intimately toward the parent, or otherwise compromises the formal nature of the interchange.

Gestures. Gestures, expressive motions or actions made with hands, arms, head, or even the whole body, are culturally based signs that are often misunderstood. They may or may not occur in conjunction with speech, but they always carry meaning. Gestures are commonly used to convey "come here," "good-bye," "yes," "no," "I don't know." In European-American culture, for example, "come here" is signaled by holding the hand vertically, palm facing the body, and moving the fingers rapidly back and forth. In other cultures, it is signaled by holding the hand in a more horizontal position, palm facing down, and moving the fingers rapidly back and forth.

"Yes" is generally signaled by a nod of the head, but in some places a shake of the head means "yes." This can be particularly unnerving for teachers if they constantly interpret the students' head shakes as rejection rather than affirmation. Teachers may want to examine gestures they frequently use or expect in their classroom, and then discuss with their students what gestures they use and what the teacher's gestures mean to them.

Facial expressions. Facial expressions carry a great deal of meaning, but that meaning is highly dependent on contexts and relationships. Smiles and winks, in particular, mean different things in different contexts. Consider the difference between a wink shared with a friend during a conversation with acquaintances and the wink a man gives a woman. Americans are often perceived by others as being superficial because of the amount of smiling they do, even to strangers. In some cultures, smiles are reserved for close friends and family.

Eye contact. Eye contact is another communication device that is highly misunderstood. Both insufficient and excessive eye contact create feelings of unease, yet it is so subject to individual variation that there are no hard and fast rules to describe it. Generally, children in European-American culture are taught not to stare, but to look people in the eye when addressing them. Teachers expect a child who is paying attention to have the eyes "up front." In some cultures, however, children learn that the correct way to listen is to avoid direct eye contact with the speaker. In the following dialogue, the teacher incorrectly interprets Sylvia's downcast eyes as an admission of guilt because, in the teacher's culture, eye avoidance signals culpability.

Teacher: Sylvia and Amanda, I want to hear what happened on the playground.

Amanda: (looks at teacher) Sylvia hit me with the jump rope.

Teacher: (turning to Sylvia) Sylvia, did you hit her?

Sylvia: (looking at her feet) No.

Teacher: Look at me, Sylvia. Am I going to have to take the jump rope away?

Sylvia: (continuing to look down) No.

By being aware that eye contact norms vary, teachers can begin to move beyond feelings of mistrust and can open lines of communication.

Communicative Distance

People maintain distance between themselves and others—an invisible wall or "bubble" that defines a person's personal space. This distance varies according to relationships. Generally, people stand closest to relatives, close to friends, and farther from strangers. This distinction is commonly found across cultures, although differences occur in the size of the bubble. South Americans stand closer to each other than do North Americans, who in turn stand closer to each other than Scandinavians do. Violating a person's space norm can be interpreted as aggressive behavior. In the United States, an accidental bumping of another person requires an "excuse me" or "pardon me." In Arab countries, such inadvertent contact does not violate the individual's space and requires no verbal apology. In classrooms, which are already crowded places, teachers can learn about students' distance requirements by organizing activities that move students ever closer to each other and asking them to signal when they are at comfortable speaking distances.

Conceptions of Time

In the mainstream culture of the United States, individuals' understanding of time may be at odds with that of students of other cultures. Hall (1959) points out that, for speakers of English, time is an object rather than an objective experience. Time is handled as if it were a material. English expressions include "saving time," "spending time," "wasting time." Not only is time a commodity, but those who misuse this commodity earn disapproval. Teachers reprove students for idling and admonish students to "get busy." Standardized tests record higher scores for students who work quickly. In fact, teachers correlate rapid learning with intelligence. Teachers allocate time differently to students in classroom recitation, giving more time for answers to students from whom they expect more.

With an awareness of mainstream U.S. conceptions of time, teachers become more understanding of students and their families whose time values differ from their own, and are willing to make allowances for such differences. In oral discourse, some students may need more time to express themselves, not because of language shortcomings per se but because the timing of oral discourse is slower in their culture. Parents who were raised in cultures with radically different concepts of time may not, for example, be punctual to the minute for parent conferences. One group of teachers allowed for this by not scheduling specific individual conference times. Instead, they designated blocks of three hours when they would be available for conferences, and parents arrived when they could.

The many varieties in language, both verbal and nonverbal, and the phenomenon of language change allow for rich and dynamic expression. The classroom is a home for the language of students, and the teacher is a liberal and stimulating language host. In a classroom that promotes English language development, the primary language is welcome as an alternative vehicle for self-expression, yet an overarching theme is the encouragement of

English as the common idiom. English, the language of one small island in Europe, is now the international lingua franca, a language that appears on most of the world's T-shirts and caps, the language used by air traffic controllers, the language of science, the official language in 63 countries, and the unofficial second language in many of the rest, the language of Shakespeare as well as of Elvis. English—with its vast store of technical terminology, its idiosyncratic spelling system, its penchant for accepting and using words from a multiplicity of cultures, and its many international dialects, including computer languages such as Basic and Pascal—is the passport to a world beyond the borders of the classroom. The sensitive teacher advances the students' language skills by accepting and promoting the students' voice. Writing journals, publishing newspapers and books, giving speeches, acting in dramas, singing songs, working within the community, debating timely issues, discussing world events . . . these literacy and language development events give students a voice to the world.

Chapter *4*

English Language Development

> . . . *the learner needs*
>   *expectation of success,*
>   *the confidence to take risks and make mistakes,*
>   *a willingness to share and engage,*
>   *the confidence to ask for help,*
>   *an acceptance of the need to readjust,*
> *and the teacher needs*
>   *respect for and interest in the learner's language, culture, thought and*
>   *intentions,*
>   *the ability to recognize growth points, strengths and potential,*
>   *the appreciation that mistakes are necessary to learning,*
>   *the confidence to maintain breadth, richness and variety, and to match these*
>   *to the learner's interests and direction (i.e., to stimulate and challenge),*
>   *a sensitive awareness of when to intervene and when to leave alone.*
>   (from *English for Ages 5–11* in Dwyer, 1991)

Language that is understandable and relevant to the learner fosters language acquisition and learning. In classroom situations, the teacher plays a central and crucial role in providing a learning environment in which language can be understood. This environment is rich with activities and materials that allow for language to be used and learned within a meaningful context. But the meaning that a teacher provides and the meaning that a student interprets are seldom identical. The teacher and the student must negotiate a compromise. The teacher not only provides information but also acts as a coach and facilitates the student's efforts toward meaning. The student receives information and actively constructs a personal knowledge framework. As the student learns a second language, the meaning that is constructed becomes a personal compromise between the native speaker's fluency and accuracy and the learner's attempts at comprehension and production. Using the most current English language development (ELD) methodologies, teachers acknowledge and build upon the student's meaningful efforts, while at the same time maintaining a challenging pace of exposure to English.

ELD teachers are knowledgeable about how their own speech patterns (delivery) can be modified to facilitate student understanding. They also have a wide repertoire of methods that provide meaningful lessons for their students. Because of the labor-intensive nature of beginning language instruction, they often have others who assist in instruction. Orchestrating teaching assistants and parent and community aides is an important part of organizing and managing an ELD classroom. This chapter defines and illustrates three aspects of teaching methodology: teacher delivery, ELD methods, and working with paraprofessionals.

TEACHER DELIVERY

In a language classroom, the focus of teacher and students is on language development. In a content classroom, teacher and students are concerned with the subject being studied. In ELD classrooms, teachers and students focus on both language and content. Through modifications in their own talk, conscious attention to clarification, appropriate questioning strategies, and an understanding of when and where to deal with grammar and treat errors, teachers can provide a rich learning environment that promotes both language and content knowledge.

Comprehensible Input

One of the primary tasks of any teacher is to ensure that students understand. In working with students who learn English at home, the teacher's task is to help them understand new concepts. English acts as an invisible medium used to accomplish this task. For students whose first language is not English, teachers are confronted with developing content knowledge through a foreign medium—English. The amount of English that is learned depends somewhat indirectly on the amount of time spent in English language development classes (see the Point/Counterpoint on page 73). It becomes the responsibility of the teacher to supply understandable language. This is Krashen's "comprehensible input" (see the input hypothesis, discussed in Chapter 1). In order to provide comprehensible input just above students' current abilities, teachers can consider four means: embedding

Point/Counterpoint: Does immersion in a second language promote acquisition?

Several methods of ESL teaching work on the *immersion* principle, in which only the target language is used in language instruction. If students hear, speak, read, and write directly in the target language, learning supposedly is quicker. But is this the case?

Point: **The more time spent in a second language context, the more language is learned.**

The time-on-task research performed by educators in the late 1970s and early 1980s promoted the idea that the more academic time was devoted to a subject, the more of that subject was mastered (Doyle, 1983). This theme has been evoked by English-only advocates, who promote English-only immersion education with the argument, "the more time spent in English, the more English is learned."

In some ways this argument is reminiscent of the mind-as-a-muscle metaphor that was common in medieval language teaching. Latin was taught as a way of disciplining the mind, on the grounds that repeated practice was the key to language learning or mental strength. Chomsky's argument (1959) against B. F. Skinner's reinforcement theory was that grammar was learned not through repeated exposure to language, drill, or practice, but through the ability of the mind to extract meaningful rules from disparate stimuli and make sense of language. Repeated exposure to language is only useful if the exposure makes sense.

Counterpoint: **Comprehensible language is more important than time.**

The principle that the more academic time was devoted to a subject, the more of that subject was mastered does not necessarily hold true for language learning. Research indicates that increased exposure to English does not necessarily speed the acquisition of English. Children who are educated in their primary language to the point where they are able to function at a high cognitive level, make sense out of academic tasks, and apply prior knowledge to learning new knowledge are able to learn a second language more rapidly.

Krashen's input hypothesis (1981b) emphasizes that classroom language that is understandable to a student will promote more rapid language acquisition than language that is incomprehensible. The more usable context the student can be provided, the more language will be learned. This means that classroom language must match the learner's level of understanding, combined with ways to make the learning familiar. The exposure to a second language must be the kind that is conducive to learning.

language within a meaningful context; modifying the language presented to the student; judiciously using paraphrase and repetition; and involving the students in multimodal learning activities. Understandable input to the student stimulates the student's language output. It is by means of this output that students actively solicit more input. Ideally, the second language acquirer has some control over the acquisition process by managing and regulating the input received. The teacher tries to "stretch" the student's proficiency by staying just slightly ahead of the language the student produces. Thus, the classroom learning becomes a two-way exchange that builds English proficiency.

To illustrate this collaboration and negotiation of meaning between student and teacher, witness the following one-to-one exchange:

Student: I put it here. (points to microscope slide on mounting platform)

Teacher: You mounted the slide.

Student: Yes, it has it—it has plant.

Teacher: You mounted a leaf on the slide?

Student: No, not leaf. The plant, um, ground (gesture to indicate under the ground).

Teacher: Oh. You mounted a plant *root* on the slide.

Student: Yes. Root.

Teacher: Can you draw what you see? (she makes drawing movements on an imaginary paper). . . . Make a drawing.

Student: Make a drawing for the root.

Language contextualization. The foregoing conversation demonstrates the basic principles of language contextualization and modification. The conversation is focused on the immediate task, using vocabulary about that task. Both the teacher and the student are negotiating meaning: the teacher, in this case, tries to understand what the student has done and then guide her to the next step; the student attempts to explain what she has already done. In the process, the teacher uses sentence structures that expand the student's output by supplying needed phrases and vocabulary. The teacher uses gestures to convey instructions. The teacher does not correct the student's speech but concentrates on understanding and communicating with the student about the task. Thus, English is being acquired through the natural process of communication. Of course, the subtle meanings that are conveyed through language structure require many such conversations before the student shows mastery. What is most important in this dialogue is that the student has used language to accomplish a task and has increased language proficiency as a by-product of this interaction.

The teacher ensures that the English provided to the student is embedded within an understandable context by focusing on the task rather than the language. This context can be a learning activity (experimenting, drawing, map-making); it can be a cooperative project (a play, a game, a group report); it can involve other contexts and persons, such as field trips or guest speakers who demonstrate specific skills and talents. Any learning extends language, and teachers do not need to concentrate on building specific lessons around language structures. Many sources are available to help teachers provide thematic or communicative topics to contextualize language. Clark, Moran, and Burrows's *The ESL Miscellany* (1991) contains topics and situations that teachers and students may find fascinating, including a list of national parks, points of interest in the United States, folk heroes, comic book heroes, well-known entertainers, industrial corporations, famous quotations, superstitions, folk songs, tongue twisters, and many other springboards for activities. Sloan's *The Complete ESL/EFL Cooperative & Communicative Activity Book* (1991) is another rich source of classroom activities that stimulate language within rich contexts.

Language modification. Language modification is an important means of creating comprehensible input in second language classes. Numerous studies have examined how teachers adapt their speech. Such adaptation has been found to exist at all linguistic levels—phonological (using precise pronunciation); syntactic (less subordination; shorter sentences that follow subject-verb-object format); semantic (more concrete, basic vocabulary); pragmatic (more frequent and longer pauses, exaggerated stress and intonation); and discourse (self-repetition, slower rate). Although these elements are widely used and have value, they have not been conclusively proved to aid comprehension. Elaboration, in which the teacher supplies redundant information through repetition, paraphrase, and rhetorical markers, may prove more effective than simplifying grammar and vocabulary (Nunan, 1991).

Repetition and paraphrase. An important part of providing a comprehensible learning environment for students is the teacher's use of repetition and paraphrase. Repetition involves not merely verbal repetition, but organizational repetition as well. Verbal repetition does not mean that the teacher repeats the same directions five or six times consecutively but that she uses the same type of direction throughout various lessons. For example, an elementary teacher may say, "Today we are going to continue our work on. . . . Who can show me their work from yesterday?" These sentences can be repeated throughout the day to introduce lessons.

Organizational repetition involves the structure of the day and the format of lessons. Lessons that occur at specific times and places help orient students to procedures. Lessons that have clearly marked boundaries—nonverbal, such as a location change or materials gathering, as well as verbal ("Now it's time to . . .")—also provide a basis for understanding. Students know what to expect and how to proceed. They are then able to turn their attention to content and language instruction (Wong-Fillmore, 1985).

Paraphrases of simple instructions can give students yet another opportunity to process spoken input. Repeating important words and phrases need not be dull. Wong-Fillmore (1990) gives an example of an important point that was communicated to students using simple, repetitious phrases.

Teacher: Who remembers the person who came to speak to us yesterday?

Class: The mayor [Diane Feinstein, mayor of San Francisco]

Teacher: Good. And what was special about the mayor?

Class: She is a woman.

Teacher: Yes! The mayor is a woman. A woman can be a mayor. What else can a woman be?

Class: President.

Teacher: O.K., a woman can be a president. What else can a woman be?

Class: Governor.

Teacher: Yes, a woman can be a governor. Very good.

Use of media, realia, manipulatives, and other modalities. Not all students are principally verbal learners. Most students can benefit from the use of media, realia, manipulatives, and other modalities—visual and hands-on activities that make language more comprehensible. For example, diagrams in science books represent structures and functions in a graphic way. Models that construct the human alimentary system make concrete the abstract process of digestion. One teacher recommends the use of a Language Master™ to communicate science concepts: the picture and vocabulary word are put on a card that contains a magnetic strip, which, when passed through the Language Master™ machine, pronounces the word. Computer-assisted instruction can be used in a similar fashion to augment visual pictures with auditory input. Particularly in science, social studies, and mathematics, the availability of concrete objects for manipulation provides a rich context for meaning-centered tasks. Table 4-1 provides a list of both object and human resources as well as multi-sensory language experiences.

Clarification Checks

Clarification checks at intervals give the teacher a sense of the students' ability to understand. A teacher might pause during instruction to ask, "Do you understand?" or "Is this clear?" Students can raise their hands if they are following. Similarly, the teacher might pause to ask a question requiring a simple response. "Show me how you are going to begin your work."

TABLE 4-1 Classroom Elements That Foster Language Learning

Object Resources	*Human Resources*	*Multisensory Language Experiences*
Picture files	Cooperative groups	Drama:
Maps and globes		Reader's theater
Charts and posters	Pairs	Role-plays
Printed material:		Dialogues
Illustrated books	Cross-age tutors	Simulations
Pamphlets		Rhythmic language:
News articles	Heterogeneous groups	Jingles
Catalogs		Rhymes
Magazines	Community resource	Chants
Puzzles	people	Poems
Science equipment		Jump-rope rhymes
Manipulatives:	School resource people	Songs
M&Ms		Song parodies
Buttons		Games:
Cuisenaire rods	Parents	20 Questions
Tongue depressors		Simon Says
Gummy bears	Pen pals (adult and child)	Password
Costumes:		Win, Lose, or Draw
Old clothing		Mother, May I?
Hats		Story telling/retelling:
Shoes		Stories heard or read
Material		Films watched
Lace		Experiences shared
		Listening activities:
		Tapes of books
		Records
		Songs
		Dictation

Reprinted with permission from "First and Second Language Learners Together in the Language Arts" by K. Weed and K. Johns, manuscript submitted for publication, 1992.

For a more complex instruction, the teacher might ask an individual student to restate the instruction using his/her own words. These clarification checks are an important means of maintaining a two-way process of instruction. Those students who seem to lack comprehension may be paired with a "buddy" who can supplement the teacher's instructions.

The teacher may also find it necessary to teach students how to verbalize their understanding. Students need to know not only what to say to signal understanding, but also how and when to send these messages. Teachers may need to find ways in which language minority students can voice their need for clarification, such as accepting questions that are written on index cards or allowing students to speak for others (Díaz-Rico, 1991). The ability to ask for help when needed involves cultural norms and discourse competence. Just as kindergarten and first grade teachers recognize that part of their task is to socialize students to school procedures, so too must

ELD teachers, at all levels, recognize that their students need to be taught the appropriate context and procedures for speaking.

Appropriate Questioning Strategies

Questions are a staple in U.S. classrooms, and it is generally through skilled questioning that teachers lead discussions and ascertain students' understanding. However, standard questioning strategies can be fraught with peril in working with language minority students. Two general areas are considered here. The first concerns the way questions are framed relative to students' proficiency levels; the second has to do with sociocultural aspects of displaying knowledge.

Generally, a teacher can consider a linguistic hierarchy of question types. For students in the "silent period," a question requiring a nonverbal response—a head movement, pointing, manipulating materials—will elicit an appropriate and satisfactory answer. Once students are beginning to speak, either/or questions provide the necessary terms, and the student needs merely to choose the correct word or phrase to demonstrate understanding: "Is the water evaporating or condensing?" "Did explorers come to the Americas from Europe or Asia?" Once students are more comfortable in producing language, "wh-" questions are appropriate: "What is happening to the water?" "Which countries sent explorers to the Americas?" "What was the purpose of their exploration?"

The common practice in teacher-directed classrooms is for students to bid to answer a teacher's question or for the teacher to call on a specific individual. Both procedures can be problematic for language minority students, who may be reluctant to bring attention to themselves, either because they see such an action as incompatible with group cohesiveness and cultural norms, or because they may be reluctant to display knowledge in front of others. Teachers who are sensitive to these cultural styles organize other means for students to demonstrate language and content knowledge, and act as observers and guides rather than as directors or controllers of student activity.

Treatment of Errors

In any endeavor, errors are inevitable, and language learning is certainly no exception. Often, people accept errors (or do not even notice them) when children are learning their first language, but teachers expend much energy noting, correcting, and designing lessons to address errors when students are learning a second language. Often no allowance is made for the learner's age, level of fluency, educational background, or risk-taking behavior. These, however, are relevant factors in determining how a teacher should deal with language errors.

In the early stages of language learning, fluency is more important than accuracy. A teacher who is uncomfortable with less than perfect speech only adds unnecessary anxiety to the developing proficiency of the ELD student. Thus, the teacher, instead of monitoring and correcting, should converse and model appropriate language. When a student says, "My pencil broken," the teacher's response is "Go ahead and sharpen it." In this interchange, language has furthered meaning despite the imperfection of syntax. Error correction is not necessary. The teacher focuses on the student's message and provides correction only when the meaning is not clear. Younger children, particularly, appear to learn more when teachers focus on meaning rather than form. Older students, who are more aware of school procedures and who are able to apply learned rules, may profit from specific lessons or feedback on recurring errors (Yorio, 1980).

Apart from the personal factors just mentioned, teachers need to be aware of the types of errors their students are making (Walz, 1982). According to Yorio (1980), errors can occur in two general categories: systematic (appearing with regularity) or random (caused by memory lapse, inattention, or inadequate rule acquisition). The teacher can observe systematic errors in the class and discuss them with the class, with small groups who display the same error, or with individuals. By observing systematic errors, the teacher will recognize that random errors do not need to be corrected.

Error correction strategies should serve to enhance the student's self-correction abilities. As mentioned before, probably the best overall strategy is for the teacher to focus on meaning and provide communicative contexts in which students can hear, produce, and learn.

Treatment of Grammar

Grammar is the organizational framework for language and as such has been used as the organizational framework for language teaching. In many classrooms, second language instruction has been based on learning the correct use of such items as the verb *to be*, the present tense, definite articles, possessive adjectives and pronouns, subject–verb agreement, and so forth (see Allen & Vallette, 1977). Ellis (1988) calls this the "structure of the day" approach (p. 136). Linguists dispute the value of such a structured approach for the attainment of grammatical competence, and some research (Dulay, Burt, & Krashen, 1982) indicates that teaching may have a very limited effect on the order of development of at least some grammatical structures. The effectiveness of formal instruction may depend on the nature of the grammatical rule that is being taught (Ellis, 1988). Students, who have acquired the first language through communicative interaction, often miss the intent of the teacher's corrective comment because they are searching for meaning, not correction.

Teachers may focus on grammar in an attempt to describe correct syntax. Too often, however, teachers misuse a focus on grammar to prescribe a narrow view of correctness, a view that may not be universally agreed on. This may inadvertently communicate to students that their usage is substandard. Greenbaum and Quirk (1990) point out that evaluations of acceptability are often made by self-appointed authorities. Grammarians prefer to view grammar as descriptive rather than prescriptive: to describe the actual language of native speakers rather than to prescribe usage. Viewing language as a process in which the teacher directly imparts a hierarchy of structures may impede students' naturalistic acquisition (Rutherford, 1987)

The effective language teacher, therefore, organizes instruction around meaningful concepts—themes, topics, areas of student interest—and deals with grammar as the need arises. This is done on an individual basis or, when the teacher notices a systematic problem among several students, direct instruction. Practice on the grammar point may be directed to a small group or, when necessary, the class as a whole.

Making Learning Strategies Explicit for Students

Whether language is being taught formally (with a focus on form), or informally (with a focus on meaning), one key to proficiency is knowing and using learning strategies. Oxford (1990) has divided learning strategies into two categories: direct and indirect.

Direct strategies. Direct strategies are those that require mental processing of English. These fall into three groups: memory strategies, cognitive strategies, and compensation strategies. *Memory* strategies help students store and retrieve new information by using such tools as applying images and sounds, creating mental linkages, reviewing well, and employing some physical response such as writing words on cards. *Cognitive* strategies include practicing sounds, patterns, or natural verbal interchanges; sending and receiving messages; analyzing and reasoning; and creating structure for input and output such as taking notes, highlighting, and summarizing. *Compensation* strategies enable learners to use English for comprehension or production despite limitations in knowledge. Guessing strategies help students to overcome limitations in speaking and writing; the use of gesture, avoidance, altering the message, or coining new words gets meaning across when language fails.

Indirect strategies. Indirect strategies use nonlinguistic means to make learning easier. *Affective* strategies help regulate emotions, motivations, and attitudes by lowering anxiety, using means of self-encouragement, and learning to gauge one's own feelings to remove learning blocks. *Social* strategies help students learn through interaction with others by making use of clarification and correction requests, interpersonal cooperation, and cultural empathy. *Metacognitive* strategies allow learners to control their own cognition, focusing new learning by paying attention, and linking new learning with already-known material. Other metacognitive strategies include setting goals and objectives, maintaining a strong purpose for learning English, seeking practice opportunities, and organizing conditions for optimal learning (physical environment, notebook, one's daily schedule). Self-evaluating and self-monitoring help to identify errors and ensure that progress is being made in learning English. Teachers can make these strategies explicit by sharing how the strategies function and providing opportunities for students to use the strategies effectively.

The Cognitive Academic Language Learning Approach (CALLA). This approach (Chamot & O'Malley, 1987) provides explicit teaching of learning strategies within academic subject areas. Its purpose is to enrich the language that students may use for academic communication while furthering their ability to comprehend the language and discourse of different subject areas. Explicit focus on learning strategies is a basic tenet of this approach. These strategies are divided into three major categories: metacognitive, cognitive, and social-affective. The *metacognitive* strategies help students to plan, monitor, and evaluate their learning processes. Teachers help students learn to preview the main concepts in material to be learned, plan the key ideas that must be expressed orally or in writing, decide in advance what specific information must be attended to, check comprehension during listening or reading, and judge how well learning has been accomplished when completed.

Cognitive strategies include using reference materials resourcefully, taking effective notes, summarizing material adequately, applying rules of induction or inference, remembering information using visual images, auditory representation, or elaboration of associations to new knowledge, transferring prior skills to assist comprehension, and grouping new concepts, words, or terms understandably. *Social-affective* strategies teach how to elicit needed clarification; how to work cooperatively with peers in problem solving; or how to use mental techniques or self-talk to reduce anxiety and increase a sense of personal competency. Table 4-2 illustrates five essential steps of a CALLA lesson. Within each of these steps, learning strategies are employed.

A useful resource for teachers to use in their classrooms is *Content Points* (Johnston & Johnston, 1990), which provides lessons in science, mathematics, and social studies. Within each lesson is an associated CALLA tip to focus students on relevant learning strategies. In a mathematics unit on triangle shapes, for example, students may be asked to group the shapes in different ways, employing the cognitive strategy of grouping and classifying. In social studies, a student may be asked to mark a globe with imaginary lines to begin to understand location and distance. This helps students learn to bring imagery to bear when remembering new information. Similarly, in a science unit, students compare a diagram of the eye with that

TABLE 4-2   Classification of Language and Content Activities Within Cummins's (1982) Framework

	Nonacademic or Cognitively Undemanding Activities	*Academic and Cognitively Demanding Activities*
Context-embedded	**I** Developing survival vocabulary Following demonstrated directions Playing simple games Participating in art, music, physical education, and some vocational education classes Engaging in face-to-face interactions Practicing oral language exercises and communicative language functions Answering lower level questions	**III** Developing academic vocabulary Understanding academic presentations accompanied by visuals, demonstrations of a process, etc. Participating in hands-on science activities Making models, maps, charts, and graphs in social studies Solving math computation problems Solving math word problems assisted by manipulatives and/or illustrations Participating in academic discussions Making brief oral presentations Using higher level comprehension skills in listening to oral texts Understanding written texts through discussion, illustrations, and visuals Writing simple science and social studies reports with format provided Answering higher level questions
Context-reduced	**II** Engaging in predictable telephone conversations Developing initial reading skills: decoding and literal comprehension Reading and writing for personal purposes: notes, lists, recipes, etc. Reading and writing for operational purposes: directions, forms, licenses, etc. Writing answers to lower level questions	**IV** Understanding academic presentations without visuals or demonstrations Making formal oral presentations Using higher level reading comprehension skills: inferential and critical reading Reading for information in content subjects Writing compositions, essays, and research reports in content subjects Solving math word problems without illustrations Writing answers to higher level questions Taking standardized achievement tests

Reprinted with permission from "The Cognitive Academic Language Learning Approach: A Bridge to the Mainstream" by A. Chamot and J. O'Malley, *TESOL Quarterly,* Vol. 21, No. 2 (1987), p. 238.

of a camera, again employing imagery to further understanding. These strategies are taught explicitly to students, with the expectation that students will spontaneously learn to generate an appropriate strategy when necessary. CALLA is a framework for teaching academic language skills and learning strategies that can help an English language learner succeed in content areas. It is intended to supply added support in English language development for ESL students, not to replace mainstream content instruction.

METHODS FOR ENGLISH LANGUAGE DEVELOPMENT

Instructing students in a second language has a long and distinguished history. Scholars in the universities and preparatory schools of Medieval and Renaissance Europe routinely learned Greek and Latin; in seventeenth- and eighteenth-century Europe, use of the vernacular became more acceptable as a medium of instruction, yet French was widely taught because it was the language of Western intellectual exchange. A well-educated person was expected to have mastered several languages; Elizabeth I of England, for example, spoke Latin, French, Spanish, Italian, and Flemish.

As scientific knowledge about the human body, mind, and language developed and changed, language teaching methodology mirrored the current thinking. When the mind was viewed as a muscle, exercise in the form of grammar drills and translations dominated language teaching. When the mind was viewed as an "empty slate," the teacher's job was to pour information into students in the form of drill and practice, particularly emphasizing oral repetition. Contemporary views of the mind hold that it has a meaning-making, pattern-seeking function. Teaching that follows this view supplies rich linguistic input in a meaningful context and encourages students to communicate ideas. Many of the techniques of past eras survive in some form in modern second language instruction—grammar-translation, audiolingual, and direct methods all use classic techniques, sometimes with a modern twist. The ESL methods advocated today include the communicative approach, the Natural Approach, Total Physical Response, and the content-based approach, as well as some lesser-known techniques. Specific ELD methods are explained in the next section, followed by methods that develop listening, speaking, reading, and writing abilities.

Methods for Beginning English Learners

Developing proficiency in English is a multifaceted task. Not only must students *read* and *write* at a level that supports advanced academic success, but they must use their skills of *listening* and *speaking* to gain information and demonstrate their knowledge. A fifth necessary skill is the ability to *think* critically and creatively. The teacher's role is to integrate these separate, but interrelated, skills in a unified curriculum that moves students from beginning to advanced proficiency in classroom English. A variety of methods are available that teach English to second language learners; these ESL methods range from an emphasis on language-for-the-sake-of-language to the other extreme, content-for-the-sake-of-content. The following discussion describes first those methods that are supported by current research on language acquisition and development and, second, those methods of historical importance.

The communicative approach. In the communicative approach, negotiation for meaning is crucial. The teacher and students work together to construct a meaningful and comprehensible shared knowledge. The teacher's role is to guide the students, organize resources, and set up procedures and activities so that a communicative process among all participants in a classroom furthers learning. This approach does not necessarily preclude formal practice (see the Point/Counterpoint on page 85). The teacher actively shares the responsibility for learning with the students and becomes a coparticipant in reaching the learning objectives. The students, in turn, take responsibility for their own learning and share that responsibility with other students and the teacher. The content of the curriculum is not prescribed, but selected and organized by the participants (Breen & Candlin, 1979; Taylor, 1983).

As students work together to communicate, the language that they use must incorporate a wide range of useful functions. At the beginning levels, students need to know how to achieve basic needs, such as borrowing a pencil or asking to go to the nurse. This language uses basic interpersonal communication skills (BICS), the language used to function in everyday interpersonal contexts. As school becomes more demanding, students must develop cognitive and academic language proficiency (CALP). Students need to know how to respond to teacher prompts intelligently, to cooperate with peers to use resources and construct group projects, and to express themselves orally and in writing. This cognitive academic language proficiency requires numerous years to develop (Cummins, 1981a), and changes in quality with each grade in school.

In order to incorporate both interpersonal and cognitive language functions, the teacher who employs a communicative approach focuses learning on content mastery, using language forms and structures to meet students' language needs.

The Natural Approach. One of the most effective communicative approaches is the Natural Approach (Krashen & Terrell, 1983, see Chapter 1 for a discussion of basic principles). This method, designed for beginning language students, is based on the assumption that, if students have enough comprehensible input, they will teach themselves how to talk (Terrell, 1981, 1982). Terrell emphasizes that, of the language skills, listening comprehension is

Point/Counterpoint: Is repetitious practice the best way to learn language?

Many of the activities that take place in English-as-a-second-language classes allow students to engage in practicing new features of the language (vocabulary, grammatical forms, interactions, etc.) in order to develop confidence and ease in English. The role of formal practice activities has changed as language teaching methodologies have been updated. What is the best kind of practice to gain specific skills in the second language?

Point: **Language skills become automatic through repeated drill and practice.**

In the behaviorist teaching methodology popular in the 1960s, "structured drills" were designed to enable students to form new language habits. These drills revolved around morphological or syntactic features. For example, pattern drills guided students through series of verb forms in highly structured ways. A typical drill might work on the present tense: "He *plays* soccer. (We) We *play* soccer. (I) I *play* soccer." It was thought that by using extensive drill, language use would become automatic and students would be able to access the forms acquired through drill practice to use in everyday interaction and academic work. These formal drill activities were considered most suitable for students at the beginning of second language acquisition.

Counterpoint: **Language is learned more readily through communication.**

When cognitive theory became popular in the 1970s, pattern drills were replaced with structured but meaningful practice activities in order for students to integrate language subskills into their internal representation. Rather than learning subskills based on forms and structures, learners were instead encouraged to acquire language strategies. These strategies included facility in communicating. Learning to carry on conversations, modifying language to fit various contexts, and choosing the best style of speech for each interaction are examples of the strategies needed for effective communication. One might think of this type of practice as "creative automatization" (Gatbonton & Segalowitz, 1988). Formal practice activities are still suitable in order to develop accurate usage; this type of practice is incorporated into activities that encourage communicative competence.

the most important for beginners. Thus, in the Natural Approach, the key element is for the teacher to provide comprehensible input and to be alert to patterns and behaviors that indicate that students are listening and comprehending. Speech is of secondary importance in the early stages.

Terrell describes three techniques that help with listening comprehension skills. The first one, Total Physical Response (TPR), is a method developed by Asher (to be explained). With the second technique, the teacher uses characteristics of people and objects in the immediate environment to help students be able to associate words with the characteristics. The important elements in this technique are context (everything talked about can be seen), intent (students know the subject and the teacher's expectations of them prior to the lesson) and key vocabulary (emphasized through intonation, pauses, and repetition). When using this technique, students will understand the *ideas* (70 percent according to Terrell), but not necessarily the *specifics* of the language. What they are learning is the important developmental step of "partial comprehension"—listening for general meaning. The third technique uses pictures rather than actual objects. The teacher describes the pictures, only expecting students to respond with yes/no or another student's name.

Once students begin to speak, teachers progress to "either/or" and identification questions. They use open-ended ("On the wall, there is a _____.") and pattern frames ("Diana likes to _____. Timoteo likes to _____. Daniel and Voltario like to _____.") sentences. Charts and advertisements are used to supplement pictures and objects.

Through the Natural Approach, Krashen and Terrell have revolutionized current thinking about second language teaching in the United States. Their influence has led to a reduced emphasis on teaching grammatical structures. Second language learning in the classroom has come to be seen as a process similar to language acquisition outside the classroom as well as to first language acquisition in childhood.

Total Physical Response (TPR). TPR is an approach to second language acquisition that is based on the model of how children learn their first language (Asher, 1982). In studying and observing children learning their first language, Asher noted three elements that he made the basis for his approach:

1. Listening, and hence understanding, precedes speaking.
2. Understanding is developed through moving the body.
3. Speaking is never forced.

In the TPR approach, instructors issue commands while modeling actions. For example, the instructor says "Stand" while standing up and "Sit" while sitting down. Students follow along with the instructor, who repeats the commands followed by the appropriate action, until students perform without hesitation. The instructor then begins to delay his or her own action to allow students the opportunity to respond and thus demonstrate under-standing. Eventually, students, first as a whole group and then as individu-als, act on the instructor's voice command alone. The number of commands is gradually increased (Asher recommends three as an optimal number of new commands). Novel commands are given that combine previously learned commands in a new way. For example, if the students were famil-iar with "Run" and "Walk to the chair," they might be given "Run to the chair." Students continue to respond in a nonverbal manner until they feel comfortable issuing their own commands.

Reading and writing are also introduced through commands. The in-structor may write on the board "Stand" and gesture to the students to perform the action. After practice with the written form in class, students can be given lists of familiar commands that they can then manipulate in their own fashion. The concrete, hands-on methodology recommended by Asher is associated with early stages of second language learning and is recommended by Krashen and Terrell (1983) for promoting comprehension in a low-anxiety environment.

Content-based ESL. Students' acquisition of content material need not be rel-egated to a secondary position while they are learning basics of a second language. For many students at both elementary and secondary levels, lan-guage instruction takes place using a content-based approach in which teach-ers employ subject matter content (Hudelson, 1989). For example, at Tho-mas Jefferson High School in Los Angeles, the program "ESL Humanitas" attempts to break down artificial boundaries between disciplines and to develop written, oral, and critical thinking skills through a writing-based curriculum. The participating students are concurrently enrolled in coordi-nated classes of ESL, biology, and U.S. history, which are linked through a sharing of themes. The content of biology and U.S. history is reinforced in the language class; students use English in the language class to read and write about the topics covered in the two content classes. The themes that are shared across disciplines include culture and human behavior, identity and self-awareness, the Protestant ethic and the spirit of capitalism, immi-gration and racial prejudice, individual and group power, and conflicts and resolutions of the atomic age. The team structure of Humanitas allows all three instructors to work with students on particular assignments. An evalu-ation of the program reported that students' writing over the course of a year showed significant improvement (Wegrzecka-Monkiewicz, 1992).

Other methods of ELD instruction. Many of the techniques of past eras still have a use in certain aspects of instruction. Modern language teachers need to be aware of past practices and incorporate appropriate elements of those practices into their instruction.

Grammar-translation method. The earliest pedagogy for second language in-struction depended largely on students' laborious translation of classical texts. The prevailing medieval European philosophy of instruction was derived from the belief that man was a sinful creature; young scholars had to be severely disciplined if they were to be saved from ignorance. Long hours bent over manuscripts completing word-by-word translations of Latin or Greek texts was considered an appropriate training that strengthened the will. An emphasis on teaching grammar accompanied translation, because both Greek and Latin were languages in which declensional word endings were necessary to establish meaning.

This instructional method was the most popular foreign language instruction in the Western world until the mid-twentieth century (Richard-Amato, 1988). Instruction was given in the students' native language, with little use of the target language; therefore, the teacher did not need to speak the target language (Celce-Murcia, 1991). The emphasis on rules of grammar and perfect translation left little room to develop speaking proficiency. The major remaining vestige of this pedagogical legacy is the tendency for second language instructors to cling to grammatical structure as the hallmark of successful second language learning. Translation of texts, particularly literature, still constitutes much of advanced second language instruction in secondary schools and universities.

The audiolingual method. As a reaction to the grammar-translation method, which focused upon reading and writing ability in a second language, audiolingual instruction was designed to create facile speakers in a second language. The predominant learning theory of the decades between 1930 and 1970 was Skinnerian behaviorism, which influenced the way people thought about language teaching and learning: If language could be learned as a process of habit formation, the appropriate response could be conditioned and available when needed. The audiolingual method used carefully ordered structures in the target language, which were incorporated into dialogues and pattern drills in an attempt to develop correct language habits by repetitious training. The role of the teacher was to direct and control students' behavior, provide a model, and reinforce correct responses (Doggett, 1986).

According to such advocates as Fries (1945), the unconscious habits that a native speaker acquires in the first language must become a different set of automatic habits in the new language. Thus, structural devices—that is, the basic sentence structure and the sound system (understanding the stream of speech and making understandable speech production)—must be built using repetition and drill. Often a language lab was used to expose students to audiotapes that they were expected to mimic. The audiolingual method can still be incorporated into the instruction of idioms and formulaic greetings and exchanges ("Hi! How are you?" "I'm fine. And you?") because these exchanges are often predictable and patterned. The weakest feature of audiolingual instruction is the lack of creative communication when patterned drills are used. The strength of the method is probably its focus on correct pronunciation.

The direct method. In the direct method, students are immersed in the target language through listening to discourse and responding to questions. Using short sentences, they eventually build up long sentence strings. This methodology, begun in the mid-nineteenth century, was based on the way children were perceived to learn their native language—through the direct association of words and phrases with words and actions (Omaggio, 1986). No translation is allowed in this method. Students are expected to understand meaning directly from the target language without using the native language. Grammar is taught inductively as students experience a variety of sentence forms. Teachers pantomime and use visual aids to convey vocabulary, and students use only the target language to convey comprehension. The culture associated with the target language is also taught inductively (Doggett, 1986). The best known user of this method is the Berlitz language program.

Suggestopedia. Georgi Lozanov, a Bulgarian psychotherapist and physician, introduced Suggestopedia as a method that would fully utilize the capabilities of the human brain. According to Lozanov (1982), the following tenets of ordinary education are contrary or inconsistent with the physiological and psychological functions of the personality: education that addresses only the intellect and not the emotional and motivational aspects of the personality; education that either isolates elements for study or that presents the whole without paying attention to the parts; and education that formalizes all learning at the conscious level, ignoring the fact that material can also be learned spontaneously and intuitively, or that considers only the paraconscious and intuitive powers of the learner. By contrast, Suggestopedia incorporates three psychophysiological aspects: the global participation of the brain, the simultaneous processes of analysis and synthesis, and the simultaneous and indivisible participation of the conscious and paraconscious processes.

Important conditions of any Suggestopedic language program are the absence of tension and the inclusion of relaxation elements. Such conditions allow students "undisturbed intellectual and creative activity" (p. 155), tapping into those mental reserves untapped in other learning environments. Concentration is directed to the whole of the teacher's message, to its communicative aspect. Pronunciation, vocabulary, and grammar remain on what Lazanov characterizes as the "second" plane. They are assimilated and learned along with the whole structure.

The Suggestopedia lesson has three phases: presession, session, and postsession. In the presession, students become familiar with key topics of the new material. The teacher explains the material briefly, being alert to create a positive mind set. The session phase uses music—classical and early Romantic music of an emotional nature; preclassical of a more philosophic nature. New material is read twice, with the teacher using intonation and behavior congruent with the mood of the music and conveying to the students that the material can be easily mastered. The postsession (which can occur at a later time) employs "elaborations" of the topic to ensure its assimilation. Elaborations can be reading the text (dialogue), songs, games, other dialogues, and conversations. Role playing is an important aspect of the program. Students can take on new identities when they wish but are never forced to perform. There is no obligatory homework, and the text-book contains "a lighthearted story with a pleasant, emotional plot" (p. 158).

The Society for Accelerative Learning and Teaching (SALT) promotes this methodology in the United States. (For more information contact SALT, Box 1216, Welch Station, Ames, Iowa 50011.) Current language instruction may benefit from Suggestopedic techniques such as the relaxation methods, the vocabulary presentation, and the use of creative skits and the involvement of students' personalities.

The Silent Way. In this method, no first language is used. Simple linguistic situations allow learners to observe and then describe the actions performed. The teacher concentrates on the students' pronunciation and word flow and encourages personal production of the language. Students use their own judgment to listen, voice, and correct their own language. According to Gattegno, the developer of the method, the teacher provides little vocabulary, yet the students are able to produce much language. Gattegno (1982) describes a typical lesson:

> The box of colored rods that the teacher places on his desk is all he carries. He opens it and draws out of it one rod and shows it to the class while saying in the foreign language the word for rod. . . . He puts it down in silence and picks up another of a different color and says the same (one or two) words again, and so on, going through seven or eight rods and never asking for anything. The intrigued students have attentively noted the events and heard some noises which to them will seem the same while their eyes see only different objects and a repetition of the same action. Without any fuss the teacher then lifts a rod and asks in mime for the sounds he uttered. Bewildered, the class would not respond, in general, but the teacher says "a rod" and asks again in mime for another effort from the class. Invariably someone guesses . . . that the teacher wants back what he gave. When in his own way the pupil says something approximating what the teacher said, the teacher may smile or nod, showing how content he is at being understood. At the next trial almost the whole class repeats the sounds for a rod. . . . The teacher does not inquire whether some students are thinking of a piece of wood, others of lifting something, or something different. (p. 197)

In this method, students must develop their own criteria for correctness. Errors are expected as a normal part of learning. Through teacher silence, students are encouraged to take the initiative and be self-reliant, and to do most of the talking and interacting (Doggett, 1986).

Listening and Speaking

As knowledge about language and language processes has developed, views have changed about the role of speaking and listening in second language learning and the manner in which to teach them. Early methods that encouraged the systematic study of grammar and phonology were based on the assumption that proficiency in listening and speaking was dependent on intensive prior study of language forms. In the audiolingual approach, for example, students listened to chunks of language—words, phrases, sentences—arranged in sequences that highlighted specific pronunciation rules. The students' task was to imitate, repeat, and memorize the patterns they heard. Many programs of second language acquisition still promote the idea that mastery of oral language must proceed other skills (see the Point/Counterpoint on page 92). More recent communicative approaches, however, emphasize the interchange of meaning as a primary focus and do not isolate speaking and listening skills (Morley, 1991a). To synthesize these extremes, students should be encouraged to express themselves freely in their second language while at the same time, being exposed to language skills through an orderly progression (Rivers & Temperley, 1978).

By the time children enter school, listening and speaking in the first language are well developed. Kindergartners have remarkable oral communicative competence and can use language appropriately in many social contexts (Pappas, Kiefer, & Levstik, 1990). This knowledge can be transferred from the first language to English when teachers provide opportunities for children to employ their range of oral language skills to communicate interpersonally and later academically. Combined with oral production is aural reception, the ability to comprehend and appreciate authentic spoken English. In addition to receiving the content of a message, listeners must also determine the speaker's intent, calling on their knowledge of the situation, the participants' role in the communication, and the goals and purposes of the interaction (Omaggio, 1986).

Speaking: Creating coherent text. Speaking involves a number of complex skills and strategies; but, because spoken language leaves no visible trace, its complexity and organizational features had previously never been realized. With the invention of the tape recorder, however, a means became available to study and analyze spoken language. Spoken discourse involves not only the stringing together of words in proper grammatical sequence, but also the organizing of those strings into coherent wholes. This produces an oral text, one that has an inherent form, meaning, and a set of characteristics that determine its purpose and function. Spoken discourse can be informal, such as conversations between friends, or formal, such as lectures or presentations. Informal conversations are interactive; speaker and listener share common knowledge and support one another with nonverbal cues. On the other hand, in a formal presentation, the speaker assumes the

Point/Counterpoint: Is oral language easier to learn?

Regardless of family background, race, or class, children learn their native language during infancy and preschool years without special tutoring or formal instruction. At this age, language is primarily oral. In the process of second language acquisition, it might be argued that language should also be primarily oral. Should second language instruction focus first on oral language?

Point: **Students should learn to speak and listen before they read and write.**

When language is used for communicative purposes, the primary means of learning is through face-to-face conversations. Much can be learned when a speaker must express the meaning of experience through oral discourse. The ability to speak and listen in a meaningful discourse context is an important means of acquiring functional language. Speakers and listeners negotiate and collaborate to construct shared meaning—one that is satisfactory to both participants. Thus, language maintains social relations, which in turn motivate and promote second language acquisition. Later, the knowledge about the second language that is acquired through oral interaction can be transferred to reading and writing.

Counterpoint: **Language skills are learned more easily if integrated.**

In many ways, relying on conversation to develop language is too simplistic. Much of language is used to enable both language learning itself and content learning through language. Performing academic tasks, for example, enables learners to talk about their activities while doing them. This means that sensory-motor interactions of all types promote language. Moreover, many learners do not rely primarily on auditory learning styles. Seeing things in writing promotes visual learning as an important means to reinforce oral learning. Therefore, an integrated approach (Pappas, Kiefer, & Levstik, 1990) that combines reading and writing with listening and speaking, acting and thinking contains the maximum possibility for success in learners with a variety of styles and interests.

listener can supply a complex background or context. The listener is less able to interact with the speaker to negotiate meaning.

Part of the role of the teacher is to help students assimilate and produce discourse not only for the purpose of basic interpersonal communication (informal), but also for the comprehension and production of cognitive/academic language (formal). Part of the necessary knowledge about discourse is how different forms of text vary in organization and tone.

Situations for spoken discourse. Students need opportunities in which they use English to exchange messages of real interest. These messages should have natural interactional contexts: to establish and maintain social relationships; to express reactions; to give and seek information; to solve problems, discuss ideas, or teach and learn a skill; to entertain or play with language, or to display achievement (Rivers & Temperley, 1978). In addition, students need numerous opportunities to interact with different conversational partners: other students, the teacher, other adults at school, cross-age peers, guests. These interactional activities are facilitated when students take responsibility and use their own resources to communicate. Teachers can be satisfied with the accuracy of students' expressions when their utterances are intelligible and communicative, and display some knowledge of the social features of discourse. Students can correct errors over time if a fluent interaction can be established and maintained.

In order for students to have the opportunity to practice and develop discourse proficiency, teachers can organize classroom activities with four basic strategies in mind:

1. Vary activities according to student ability and preferences.
2. Provide multiple opportunities for students to interact.
3. Provide an integrated context in which students can talk.
4. Teach conversation and group skills (Scarcella, 1990).

By varying activities and conversational partners, teachers can ensure that students are not pressured to use language that is too far beyond their discourse ability. When subject content is organized around themes, students use vocabulary, concepts, and structures in several different contexts and have multiple opportunities to speak on a theme.

Resources for spoken discourse. Teachers can provide opportunities for oral discourse, ranging from those that are carefully constructed to those that are completely student-generated. Several texts are available to help teachers include speaking activities in their daily lessons.

Cooperative Learning: Resources for Teachers (Kagan, 1989) provides numerous activities that help students learn important conversational and group skills such as taking turns, interrupting, asking for clarification, looking interested, and changing the topic of conversation.

"Oral communication in TESOL: Integrating Speaking, Listening, and Pronunciation" (Murphy, 1991) provides a wide range of activities for actively teaching oral communication. These include problem solving in small groups, enacting sociograms, and practicing persuasive or entertaining speeches.

Getting Students to Talk (Golebiowska, 1987) contains detailed classroom plans and lessons that involve students in many useful social situations: lodging a complaint, reassuring somebody, apologizing, and accepting/rejecting an offer for help.

Jazz Chants and subsequent jazz chant books by Carol Graham (1978a, 1978b, 1986) offer entertaining verbal interchanges set to catchy rhythms. Students soon request their favorite segments, such as the toe-tapping singalong, "I'll have a chicken salad sandwich on toast" or the woeful, "I'm sorry, I'm so sorry, I'm really sorry, I'm terribly sorry." Graham (1988) has also put fairy tales into jazz chant form so that younger and less proficient students have the opportunity to work with longer texts.

Real Conversations (Larimer & Vaughn, 1993) is organized around competencies that can be rehearsed via simulated exchanges at such locations as the drugstore, on the street, or at a fast food restaurant.

Conversation Inspirations for ESL (Zelman, 1986) is an invaluable source of conversation topics (1,200, according to the Introduction) that are arranged into six types of activities: role-plays, interviews, chain stories, talks, problems, and discussions.

Can't Stop Talking (Rooks, 1990) presents serious and challenging dilemmas for students to solve. Students take on the roles of those involved in solving such problems. Examples include "Making the Punishment Fit the Crime!" and "Let's Put Some Pizzazz in the TV Schedule!"

Table 4-3 has organized representative oral activities into the three categories suggested by Allen and Vallette (1977). These categories range from tightly structured on the left to freely constructed on the right.

Improving oral proficiency. English-as-a-second-language students must have a comprehensible control of the English sound system. Pronunciation involves the correct *articulation* of the individual sounds of English as well as the proper *stress* and *pitch* within syllables, words, and phrases. Longer stretches of speech require correct *intonation* patterns. (Pennington & Richards, 1986). However, the goal of teaching English pronunciation is not necessarily to make second language speakers sound like native speakers of English (Celce-Murcia & Goodwin, 1991). In fact, the goal of the learners themselves often has more to do with their eventual approximation of native speaker pronunciation than do special teacher-directed exercises. Some English learners do not wish to have a native-like pronunciation but prefer instead to retain an accent that indicates their first language roots and allows

TABLE 4-3   Formats for Oral Practice in the ELD Classroom

Guided Practice	*Communicative Practice*	*Free Conversations*
Formulaic exchanges:	Simulations	Discussion groups
greetings	Guessing games	Debates
congratulations	Group puzzles	Panel discussions
apologies	Rank order problems	Group picture story
leave-taking	Values continuum	Socializing
Dialogues	Categories of preference	
Mini-conversations	opinion polls	
Role plays	survey taking	
Skits	interviews	
Oral descriptions	Brainstorming	
Strip stories	News reports	
Oral games	Research reports	

them to be identified with their ethnic community (Morley, 1991b). Still others may wish to integrate actively into the mainstream culture and thus are motivated to try to attain a native accent in English. Teachers need to recognize these individual goals and enable learners to achieve a quality of pronunciation that does not detract significantly from their ability to communicate.

Over a period of many months, teachers may find that students' attempts to reproduce correct word stress, sentence rhythm, and intonation may improve by exposure to native speaker models. Particularly with younger students, teachers may not explicitly teach such discourse patterns but instead may allow for interactive contact with native English speakers to provide appropriate patterns. The teacher's role, in this case, is to create a nonthreatening environment that stimulates and interests students enough that they participate actively in producing speech. In other cases, however, teachers may want to intervene actively. Clarification checks may be interjected politely when communication is impaired. Correction or completion by the teacher may be given after the teacher has allowed ample "wait time." Older students may be given the task of comparing speech sounds in their native language with a sound in English in order to better understand a contrastive difference. Students' attempts to produce English may be enhanced if they are encouraged to produce alternative vocabulary, simplified sentence structures, and approximate sounds to English.

Listening: Making meaning from speech. Part of the knowledge needed to comprehend oral discourse is the ability to separate meaningful units from the stream of speech. Although listening has been classified along with reading as a "receptive" skill, it is by no means a passive act. The cognitive approach to learning encourages us to view listening as an act of constructing meaning. Listeners draw on their store of background or prior knowledge and their expectation of the message to be conveyed as they actively work at understanding conversational elements. The role of the teacher is to set up situations in which students feel a sense of purpose and can engage in real communication. In this way students can develop a personal agenda—their own purposes and goals—for listening, and the English that they acquire is most useful in their daily lives. Although the current emphasis is on communicating for authentic purposes, a number of guided listening techniques that come from more traditional language teaching methodologies may be helpful for teachers. Activities will be discussed under the categories "listening to repeat," "listening to understand," and "listening for communication."

Listening to repeat: The audiolingual legacy. In audiolingual language teaching, the learner is asked to listen in order to reproduce a model accurately. A common audiolingual strategy is "minimal pair" pattern practice in which students are asked to listen to and repeat simple phrases that differ only by one phoneme—for example, *It is a ship/It is a sheep. He is barking/He is parking.* Another typical listen/repeat format is "backwards buildup." Students are given the end of a sentence or phrase to repeat; when they are successful, earlier parts of the sentence are added until the complete phrase is mastered *(store/the store/to the store/walked to the store/Peter walked to the store).* This procedure not only addresses word pronunciation, but also provides students with practice in sentence intonation patterns. The chief drawback to the method is that the emphasis on pieces of language and not on meaning discourages understanding. Rivers and Temperley (1978) provide a wealth of exercises consonant with the audiolingual approach.

Listening to understand: The task approach. Gradually, listening to repeat was replaced with other uses for listening as the audiolingual tradition faded. Instead, students were asked to perform tasks such as writing the correct response or selecting the correct answer to demonstrate comprehension (Morley, 1991a). To be successful, they had to listen carefully. Typical classroom tasks are listening to an audiotape and completing true/false exercises based on the content; listening to a prerecorded speech and circling vocabulary items on a list as they appear in the text; and listening to a lecture and completing an outline of the notes.

Listening for communication: The comprehension approach. Language teaching methods have begun to emphasize the interactional aspect of language and to recognize the importance of the listener's construction of meaning. The central focus on "communicative competence" emphasizes that the desire for meaningful human interaction is the real impetus for language acquisition, and any activity that furthers this goal will promote language learning. During the process of learning a second language, listening is seen as a

TABLE 4-4　Activities for Listening Comprehension

Repetition	Understanding	Communication
Pattern practice Minimal pair Backwards buildup Dialogues Skits Poems, songs Jazz chants	Answer orally to factual questions about an oral text (sentence, dialogue, paragraph, talk, lecture) Answer in writing to questions about an oral text Answer orally with yes/no single words, short phrases	Games (Twenty Questions, Pictionary, Password) Open-ended sentences Conversation starters

necessary first stage. During the initial "silent period," learners actively listen to make sense of the new language. They segment the sound stream, absorb intonation patterns, and become comfortable in the second language environment. Students are no longer expected to mimic previously prepared speech or to respond to comprehension checks.

Asher's Total Physical Response (TPR) and Krashen and Terrell's Natural Approach are models for this communicative approach. Either through physical movements or through observation and manipulation of objects and pictures, students listen to language being used in a communicative context. They are not expected to produce language initially, but they do demonstrate comprehension through nonverbal means. With this methodology, academic subjects can be included, even in the early stages of language acquisition.

Interviews are often used to augment listening skills in the communicative approach. *The Complete ESL/EFL Cooperative and Communicative Activity Book* (Sloan, 1991) offers various interview formats and subjects that can be used cooperatively among students. Listening can also be used in problem-solving situations. Teachers can give students riddles, logic puzzles, and brainteasers as well as more traditional mathematical problems to listen to and solve (Morley, 1991a). Listening, far from a mere receptive skill, can be successfully combined with other language modes as part of an integrated approach to English acquisition.

Table 4-4 provides listening comprehension activities within each of the three categories discussed.

Literacy

Reading and writing have traditionally been viewed as separate but related skills and have often been taught in separate contexts. Now, however, research and classroom practices have shown that reading and writing, along with listening and speaking, are all interrelated. *Integrated language arts* is a term that has been used to label the practice of unifying language teaching across the four modes. *Whole language* is another term associated with this integrated teaching. However, advocates of whole language see this approach as more than integrated language teaching (Goodman, Bird, & Goodman, 1991; Edelsky, Altwerger, & Flores, 1991). "What began as a wholistic way to teach reading has become a movement for change, key aspects of which are respect for each student as a member of a culture and as a creator of knowledge, and respect for each teacher as a professional" (Rigg, 1991, p. 521).

Whole language instruction is beginning to affect the teaching of ESL not only in elementary schools but also at the secondary level. Whole language focuses on literacy and the process of learning rather than on the products. Whole language instruction uses authentic texts and activities that evolve from the daily life of students. Students are encouraged to see themselves as producers of knowledge, experimenting and taking risks with their learning, unafraid to make errors. Teachers are encouraged to make informed decisions about teaching and learning, reading and writing (Searfoss, 1989). This whole language philosophy is particularly relevant and important for language minority students, whose previous schooling may have been fragmented and disengaging (Crawford, 1991).

Although reading and writing are considered to be intricately intertwined, they will be treated in two separate sections here. Overlaps between the two will be evident.

Reading: Making sense of the written word. Many teachers consider reading to be the intellectual foundation of academic work. However, reading is a process that involves much more than merely decoding text; it is a construction of meaning. Meaning does not exist on the page, independent of the reader. The construction of meaning is an interaction between the text and the reader's experience. This constructive process requires that readers be able to draw upon short- and long-term memory to match the meaning of the text to their prior knowledge, linguistic ability, and experience (Barnitz, 1985; Rumelhart, 1977, 1980). They must also be familiar with the discourse community from which the text is drawn. Thus, through acquiring and practicing literacy, readers are dealing with more than the mechanics of reading and comprehension. They are going beyond the narrow act of "reading" itself. They are acquiring knowledge. This process can be accomplished more effectively through reading in a larger context, in which students engage in group activities, work collaboratively, and read and write texts for communicative purposes.

A focus on the importance of the mechanics of reading and comprehension has resulted in reading approaches based on sight vocabulary and phonics instruction. These methods often present words without a context (assuming that vocabulary is necessary for decoding) and sounds in isolation (assuming that words can be understood by knowledge of the sound strings). In contrast to this bottom-up view of reading in which texts are understood by assembling the smallest pieces first, recent researchers emphasize that reading entails predicting and synthesizing meaning in a top-down manner, using syntax, context, intention, and purpose as cues (Goodman & Burke, 1980; Williams & Snipper, 1990). The following strategies and techniques explain ways in which teachers can help ELD students interact with written texts to acquire the knowledge they seek.

Prereading. As a means of connecting the learner with the cultural context of a book or passage, prereading activities give learners the background information they need to be able to interact effectively with the text. These prereading activities may include group brainstorming; use of pictures, charts, and realia; field trips, nature walks, guest speakers, and other types of community contacts; and/or recall of previous readings on related topics. Such experiences help students to build their knowledge of the topic and to anticipate the content of the text. They further allow students to understand vocabulary and concepts within a rich linguistic environment so that the whole of the text is comprehensible, not merely individual vocabulary items.

Initial reading instruction. According to Thonis (1981), all methods of reading instruction can be grouped into three major categories: synthetic approaches, analytic approaches, or a combination of these two, sometimes called eclectic. A synthetic approach builds meaning from units such as letters, sounds, and/or syllables. Traditional reading methods teach children the sound of letters (phonics instruction) or the names of the letters of the alphabet. This approach works better in languages in which the speech–print correspondence is regular, such as Spanish. Such an approach emphasizes knowing specific elements of the code (sounds, symbols) and how those elements are combined. It assumes that once such knowledge is mastered, texts can be read for meaning.

An analytic approach focuses on whole words and meaningful sentences. One widely used example of the analytic approach is the Language Experience Approach (LEA). Students respond to events in their own words, which the teacher writes down and reads back so that students can eventually read the text for themselves. This approach draws upon the topics that the students find relevant and interesting and provides them with their own whole phrases or sentences. The importance of this method in ELD cannot be overemphasized. It connects students to their own experiences and activities by having them express themselves orally; it reinforces the notion that sounds can be transcribed into specific symbols and that those symbols can then be used to recreate the ideas expressed. Importantly, when the students dictate their ideas to the teacher, their exact words must be used, for three reasons. First, the purpose of LEA is to produce reading material that students can read. Exactly transcribed text reflects the students' ideas, in phrases created by the students. Second, the purpose of LEA is to focus on the experience itself, not on grammar points that may become evident. A discussion of grammar points either during the transcribing process or on initial reading will move away from an emphasis on meaning. And, third, by writing the students' exact words, the teacher has an account of actual usage. Successive LEA lessons provide a record of students' progress (Rigg, 1989).

Whole language has been considered by some to be an analytic approach because students are exposed to complete texts rather than isolated language units. Whole language proponents, however, would see this as a miscategorization because they interpret *analytic* as a term connoting a reduction to discrete skills, and such reduction is contrary to whole language philosophy. Furthermore, whole language is not an approach but a philosophy based on an understanding of language, language learning, and learning itself (Edelsky et al., 1991; Goodman, 1986).

An eclectic approach combines successful elements of both synthetic and analytic approaches to promote reading proficiency. Basal reading texts and manuals often attempt to present an eclectic package so that teachers can choose a method that best fits the needs of the individual student.

Perceptive teachers are aware of elements in the various approaches that may cause problems for language minority students. For example, even though students may be able to express themselves well orally, a phonics method may be a disaster because students cannot discriminate isolated sounds. On the other hand, texts using whole words and sentences may be equally hazardous if the material portrays experiences totally outside students' frames of reference. Generally, knowing the students' level of language development in both the native and second languages and their previous experience with literacy helps teachers decide on appropriate English literacy experiences.

Literature-based curriculum. A curriculum that relies on authentic works of literature written in English is valuable to ELD students in a number of ways. Literature offers language that is not created solely for a teaching purpose but that is a genuine sample of English prose intended for native speakers. Literature is culturally enriching, allowing English learners to deepen their understanding of their English-speaking environment. It depicts people from many social backgrounds and shows implicitly or explicitly what they buy, believe in, fear, and enjoy. Literature of a historical period helps students participate in the past. Literature also enriches the understanding of feelings, lending insight into characters' actions, experiences, and perceptions. Literature is personally involving, bringing learners to a focus on characters and settings that stimulate the imagination and lead to the exploration of new territory (Collie & Slater, 1987). Literature also stimulates oral language development as students participate in reading and writing activities, and, on a more basic level of skill development, it familiarizes them with left-to-right text direction, the print characteristics of books in English, and the appreciation of illustrations and graphics (Heald-Taylor, 1986).

The interests, needs, cultural background, and language level of students determine what sort of literature is suitable in the ELD classroom. The primary criterion, however, is that students have a personal interest in the literary work. Such interest can push them on to increasingly challenging material. Works that are too difficult—linguistically, conceptually, or culturally—may not be enjoyable. The teacher's role is to spark interest and guide students to share insights and understandings. Student-centered activities can support students' sharing literature and learning its value (Collie & Slater, 1987).

Often students are pleased to find English language books that reflect their own traditions and culture. Such books are an entrée into the world of reading in English. Several sources provide lists of books appropriate for various ages, interests, and abilities of students. *The Literature Connection* (Smallwood, 1991) features an annotated multicultural booklist crosslisted in several categories as well as lesson ideas. *Teaching Multicultural Literature in Grades K–8* (Harris, 1992) has chapters on different ethnic groups in the United States. The invited authors explain their respective group's experience in the United States and suggest literature that reflects that experience. The California State Department of Education has published *Recommended Readings in Literature* (1988b; addendum, 1990), which also notes those titles featuring various cultural experiences.

Often, a literature-based curriculum is confused with a whole language approach. An important distinction must be made between whole language and the use of literature as an instructional focus. Whole language teaching involves a stance that accepts students' language products and encourages authorship on the part of students. Merely reading and responding to literature does not fulfill the added mandate of whole language—to empower the students as voices worthy of note (Goodman, Hood, and Goodman, 1991). Whole language instruction does not necessarily require literature; instructional materials may include a range of real sources, starting with those familiar to the learner—signs, cereal boxes, T-shirts—then moving into the more connected text found in books (Goodman, 1986).

A whole language approach for English second-language learners can make use of predictable stories or pattern books. A typical group reading experience uses a big book, an enlarged format story designed to be used by a group. When students read together and share a story, they feel assured of being able to read that book for themselves later on. Often students are asked to predict what a story is about by a preview of the cover. This elicits students' personal knowledge and arouses interest. As the reading experience unfolds, students hear the full story without interruption. Later, students talk about the book in groups and discuss the story page by page.

This cycle of predicting, reading, and confirming or revising the prediction mirrors the cognitive cycle that children use to enjoy literature. Stories that involve patterned language such as repetition and rhyme increase children's ease in recognizing words and eliciting emotional involvement. Creative activities based on reading, such as role playing, writing new endings, making puppet shows, or writing to the author, are ways children can expand on their reading and integrate other skills. Predictable texts and pattern books lend themselves to integrated language experiences as children write their own stories, folktales, sequence books, and so forth. Many books with predictable texts also include multicultural themes and beautiful illustrations. Two sources for predictable texts are Whole Language Resource Books from Scholastic and the Literacy 2000 materials from Rigby. Scholastic also carries several brief booklets for teachers and parents on whole language teaching.

Genres: Patterns and purposes. Readers need to be aware that written texts— various types of composition—are composed for different purposes and audiences. Teachers can help students understand text not only by involving them in prereading activities, but by also helping them understand the purpose and audience for which a text is written. Each genre or type of writing has specific characteristics that, once known, act as guideposts for the reader in understanding text. Each text has a characteristic discourse pattern that is used to supply information in a specific context. For example, a menu at a restaurant and the instructions on a bottle of aspirin are texts that have very different purposes and structural characteristics. By exposing students to a variety of texts and helping them discover the similarities and differences among genres, teachers are enabling students to build their knowledge of English text. Stories, poems, plays, fantasies, romances, newsletters, recipes—literary discourse is as varied as the teacher is imaginative. Students of English can benefit by a wide exposure to the writing featured in English-speaking cultures.

Techniques for students without literacy in first or second languages. Preliterate students are those who have not yet learned to read or write in any language. This includes preschoolers without a knowledge of print, older students without previous schooling, and the partially literate who may have acquired some decoding skills in their primary language but whose overall level of literacy does not provide them useful access to print. For those students preliterate in their native language, reading programs in their native language should be continued systematically until the fourth grade level (Williams & Snipper, 1990). Along with this native language instruction, students may receive exposure to the printed word in English. By reading stories from their own culture in English, students learn about English print through known material. Because the concept load is minimized, students can concentrate on language. Older preliterate persons can also be taught with a literature-based curriculum if the texts are chosen for interesting and familiar material.

It is especially important for preliterate students to begin to read on their own, even though they may not understand every word. A beginning step is for teachers to read aloud from works of literature to show students that writing can be translated into oral speech and that books are made for knowledge and enjoyment. Students can also listen as others discuss the book and can increase their vocabulary by hearing words in context. Even science, history, and math students in upper grades can profit from hearing text; reading parts of texts aloud makes them more accessible to students (Law & Eckes, 1990). The Language Experience Approach (LEA) is highly recommended for preliterate students at all levels.

Writing: Communicating ideas on paper. Writing is more than an exercise for the teacher to assign and critique. It is an opportunity for students to link with the social and cultural heritage of English and to begin communicating effectively across cultures. At the heart of the classroom writing task is its relation to the real world. Through writing, students perform a purposeful social action, an action that takes them beyond a mere school assignment. Communicating with one another, with others outside the classroom, with home and family, with presidents and corporate officers, with city officials and nursing home residents establishes real discourse and helps students to convey information that is real and necessary. This is the essence of writing as a communicative task.

The writing process. Many teachers, focusing on the written "product," have students produce a composition that demonstrates technical competence. This ignores the social aspect of language and, moreover, ignores the process of writing. A process view of writing has become increasingly accepted as an alternative to the "product" view. The shift from a focus on product to a focus on process is "the most significant single transformation in the teaching of composition" (Kroll, 1991, p. 247). It changes the way students compose, provides situations where language can be used in a meaningful way, and emphasizes the act of writing rather than the result. Donald Graves has been instrumental in encouraging an acceptance of this process view. His book, *Writing: Teachers and Children at Work* (1983) offers a rich resource for classroom teachers in organizing writing according to the process view. Although written for the mainstream classroom teacher, this book is a fundamental resource for all teachers working with children and language.

The process approach involves several stages: the planning or prewriting stage, the writing stage, and the editing stage. During prewriting, children are involved in oral language experiences that develop their need and desire to write. These activities may include talking and listening about shared experiences, reading literature, brainstorming, or creating role plays or other fantasy activities (Enright & McCloskey, 1988). Such activities encourage students to generate and organize their ideas.

The drafting stage involves writing quickly to capture ideas. Students do the best they can in spelling, vocabulary, and syntax without a concern for accuracy. This is followed by as much rewriting and redrafting as necessary. Students can help each other by sharing and discussing the content of their writing and the clarity of expression. This interaction helps students to expand their ideas and communicate more expressly before the editing step perfects the form and grammar.

In the last stage, editing, students are helped to fix up their mechanics of usage and spelling, particularly when their writing is going to be shared in a formal way. If a perfected or final version is not necessary, students may file their rough drafts in a portfolio. The process has generated writing that is satisfying in its ability to capture and share ideas—the essence of writing for the purpose of communication. If, however, the writing is published or publicly shared, students also achieve the pride of authorship. Ways of publishing may vary: a play performed, a story bound into a book for circulation in the class library, a poem read aloud, an essay posted on a bulletin board, a video made of a student reading aloud, a class newspaper circulated to the community (Enright & McCloskey, 1988).

The writing workshop. The process approach to writing is most successful within an environment of collaboration. Students have frequent opportunities to draw upon prior knowledge and experience, to share with one another as they compose and revise, and to view the teacher as a resource for advice and support. Williams and Snipper (1990) label this approach "the classroom as workshop." In such a workshop environment, students assume a great deal of responsibility for their own learning. The teacher's role is to ensure that students are working on projects of interest to them and that materials and resources are available. In these workshops, ELD students can draw on native English-speaking students, not just the teacher, as a resource, and, in turn, can use their own experiences to enrich their writing and that of their peers (Samway, 1992).

The teacher, then, becomes a facilitator and listener. The main task for the teacher is to work with students on their progress in writing during the conference. The teacher sets aside specific times for individual conferences and *listens* to each student talk about the work in progress. The conference always begins with the teacher commenting and asking questions about the content of the writing. She then listens to the way the student talks about the writing. Cues to aid the student toward developing writing proficiency come from the student's own words, not from a preset series of curriculum objectives. Teachers ask "following" questions (those that follow or reflect the student's comment) aimed at leading the student toward control of the topic; "process" questions that help the student organize and focus the writing; and "basic" questions that ask the student to focus on the basic structure (Graves, 1983). The questioning serves a dual purpose: to help the teacher understand the student's topic and focus and to model appropriate questions that students can later ask themselves as they integrate the principles of putting their thoughts on paper.

Conferences are not feasible for every piece of student writing. In written feedback, however, teachers can continue to be supportive. They respond to the students' intentions, the content of the writing, rather than surface grammatical problems. Surface grammatical errors will not disappear within one semester or even one year, but general language proficiency will be enhanced by the shift in focus from grammar to meaning. A procedure recommended to use with ELD students includes the following steps:

- Skim a student's paper before writing comments.
- Address the student by name when writing comments.
- Recognize the major strength(s) of the paper, along with sentences or paragraphs that are particularly effective or important.
- Phrase any comments tentatively ("perhaps," "do you think").
- List questions and suggestions for change. Students should work at solving major problems of development, organization, and style—they do not benefit much when the teacher solves these *problems.* (Peitzman, 1989)

A technique used by one ELD teacher when reading papers outside of class is to give students oral feedback through the tape recorder ("Human Touch," 1993). As this teacher reads each composition, he thinks aloud, reacting to student ideas and writing style. He finds that he spends the same amount of time talking as he would writing on the paper, yet gives students more personal feedback.

Teachers who value collaborative learning encourage students to assist one another in the feedback process. Peer response often increases students' abilities to analyze their own drafts. However, simply putting students together in groups and having the group members react to the strength and weaknesses of a paper read aloud is not a format that is likely to be successful (Kroll, 1991). Peer response in the ELD classroom must be modeled and taught in order for it to be useful. One way to shape peer response is to give students a short list of questions that they must address as they read each other's papers. This might include a checklist of necessary attributes. Working with a sample essay as a group, students can collectively use the list until each is capable and confident enough to apply the list alone. Leki (1990) draws a distinction between peer response to writing and editing. Teachers may wish to help students understand that peer response should include feedback about the content, point of view, and tone of the work. This helps to focus on the communicative content of the writing and draws students together in a more respectful sharing of the messages they intend. Editing is a later step, which may or may not involve the student's peers.

Editing takes place after the message is intact and the student has formu-
lated and written down all appropriate thoughts.

In the early stages of acquiring English, fluency is a much more vital
goal than accuracy in the process of writing. Many teachers, however, view
their role as that of judge: They decide when to correct errors, who will
correct errors, which errors to correct, and how to correct errors (Kroll, 1991).
With ELD students, the teacher must consider the level of students' general
language proficiency before decisions about error correction can be made.
Law and Eckes (1990) suggest that with younger children and newcomers,
it is best to encourage expression of ideas without correcting grammar. Feedback helps clarify ideas and intent. A focus on quality and correctness is a
matter of priorities. Students should be rewarded for their courage in trying new formats and more complicated sentence syntax. By celebrating the
effort that sometimes results in mistakes rather than judging the mistake,
teachers can set a tone of encouragement for risk taking. Error correction is
a process of tactfully bringing students to enjoy perfecting their control over
vocabulary, grammar, and usage. Correcting an essay is like fine tuning an
engine: An essay must "run" before a tune-up is needed (Gadda, Peitzman,
& Walsh, 1988).

The writing classroom: A case study. As the bell rings, students in Maxine
Grimm's ELD class take their seats and begin writing in their journals.
Ms. Grimm turns on a tape player, and the music of Liszt provides a
background atmosphere. A writing prompt on the board directs students to write about an incident where they attended a party and at
first felt uncomfortable. After ten minutes, the students count the number of words written and record the information on a fluency chart.
Once a week, Ms. Grimm reads these journals and writes comments,
opening a dialogue with the student about thoughts and feelings that
are evident. She does not correct grammar or spelling, but focuses on
what the student is trying to say.

Although Ms. Grimm is encouraged that students' writing fluency
is increased, she worries that by allowing the students to write freely in
their journals, she is not spending sufficient time in correcting errors in
students' writing. There is much individual variation in the errors and
the fluency in the personal journals. The Spanish-speaking students
seem to have difficulty using the journal to express personal feelings.
This may be because the recently immigrated students rarely keep dia-
ries or journals in Spanish—it is not a part of their literacy experience in
their native culture. In contrast, several of the Japanese exchange students in this class have asked Ms. Grimm to help them obtain English-
speaking pen pals so that they may maintain their English skills once
they have returned to Japan.

The newest class member is a Romanian orphan who has been
adopted by a local family. Sophia's journal entries show minimal effort

in using written English. When the students chart their daily word count, Sophia remains silent and does not complete the chart. Other students seem to be aware of Sophia's discomfort.

In an article in a recent *CATESOL Journal* (Lucas, 1991), Ms. Grimm read about individual differences in classroom personal journal writing. Those personal characteristics mentioned in the article, such as language habits, motivations, social needs, and habitual approaches to problem solving, are quite apparent in the differences shown by her students as they write. Ms. Grimm is now slowly moving away from assigned topics, allowing students to write on items of interest or concern to them. For those students who are not comfortable with that degree of independence, Ms. Grimm has brought in topics related to areas of study. She has also used a simple workbook called *This Is Me* (Claire, 1990) designed for new students of English. Ms. Grimm suspects that Sophia may be preliterate and that she needs very simple yet stimulating materials to begin learning English.

Thus, Ms. Grimm is finding support for her program in the professional items she reads. She believes she is helping the students in their writing ability, and she has evidence to support this belief. She recognizes that part of her uneasiness stems from the different philosophical stance she has taken toward education in general and language teaching in particular—a stance that departs significantly from her own background as a student and beginning teacher.[1]

Teaching ELD writers: Factors to consider. Writing is not always an easy process to master. In any class, students' willingness and motivation to tackle writing activities vary. With ELD students, additional factors can affect students' motivation in learning English in general and writing in particular. Specific information about immigrant students is important: their nation of origin, age upon arrival in the United States, amount of prior schooling; and difficulties in the journey. Additionally, the reasons why the students are in an English-speaking environment can be extremely important: Were they forced to emigrate from their home countries because of adverse conditions such as war or famine? Were their families seeking political asylum, or were they seeking better economic conditions? Another factor to consider is how the student's ethnic, racial, or national group is accepted in mainstream U.S. society. Some groups are well received, but others do not fare as well. The rural or urban background of the student can also make a difference. A student coming from an area of little technological development will be facing a much different adjustment situation than will one who comes from a cosmopolitan city (Leki, 1992; Scarcella, 1990).

---

[1]Adapted with permission from "Constructivist Theory into Practice in a Secondary Linguistic Minority Classroom: Shared Teacher and Student Responsibility for Learning" by W. Waters, unpublished paper, 1987.

Besides these general background factors, specific ones regarding the students' literacy background are important to keep in mind: To what extent is literacy practiced in the home? How is it practiced? What is the child's role in literacy practices in the home language? In English? In some families, literacy might consist of shared letter reading and writing. In families with non-English-speaking adults, school-age children may be encouraged to become competent readers and writers in order to help parents read official papers and fill out documents (Hudelson, 1986).

Although these factors need to be considered in planning school experiences, ELD teachers should not postpone writing instruction until some optimal time when students are "ready." Contrary to the traditional belief that students must have "mastered" the oral language before being able to write, research indicates that children are able to write using whatever knowledge of English they possess. As their control of English grows, their growth is reflected in their writing. To encourage student writing, teachers need to have students write on a daily basis in different genres and for a variety of tasks. Students should be allowed to develop ideas and focus on the content without regard to mistakes. Reluctant writers and beginning students can be given numerous short writing tasks throughout the day (Simmons, 1989).

Transferring literacy from first to second languages. During the era in which the audiolingual method of second language instruction was in vogue, it was customary to anticipate that certain learners would experience predictable kinds of difficulties in learning English depending on their first language. For example, it is difficult for native speakers of Japanese to distinguish the phonemes /r/ and /l/, because Japanese does not feature such a distinction. Likewise, native speakers of Mandarin or Cantonese forms of Chinese might have difficulty mastering the definite and indefinite article in English because Chinese employs a very different way of marking nouns. This reasoning about predictable difficulties, called *contrastive analysis,* is no longer a primary strategy in second language acquisition theory. Contemporary views deemphasize L1—L2 transfer or interference and instead emphasize meaningful communication in the second language.

The idea of contrasting the native language with English in order to predict possible interference or transfer has been carried into the domain of writing instruction. *Contrastive rhetoric* is a term used to denote the process of understanding ELD students' writing by comparing typical texts in the native language with that of English (see Grabe & Kaplan, 1990). Kaplan (1967) indicates that a language such as Arabic may show a text structure that depends upon elaborate parallel structures and embedded references to moral teaching to create points of rhetoric. Arabic students learning English tend to use very little in the way of subordinating structures and instead rely on parallelism and metaphor. Other writing instructors have commented that Chinese students tend to use circular rhetoric structures when writing in English, and use relatively few linear or "logical" beginning-to-end arguments such as are common in English texts. Teachers of writing may find their students' thought structures more understandable by noting what a typical rhetoric structure in the primary language contributes to thought.

Written discourse strategies. Writing within a classroom can serve a range of purposes. If all writing assignments are teacher-directed, then writing takes the flavor of strictly academic work with the characteristics of such labor: teacher-selected topics that may be of little interest to the student, assigned for the purpose of increasing skills without a concern for communication. If the writing takes place within the context of thematic units, then writing topics can be student-generated, with the purpose of increasing the general fund of knowledge about the theme. Other purposes for writing may be interpersonal communication: pen pals, notes, requests for information from community sources, lists, texts for student publications, and entertaining stories.

When the audience changes, student writing changes. Instead of the teacher being the sole reader and critic, students write for each other and for people beyond the classroom. Peer responses and responses from others become an important measure of communicative success and can lead to increased effort and interest. As students write, they learn to consider the effect of their writing on the audience, making their thoughts understandable to others.

The use of a variety of genres provides a means for teachers to maintain student interest and motivation in writing. Not all classroom writing needs to be confined to the one-page essay. Just as students can be encouraged to read many kinds of fiction and nonfiction, they can also write longer and more engaging works—mysteries, Western stories, fantasies, science-fiction, historical fiction, romances, biographies, how-to manuals, editorials, advertisements, commentaries, reviews of books, films, and movies, newsletters, recipes—the list is as extensive as a teacher's creativity. Each of these genres has a typical discourse pattern that makes the genre predictable. Each genre's organization relies on a particular order of words and phrases. By using the pattern and organizational features, students can learn the logic of stories and thus transfer this logic to the linear organization of text that is characteristic of English writing.

A beginning step for teachers to use in helping students learn about purpose, audience, and genre may be reader response. In this technique, students respond in writing to texts that they have read. As students learn that their writing can voice their response to the texts they read, they begin to understand that others can learn from their writing if it is clear and understandable. The awareness that a reader will respond to their writing helps them provide a structure that shapes thinking. In *Stories to Tell Our Children,* Weinstein-Shr (1992) presents brief reading selections that capture

TABLE 4-5   Reader Response Questions for Fiction and Nonfiction Works

Response to Fiction	Response to Nonfiction
How did the piece make you feel?	What does this piece remind you of in your own life?
Is any character in this work like you? Why do you say this?	Did this piece make you think of any thing else you have read or heard about?
Was there anything about this piece that confused you?	When you think about this piece, what picture or image comes to mind? Describe it
What about this piece made you want to keep reading?	Did your feelings about what you read change as you were reading? If so, explain how.
Before you started reading this piece what did you think it would be about? Were you right?	What was most important in this piece?
If the author of this piece were in this classroom right now, what would you like to say to him or her?	

Reprinted with permission from *Developing Writers: Process, Craft, Collaboration* by N. Farnan & L. Feam, 1991, San Diego State University Developmental Writing Institute, San Diego, CA.

the feelings of immigrants from many cultures. Topics such as neighbors, marriage, music, friends, and grandchildren serve as prompts in a multi-cultural class. Another excellent source of writing prompts is Blot and Davidson's (1988) *Put It in Writing*, which offers reading selections that range from vignettes about cultural adjustment to problem-solving interactions between individuals. These multicultural reading selections can draw forth from students thoughtful and meaningful responses that make writing more purposeful. Table 4-5 provides examples of questions to guide student responses. These questions can be adapted to various genres of fiction and nonfiction.

The teacher's role is that of orchestrator—setting up cooperative groups of students to work on reading, listening, speaking, or writing tasks. The complexity of organizing an ELD classroom falls primarily on the teacher. To make this task easier, teachers often call upon others to assist in tutoring, coaching, monitoring, and motivating students. Working with a variety of aides can be a definite asset, and can provide ELD teachers with additional help.

WORKING WITH PARAPROFESSIONALS

Paraprofessional educators may be instructional aides, volunteers from the parent community, tutors from other grades, or senior citizens and other community volunteers. Students from high school service organizations or university students may work in classrooms as part of community outreach programs. Language teaching is a labor-intensive enterprise, and having a variety of assistants means that more can be accomplished during school time. Involving para-educators requires careful organization to recruit skillful helpers and to utilize them effectively. Prudent planning is needed to maintain high quality instruction and to ensure that assistants in the classroom feel valued.

Organizing for Assistance

A paraprofessional works alongside the teacher to assist in preparing materials, doing clerical work, monitoring small groups of students, giving tutorial help, or providing basic instruction under teacher supervision. Many bilingual education programs rely upon teacher aides to deliver primary language instruction; or, in a classroom in which the teacher delivers the primary language instruction, the aide may be involved with pull-out ELD tutoring for those students most in need of English instruction. The quasi-instructional duties, such as tutoring and assisting small groups of students, provide an extension of teacher expertise. It is the teacher's responsibility to see that instructional quality is maintained, that the aide is effective in promoting student achievement, and that students receive as rich instruction from the aide as they might from the teacher.

Although aides who are hired and placed by the school district or principal are often assigned to classrooms without prior input from the teacher, at other times the teacher can choose who will be helping. The strongest criteria are that an aide be reliable, helpful, and sincerely desire to work with students (Charles, 1983). Beyond these personal characteristics, paraprofessionals in bilingual and ELD classrooms should possess good English language skills, a working knowledge of classroom management, and "cultural savvy"—an understanding of both the host culture and the students' (Law & Eckes, 1990). Volunteers who speak the students' native language(s) can be selected to serve as role models, giving a greater sense of worth to language minority students. Although it is certainly desirable for the volunteer to have good English-language skills, those who do not speak English well can read to and with children in the primary language or can preteach necessary subject matter vocabulary and concepts that will subsequently be taught by the teacher in English.

To locate classroom volunteers other than district-provided personnel, teachers may approach other colleagues to request that older students be assigned as cross-age tutors. Helpful peers with good English abilities can be used as "buddies." Parents may be recruited through invitations sent home with students or through personal contacts at open house activities, student conferences, or home visits. The local high school and university can be contacted for a list of outreach organizations and names of contact people. Also many communities have a city worker to coordinate senior citizen activities. This person can be contacted to suggest volunteers.

Classroom professional teachers have responsibility for all instruction and classroom behavior. By right of their position, they have authority in these areas. Disciplining students in groups supervised by the aide is certainly the responsibility of the aide; the teacher must support such discipline while ensuring that students are treated with courtesy. Instruction provided by the aide likewise is valid and important and should be considered as such by the students. However, ultimately smooth management and major teaching in the classroom rests on the teacher's shoulders.

Often, teacher assistants who are brought into the classroom to offer primary language instruction may share the students' cultural background. These individuals can provide valuable linguistic and emotional support for students as they learn English. On the other hand, such aides may subtly modify the teacher's educational intentions (Williams & Snipper, 1990). For example, Mr. Burns, a fifth-grade teacher in a bilingual classroom, had a Laotian aide who was the mother of four students in the school. While working in cooperative groups, the students were expected to exchange ideas and information, compose and deliver group reports. Mr. Burns began to notice that the Laotian students did not speak voluntarily but waited to be called on. In observing the aide work with these students, he found that she discouraged students from speaking unless they received permission to do so. In a conference with the aide, Mr. Burns discovered, to his chagrin, that she believed that speaking out undermined the teacher's authority. The aide and the teacher came from different cultural backgrounds, with different views of what constitutes respectful behavior. A compromise had to be negotiated that would encourage students to develop speaking proficiency.

Planning Assisted Lessons

All individuals working with the teacher provide a challenge in planning activities and monitoring student achievement. Teachers who value the help provided by assistants must be willing to invest time in both planning and supervising, in order for such individuals to be employed effectively.

The tasks carried out by the aide should be planned by the teacher. A paraprofessional should not be expected to plan and prepare materials without teacher supervision. Moreover, student achievement should not be evaluated solely by the paraprofessional; this is a responsibility of the classroom teacher. ELD materials are available that provide a wide range of activities suitable for paraprofessional use, particularly the *Bridge to Communication* series from Santillana Publishing Company.

All para-educators should have a classroom space provided for their tutoring or group work. Often, aides are given a table or desk where the teacher places materials for the paraprofessional's use. The teacher should arrange work that allows classroom aides to make the greatest contribution during the hours they work (Williams & Snipper, 1990). The number of students for which an aide is responsible may vary during this period, from one-to-one tutoring to supervising the entire class while the teacher is involved in conferences or individual student contact. Should the aide be unavailable, the teacher must have backup plans so that the day's activities can be modified.

It is not easy to be a classroom assistant and to work under someone else's supervision. Feeling accepted and valued is an important component of the sense of belonging that makes the role rewarding. Making the aide feel part of the instructional team is an important aspect of morale. To do this, aides need to be engaged in meaningful work from which they can derive a sense of accomplishment. Their duties should not be relegated to tedious and menial tasks. They need to be given clear directions and understand not only what is expected of them but also what is expected of the students. It is important that they participate in the instructional planning and can be involved in seeing certain activities through to closure. They are also a source of valuable feedback to the teacher on students' needs and accomplishments. For their efforts, paraprofessionals deserve appreciation, whether it is a spoken "thank you" and a pat on the back or an occasional gift or token of esteem (Charles, 1983).

The ELD classroom is a complex environment. The classroom teacher orchestrates a wide variety of language acquisition activities, involving students whose English language abilities vary greatly. Within a single class period, a teacher may employ many differing methods depending on the communicative goals desired. Teaching assistants can help teachers meet the needs of particular groups of students. The joy of working in classrooms with English learners lies in the progress that students make daily.

Chapter 5

Content Area Instruction

School started the day after Labor Day. Our enrollment suddenly included 150 Hmong who had recently immigrated to our school district. We had neither classrooms nor teachers to accommodate such a large influx, and no one was qualified to deliver instruction in Hmong. By October, it was obvious that our policy of placing these students in regular content classes was not working. The students were frustrated by their inability to communicate and keep up with classwork, and teachers felt overwhelmed and inadequate to meet the needs of students who were barely literate and did not know English. A typical student was Khim, who, though better off than most Hmong because she could communicate her basic needs in English, could not cope with the reading and writing demands of eleventh-grade history, math, and science. She did not have the background knowledge or the study skills required for these classes and thus could not meet graduation requirements. On October 15, the faculty meeting was abuzz with discontent and resolve: We needed a new approach to delivering classes for the language minority students who were our new challenge. (High school teacher journal entry)

This vignette illustrates the situation facing many schools and teachers today. Modified content area instruction, sometimes called sheltered instruction, is an approach used in multilinguistic content classrooms. The term *sheltered* suggests that students are given additional language and academic support, rather than being expected to "sink or swim" in a content class designed for native English speakers. Sheltered instruction may take place in mainstream classes made up of native and nonnative speakers of intermediate proficiency, or in classes consisting solely of nonnative speakers who operate at similar English proficiency levels (Richard-Amato & Snow,

1992). For these language minority students, primary language instruction may be the ideal option; but if there are small numbers of students representing a wide variety of languages, bilingual program models may not serve them effectively.

Sheltered English, or specially designed academic instruction in English (SDAIE[1]), combines second language acquisition principles with those elements of quality teaching that make a lesson understandable to students (Sobul, 1994). Such instruction enables them to improve listening, speaking, reading, and writing through the study of an academic subject. SDAIE is the preferred method used by both intermediate and high schools when native language instruction is not available or is offered only in Spanish (Minicucci & Olsen, 1992b). A SDAIE classroom has subject content and objectives identical to those of a mainstream classroom in the same subject, but the instruction is modified for those who have a nonproficient command of English. The distinction between SDAIE and content-based English instruction is that SDAIE features content instruction taught by content area teachers with English language support. Content-based ESL features the use of content area materials as texts for ESL lessons.

SDAIE teachers provide a context for instruction that is rich in opportunities for hands-on learning and student interaction. Teachers devote particular attention to communication strategies. Variety in instructional techniques helps students to master demanding content areas. By altering the means of presenting material to make it more accessible and understandable, the teacher maintains a challenging academic program without watering down or overly simplifying the curriculum.

PRINCIPLES OF SPECIALLY DESIGNED ACADEMIC INSTRUCTION IN ENGLISH

Language minority students can succeed in content area classes. They do not need to learn English by studying it formally as an isolated activity. If they can follow and understand a lesson, they can learn content matter, and the content area instruction becomes the means for acquiring English. Basically, SDAIE has four goals: that students learn English, learn content, practice higher level thinking skills, and advance their literacy skills (Law & Eckes, 1990). To accomplish both content and language learning goals, teachers organize instruction around these principles (see Hudelson, 1989):

---

[1] The term SDAIE will be used in preference to Sheltered English. Sources cited that refer to Sheltered English will be used interchangeably with those referring to SDAIE despite Sobul's (1994) important effort to distinguish Sheltered English from SDAIE.

- *Active participation:* Students learn both content and language through active engagement in academic tasks that are directly related to a specific content.
- *Social interaction:* Students learn both content and language by interacting with others as they carry out activities.
- *Integrated oral and written language:* Students become more able language learners when language processes are integrated in a variety of ways and for a variety of purposes.
- *Real books and real tasks:* Students learn to read authentic texts and to write for useful purposes.
- *Background knowledge:* Students' prior knowledge of a topic may be activated through classroom activities drawn from a variety of language sources.

In general, sheltered instruction incorporates fundamental principles of good teaching—the ability to communicate, to organize instruction effectively, and to modify complex information to make it understandable to students.

COMMUNICATION SKILLS

Teachers in SDAIE classrooms use language to further knowledge acquisition. They attempt to bridge the gap between their own language ability and that of their students by planning for instruction that ensures students are concurrently learning both English and academic content (Watson, Northcutt, & Rydell, 1989). They use language to further learning rather than to focus on language itself.

Modifying Teacher Talk

The organization of discourse is important for language acquisition in content classes. "Teacher-fronted" classrooms (Harel, 1992) are dominated by teacher talk. The teacher takes the central role in controlling the flow of information, and students compete for the teacher's attention and for permission to speak. In these classrooms, language minority students are dependent on their ability to understand the teacher's explanations and directions. A cooperative learning classroom, by contrast, permits students greater flexibility in the flow of information (Slavin, 1991). Students may have an easier communication task when they talk and listen to their peers. In cooperative learning classrooms, the style of teacher talk often changes: Teachers assist students with the learning task (emphasizing content) rather than providing error correction; moreover, teachers give fewer commands and impose less disciplinary control (Harel, 1992).

When teachers provide directions and explanations, they modify their manner of speaking in order to increase understandability. A major way of modifying talk is by providing comprehensible input. As described in Chapter 4, teachers achieve comprehensibility by embedding language in a meaningful context; using paraphrase and repetition, using media, realia, and manipulatives; and modifying their speech. For example, words may be presented in a rich context of pictures and objects that students use in performing tasks. Content vocabulary can be written on the board or on wall charts. Once introduced, vocabulary items are used in multiple ways over a period of weeks and months to build recognition and usage. By continuous work on ever-expanding concepts, students learn shades of meanings and synonyms.

Teachers can monitor their own language usage and reduce the amount of their talking in the classroom. They can modify their language by slowing their delivery, which, when combined with clearer articulation, allows English learners greater opportunity to separate words in a sentence and process the language. Krashen (1980) compares this to other kinds of language simplification such as caretaker speech and foreigner talk (a term coined by Ferguson, 1975). Many native speakers unconsciously alter and simplify speech addressed to a nonnative speaker by slowing their speech, and teachers can do this consciously.

Another means of modifying input is by exaggerating intonation and placing more stress on important new concepts. Again, this is similar to caretaker speech, in which nouns and verbs in a sentence are emphasized more than the smaller function words (*the, a, in, on*). The use of exaggerated stress and intonation allows the teacher and student to share a focus on the topic at hand and to continue or extend an instructional conversation for as long as needed (Richards, 1978).

Providing Linguistic Cues

Teachers of language minority students can give ample verbal cues to students about the organization of lessons. They can change their tone of voice when an activity must end, allow adequate time for students to make the transition from one activity to another, and then clearly signal the start of a new activity by predictable phrases and emphatic voice tone (Wong-Fillmore, 1985). In addition, before students begin an activity, teachers can familiarize them with a list of instructions. These can be written on the board using special care to write legibly. At the close of the lesson, teachers can use visual reviews, paraphrase the salient points in summary form, and have students provide oral summaries themselves (Short, 1991).

Teacher directions that promote organization and management in the classroom can be made accessible to language minority students. One technique is for the teacher to determine the ten most frequently used directions and to assign the language minority students the task of memorizing them. The teacher might also learn how to say all or some of these ten simple directions in the students' language(s). This helps students to overcome the anxiety of not understanding a teacher's directions and provides a bond between teacher and students as the students recognize and appreciate the teacher's attempts to include them and know something about their language.

In an SDAIE classroom, a good teacher is a "great communicator"!

ORGANIZING FOR INSTRUCTION

Each phase of a lesson, from planning through evaluation, can include some special modification for language minority students. Specific suggestions follow for distinct lesson components: preplanning curriculum; developing objectives; selecting, modifying, and organizing materials; instructing; evaluating student achievement; and providing follow-up.

Preplanning Curriculum

A clear format for instructional planning and implementation is a must in the SDAIE classroom. In planning the year, the teacher needs to specify learning goals and identify competencies students must develop. Each content area has specific curricular goals that are determined by state agencies, district planners, or school officials and teachers. These content area goals must be considered in the yearly plans. In addition, a SDAIE course also includes language acquisition objectives and takes into account particular language demands of the content area. Some examples of these demands are reading textbooks, completing worksheets, writing reports, doing library research, and solving mathematical and scientific word problems.

Language and content teachers can work together to identify and plan for the language and content needs. Language teachers can assist content area instructors by suggesting modified ESL techniques such as Total Physical Response to demonstrate vocabulary, incorporating music and jazz chants on subject area topics, and implementing sustained silent reading sessions with content area materials (Short, 1991).

The yearly plans may include objectives in more than one content area. Students placed in a high school biology class may be helped to learn content by the use of art activities. High school math that incorporates abstract designs is another use of art to teach content. Music can also be analyzed as a math activity, thereby enriching one content area with another. A recent approach to middle school instruction encourages teachers to plan thematic units that integrate basic skills and content areas (Short, 1991). Elementary teaching is particularly enriched by and lends itself to cross-subject thematic units.

By keeping in mind the language needs of the students and the curricular program for the subject, the teacher may plan themes that build on each other. In this way, students are able to take advantage of previously learned concepts and language as they continue through the year. Topic-related vocabulary and concepts are repeated throughout the various thematic materials allowing students to become increasingly able to communicate their ideas on these topics. By offering students a rich array of text types, formats, and activities, teachers can help students move to higher levels of language processing. These various sources help students to find the learning more meaningful and the contexts increasingly understandable (Brinton, Snow, & Wesche, 1989).

Examples of thematic units appropriate for elementary school students can be found in *Integrating English* (Enright & McCloskey, 1988). *Finding Out/ Descubrimiento* (De Ávila, Duncan, & Navarrete, 1992) is a bilingual science and mathematics curriculum designed for interactive small group work. *ESL through Content Area Instruction* (Crandall, 1987) provides guidelines for planning mathematics, science, and social studies lessons along with samples of specific lessons. Table 5-1 illustrates planning for a unit on life cycles in which students are actively engaged in discovery and literacy events.

Developing Objectives

Objectives are necessary to guide teaching. A lesson with a clear objective focuses the instruction by concentrating on a particular goal and guides the teacher to select those learning activities that accomplish the goal. If the teacher is not clear on the objectives of a lesson, then it is difficult to assess student learning. Skillful teachers incorporate students' interest and knowledge into the objectives so that students can participate effectively.

Planning begins with the grade level or content objectives recommended by the state curricular framework or district curriculum guides. The teacher divides these overall goals for the year into units. These units are further divided into specific lessons. Each lesson contains the essential content area objectives.

Effective SDAIE lesson plans not only accomplish content objectives but also increase language skills. Language objectives are included and coordinated with the content objectives. The objectives for the life cycles unit mentioned in Table 5-1 would include the following:

Science:

> To study the life cycles of various animals
> To compare life cycles for similarities and differences
> To study the effect of the surrounding environment on an animal's life cycle.

TABLE 5-1   Life Cycles (Social Studies, Science and Technology, Personal Development)

Engaging children
   Read texts, discuss (with particular attention to life cycles).
   Games: Frog races; the tadpole game
   Make "life lines" to share special events in children's lives. Continue to show events children see happening in the future.

Preparing to find out
   Chart about butterflies: "What We Know/What We Want to Find Out"
   Make clay models to show butterfly life cycle.
   Q: What other animal life cycles do you know about?
   Collect various materials about these animals and decide which one to study.
   Prepare questions for zoo staff.

Shared experiences
   Set up Vivarium. Collect caterpillars or eggs. Continuing observation, sketching, and note taking. Begin journal.
   Excursion to zoo. All visit the butterfly enclosure. Talk by zoo staff. Groups visit specific areas and zoo classroom to find out more about other animals' life cycles.

Gathering, sorting and presenting
   Q about specific animal: What do we know? What do we need to find out about its life cycle?
   Collect general info about animal to add to info gained at zoo.
   If appropriate, use magnifying glass to observe animal.
   Complete labeled drawings.
   Sort info using appropriate headings (characteristics, habitat, movement, skin covering, food, communication, growth).
   "Animal Facts" pages for presenting info.
   Write own animal life cycle report (information narrative form).

Drawing conclusions, reflection, and action
   Revisit statements ("What We Know/ . . . Need to Know")—review and revise
   Write questions for quiz cards.
   Write true/false statements.
   Write sentence beginnings; read to others, who have to supply an ending ("A caterpillar shed its skin because . . .")

Reprinted with permission from *Understanding Whole Language* by D. Hornsby, Workshop presentation, Riverside, California, 1991.

To study the ways in which humans have influenced the life cycles of various animals.

Language:

To use strategies for reading nonfiction text

To understand the purpose and use of an index

To learn note-taking skills

To compare the report genre with the informational narrative genre

To construct in a small group an informational narrative about the life cycle of butterflies

To write individually an informational narrative or a report about the life cycle of a chosen animal

To read and interpret diagrams to assist in the comprehension of factual text

To study the ways in which authors and publishers use graphics and layout features in factual text (Hornsby, 1991)

Selecting, Modifying, and Organizing Materials

A critical aspect of any lesson is the proper selection and use of materials. Textbooks have become a central tool in many classrooms, and the SDAIE teacher must select, modify, and organize text material to best accommodate the needs of language minority students.

Selecting materials. Selecting materials involves an initial choice of whether the teacher wishes to have one primary content source or a package of content-related materials (chapters from various texts, video- and audiotapes, magazine and newspaper articles, encyclopedia entries, literary selections). Regardless of what is chosen, however, the teacher must consider two main criteria: Are the content objectives for the lesson adequately presented by the material? Is the material comprehensible to language minority students?

To present the content sufficiently, the text must be up to date and thorough in its treatment of the desired material. The tasks required of students should be appropriate to the discipline and should promote critical thinking. The style of the text should be clearly organized, with attractive print and layout features that assist students' comprehension. Study questions and other guides should be included, along with a teacher's guide and/or answer key. The text should appeal to a variety of learning styles. Sources represented in the text should include various literary genres (e.g., narrative, descriptive, analytic).

To make the text comprehensible, the language should be straightforward, without complex syntactic patterns, idioms, or excessive jargon. New content vocabulary should be clearly defined within the text or in a glossary.   Diagrams should show vocabulary pictorially. Graphs and charts need to be clearly labeled. Overall, the text should engage the student. For further guidelines on selecting texts for content-based courses, Brinton, Snow, and Wesche (1989) provide a checklist. Chapter VII of the *Foreign Language Framework* (California State Department of Education, 1989) lists criteria for evaluating instructional materials in ESL.

Content area teachers must also consider the use of primary language resources such as dictionaries and books in helping students to understand concepts. English learners in the content class are continually exposed to new content material and often find a native language dictionary helpful. Students may bring two dictionaries to class: a bilingual dictionary and a dictionary in their native language with definitions. For an elementary student, picture dictionaries such as Amery and Milá's *The First Thousand Words in Spanish* (1979) and Amery's *The First Thousand Words: A Picture Word Book* (1979) have been found to be very useful. The teacher should ensure that the students know how to use the dictionary; if they do not, a lesson can be prepared on dictionary use. Other primary language resources such as encyclopedias, textbooks, and illustrated charts can supply support for teaching content area concepts.

Modifying materials. Modifying materials may be necessary to assist English learners in comprehending connected discourse. Beginning English learners in a content area classroom may need special textual material, such as excerpts taken from textbooks or chapters from the readings that have been modified. In modifying text, the goal is to improve comprehensibility without watering down the curriculum. Through the use of simplifications, expansions, direct definitions, and comparisons, elements that aid in comprehension can be built into a text. The following examples, from Richard-Amato and Snow (1992), come from a history lesson:

> *Simplification:* "The government's funds were depleted. It was almost out of money."
>
> *Expansion of ideas:* "The government's funds were depleted. It had spent a lot of money on many things: guns, equipment, help for the poor. It did not have any more money to spend on anything else."
>
> *Direct definition:* "The government's funds were depleted. This means that the government spent all of its money." (p. 151)

For beginning English learners, present, simple past, and simple future verb tenses as well as commands can be used to eliminate complexity. The word order in sentences should rely on the common subject–verb–object format, with few subordinating clauses. The <u>verb + not</u> structure is more easily understood than other negations such as *hardly, no longer,* and *no more.* Paragraphs should be carefully structured so that the main idea is easily recognized and supporting information follows immediately. Markers for logic structure should be simple: Terms such as *first, next,* and *then* indicate sequence; *but* indicates contrast; *because* indicates cause and effect. These adaptations increase readability. As students' language proficiency increases, so should the complexity of their reading material. The goal is to move students toward the ability to work with unmodified texts.

Rewriting text selections to increase readability for language minority students requires a sizable time investment. An alternative approach is to supply an advance organizer for the text that brings out the key topics and concepts, either in outline form, as focus questions, or in the form of concept maps. Changing the modality from written to oral is another possible modification. By reading aloud, the teacher models the process of posing questions while reading to show prediction strategies used when working with text (Addison, 1988). Selected passages can be tape-recorded for students to listen to as they read along in the text. If modified text is necessary, some of the native English-speaking students can be assigned the task of simplifying the textbook by rewriting portions. This serves as a review for the students who do the rewriting. They can also be asked to duplicate their class notes for the benefit of the language minority students (Richard-Amato & Snow, 1992).

Organizing materials. Organizing materials increases clarity. When a variety of materials is used rather than one main text, care should be taken to sequence the materials in a structured way, so that each concept is clearly explored. Text components should be grouped by concept, to demonstrate similarity and contrast in points of view, genre, or presentation.

"Acculturation" as a theme in social studies can draw on a wealth of material that includes primary documents, personal histories, and literature. Students who research specific concepts related to acculturation such as immigration, assimilation, culture shock, job opportunities, or naturalization, may find that each document features a unique voice. A government document presents a formal, official point of view, whereas a personal or family story conveys the subject from a different perspective. In addition, numerous pieces of literature such as Bunting's (1988) *How Many Days to America?* or Yep's (1975) *Dragonwings* offer yet another point of view. The teacher's role is to help students recognize the similarities of concept in various genres.

In a biology class, pictures both in the text and on the walls can complement the text. The teacher can use these for discussion and then guide students to texts that amplify the concepts. For example, when teaching about the parts of a flower, a teacher may refer students to the explanation in the text (paragraph form), a diagram of a flower in the text (graphic form), a wall chart with a different flower (pictorial form), a text glossary entry (dictionary form), and actual flowers that students can examine. Through these numerous media, the concepts *petal, stamen, pistil,* and *sepal* are understood and provide a basis for future study about life forms. The teacher's task here is to ensure that these multiple sources are organized to communicate clearly each concept. The various materials are organized to ensure that concepts build on one another as the subject matter becomes more complex.

Instructing

Once general content themes have been selected and objectives determined, the teacher working with language minority students provides instruction in three steps: preparation, presentation, and practice (Chamot & O'Malley, 1987, 1989). Within these steps, content-area topics and language development activities are combined.

Preparation. Preparation for the new concepts begins with experiences that focus the students' attention on the topic, get them ready to learn, and connect that learning to what they already know. By determining what prior knowledge students already have, the teacher can assess what background knowledge needs to be taught and what can be assumed. Graphic organizers help students to structure their ideas. Preteaching vocabulary exposes students to essential terms that may be lacking or gives them the English equivalent for concepts they know in their native language.

Experiences that arouse interest and attention to a new topic may include field trips, guest speakers, films and movies, experiments, classroom discovery centers, music and songs, poetry and other literature. By engaging in these experiences and talking with the teacher and others, students can focus on the topic and begin to associate what they already know with these new experiences. In order to deepen these experiences, the teacher can guide the students to talk and write about them. This prewriting can be shared with others. Once the students have had these experiences, the teacher can give an interest survey composed of general issues about the topic (see Table 5-2). This survey addresses some of the major themes in a chapter in a sixth-grade social studies text. Students check the box that best indicates their interest in the particular item. The teacher is then able to organize instruction and use of the text based on student responses.

Prior knowledge of a topic may be tapped to determine the extent of students' existing concepts and understandings. Many students may have experiences to share that are relevant to the topic of the lesson. This allows them to place new knowledge in the context of their own episodic memories rather than storing new information solely as unrelated concepts. Some prior knowledge may include misconceptions; there may be some "unlearning" that has to take place. Also, some prior knowledge may be based on experiences and conceptualizations of the student's home culture that are beyond the teacher's experience. Background knowledge may be activated or developed through classroom activities that include all of the language processes. Brainstorming and KWL (What do I *k*now? What do I *w*ant to learn? What have I *l*earned?) procedures are two such activities. If there is little prior knowledge about the topic at hand, students will need more instructional support, probably in the form of more experiences and materials, help in focusing and sustaining attention, and explicit instruction.

Brainstorming is one strategy to determine how much students know about the topic. Brainstorming can be done either as a whole class activity or within student groups. The essential element in any brainstorming session is that all ideas be accepted. This is especially true for language minority students. A comment made by a student may be highly relevant within

TABLE 5-2 Interest Survey

	What Do You Think?		
	Ho-hum	That's Interesting	That's a Problem
1. Many African nations gained independence in the 1960s.			
2. There is often a conflict within individuals between tribal loyalty and national loyalty.			
3. There are about 250 ethnic groups in Nigeria alone.			
4. Pidgin English is the lingua franca of West Africa.			
5. In many African groups, the women do the planting and harvesting and the children perform specific chores.			
6. Some African countries have rich natural resources, while others have almost none.			
7. Africans practice a variety of religions, including Christianity and Islam.			
8. About 25% of the population of Nigeria live in urban areas.			
9. Some people in the United States hate Africans.			
10. It is difficult to say exactly what an African is.			

that student's experience or cultural background, but may appear inappropriate to the teacher. The teacher needs to accept the comment and then, in the follow-up to brainstorming, ask the student to give more detail about the comment. "Can you tell me more about what you said here?" allows the student to explain without feeling there was something amiss with the comment. Once ideas are exhausted, the students and teacher together can organize the list, grouping and selecting appropriate category labels. The class and teacher then have a beginning model from which they can work and learn.

Another method not only taps into what students already know but also ascertains what they would like to learn. The students again list everything they know about a topic. They then tell the teacher what they would like to learn. When the unit is completed, they return to the chart and talk about what they have learned. The chart is kept up throughout the duration of the unit, and students refer to it from time to time. They have the opportunity to make additions and changes. In the initial "this-is-what-we-know," it is important for the teacher to write what the students say, even if the information is incorrect. Such information will be corrected in a natural way during the unit, allowing students to see that ideas and facts need to be investigated and substantiated.

Graphic organizers help students order their thoughts by presenting ideas visually. Semantic mapping is a way of presenting concepts to show their relationships. After a brainstorming session, the teacher and students could organize their ideas into a semantic map, with the main idea in the center of the blackboard and associated or connected ideas as branches from the main idea. The teacher and students collaborate to put together supporting ideas, using brainstormed words to capture details. Alternatively, a teacher could be more directive in creating a map by writing the central topic and branching out from it with several major subtopics. Students could provide information that the teacher then writes into the appropriate category. Figure 5-1 shows the results of a brainstorming session after second grade students had heard *Cloudy with a Chance of Meatballs* (Barrett, 1978). They brainstormed on the questions "What junk food can you think of?" and "What is in junk food that our bodies don't need?"

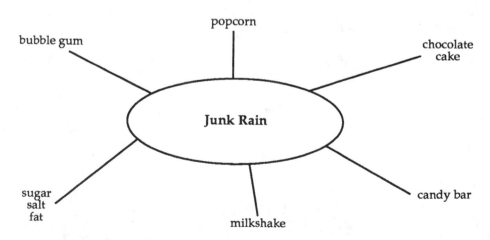

FIGURE 5-1 Semantic Web Created While Brainstorming "Junk Food" after Reading *Cloudy with a Chance of Meatballs*

Preteaching vocabulary is necessary for those special content terms that are unique to each subject. Students need to know these words in order to read a text, to comprehend classroom instruction, and to develop further knowledge in the content field. Whenever possible, students should have direct, firsthand experiences with concrete objects to use as referents for words that will be studied directly. Then the teacher and students can generate a list of terms. From this list, students can use dictionaries to supply meaning, search the text for the terms and draw definitions from the context, work with a Language Master™ or computer program that uses the new terms, or make connections between new words and previously learned words by finding synonyms, cognates with the home language, or word stems and prefixes.

Presentation. Presentation of the lesson involves extending students' existing knowledge. This is normally accomplished through a variety of means including lecturing, demonstrating, and working with text. With language minority students, a key to all verbal presentations is to supplement them with visual stimuli.

Lecturing, which should be kept to a minimum, is supplemented by the use of manipulatives and visual backup as teachers write key words and concepts on the chalkboard or butcher paper, use graphs, pictures, maps, and other physical props to communicate, or imaginatively use the overhead projector. Lectures need to be well organized and succinct, supplying only the knowledge that students need in order to extend or modify their previous knowledge or clarify misunderstanding. Verbal markers provide structure during the lesson so students can understand what is expected of them. Markers for key points such as "now, note this," "for instance," or "in conclusion" cue students to material that is especially important. Terms such as *first, second,* and *last* clearly mark the steps of a sequence. Occasionally asking students to "vote" on their understanding of what has been said by a show of hands helps to maintain interest and check for understanding. Depending on student response, teachers may need to rephrase questions and information if the students do not understand the first time.

Demonstrating new concepts can involve hands-on, show-and-tell explanations in which students follow a careful sequence of steps to understand a process. This can include having students work with materials at their seats in order to accompany the demonstration. Again, the key is for the teacher to be succinct in explanations and to continue to use the chalkboard or overhead to write key terms, concepts, and/or sequential elements.

Working with text can be problematic for language minority students. Teachers must be aware of the text structure as well as the content material so as to facilitate students' interaction with the text. An overview or "walk-through" of the text calls attention to the structure of the assigned chapter(s) including the main headings, subheading, maps, graphs, and pictures that are included to assist comprehension (Law & Eckes, 1990). The teacher may also provide a framework or outline to help students look for main ideas.

If students are permitted, they should be taught to highlight carefully, marking only the main idea in a paragraph. It may be helpful to introduce students to a systematic approach to studying instructional texts, such as Thomas and Robinson's (1972) SQ4R, an acronym for *survey, question, read, reflect, recite,* and *review.* This encourages students to scan a text before reading, paying attention to headings and subheadings to look for major topics. Headings are used to invent questions using the *wh-* words: *who, what, why, where, when.* Then students read the material. They reflect on what has been read, trying to relate the material to information already known. Asking and answering questions (recite) puts the major ideas into focus. Finally, an active review necessitates rereading only material that has not yet been learned.

Teachers should also familiarize students with the difference in the style and structure of texts depending on the particular discipline. Stories have a rhetorical style based on characterization, plot, and setting; in contrast, expository writing uses such devices as cause and effect, comparison and contrast, and main ideas with additive details. Content texts are more information-packed than stories; have specialized organizing principles that may be discipline-specific; and use abstract, specialized, and difficult vocabulary. The language may feature complex sentence structures, and reference may be made to background knowledge that is restricted to that discipline (Addison, 1988; Gunderson, 1991). Visual aids (graphs, maps, charts) may be unique to each discipline, and, although certainly valuable for language minority students, can cause interpretation difficulties if not specifically addressed.

Teachers can assist students in acquiring the specific skills needed to understand discipline-based reading. General skills such as finding the main idea, locating topic sentences, making inferences about content, and locating answers to specific questions are skills useful to many nonfiction texts. Critical thinking skills help students evaluate content, recognize the purpose of the author, and determine the accuracy of information. Technical reading skills are necessary to read and interpret diagrams, written problems, formulae, charts, tables, and graphs. Teachers can suggest that students adjust their reading rate, scanning and skimming for specific information. These skills help students comprehend technical material and authentic texts (Gunderson, 1991).

Practice. Practice is incorporated into the lesson plan to allow students to understand more fully through participation in experiments and other hands-on experiences. Practice can be carried out in both group projects and individual learning opportunities.

Group practice can involve cooperative learning activities, both formally and informally structured. Cooperative learning has been used successfully with language minority students to provide a noncompetitive, equal opportunity environment (Holt, Chips, & Wallace, 1992). In the "Complex Instruction" model (Cohen, Lotan, & Catanzarite, 1990), students are assigned well-defined roles that rotate among all members. Equal opportunity at all roles eliminates notions of high and low status within the group. Students further practice cooperative rules while working with content materials. These rules include:

- You must complete each activity and worksheet.
- Play your role in the group.
- You have the right to ask anyone in your group for help.
- You have the duty to assist anyone who asks for help.
- Everyone helps. (Cohen, DeAvila, Navarrete, & Lotan, 1988)

Thus, if a student has difficulty performing the role of reporter because of limited use of English, for example, other members of the group have the responsibility of seeing that this youngster can carry out the assigned role. Students hear and produce English in a nonthreatening, secure environment, in a supportive, friendly climate that encourages a boost in self-esteem. In this way, they adjust to the culture of the school and also to the knowledge culture of the content discipline (Johns, 1992).

Group practice can also include writing through such activities as the Guided Writing Procedure (Searfoss, Smith, & Bean, 1981). This procedure allows students to write what they know about a topic using a brief outline and quick-writes. Using a teacher-designed checklist that addresses content, organization, style, and mechanics, the drafts are quickly read and analyzed. A second draft incorporates more content-related material; a third draft, even more content. Thus guided writing builds knowledge. Another writing activity can involve the community outside the classroom. Trueba, Moll, and Díaz (1982) incorporated a series of modules that linked expository, school-sanctioned tasks to community issues and concerns. This relevant, authentic communication allowed students to practice writing within a content framework that the community deemed important.

Language minority students need to become familiar with what Kinsella (1992) calls "key direction" words: *analyze, compare, contrast, define, describe, discuss, explain, evaluate, illustrate, justify, state,* and *summarize.* By initially working together to complete short tasks that incorporate these different words, they can become familiar with these terms. Teachers can then use the overhead projector to share work samples generated from the tasks, and the class as a whole can pinpoint specific examples of these direction words within their appropriate contexts and in conjunction with content material. Other important learning strategies, such as lecture note taking, vocabulary expansion, and summarizing, can be practiced in small groups and then discussed in teacher-led whole group sessions. In this manner, language, content, and learning strategy objectives are constantly being incorporated throughout lessons.

Students may need *individual practice* for learning strategies in specific content areas. *The Content Connection* (Schrega, 1991) incorporates five-part units in which students first complete a simple vocabulary exercise. Then they display basic knowledge through short activities (talking about first aid, reading prescription labels). Third, they read more extensive informational text segments. Fourth, they write, take notes, or interview each other. Finally, they relax with content-related puzzles and games. A variety of strategies are incorporated into these lessons to help students recognize and discuss content-related language and concepts. Another lesson model, CALLA (discussed in Chapter 4) includes a variety of strategies to assist students in self-monitoring, organizational planning, using resources and reference materials, grouping, summarizing, using imagery, information representation, cooperation, and questioning for clarification.

Individual work also expands the students' ability to follow through on their specific areas of interest. Once areas of inquiry have been determined through preteaching activities, students can choose specific topics that they want to pursue. The teacher's role is to facilitate their access to resources and their ability to direct their focus.

Integrated learning: A case study. With "Fish" as a thematic topic, students in Patti Hurren's fourth- and fifth-grade ESL class developed an array of learning activities that incorporated objectives from literature, math, and art. Before introducing the place of "fish" in the classification of animals, Ms. Hurren encouraged students to classify various objects from their own collections (stickers, stamps, coins). They made tree diagrams to represent the organization of these objects. They then moved to classifying "pets" and noted the place of fish in their organization charts. At this point, Ms. Hurren discussed with the students their concepts of animal classification, and together the class developed an initial animal classification diagram. A large picture of a fish, labeled with important parts, was introduced and students were given several opportunities to compose oral sentences based on this diagram. A coherent text that described the goldfish was eventually produced by combining individual students' sentences. The students and the teacher were all involved in the spoken, organizational, and written stages so that students' language abilities were developed. Information books and literature, art projects and field trips were used to provide opportunities to develop both concepts and language. Colorful fish prints extended the unit into graphic design. (Early, 1990)

Evaluating Students' Understanding

After students have had the opportunity to learn new material in a meaningful way, they can share their discoveries in a variety of manners: learning centers; art projects; dramatic, visual, or oral presentations; readers' theater; slide or video shows; maps and graphs—the possibilities are endless.

A more teacher-directed means of evaluating student learning is to give students sample tasks based on specific learning strategies taught. Reading short passages to capture the main idea, briefly defining vocabulary from context, scanning text for a target idea, or checking a diagram for a specific fact can evaluate whether students have mastered learning strategies. Evaluating for mastery of a lesson is less formal than testing. It provides feedback to the teacher about the success of a lesson rather than assessing each student's specific progress.

Following Up the Lesson

Content expansion is a key component of a lesson. Activities need to relate directly to the focus topic and reinforce the principle of utilizing content concepts to develop language. Students have a chance to integrate new concepts with the old, using such follow-up activities as projects, interviews with community members, letter writing campaigns, or posters that enrich the classroom-based content.

The *Bridge to Communication* curriculum developed in the San Diego Unified School District (Santillana, 1992) includes content expansion activities in language arts, science, and social studies. For example, the Primary Level B curriculum contains a unit called "Transportation of Long Ago." After a lesson focus on content vocabulary, such as *chariot, rowboat, stagecoach, covered wagon, pony express,* and *clipper ship,* students are given a cooperative task to decide which modern means of transportation is most likely to become outdated in the future. For follow-up activities in art, students design a vehicle of the future. In language arts, they draw pictures of transportation from different periods in history and make a class book that displays these pictures on a timeline accompanied by a brief explanation. To develop oral proficiency, students are challenged to become salespersons and to "sell" an antiquated means of transportation to another student using display advertisements that they have created. These expansion activities develop alternative ways of expressing content area knowledge and thereby encouraging a variety of skill expression in students.

CONTENT AREA APPLICATION

Traditionally schools have been organized around subject areas—mathematics, social studies, science, language. Such organization can allow a teacher to pursue an area of interest and to specialize in a content area, devoting time to gathering content-specific knowledge and materials. The division of knowledge into subject areas is reinforced by the availability of such knowledge in designated textbooks. Such organization, on the other hand, can obscure the overlapping and integrated nature of knowledge. A recent trend in many public schools has been to recognize the wholeness of knowledge and to organize instruction around broad themes. Based on students' interests and questions, these themes engage students in meaningful activities that focus on the area of inquiry rather than a specific skill. Students learn math, science, and social studies by researching, reading, and experimenting to answer real-world questions that they have posed themselves. This view is student-centered rather than teacher-centered and involves as much student–student interaction as teacher–student. The "question-driven" format forces a reconceptualization of the curriculum away from a narrow focus on subject areas to broader concepts that connect to significant ideas and issues (Freeman & Freeman, 1992a, 1992b). For second language learners, this reconceptualization is felicitous as it allows for more interactive engagement with a number of other speakers, for continuous concept development, and for an expanding base of vocabulary and language structures that can be used in a variety of contexts.

The move to a thematic approach to instruction has taken place primarily at the elementary level, but middle schools have also been reorganizing so that content teachers can collaborate on instruction and can work together with the same groups of students. High schools, however, have tended to retain classes organized around subject areas. Academic work at the secondary level is particularly challenging for students whose native language is not English. Modifying instruction for these students at the high school level is imperative in order for these students to have access to the core curriculum and to be able to graduate with the same depth of knowledge as their native English speaking peers. Each content area has specialized vocabulary (consider, for example, the different meanings for *foot* in mathematics, biology, geography, furniture construction, poetry, theater) and particular graphic and verbal means for organizing information. In the following section, a case study will first be presented to illustrate some of the do's and don't's of SDAIE instruction. Then, individual content areas will be discussed with emphasis on appropriate strategies for the integration of language and academic skills.

Social Studies

Social studies is a content domain that is heavily dependent on language proficiency. Students benefit from cooperative settings in which those who need language help can rely on their peers (Olsen, 1992b). In addition, students may need help with study skills. The following examples show how SDAIE techniques are employed in history and social studies classes.

A sheltered history class: A case study. Gabriela, who finished high school *(la preparatoria)* in Mexico, had arrived in California only six weeks previously. She struggled to make sense of classroom activities in U.S. History, one of the "sheltered" classes she was taking at Capital High. Gabriela's ESL 1 teacher identified her as being at the early production stage of language proficiency, yet she was being asked to function in a history class where all presentations, readings, and written assignments were done in English. The bilingual history teacher, Mr. Ortega, sometimes accepted students' questions and/or responses in Spanish, but three out of the thirty-one students in the class were not Spanish speakers.

Mr. Ortega asked Gabriela to retake a test when she received an "A." His suspicion of cheating was unfounded, however, because she was able to explain orally all of the test items in Spanish. Gabriela was happy to explain her note-taking and test-taking strategies to her teacher. She said that she copied every word that the teacher wrote on the blackboard, even though she understood very few of them. When she got home, she asked her U.S. cousins to translate the words into Spanish so she could study them and then memorize the English words. Gabriela explained that she could rarely follow oral activities in class because she was too busy taking notes, and the teacher spoke too quickly. She depended almost entirely on the text and translated class notes for information. Students were not allowed to take the class set of books home, so Gabriela spent most of her time studying her notes. High school in Mexico had been even more demanding, so this chore did not seem onerous.

Mr. Ortega encouraged Gabriela to see him after class whenever she had questions about class activities. At that time, he explained difficult concepts in Spanish whenever necessary. He also encouraged her to try to listen to his explanations rather than read or write as he spoke in class. He told her that he underlined key items on the board as he spoke, and he always explained test formats and content.

Gabriela was highly motivated and well educated. Her prior knowledge enabled her to make comparisons between the U.S. and Mexican systems of government and to make connections between the histories of the adjoining countries. This "sheltered" class, however, did not provide enough linguistic support for her needs, despite occasional tutoring by her teacher. Gabriela would have benefited from the use of more audiovisual support and vocabulary and concept development strategies in Mr. Ortega's presentations. Since this class contained students with a wide range of English language proficiencies, she would have learned more English through formal and informal collaborative activities with her fellow students—activities that focused on historical issues and students' experiences (Giacchino-Baker, 1992).

The thematic approach in elementary school. Thematic units can be used to provide a natural environment for the practice of language skills as students learn concepts in the elementary social studies curriculum. Students studying a fifth-grade unit on "Settlement of the West" can examine the legal issues involved in the Treaty of Guadalupe-Hidalgo, compare the various cultures that came into contact in the Southwest, delve into the history of land grant titles, and pursue many more issues of interest. Through means such as filmstrips, films, videos, computer simulations, literature, nonfiction texts, and oral discussions, students are able to develop conceptual knowledge. Such a unit would incorporate history, geography, sociology, economics, values, information-seeking skills, group participation, and perhaps dramatic skills as students act out the signing of treaties and other cultural events.

For history to come alive for language minority students, specific strategies can increase their ability to understand the content. Graphic organizers provide students with visual means to represent their content knowledge. A timeline can be used to place important events in chronological sequence. A population graph can show the effect of events on people, and maps can place significant events in their geographical locale. Pictures from a variety of sources can bring past events to life. Skills in working with text, such as previewing a social studies chapter by following the visual material (pictures, charts, diagrams) or scanning for specific information help students to identify main concepts. Classmates can help each other evaluate the information they read in order to write group reports. Johnston and Johnston's *Content Points* (1990) offer a variety of specific strategies for social studies content units that are based on Chamot and O'Malley's CALLA strategies.

Once students have engaged in the study of geography, lifestyles, economics, politics, and the daily lives of people within a country, they can then create their own fictional country. They can choose to present written as well as visual material. Maps of various types might display land forms, bodies of water, and other geographical characteristics. Illustrations of housing, clothes, and ceremonies can be included. A written description of the people and their social rules is important. Creating a new country also promotes group projects and interdependence so that these issues can become items for class discussion as well (Pérez & Torres-Guzmán, 1992).

Social studies topics in particular have been difficult for language minority students because the topics are generally abstract, cognitively complex, and highly language dependent. Therefore, the use of visuals, hands-on props and manipulatives, and other projects to supplement the lesson content is a necessity. However, the teacher must be aware that the use of such materials may inadvertently be misused to water down content, a practice that decreases the information available to students rather than increasing the students' ability to comprehend a complex content. To avoid such a situation, cooperative learning can be used to structure the classroom so that language minority students have increased opportunities to verify their comprehension by receiving explanations from their peers and sharing prior knowledge. Encouraging students to exchange information helps them to clarify and familiarize themselves with the lesson content. In this way, students are involved in their own learning and teachers can rely less on lectures and worksheets. In *Whole Language for Second Language Learners* (1992b), Freeman and Freeman offer an excellent example of a social studies lesson on communities that combines whole language philosophy with cooperative learning.

When designing the social studies curriculum, it is important that the underlying concepts be repeated. Teachers should start with the most basic concepts and gradually develop related ideas into broader areas of study. In this way the learners are given the opportunity to acquire new knowledge in a coherent and relative fashion.

Literature

Teachers using literature in their classrooms or those whose main focus is to teach literature may find that English-language literature does not elicit the same responses from language minority students as from native English speakers. By selecting materials judiciously, slowing the pace slightly, portioning work into manageable chunks, and increasing the depth of each lesson, the teacher can ensure that language minority students have a fulfilling experience with literature.

An appropriate selection of genre may be one way to help language minority students develop their conceptual and linguistic schemata. The literature curriculum can be a planned sequence that begins with familiar structures of folktales and myths and uses these as a bridge to more complex works of literature. Myths and folktales from many cultures are now commonly available in high-quality editions with vibrant illustrations. These tales often evoke a familiar response from students despite their various nationalities. Students can move from these folktales and myths to selected short stories by authors of many cultural backgrounds, then to portions of a longer work, and then to entire works (Sasser, 1992).

A common framework now used in working with literature is "into, through, and beyond." *Into* activities activate students' prior knowledge by drawing from their past experiences or develop background knowledge through new experiences. Film, text, field trips, and visual aids can be interwoven to clarify and enhance meaning and help students appreciate the work. Once students are ready for the text, they can make predictions about the story. Some teachers put these predictions into "time capsules" that can be opened and analyzed once the text has been read. Students can discuss what happened later in the book to confirm or disprove their original predictions.

In order to help students *through* the text, teachers find reading aloud a useful strategy. This gives the students an opportunity to hear a proficient reader, to get a sense of the format and story line, and to listen to the teacher "think aloud" about the reading. A commercial tape recording of a work of literature can be obtained for listening and review or native English-speaking students or adult volunteers may be willing to make a recording.

To sustain students' interests in a longer work of literature, class time may be used to recapture the narrative to date and compare students' understanding of the assigned reading. A preview of the next assignment can feature interesting aspects of the new passage. In *Literature in the Language Classroom,* Collie and Slater (1987) suggest several ways in which a teacher can structure literature homework. One suggestion is the "gap summary," a technique in which the teacher provides an almost-complete and simply phrased description of the main points of the section assigned for home reading. Gaps are usually key words or expressions that only a reading of the passage can reveal. This gives students a focus for their reading assignment.

Many kinds of graphic organizers can also be used to help students focus their thoughts and reactions to an assignment. Semantic webs, T-graphs (which cite selected passages and ask for students' reactions), and Venn diagrams allow students to organize their understandings of the text. To tie together students' appreciation of the longer text, an ongoing diary of what each character is feeling helps students step within the character. Students can also be encouraged to make inferences about missing aspects of the story: What were the characters like at school? What were their favorite subjects? Did they have friends? Were they close to their parents?

Beyond activities are designed to extend the students' appreciation of literature. Authentic written responses encourage students to reflect on the piece of literature and to express their interpretations to an audience beyond the classroom. Poems can be written and shared with other classes or parents at a "Poetry Night." Reviews of literature works can be written for the school or classroom newspaper. Letters can be written to authors expressing students' reactions to the story or to pen pals recommending certain pieces of literature. Students can pretend to be movie critics and view the film representation of a text studied in class. They can then compare the differences and draw conclusions about the pros and cons of the different media. Favorite parts of selections can be rewritten as a play and enacted for other classes as a way to encourage other students to read that piece of literature. Students can plan a mock television show and devise various formats that include ideas from the literature studied. For example, a weather announcer can talk about the weather and climate, a newscaster can give the latest update on the characters, and a game show host can ask contestants to answer questions or to act as characters or objects in the story.

Teachers working in mixed-ability classrooms can plan group activities that help students in different ways. Students can work in homogeneous groups when the goal of the activity is accuracy and in heterogeneous groups when the goal is fluency (Peck, 1992). For example, to develop accuracy, first-grade students can listen to a reading of the story *The Three Little Pigs.*

A group of beginning students can retell the story using pictures and then talk about the pictures. Intermediate students can retell the story to the teacher or a cross-age tutor. The teacher writes their story for them, and then students can reread, illustrate, and rearrange the story from sentence strips. A group of more proficient students can create a new group story.

Heterogeneous groups encourage language development when fluency is a goal. Mixed groups of children can experience activities in learning centers and talk about the experience with one another. In *Literature and Cooperative Learning,* Whisler and Williams (1990) detail a variety of cooperative learning activities that have been adapted for the literature classroom.

Mathematics

The National Council of Teachers of Mathematics' (NCTM) publication *Curriculum and Evaluation Standards for School Mathematics* (1989) lists learning to communicate mathematically as one of its five major goals. For nonnative speakers of English, specially designed activities and teaching strategies must be incorporated into the mathematics program in order for all students to have the opportunity to develop their mathematics potential. The difficulties that language minority students have with the language of mathematics lie in four major areas: vocabulary skills, syntax, semantics, and discourse features.

Vocabulary in mathematics includes words of a technical nature such as *denominator, quotient,* and *coefficient,* and words such as *rational, column,* and *table* that have a meaning different from everyday usage. Often two or more mathematical concepts combine to form a different concept: *least common multiple, negative exponent.* The same mathematical operation can be signaled with a variety of mathematics terms: *add, and, plus, sum, combine,* and *increased by* all stand for addition. Moreover, special symbols are used to stand for vocabulary terms (Dale & Cuevas, 1992).

Syntax problems occur when students try to translate directly from English word order to the corresponding mathematical expression (Dale & Cuevas, 1992). For example, the expression "8 divided by 2" might be translated as $8\overline{)\,2}$; however, the correct expression is $2\overline{)\,8}$. This may pose difficulty for students who tend to write mathematical sentences in the same manner in which they read and write English. A further difficulty is the complex sentence structures often used in mathematical problems to signal logical connectors and other propositions. For example, "if . . . then," "either . . or" statements must be translated into logical symbols before problems can be completed, posing additional linguistic difficulty for language minority students.

Semantic problems occur when students are required to make inference from natural language to the language of mathematics. Students need to be able to identify key words and determine how other words are linked to the key words. For example, in the problem "Five times a number is two more than ten times the number," students must recognize that "a number" and "the number" refer to the same quantity. However, in the problem "The sum of two numbers is 77. If the first number is ten times the other, find the number," students need to know they are dealing with two numbers (Dale & Cuevas, 1987).

Discourse features that are unlike natural language characterize the texts used in mathematics. The tendency to interrupt for the inclusion of formulae is confusing and perhaps frightening to the reader of mathematics textbooks. Such texts require a reading rate adjustment because they must be read more slowly and require multiple readings. Charts and graphs are an integral part of the text, not a supplement, and technical language has precise, codified meaning. Reading such text may require up-and-down as well as left-to-right eye movements. Unfortunately, most students receive very little explicit instruction in mathematics text processing (Bye, 1975).

Strategies for reading math texts and for supplementing students' math with language instruction involve more student interaction and small group work. Students need to be encouraged to think aloud about mathematics and talk with one another about the processes involved. In this way, they use language as a tool for tackling mathematics concepts (Crandall, Dale, Rhodes, & Spanos, 1987). Working in groups, students can discuss with one another the activities in which they engage at math centers or stations in various parts of the classroom. This gives them an opportunity to try out ideas and learn various mathematical strategies from their peers. For older students, weekly worksheets can be provided by the instructor that list the terms being used in the current chapter; give directions for oral discussion; offer specific problems to explain or work on as a group; and/or give directions about the assignments or oral reports (Quinn & Molloy, 1992). Language and mathematics content can also be processed simultaneously by having the students carry out authentic problem solving such as checking a telephone bill for accuracy or scanning text to select necessary information to solve a mathematics problem (Johnston & Johnston, 1990).

A teacher whose classroom contains students in various stages of language acquisition can modify comprehension questions and tailor these questions to elicit different responses. For example, when showing students a box holding four red cubes and three blue ones, the teacher may ask a preproduction student questions such as "Are there more red or blue cubes?" (The answer can be expressed by holding up a red or blue card.) To students in the stage of speech emergence, the question can elicit the response "blue" or "red." For those students in intermediate stages of fluency, a harder question might be: "Do you think that more than half the cubes are blue? More than 50 percent?" Bosnos's "Mathing: A Whole Language Process" (1991) is a rich source to guide teachers in thinking about mathematics.

Science

Science is a way of thinking and doing as well as a body of knowledge (American Association for the Advancement of Science, 1989). Science learners can engage in concrete experiences, work together as they learn to think critically and analyze information, and use language creatively to form a conceptual base for science. Hazen and Trefly (1991) offer "20 Great Ideas in Science" that can be used as a foundation for thematic units. These concepts integrate physics, biology, chemistry, earth/space science, and other disciplines to foster thematic teaching. When students are able to connect ideas both within the broad fields of science and across other subjects, they are encouraged to make multiple connections and tap their own world views.

Language minority learners bring multiple views of the world to a learning setting. Their prior experiences, personal and cultural, offer insights into the domain of science inquiry. Teachers need to recognize that as language minority students construct science knowledge, they have linguistic and cultural demands placed on them over and above those placed on native English-speaking students (Kessler & Quinn, 1987; Kessler, Quinn, & Fathman, 1992). Therefore, specific strategies need to be incorporated to facilitate the language minority students' science learning. Using sensory materials that can be touched and manipulated assists comprehension. Expressing ideas and accepting feedback in a non-threatening environment helps students understand the relevance of new topics. Frequent group activity in the science classroom makes learning the product of team efforts. Problem-solving experiences under the guidance and support of the teacher build subject specific knowledge and vocabulary recognition. Effective science teaching is based on investigation and questioning. Using language to carry out these questioning and exploratory activities fosters second language acquisition as well as content knowledge.

In addition to the experiments and problem-solving experiences in which students need to engage to acquire scientific concepts, they also have to read science textbooks. The four major areas (vocabulary, syntax, semantics, discourse features) detailed in the section on mathematics are also relevant for science. Furthermore, language minority students need to understand the structure of scientific writing. Generally science articles "describe a process"; a hypothesis is made, data are gathered, ideas are confirmed, and conclusions are reached. A number of types of text structures are common in science content materials. The cause–effect structure links reasons with results or actions with their consequences. The compare–contrast text pattern examines the similarities and differences between concepts. The time order text structure shows a sequential relationship over the passage of time (Pérez & Torres-Guzmán, 1992). To assist in their comprehension, students can receive special training in following written instructions for procedures or experiments and can be shown ways to organize their recognition of science vocabulary.

Diagrams and charts are graphic organizers that can explain classification and scientific processes. Other kinds of information in graphic aids are raw data as expressed in pie charts, bar graphs, tables, and maps. Comparative and descriptive data can be shown in pictures, interaction diagrams, and technical illustrations (Gunderson, 1991).

If the teacher feels the need to lecture, a helpful strategy for language minority students is to videotape the lesson. Students should be encouraged to listen to the lecture, concentrating on understanding and writing down only questions or parts of the lecture they do not understand. Later, the videotape is played and the teacher and several students take notes on the board. The teacher can model the type of outline that emphasizes the main ideas and clearly indicates supporting details. The students use whatever strategies are comfortable for them, including use of their native language. After a few minutes, the videotape is stopped and the notes compared. The discussion then highlights various note-taking strategies and provides new strategies for everyone involved. This activity can be used on a periodic basis to determine students' ability in comprehending lectures and taking effective notes (Adamson, 1993).

English learners may not be able to speak before the entire class either because of shyness or because of limited oral proficiency. Teachers can check students' understanding of content materials by conducting non-verbal reviews (Cochran, 1989).

- Several students can be called to the board simultaneously to work a problem.
- Class members can respond to true/false statements by holding their thumbs up or down.
- A designated physical response (such as standing up or sitting down) can show agreement or show which of two options students prefer.
- Students can raise previously made flash cards in response to an identification question (flashcard sets can consist of geographic regions, parts of a microscope, and so on).

Teachers of students with limited oral English proficiency frequently worry that their students do not contribute enough to group discussions. Native English-speaking students may dominate a learning group by out-talking other students. Kagan (1989) describes a strategy that can equalize the conversation in a cooperative learning group. Each person uses his or her pen or pencil as a designated marker that serves as a pass to speak. The student wishing to speak puts the pen in the middle of the group table. The next person who wishes to talk then puts down a pen. This technique gives each group member an equal opportunity to be heard. When everyone has taken a turn, the pens are picked up and another round of speaking can begin.

Art and Music

Art is often used as a medium for language minority students to illustrate their understandings of concepts. Ideas that were originally presented in linguistic form can be translated into the artistic medium so that students can demonstrate their comprehension. However, art lessons in themselves can be used to help students develop language skills. As a stimulus for native/nonnative speaker interaction, those students or community members with art skills to teach or knowledge of a traditional craft can be invited to share with a class. Students can listen, question, and learn. Children can learn the method and especially the spirit in which the art form is made and then create their own artwork. They can then share the artwork with other students or can write round-robin reactions to others' art works (Schuman, 1992).

These same methods of sharing reactions to an art work can be true for students' appreciation of music. Dobbs (1992) suggests that, whenever possible, music should be presented to students in a live format rather than recorded. In this way, students have the opportunity to interact with the musician, and the sources are authentic. Once students have listened to and enjoyed the music, it may be helpful to allow them to read along or take the lyrics of the songs with them.

Physical Education

Physical education activities can be carefully structured to motivate students' cooperation and sense of group cohesiveness. This is particularly important in a class in which English learners of various cultures are together. Torbert and Schneider (1992) call these activities Positive and Effective Multicultural Interaction (PEMI). Bonding among students occurs over time using games that encourage collaboration, group identification, equalization of opportunity rather than elimination, a focus on participation rather than winning, and inclusion of players at various ability levels. An example of such an activity is "Chaotic Team Juggle" in which students toss 8 to 15 soft "trash" balls (made of loosely packed paper held together with a rubberband or two). The only rule in tossing is that the passer must make eye contact with the receiver before throwing. There are so many balls (about one for every three students) that students are constantly involved, and the eye contact "seems to support a subtle bonding effect between players" (p. 359).

Several games and activities successfully combine linguistic and sensory-motor stimulation. A game such as "Hot Potato" can help students learn parts of the body while involved in an engaging activity. The leader gets students thinking by asking them what they'd do if a hot potato came near them. The leader then pushes the ball, warning students not to let it touch any part of their body. They must push it away with their hand only. As the ball is pushed around and across the circle, students usually chime in with "Watch out, it's coming to your leg" and other such warnings. Singing games, such as "Did You Ever See a Lassie" and "A Hunting We Will Go" are particularly appropriate for language minority students. For a detailed handbook on physical education activities for elementary students, see *Games, Contests, and Relays* (Martin, 1981).

Instructional Needs Beyond the Classroom

To be successful in their academic courses, language minority students need assistance from organizations and volunteers outside of the classroom. This assistance can come from academic summer programs, additional instructional services such as after-school programs and peer tutoring, and Dial-A-Teacher for homework help in English and in the primary language. Support in the affective domain may include special home visits by released time teachers, counselors, or outreach workers and informal counseling by teachers. Monitoring of academic progress by counselors helps to encourage students with language needs (Romero, 1991).

Escalante and Dirmann (1990) explicate the main components of the Garfield High School Advanced Placement Calculus course in which Escalante achieved outstanding success in preparing Hispanic students to pass the AP Calculus examination. Importantly, Escalante's success was not solely due to outstanding classroom teaching; he was the organizer of a broad effort to promote student success. In his classroom, he set the parameters: He made achievement a game for the students, the "opponent" being the Educational Testing Service's examination; he coached students to hold up under the pressure of the contest and work hard to win; and he held students accountable for attendance and productivity. But beyond this work in the classroom was the needed community support. Community individuals and organizations donated copiers, computers, transportation, and souvenirs such as special caps and team jackets. Parents became involved in a campaign against drug use. This helped Escalante to stress proper conduct, respect, and value for education. Past graduates served as models of achievement. They gave pep talks to students and acted as hosts in visits to high-tech labs. The support from these other individuals combined to give students more help and encouragement than could be provided by the classroom teacher alone. Students saw concentrated, caring, motivated effort directed toward them—something they had not previously experienced. The results were dramatized in the unforgettable feature film *Stand and Deliver*.

Escalante's successful mathematics program at Garfield High School involved much more than excellent classroom instruction. Not surprising, however, are the features of SDAIE that are incorporated in his teaching: cooperative student learning, use of realia and visual support for instruction, modification of teacher talk to provide comprehensible input, and extensive attention to specific mathematics vocabulary. This instructional enhancement opens the door to success for English second language learners.

Chapter *6*

Theories and Methods of Bilingual Education

When we hear the child speak, we see only what is above the surface of the water, the water lily itself. But the roots of the mother tongue lie deep beneath the surface, in the more or less unconsciously acquired connotative and non-verbal meanings. When the child learns a foreign language, that language easily becomes . . . a splendid water lily on the surface which superficially may look just as beautiful as the water lily of the mother tongue. . . . But it is often the case that for a very long time the second language is a water lily more or less floating on the surface without roots.

If at this stage we allow ourselves to be deceived by the beautiful water lily of the foreign language into thinking that the child knows this language . . . well enough to be able to be educated through it . . . the development of the flower of the mother tongue may easily be interrupted. If education in a foreign language poses a threat to the development of the mother tongue, or leads to its neglect, then the roots of the mother tongue will not be sufficiently nourished or they may gradually be cut off altogether. . . . [A] situation may gradually develop in which the child will only have two surface flowers, two languages, neither of which she commands in the way a monolingual would command her mother tongue. . . . And if the roots have been cut off, nothing permanent can grow any more. (Skutnabb-Kangas, 1981, pp. 52–53)

Bilingual education has existed in the United States since the colonial period, but over the two centuries of U.S. history it has been alternately embraced and rejected. The immigrant languages and cultures in North America have enriched the lives of the people in American communities, yet periodic waves of xenophobia and language restrictionism have virtually eradicated the capacity of most U.S. citizens to speak a foreign or second language. For language minority students, English-only schooling has brought difficulties, cultural suppression, and discrimination even as English has been touted as the key to patriotism and success. Only as recently as 1968 did Congress signal its first commitment to bilingual education by enacting the Bilingual Education Act as a means of addressing the needs of students whose first language was not English. Beginning in 1970, landmark court cases mandated special language instruction for children with a limited command of English.

Despite the argument—and the evidence—that bilingual education helps students whose home language is not English to succeed in school, bilingual education continues to be an area of contention. Knowledge of a foreign language is not the accepted norm for much of U.S. society, and those individuals who speak languages associated with immigrant status are looked upon with disfavor. Furthermore, many people feel that any tolerance of linguistic diversity undermines national unity. However, the tide has turned away from the idea of the United States as a "melting pot," in which all cultural and linguistic diversity is melted into one collective culture and language, toward the notion of the "salad bowl," which features a mixture of distinct textures and tastes. Thus, bilingual education in the 1990s has become bilingual/bicultural education, and is rapidly becoming multilingual/multicultural. The classrooms of the United States are increasingly diverse, with students coming from many countries of the world to be educated as Americans. The challenge to any English language development program is to cherish and preserve the rich cultural and linguistic heritage of the students as they acquire English. One means of preserving and supplementing the home languages of our nation's children is through bilingual education. Bilingual education has been considered by many to be a teaching method, but it can also be considered a policy: a way in which instruction is organized and managed (see Figure I-1).

FOUNDATIONS OF BILINGUAL EDUCATION

The progress of bilingual education in the United States has advanced on three fronts: cultural, legislative, and judicial. Culturally, the people of the United States have seemed to accept bilingualism when it has been economically useful and to reject it when immigrants were seen as a threat. Legislative and judicial mandates have reflected this ambivalence. In periods when the economic fortunes of the United States were booming, European immigrants were welcome and their languages were not forbidden (immigrants of color, however, faced linguistic and cultural barriers as they strove for assimilation). In times of recession, war, or national threat, immigrants, cultures, and languages were restricted and/or forbidden.

Periodically throughout history, English has been proposed as the national language, yet this has never been enacted into law. The United States has no official language.

Because the states reserve the right to dictate educational policy, bilingual education has depended on the vagaries of state law. When the U.S. Congress enacted legislation to begin Title VII of the Elementary and Secondary Education Act, federal funding became available for bilingual education programs. Almost simultaneously, the courts began to rule that students deprived of bilingual education must receive compensatory services. Together, the historical precedents, legislative initiatives, and judicial fiats combined to establish bilingual education in the United States.

Historical Development of Bilingual Education

Early bilingualism. In 1664, at least eighteen colonial languages were spoken on Manhattan Island. German, Dutch, Swedish, and Polish could be heard in the armies of the American Revolution, and Spanish was dominant in the Spanish lands of the New World. Bilingualism was common both among the working and educated classes, and schools were established to preserve the linguistic heritage of new arrivals. The Continental Congress published many official documents in German and French, and German schools were operating as early as 1694 in Philadelphia. By the mid-1880s, public and parochial German schools were operating in Baltimore, Cincinnati, Cleveland, Indianapolis, Milwaukee, and St. Louis; by 1900, over 4 percent of the United States elementary school population was receiving instruction either partially or exclusively in German. Other language groups were also able to obtain legal authorization for educational services. In 1847, Louisiana authorized instruction in French, English, or both upon the request of parents. The Territory of New Mexico authorized Spanish-English bilingual education in 1850 (Crawford, 1991).

Language restrictionism. While there were several such pockets of acceptance for bilingual education, other areas of the country effectively restricted or even attempted to eradicate immigrant and minority languages. Under an 1828 treaty, the U.S. government recognized the language rights of the Cherokee tribe. Eventually, the Cherokees established a 21-school educational system that used the Cherokee syllabary to achieve a 90 percent literacy rate in the native language. In 1879, however, the federal government forced the Indian children to attend off-reservation, English-only schools where they were punished for using their native language. In the East, as large numbers of Jews, Italians, and Slavs immigrated, descendants of the English settlers began to harbor resentment against these newcomers. New waves of Mexican and Asian immigration in the West brought renewed fear of non-English influences. Public and private schools in the new U.S. territories of the Philippines and Puerto Rico were forced to use English as the language of instruction (Crawford, 1991).

World War I brought anti-German hysteria, and various states began to criminalize the use of German in all areas of public life (Cartagena, 1991). As World War I ended, Ohio passed legislation to remove all uses of German from the state's elementary schools, and mobs raided schools and burned German textbooks. Subsequently, fifteen states legislated English as the basic language of instruction. This repressive policy continued in World War II when Japanese-language schools were closed. Until the late 1960s "Spanish detention"—being kept after school for using Spanish—remained a formal punishment in the Rio Grande Valley of Texas, where using a language other than English as a medium of public instruction was a crime (Crawford, 1991).

Assimilationism. Although the U.S. Supreme Court, in the *Meyer* v. *Nebraska* case (1923), extended the protection of the Constitution to everyday speech and prohibited coercive language restriction on the part of the States, the "frenzy of Americanization" (Crawford, 1991) had fundamentally changed public attitudes toward learning in other languages. European immigrant groups felt strong pressures to assimilate and bilingual instruction by the late 1930s was virtually eradicated throughout the United States. This assimilationist mentality worked best with northern European immigrants. For other language minorities, especially those with dark complexions, English-only schooling brought difficulties. Discrimination and cultural repression became associated with linguistic repression.

After World War II, writers began to speak of language minority children as being "culturally deprived" and "linguistically disabled." The "cultural deprivation" theory rejected genetic explanations for low school achievement for language minority students and pointed to such environmental factors as inadequate English language skills, lower class values, and parental failure to stress educational attainment. On the basis of their performance on IQ tests administered in English, a disproportionate number of language minority children ended up in special classes for the educationally handicapped.

Rebirth of bilingual education. Bilingual education was reborn in the early 1960s in Dade County, Florida, as Cuban immigrants, fleeing the 1959 revolution, requested bilingual schooling for their children. The first program at the Coral Way Elementary School was open to both English and Spanish speakers. The objective was fluency and literacy in both languages. Subsequent evaluations of this bilingual program showed success both for English-speaking students in English and Spanish-speaking students in Spanish and English. By 1974, there were 3,683 students in bilingual programs in the elementary schools and approximately 2,000 in the secondary schools (Hakuta, 1986).

The focus of bilingual education on dual-language immersion and developmental bilingualism that had been featured in the Dade County bilingual programs was altered when the federal government passed the Bilingual Education Act of 1968 (Title VII, an amendment to the 1965 Elementary and Secondary Education Act). This act was explicitly compensatory. Children who were unable to speak English were considered to be educationally disadvantaged, and bilingual education was to provide the resources to compensate for the "handicap" of not speaking English. From its outset, federal aid to bilingual education was seen as a "remedial" program rather than an innovative approach to language instruction (Crawford, 1991). The focus shifted again in 1989, when developmental bilingual programs were expanded. Maintaining and developing the native language of students became an important goal for bilingual education.

The English-as-official-language movement. This movement has supplied the chief opposition to bilingual education in the late twentieth century. The goals of the English-only movement are the adoption of a Constitutional amendment to make English the official language of the United States, repeal of laws mandating multilingual ballots and voting materials, restriction of bilingual funding to short-term transition programs, and universal enforcement of the English language and civics requirement for naturalization (Cartagena, 1991). One English-only organization, U.S. English, claims 200,000 members who operate a political action committee that presses for adoption of English-only amendments. Senator S. I. Hayakawa, honorary chairman of the U.S. English Initiative, articulated the philosophy of the organization:

> We have unwisely embarked upon a policy of so-called bilingualism, putting foreign languages in competition with our own. English has long been the main unifying force of the American people. But now prolonged bilingual education in public schools and multi-lingual ballots threaten to divide us along language lines. (cited by Galvan, Macias, Magallan, & Orum, 1986)

U.S. English has financed the drive at the state level to have English as the official language of each state. For example, U.S. English spent more than $700,000 on Proposition 63 in California. This 1986 ballot initiative, which passed by a three-to-one margin, instructed public officials "to ensure that the role of English as the common language in the State of California is preserved and enhanced." Critics of this initiative charge that the climate created by this measure was responsible for California's failure to reauthorize a bill mandating bilingual education in the state. In 1987 and 1988, similar proposals were considered by voters and lawmakers in 39 states and passed in 8, bringing the total of "official-English" states to 16 (Crawford, 1991). Proponents of the U.S. English policy consider the proliferation of bilingual education a move to polarize the United States by institutionalizing official bilingualism—that is, coequal status for Spanish in the United States. Although this movement finds a receptive ear among Americans of diverse backgrounds and political persuasions, this espousal of English is not as benign a concept as might be believed. At various times, the leaders of U.S. English have advocated the abolition of 911 operators and health services, endorsed "English-only" rules in the workplace, petitioned the Federal Communications Commission to limit foreign language broadcasting, protested Spanish-language menus at McDonald's, and opposed Pacific Bell's publication of Yellow Pages in Spanish and Chinese (Crawford, 1991).

Emergence of a new nativism. Many U.S. communities are feeling the pressure of increased immigration. The annual number of legal immigrants to the United States has doubled since the mid-1960s, and most newcomers are from underdeveloped nations in the Third World. The English-only movement, an outgrowth of the immigration-restrictionist lobby, has used language as a symbol of national unity (Crawford, 1991). Since the mid-1980s, language loyalties have become a subtle means of reframing racial politics, and bilingual education has become an integral part of the issue. The English-only lobby has labeled "un-American" the effort to provide language support to language minority speakers. The English-only movement also plays on the fears of monolingual English teachers, raising the spectre that the effort to recruit qualified teachers, redesign curricula, and reorganize class schedules to provide a bilingual program will lead to reassignment and loss of status for non-bilingual staff. Bilingual education is a subject that is bound up with individual and group identity, status, intellect, culture, and nationalism. As a people, Americans have limited experience with bilingualism, and some find it hard to justify spending resources on dual language instruction.

Bilingualism in the modern world. Many countries in today's world are officially bilingual, including Canada, Belgium, Finland, Israel, Cameroon, Switzerland, Ireland, and India. Official bilingualism, however, does not imply that all inhabitants of a country are bilingual; it simply means that more than one language may be used in government or education. However, in areas such as Europe or West Africa characterized by economic trade and interdependence, bilingualism, and even multilingualism, is a fact of daily life. In the global society, proficiency in more than one language is a highly desirable trait (Glick, 1988).

Legal Evolution

The use of English and other languages in public life, particularly language use in the schools, has been affected by "cycles of liberalism and intolerance" (Trueba, 1989) in which conflicting beliefs and policies about language have influenced legislation and judicial actions.

Federal law and judicial decisions. The first federal law relating to bilingual education was the 1968 Bilingual Education Act (Title VII), which authorized $7.5 million to finance 76 projects serving 27,000 children. The goal of these funds was to support education programs, train teachers and aides, develop and disseminate instructional materials, and encourage parental involvement. The second wave of federal support for bilingual education came in the 1970s as a response to civil rights activism. In 1970, the Office for Civil Rights informed school districts with more than 5 percent national origin-minority children that the district must take affirmative steps to rectify these students' language deficiencies. The memo mandated that districts offer some kind of special language instruction for students with a limited command of English; prohibited the assignment of students to classes for the handicapped on the basis of their English language skills; prohibited placing such students in vocational tracks instead of teaching them English; and mandated that administrators communicate with parents in a language they can understand.

The federal courts began to enforce Title VI of the Civil Rights Act, which outlaws discrimination in federally supported programs. In *Serna* v. *Portales Municipal Schools*, a 1972 case, a federal judge ordered instruction in native language and culture as part of a desegregation plan. In *Ríos* v. *Read* (1977), a federal court decided that a New York school district had violated the rights of language minority students by providing a bilingual program that was based mainly on ESL and that included no cultural component (Crawford, 1991). Finally, in 1974, in the landmark *Lau* v. *Nichols* case, the U.S. Supreme Court ruled:

> There is no equality of treatment merely by providing students with the same facilities, textbooks, teachers and curriculum, for students who do not understand English are effectively foreclosed from any meaningful education.

Although no specific remedy was mandated, the U.S. Office for Civil Rights began to visit school districts with large numbers of language minority children to ensure that districts met their responsibilities. In 1975, the U.S. Commissioner of Education announced the so-called Lau remedies, guidelines that told districts how to identify and evaluate children with limited English skills; what instructional treatments to use; when to transfer children to all-English classrooms; and what professional standards teachers need to meet (Office for Civil Rights, 1976).

The Equal Educational Opportunities Act (EEOA) states that:

> No individual can be denied equal educational opportunity on account of race, color, sex, or national origin by . . . (f) the failure of an educa-

tional agency to take appropriate action to overcome language barriers that impede equal participation by its students in its instructional program.

Several federal cases have tested this statute. In *Castañeda* v. *Pickard* (1981), the Fifth Circuit Court outlined three criteria for programs serving language minority students. District programs must be:

- Based on "sound educational theory"
- "Implemented effectively" through adequately trained personnel and sufficient resources
- Evaluated as effective in overcoming language barriers

Qualified bilingual teachers must be employed, and children are not to be placed on the basis of English language achievement tests. *Idaho Migrant Council* v. *Board of Education* (1981) mandated that state agencies are empowered to supervise the implementation of federal EEOA requirements at the local level. *Keyes* v. *School District #1* (1983) established due process for remedies of EEOA matters. *Gómez* v. *Illinois State Board of Education* (1987) gave state school boards the power to enforce state and federal compliance with EEOA regulations. Taken together, the rulings supported the EEOA provisions. Children may not sit in classrooms where they cannot understand instruction, and districts must properly serve students who are limited in English. In none of the rulings did the courts mandate a specific program format, but in all they clearly upheld the notion that children must have equal access to the curriculum.

State law. Although federal protections of the rights of limited-English-proficient students are still in effect, many states have weakened or eliminated their requirements regarding bilingual education. California, with a school enrollment of over one million limited-English-proficient children, has no mandate for bilingual education. As of June 1987, twelve states mandated bilingual education, and twenty-one states offer teacher certification in bilingual education. Only West Virginia prohibits bilingual education.

Educational Issues

What obligation does a community have toward newcomers—in particular toward nonnative, non-English-speaking children? When education is the only means of achieving social mobility for the children of immigrants, these young people must be given the tools necessary to participate in the community at large. When school dropout rates exceed 50 percent among minority populations, it seems evident that the schools are not providing an adequate avenue of advancement. Clearly, some language minority students do succeed: Asian students are overwhelmingly represented in college attendance, whereas Hispanics are underrepresented (Suarez-Orozco, 1987). Some states are addressing the obligation to educate all students more than others are. California, for example, in its *Model Curriculum Standards* (California State Department of Education, 1985) has established high-level guidelines for every subject and encourages that these guidelines be applied to all students. Nevertheless, children continue to receive differential treatment in the public schools. The structure of schooling creates equity problems, all the way from the tracking procedures that segregate students of "lower" ability from those of "higher" ability to the day-to-day operation of classrooms, in which some students' voices are heard while others are silenced. These structural components of schools must be addressed lest the belief continue that achievement problems reside solely within students.

The success and/or failure of ethnic minority students has caused concern and has prompted various explanations for students' mixed performances. A genetic inferiority argument assumes that certain populations do not possess the appropriate genes for high intellectual performance. The cultural deficit explanation attributes lower academic achievement to deficiencies in the minority culture. The cultural mismatch perspective maintains that cultures vary and that some of the skills learned in one culture may transfer to a second but that other skills will be of little value or, worse, will interfere with assimilation to the new culture. The contextual interaction explanation posits that achievement is a function of the interaction between two cultures—that the values of each are not static, but adapt to each other when contact occurs.

In schools, three phenomena occur in which minority students are disproportionately represented: underachievement, dropping out, and overachievement. These phenomena may be occurring because of the ways schools and classrooms promote unequal classroom experiences for students. In response to the perception that some students "underachieve" or "overachieve" or "drop out" or are "pushed out," schools have designed various mechanisms to help students to succeed. Some of these have been successful, others problematic.

Underachievement. Several measures of achievement reveal discrepancies in the achievement of Whites in comparison with ethnic minorities. On the National Scholastic Aptitude Test in 1990, the average scores for Whites on the verbal subtest exceeded those of all ethnic minority groups (Hispanics, Blacks, Asians and Pacific Islanders, American Indians and Native Alaskans) by 30 to 90 points. With the exception of Asians, all ethnic groups were lower than Whites on the mean score of the mathematics subtest (Waggoner, 1992). Ethnic minority groups, except for Asians, attain lower levels of education. Hispanics, for example, are particularly hard hit by the phenomenon of educational underachievement. Census data indicate that in 1987, 8.6 percent of all Hispanics over age 25 were college graduates, as compared to 20.6 percent of the same age cohort among the non-Hispanic population in the United States. Moreover, Hispanics represent 5 percent of total enrollment in institutions of higher education compared with 79.3 percent represented by Whites (non-Hispanic). Hispanics constituted 3.2 percent of graduate enrollment in 1986 compared to Black enrollment, which represented 5 percent of the total. Of those Hispanics enrolled in college, a disproportionate number are enrolled in community colleges, 54.4 percent compared to 36 percent of Anglo students and 42.7 percent of Black students. Hispanics represent only a small number of faculty members and administrators in higher education; they hold 3.3 percent of such positions. They are more likely to be instructors than professors, and women are much less often represented than men (Nieves-Squires, 1991). Low educational levels have resulted in poor subsequent incomes and a lower likelihood of high-prestige occupations. A recent survey by the Hispanic Association on Corporate Responsibility found that Latinos hold only 81 of 11,881 executive positions in the top 500 industrial corporations in America (Fortune 500) (Ross, 1993).

A study by the U.S. Commission on Civil Rights (1978) found that Asians were frequently "overqualified" for their jobs and that Whites with lesser qualifications held the same jobs as Asians. Thus, it is unclear that underachievement is the real problem. Even ethnic minorities who achieve in school may not be able to attain positions of responsibility in society. The contextual interaction approach would connect the exploitation and discrimination in society with underachievement in schools.

Dropouts. There is a disparity in graduation and dropout rates among various ethnic groups in the United States. According to 1980 census data, graduation rates among persons in California over 24 years of age varied as follows: 77 percent of Whites, 76 percent of Asians, 69 percent of Blacks, 66 percent of Native Americans, and 44 percent of Hispanics graduated from high school (Sue & Padilla, 1986). Table 6-1 shows the dropout rates by ethnicity for eighth- through tenth-graders from data compiled from 1988 through 1990.

Hispanic students continue to have the highest school dropout rates of any group for the United States as a whole. According to the Policy Analysis Center of the National Council of La Raza (1990), about 40 percent of Hispanics age 19 and older are not enrolled in school and have no high school diploma. By age 16 or 17, almost one in five (19.5 percent) has left school without a diploma, compared with fewer than one in sixteen Blacks (6.0 percent) and one in fifteen Whites (7.1 percent). Of all Hispanic subgroups, Mexican-Americans have the lowest level of academic attainment and Cubans the highest; only 50 percent of the young adult Mexican-American population aged 25 to 34 has completed four or more years of high school, compared to 84 percent of Cubans.

Current studies that have compared the educational success of various

TABLE 6-1   Dropout Rates, 1988–1990, Eighth- to Tenth-Grade Students in the United States

White	Hispanic	Black	Asian/Pacific Islander	Native American
5.2%	9.6%	10.2%	4.0%	9.2%

Source: U.S. Department of Education (1992b).

minority groups have noted two important trends. One trend recognizes that the relationship between the individual and the social group impacts academic socialization. Sociolinguists and ethnographers have shown that lifestyles of various social groups and varied sociocultural settings lead to diverse ways of acquiring and utilizing literacy. This diversity is not necessarily considered in school settings. A second trend identifies ways in which minorities are disempowered by schools and ways in which the resultant lack of achievement can be reversed (Moll and Diaz, 1987; Trueba, Cheng, & Ima, 1993).

If school is responsible for the social and economic success of students (the data on Asian achievement lead us to believe that schooling is necessary but not sufficient for minority achievement), and schools disenfranchise many students who drop out or underachieve, then we must ask why schools maintain certain individuals in a situation of disempowerment. The sociological and sociopolitical conditions for this disempowerment are complex, but research shows that classroom factors, including discourse and interaction patterns, combine with family, culture, and language variables to affect school achievement. Moreover, knowledge about these factors is not enough in itself. Teachers must examine how their own beliefs and teaching behaviors affect children's achievement and how certain school organizations contribute to the problem or the solution.

Overachievement. The prevailing public image of Asian newcomer students represents them as largely successful in acquiring English language skills. The term *model minority* has been evoked for Asian-Americans, connoting a "super group" whose members have succeeded in U.S. society despite a long history of racial oppression. Asian students are seen as academic superstars who win academic distinction and are overrepresented in elite institutions of higher education (Suzuki, 1989). This stereotype, however, does not represent the full range of Asian newcomer students. Many never learn English well enough to enter mainstream classes and drop out prior to high school graduation. Trueba et al. (1993) hold that foreign-born Asian groups who were not exposed to the English language prior to their entry in the United States are the most neglected group in U.S. schools. The labor force in the United States employs large numbers of undereducated Asian young men, many of whom are employed "under the table" in exploitive conditions. Official unemployment figures for Asians are higher than those for Whites and Hispanics, and approach the figures for Blacks (32 percent). Unemployment problems and poverty keep Asians at the bottom of the social structure.

The heterogeneous group covered by the term *Asian* contains many subgroups with differing degrees of educational success. Among the Southeast Asian students, the Khmer and the Lao have a grade point average (GPA) below that of White majority students, whereas Vietnamese, Chinese-Vietnamese, and Hmong students are well above this GPA. Japanese, Korean, and Chinese students are also well above White students in terms of GPA. For those Asian students in postsecondary education, the fields of study selected at both the graduate and undergraduate levels are predominantly engineering, physical sciences, mathematics, and computer sciences. At the graduate level, Asians additionally choose dentistry, medicine, optometry, and pharmacy. This selection seems to target occupations that have high status and in which communicative language skills are less needed (Trueba et al., 1993).

Two general factors may contribute to academic success for certain minority groups: the groups' views about the place of education for the group, and the school's bias toward viewing the group as academically successful. In the first instance, the success of the Punjabi (Sikhs from rural northwest India who settled in northern California), for example, may be due to the groups' resistance to assimilation into mainstream society and to the strong family support for students who are harassed or experience other cultural conflicts in the schools (Gibson, 1987).

In the second case, school personnel may act toward Asians in ways that support the model minority attribution. Wong-Fillmore (1980) documents the behavior of Chinese students as being more in accord with teachers' expectations than, for example, that of Hispanic students. Asian children may comply with authority, but this compliance may afford them less opportunity to acquire the networking and social skills needed to advance in the workplace.

Teachers can actively move away from the model minority myth in their practices and interactions through a number of specific actions. They can treat students as individuals and not ascribe high or low expectations to them as members of groups based on national origin or ethnicity. By recognizing that Asian/Pacific American students speak different languages and come from different cultural areas, teachers can avoid lumping them together as one homogeneous group. Instead, teachers who take time to learn about the languages and cultures of these students will appreciate their differences. Once the school determines which languages are spoken, teachers can advocate for providing guidance counselors, homework tutors, and parent advocates who speak those languages. Asian/Pacific American students should not be treated either better or worse, than other students; this practice not only is unfair to other students, but also can lead to extramural animosity and violence directed toward Asian/Pacific American students (Nash, 1991).

Placement. Educators have responded to these educational issues by developing special programs and procedures and/or by placing students in special classes.

Special education. Culturally and linguistically different students have been disproportionately referred to and placed in special education programs (Cummins, 1984; Rodriguez, Prieto, & Rueda, 1984). Explanations for this overreferral include the following: low level of acculturation, inadequate assessment, language problems, poor school progress, academic/cognitive difficulties, and special learning problems (Malavé, 1991). Biased assessment has resulted in negative evaluation of language minority students, largely because intelligence testing has been derived from models of genetic deficiency, cultural deprivation, and other deficit models (Payan, 1984; Rueda, 1987).

In situations where students are legitimately placed in special education classes, Bransford and Baca (1984) recommend alternative bilingual special education model programs that build on the students' language and cultural strengths. Successful instructional programs for culturally and linguistically diverse special education students focus on building higher order thinking skills; encouraging creative tasks that allow the expression of ideas through the native culture and language; providing student-to-student interaction and meaningful social contact; using comprehensible input in the second language; and allowing enhanced social contact with native speakers and mainstream students (Malavé, 1991).

Retention/promotion. Many language minority students begin falling behind their expected grade levels almost immediately upon entering school. Whether because of language differences, frequent family moves, or poor schools and teachers in predominantly minority areas, many Hispanic students, for example, fail grades early on and are retained or placed in remedial courses. According to 1980 census data, in grades 1 through 4, 28 percent of Hispanic children are enrolled below the normal grade level, compared to 20 percent of Anglo (non-Hispanic White) children. Between the fifth and eighth grades, nearly 40 percent of all Hispanic students are behind grade level, compared to 25 percent of Anglos. By the ninth and tenth grades, 43 percent are behind. The proportion drops to 35 percent in the eleventh and twelfth grades, mostly because many students have dropped out. In high school, only about 37 percent of Hispanic students are enrolled in college preparatory courses—and even then they tend to take fewer of the difficult mathematics and science courses (Fields, 1988). A 1986 report from the National Council of La Raza indicates that only 53.3 percent of all Mexican-Americans graduate from high school, and 17.1 percent of Mexican-Americans have less than a fifth grade education (National Council of La Raza, 1986).

Tracking. Students are offered very different types of instruction depending on their placement in academic or "general" education courses. To justify this, educators have argued that tracking is a realistic, efficient response to an increasingly diverse student population. However, critics, (e.g., Goodlad, 1984) have argued that tracking is discriminatory and should be abolished. Poor minority students are often overrepresented in low, special, or vocational tracks, whereas middle-class White students are overrepresented in high, mainstream, or academic tracks, thereby reproducing the unjust socioeconomic differentiation in the wider society. Studies, however, have been inconclusive on the effects of tracking (Page, 1991).

Segregation. A study conducted by the National School Boards Association (Fulwood, 1992) revealed that Hispanic students are significantly more segregated than Blacks in U.S. schools. The study, based on 1988 data from 40,000 schools gathered by the Office for Civil Rights in the U.S. Department of Education, found that the nation's Latino school enrollment has soared from less than 1 in 20 students to more than 1 in 10 in 1989. Since 1970, the percentage of Whites in the school of the typical Hispanic student has fallen by 12 percent, while the level has remained relatively stable for Blacks. Particularly striking are the data about the increase in educational isolation of Hispanics in California. These students, in 1988, were in schools with fewer non-Hispanic Whites than were Black students in Alabama or Mississippi. The report charges that a virtual vacuum of federal leadership has eviscerated mandatory desegregation programs, with a resulting resurgence of school segregation across the land. This creeping increase in school segregation makes it difficult for language minority students to be grouped with native speakers of English during the school day.

Compensatory education programs. The Bilingual Education Act was successful largely because bilingual education was presented as a compensatory program, one that would help students whose English was limited. A compensatory view of bilingual education assumes that students whose native language is not English are deprived. Such a view reveals a condescending attitude toward language minorities and makes maintenance of the primary language less desirable (Williams & Snipper, 1990).

At the federal level, another major compensatory program is Chapter 1 of the Elementary and Secondary Education Act (ESEA), which provides funding for low-income students. To date, language minority students have been largely excluded from access to Chapter 1 programs because of the designation of language deficiency. Under the reauthorization of the ESEA in 1994, the exclusion of language minority students from Chapter 1 programs may be abolished, allowing language minority students increased access to compensatory funds under Chapter 1. This may remove the compensatory designation for bilingual education, permitting an increased emphasis on primary language development.

ESL as compensatory education. Because of the emphasis on a rapid transition to English, bilingual education has traditionally been confined to grades K-3. In recent years, however, with the influx of primary language students of high school age, bilingual education has become necessary for older students as well. As a part of these programs, a portion of the instructional day has been reserved for ESL instruction. ESL, unfortunately, has been identified with remediation of linguistic deficiencies. Too often, the ESL instruction is given by teaching assistants who have not had professional preparation in ESL teaching, and the instruction has consisted of skill/drill worksheets and other decontextualized methods.

Submersion in English is too often an alternative to bilingual education: Language minority students are placed with native speakers in classrooms where teachers have no training in language teaching pedagogy or sheltered content practices. Research has shown that parents of students in submersion programs have been less involved in helping their children with homework than parents of students in bilingual programs (Ramirez, 1991). Thus viewing ESL as remedial education or expecting children to acquire English without help has long-term adverse consequences for school achievement.

Teacher expectations and student achievement. Jussim (1986) offers a general framework for the relationship between teacher expectations and student achievement. Teachers develop initial expectations based on a student's reputation; on previous classroom performance; or on stereotypes about racial, cultural, and linguistic groups. These expectations, which often resist change despite evidence to the contrary, form the basis for differential treatment of students and for the rationalization for such treatment. Students, in turn, react to this differential treatment in ways that confirm the teacher's expectations. Thus, teachers have a high degree of effect on student achievement: Student effort and persistence are shaped, in part, by students' perception of the teacher's expectation.

Teachers' expectations for student performance are culturally based, as are their criteria for evaluation. Pedagogical training may enable teachers to organize instruction that more accurately allows diverse students access to the curriculum.

As an Anglo teacher in a reservation school, Patricia Osborn was acutely aware that her Native American students disliked writing in English. She often noted that these pupils had difficulty developing ideas when writing essays, and seemed to lack organization. As she sat down with David Littlebear, principal at the school, she reviewed her critique of the students' writing. "They don't develop a topic from beginning to end," Patricia complained. "There is little sequence, whether time-order, cause and effect, problem-solution, or comparison and contrast. I have difficulty getting them to summarize the main points at the end of the writing."

David Littlebear replied, "In tribal speaking, our elders seldom address a topic directly. Suggestions are made indirectly and the listener must make the connection. The speaker does not presume to point out the relevance of the example to the topic. The presentation is more of a collage of related ideas with the inclusion of references to stories and narratives that members of the culture share. Before you conclude that the students cannot write, try to develop a kind of writing that incorporates the speaking style of our people. Perhaps then the students will measure up to your expectations." (Scafe & Kontas, 1982)

In this case study, the Native American students were modeling writing based on experience with public speaking that is not linear in progression. Because of their stature, tribal elders may not be required to verify their sources explicitly. Credence is not determined by citing written proof, because for generations, transmission of the culture was maintained through the spoken word (Scafe & Kontas, 1982). Teachers from the dominant white culture prescribe behaviors for success with which minority students may have little experience or practice; in some cases, this behavior may be directly contrary to accepted behaviors in other cultures.

Empowerment of language minority students. School programs that recognize the rights and abilities of minority students and strive to reverse the discriminatory patterns of the society at large have proved more successful in helping these students through the schooling process (Cummins, 1984, 1989). Sociolinguists and psychologists, using ethnographic approaches, have studied the process of minority disempowerment as well as the transition to empowerment. Adaptive strategies are available that can assist teachers and decision makers in schools to help minorities gain control of their lives through participation in social and cultural institutions (Trueba et al., 1993).

"Minority students are 'empowered' or 'disabled' as a direct result of their interactions with educators in the schools" (Cummins, 1984, p. 58). Cummins found the following characteristics in programs that provided success for language minority students:

- Minority students' language and culture are accepted and incorporated into the school program.
- Minority community participation is encouraged as an integral component of the school program.

- Instructional interactions encourage students to use language in order to construct their own knowledge.
- Educators become advocates for minority students by focusing on the effect of the school context on students' achievement rather than claiming problems lie within students.

"Empowered" behaviors, in some ways, are opposite to those that teachers normally encourage. Teachers who expect and demand that students enter the room quietly, sit at their desks waiting for instructions, and speak only when spoken to are promoting the internalization of submissiveness and dependency, a process that results in lack of power over oneself. The opposites of these demands actually promote self-esteem by requiring students to set their own goals, learn independently rather than exhibit learned helplessness, and feel confident in their own academic and personal talents. Because minority students' school failure is rooted in the power structure of schools, real change in the education of minority students is likely to occur only through direct challenges to the structure of schools. Cummins (1990) suggests that this change might take place by shifting competitive social structures to cooperative ones. Cooperative learning activities in the classroom represent perhaps the best example of "cumulative empowerment" (p. 11).

Policies used to control those who are not in power establish a subordinate role that these groups are expected to accept. Many minority students are identified as "at risk," a term that perpetrates the language of deficit (Ginsburg, 1986). Flores, Tefft Cousin, and Díaz (1991) contrast deficit views with empowerment views. Table 6-2 highlights these differing assumptions. Incorporating positive attitudes about minority children into day-to-day pedagogy can change teachers' behaviors by communicating expectations for positive outcomes.

Parent and Community Participation

Teachers sometimes feel frustrated that they are not as successful as they could be in involving parents of language minority children in the educational process. In turn, parents sometimes may feel that the school does not welcome or understand their attempts at involvement. Many avenues exist for teachers to establish a strong sense of community with parents, and successful models for parent involvement have demonstrated that parents of language minority children can work with teachers to build academic success.

Parent empowerment. The Parajo Valley Family Literacy project in Watsonville, California, is a classic case of parental empowerment. The Parajo Valley School District serves a mostly rural population in the area surrounding Watsonville, California. Half of the students in the district are Hispanic:

TABLE 6-2   Contrasting Assumptions about Minority Children's Schooling

Deficit View	*Empowering View*
Language minority children have a language deficit and lack experiences. This causes them to have learning problems.	Language minority students are proficient language users and bring many experiences into the classroom.
"At-risk" students need to be separated from "regular" students and given compensatory education in a structured skill based program.	Students can be successful in regular classroom programs with rich integrative curriculum.
Standardized tests can accurately identify and categorize "at-risk" students.	Students' language use in authentic settings can form the basis for assessment.
"At-risk" students have problems because their parents do not care, do not read, or do not work with them.	Parents of language minority children are interested in their children's school success and can be partners in the school experience.

26.9 percent are migrant children; one-third of all students do not speak English fluently; and the dropout rate for Hispanics in the district is 53.6 percent. Project founder Dr. Alma Flor Ada, an author of children's books and director of the University of San Francisco's Multicultural Program, designed a parental involvement program that would help parents recover a sense of dignity and identity. Ada worked first with students in a "meet the author" program in which she told her stories and explained her feelings about writing in Spanish. Then Ada used children's literature as the stimulus for parent meetings. Invitations to the library were sent in Spanish and transportation was provided for parents if needed. Children of all ages were invited in a parallel program featuring films and story-telling. Ada selected five children's books to read to parents in the first session and in subsequent sessions parents shared their experiences and discussed children's books. Videotapes showing parents discussing and enjoying the books were circulated in the community. Parents eventually replaced teachers as facilitators in the discussions, and parents were encouraged to write their own stories. As a result, those parents increased in self-confidence and self-expression. They gave presentations at regional migrant education conferences and circulated lists of books to buy in Spanish. The major components of this project were the collaboration of the school and parents in a shared enterprise and the reciprocal interaction between parents and children that encourages both to enjoy literature (Ada, 1989).

Involving parents in the school. Parents are the experts on their children, with the advantage of knowing them as individuals and not in a large group setting. They are also experts in their respective ways of life. By involving parents in the classroom, teachers can honor the lives of students and their parents, and in addition, can enrich their own understanding of the individual child and the child's group. Parents can be invited to the classroom to demonstrate some of their knowledge. This can include physical manifestations of that knowledge: making a kite, paper flowers, a piñata; demonstrating a craft; singing songs or telling stories in the native language. It can also take other forms: teaching some of the important greetings; explaining views toward adults; demonstrating nonverbal behaviors. Teachers should be concrete and specific in requesting parents' contributions, and, when inviting parents, should specify a particular day with the time flexible. It may be necessary for the teacher to offer the parent reciprocal help by sitting with a preschool child while the parent shares with the class. On a larger scale, a group of teachers may be able to host successful parent groups or meetings. Discussing topics of major interest for all, sharing books that facilitate communication between generations, or writing family histories with parents are activities the whole community can enjoy. Teachers can also send home activities that will involve parent–child communication, such as asking for a saying or proverb, eliciting an anecdote from the family's history, or having the children read stories they have written. One teacher created a family history project that became the basis for classroom units on Guatemala, Nicaragua, and the Mexican Revolution.

Parental support for bilingual education. Some teachers have had the experience of parents requesting English immersion programs for their children rather than bilingual programs. Parents need to understand that primary language instruction helps children build a cognitive foundation for subsequent instruction. School bilingual advisory committees often perform an informative function for parents in schools with federally funded bilingual education programs (see Bilingual Education Office, 1987). Teachers may need to explain the benefits of bilingual education in order for parents to be supportive. During the annual parent meeting at the California Association for Bilingual Education conference in 1992, many parents talked about their desires for school involvement. Here are some of the parent requests (Olsen, 1992a):

- Ways we can help the children more
- Information about parents' rights under Title VII legislation
- More presentations about programs offered by the school
- More tutoring programs and workshops about evaluation and grading
- Bilingual teaching techniques
- Material translated into other languages
- Information about model schools with excellent parental involvement
- Updates on bilingual education legislation

- Programs that combine work with university study
- Primary language speakers at school meetings
- Information on double immersion programs (English-speaking children in Spanish bilingual programs)

The community can also support bilingual education by the involvement of voluntary associations and community organizations. In several communities in southern California, the Hispanic Chamber of Commerce and the local Kiwanis and Rotary clubs offer scholarships to teachers' assistants to further their preparation as bilingual teachers. The school district can offer bilingual high school students programs of work/study in which they work as paid teacher's assistants during the school day. A climate of support for bilingual education can be created by feature articles in local newspapers and newsletters about children's achievements in the schools, prizes children have won, literature and art exhibitions featuring students, and publication of students' stories written in both languages. Children can be invited to the local library to offer their stories, books, and poetry to other children, again in both English and the primary language. In this way, support for bilingualism and bilingual education programs is orchestrated in the community at large.

ORGANIZATIONAL MODELS: WHAT WORKS FOR WHOM?

Bilingual education is an umbrella term used to refer to various types of programs and models. It is a term used in two ways: first, for education that promotes academic and linguistic development in two languages, and second, to denote programs that include students who speak languages other than English. In the first instance, bilingualism is being fostered; in the second, language minority children are present but bilingualism is not a goal of the curriculum (Baker, 1993). Obviously, the school experience for language minority students varies depending on the aim of the program in which students participate. The program can support and extend the home language and culture, or it can consider the students' language and culture irrelevant to schooling.

Within the distinctions outlined here, program models vary in degree. Where bilingual education is not even nominally implemented, many language minority students are offered a submersion curriculum; that is, they are expected to function academically in English along with native English speakers from the time they first enter school. In a transitional bilingual education (TBE) program, students are educated in their home language until the English they are learning is presumed to be adequate to place them in an English-only classroom. A maintenance bilingual education (MBE) program fosters the use of the students' home language(s) and strengthens their sense of cultural identity. Double immersion programs offer academic instruction in a second language to language majority students as well as a maintenance education for language minority students. Factors to consider in these various program models are the amount of time each language is used for instruction, the subject areas that are taught in the primary and/or second language, and the methods used for instruction.

Submersion

The default mode for educating language minority students in U.S. classrooms is commonly *submersion*. Students in such a program receive instruction in English, with English monolingualism as the goal. The associated social difficulties experienced by minority students in a language majority classroom are not addressed. As a result, the strongest of these language minority students may survive or even succeed academically (they "swim"), but the majority of the students do not have the cognitive and academic foundation in the primary language at the time of education in English and thus do not attain the level of success educators might wish (they "sink"). Submersion programs are often confused with immersion programs.

Pull-out ESL. Associated with the submersion model is the separation of language minority students for remedial instruction in English. This often takes the form of separate half-hour per day classes in which students leave their home classroom and receive instruction in vocabulary, grammar, oral language, and/or spelling. Such instruction rarely is integrated with the regular classroom program; and, when they return to the home classroom, children usually are not instructed on curriculum they missed while they were gone. This lack only exacerbates an already difficult learning situation. However, because pull-out programs are fairly simple to administer and require little or no additional expense (Baker, 1993), they remain an attractive model for schools faced with increasingly complex challenges and tightening budgets.

Structured immersion. Structured immersion or SDAIE is a program model that keeps language minority students in their respective classrooms and provides specially designed academic instruction in English. Because students are still being educated in the same classroom with language majority students, the manner of instruction becomes critical. A pedagogy that encourages interaction among all students and active student participation in learning is essential so that all students—language minority and majority—have opportunities to share and learn. The environment takes on added importance as a means of providing visual and kinesthetic stimuli. To promote a sense of belonging and acceptance, the teacher may initially accept student work in the home language, attempt to learn a few greetings in the students' language, and allow language minority students to take on the teaching role in their language to sensitize language majority students (and the teacher) to the daily situation they face as second language learners. Unless these conditions prevail, the program is indistinguishable from submersion and students are left on their own to sink or swim.

Transition

The overriding goal of transitional bilingual education (TBE) programs is to mainstream students into English-only classrooms. In the past, it was often believed that students should be transferred to all-English instruction as rapidly as possible (see the Point/Counterpoint on page 166). Most of these programs last only two to three years, long enough for students to achieve basic interpersonal communication skills (BICS) but not long enough for children to build cognitive academic language proficiency (CALP) either in their native tongue or in English. As a consequence, they may not be able to carry out cognitively demanding tasks in English, and may be considered to be "subtractively bilingual."

Two TBE program models are early-exit and late-exit. In *early-exit* programs, there is some initial instruction (30 to 60 minutes per day) in the child's primary language, usually consisting of reading skills. All other instruction is in English; the primary language is used only for support. By grade 2, virtually all instruction is in English, and students are mainstreamed into an English-only classroom by the end of second grade. *Late-exit* programs offer students a minimum of 40 percent of total instructional time in the primary language—in reading, language arts, mathematics, social studies, and/or science. Even though students may be reclassified as fluent English proficient, they remain in the late-exit program through the sixth grade (Ramirez, 1992).

Maintenance

A bilingual program that supports not only education and communication in the students' primary language, but also students' heritage and culture, is a maintenance bilingual education (MBE) design, also known as developmental bilingual education. The major assumption in such a program is that bilingualism is a valuable asset, not only for the individuals who are bilingual but for society as a whole. Students in an MBE design are not quickly transitioned but are encouraged to be proficient in both English and their native tongue. This enhances self-concept and pride in the cultural

Point/Counterpoint: Should bilingual students be taught in English as soon as possible?

Many teachers and parents look upon instruction in the primary language as a temporary necessity from which a student should be weaned as rapidly as possible. Do bilingual students benefit from rapid transition to all-English instruction?

Point: **Bilingual students will progress faster in classes taught in English.** The effectiveness of bilingual education programs has been repeatedly debated. Baker (1987) reviewed research to date and found that many studies comparing bilingual education to other program models contained contradictory evidence. Overall, Baker's view is that research in bilingual education has not confirmed its usefulness. Willig (1985) disputes that claim. Comparing 23 studies of bilingual education, Willig found that previous research used to document the failure of bilingual education actually shows small to moderate differences favoring extended primary language instruction. A longitudinal study (Ramirez, 1992) comparing early-exit programs (transition to all-English instruction by grade 2), late-exit programs (students receive 40 percent of their instruction in their primary language until sixth grade), and structured immersion programs (all-English instruction, employing primary language–receptive teachers and English language development methods) found that students in early-exit and immersion programs initially had better reading skills in English, but differences across programs faded by grade 6.

Counterpoint: **Bilingual students who remain in primary language instruction have more success in school.**

Ramirez (1992) reported that students in late-exit bilingual programs have higher mathematics skills by the end of grade 6 than those in early-exit and structured immersion programs. Moreover, students in late-exit bilingual programs show gains in reading scores that suggest an eventual approximation to those of mainstream students. One additional advantage of late-exit bilingual programs is that parents of students in these programs were better able to provide academic assistance to their children and thus better able to help their children to maintain high levels of academic performance in school. This advantage translates to lower dropout rates in middle and high school, resulting in long-term academic success.

Many studies that concentrate on school achievement fail to document an important variable: the effect of self-esteem and cultural pride achieved by children in late-exit bilingual programs that affirm cultural heritage. This factor is often ignored in classes taught solely in English.

background. Dool Elementary School in Calexico, California, features such a model, with a high degree of academic success for students.

A particularly compelling use of maintenance bilingual programs is in the education of Native Americans. There are now 22 tribally controlled community colleges and 74 schools operated by Native American organizations under grants or contracts with the Bureau for Indian Affairs. Cultural and linguistic preservation is a high priority for these schools (Reyhner, 1992). The attempt to increase the number of speakers of Native American languages is sometimes called "restorative" bilingual education. Primary language maintenance is carried out in school systems in the U.S. possessions of Guam and the Marshall Islands, as well as in the state of Hawaii.

Immersion

Immersion education also provides academic and language instruction in two languages over a period of years. The goal of immersion programs is for students to be proficient in both languages—to achieve additive bilingualism. The term *immersion* has come from program models in Canada, where middle-class, English-speaking children are instructed in French. Krashen (1991) calls these Canadian-style immersion (CSI) programs. In the United States, English-only submersion programs for language minority students are sometimes mischaracterized as immersion. This misconception has led to confusion. Canadian immersion is not and never has been a monolingual program, because English is incorporated into the programs both as a subject and as a medium of instruction (Lambert, 1984). In addition, the social context of French immersion is the upper middle class in Quebec Province, where both English and French have a high language status for instructional purposes.

Enrichment immersion. In the United States, a comparable social context to Canadian-style immersion is found in the exclusive private schools of the upper class in which foreign languages are highly supported, even to the extent of instruction being delivered directly in a foreign language. This program model might also be labeled *enrichment immersion*.

Double or two-way immersion. The enrichment immersion model is inadequate for language minority students in the United States because the low status of the students' primary language puts it at risk for suppression (Hernández-Chávez, 1984). A two-way immersion model enhances the status of the students' primary language.

In the double or two-way immersion design, a high level of academic instruction is achieved in two languages with both language minority students and English-only speakers. Both groups of students participate in content area instruction in the minority language as well as in English, although the two languages are not mixed. Both groups receive language instruction in both their native and the second language. This approach has been successful in Cincinnati, Ohio, with a mixed English-only population of White and African-American students using both French and Spanish as the target second language (Genesee, 1984).

Individualized Instruction

In situations where not enough children of a particular language group are in the same grade, provisions are made for an Individual Learning Program. In the state of California, such a program must minimally provide English language development, including reading and writing skills; primary language instruction in mathematics and language arts in order to sustain academic achievement until students transfer to English; and multicultural education (Bilingual Education Office, 1987).

Newcomer Centers

Many language minority students are new to the United States and may need some cultural orientation in conjunction with their entry into U.S. schools.

> They walk into schools foreign in structure, assumptions and even in basic approaches to learning. Finding their way through the school campus, figuring out what is expected, and learning how to be an American student are major challenges to newly-arrived immigrant students, and most are shocked at what they encounter here. (Olsen & Dowell, 1989, p.10)

Some school districts offer orientation support to newly arrived immigrant students. These programs may extend a general welcome to new students and provide information in the primary language about the United States schooling system. Peer guides may be available. New students may also need an orientation to the community and information about where to go and whom to see for nonschool matters.

Newcomer students in U.S. schools face several challenges in their attempt to succeed academically and to adapt to American society. Many students find regular school settings difficult because many of them come from parts of the world where they received little, if any, formal education. The vast majority of newcomer students are classified as limited-English-proficient by the assessments that are performed upon entering. Some may be virtually illiterate in their native language or have not received age-appropriate education. The grading system and social customs in U.S. schools may be alien to them. The hardships of their immigration experience may have undermined their sense of self-confidence. During their period of adjustment, they need an emotionally safe educational atmosphere that fosters rapid language learning, acculturation, and enhancement of self-esteem (Friedlander, 1991).

Various models of newcomer centers include the following:

- School-within-a-school versus self-contained, separate site
- Full-day versus half- or part-day programs
- Single language versus multilingual programs

Each of these models has strong and weak points. In general, models that allow some degree of interaction with English-speaking peers and equal access to regular school activities make it easier for newcomer students to make the transition from these special programs to a mainstream environment (Friedlander, 1991).

An important activity of newcomer centers is assessment of students for appropriate academic placement. This assessment should occur rapidly upon enrollment and should take place in the native language. The assessment staff needs to have comparative knowledge of the United States' and other countries' educational systems and must be sensitive to the experiences of the incoming immigrant students. The assessment staff also needs to know the academic opportunities available for immigrant students and should offer parents additional orientation. This assessment should be flexible and ongoing to allow immigrant students maximum opportunity (Olsen & Dowell, 1989). For information about specific newcomer centers and schools, *Bridges: Promising Programs for the Education of Immigrant Children* is a helpful resource.

Secondary Bilingual Programs

More than a quarter of a million language minority students are enrolled in California's secondary schools (96,060) in grades 7–8 and 164,338 in grades 9–12 (California State Department of Education, 1990). Statewide, 96 different language groups are represented among the language minority population with 68 percent Spanish-speaking, 20 percent speaking Asian languages, and 20 percent other. Besides the numbers of language minority students enrolling in secondary schools, another issue is number of previous years of schooling. Some students who enroll at age 15 or 16 have little if any prior schooling; other language minority students enroll with excellent educational backgrounds. Some students will maintain enrollment and complete the full sequence of ESL courses but may be unable to compete in challenging academic classes. For these students, schools sometimes maintain unrealistic expectations and fail to meet their needs for support services (counseling, flexible scheduling). Textbooks may not be adapted for language minority students, and assessment procedures may be limited. The program approaches for secondary language minority students include mainstream placement (submersion), sheltered English-only or primary language combined with sheltered English, and content instruction in the primary language. For the most part, access to the core curriculum is difficult for secondary students with limited English proficiency. Teachers must be willing to participate in special training programs that offer a range of incentives for them to offer additional support to students who need it (Minicucci & Olsen, 1992a).

Research Studies on Program Effectiveness

California has many examples of successful bilingual programs. Krashen and Biber's *On Course* (1988) profiles six exemplary programs. The California Office of Bilingual Education also features successful programs and models in their *BEOutreach* publication. One such program is Project OCEAN, coordinated by the staff at the Alameda County (California) Office of Education. It offers language minority students in grades K–6 an opportunity to study marine science. The project includes "Oceans Week," an innovative exploration in science concepts in thematic curriculum units. The majority of students enrolled in the program have the following primary languages: Cantonese, Khmer, Vietnamese, and Spanish (Martel, 1991). Another program for primary language development teaches 130 Hmong speaking students in grades K–8 to read and write in their home language. The program also trains credentialed teachers and Hmong instructional aides in innovative methods for teaching reading and writing, and provides training for parents (Kelly, 1991).

INSTRUCTIONAL STRATEGIES

Research on the effectiveness of bilingual education has focused primarily on the central question: Do certain features characterize effective bilingual instruction in different settings? The significant bilingual instructional features that have been identified include the use of active teaching behaviors that result in maximum on-task time for students, the active use of cultural referents from the students' home culture during instruction, the use of two languages to mediate instruction, and the integration of English language development with regular in-class instruction (Milk, 1985).

Good classroom teaching must be a part of a bilingual classroom in the same way that good teaching is required in any classroom. When students are viewed as active participants in the learning process rather than empty receptacles to be filled with knowledge, then teachers organize classroom experiences for "reciprocal interaction." Teachers are guided by beliefs that their role involves the following (Cummins, 1986):

- Genuine dialogue between students and teacher, both oral and written
- Guidance and facilitation rather than teacher control of student learning
- Encouragement of student–student talk in a collaborative learning context
- Development of higher level cognitive skills rather than mere factual recall
- Meaningful language use by students rather than correction of surface forms
- Integration of language use and development in all curricular areas rather than their separation into separate subjects
- Generation of intrinsic rather than extrinsic motivation

Teachers also recognize the importance of incorporating students' culture(s) into classroom tasks. Suggestions on this will be provided in Chapter 10. In characterizing effective bilingual instruction, the following sections will focus on the use of two languages and exemplary means of classroom organization.

Language Management

If instruction is to be effective for children who potentially can function at a high level in two languages, the use of these languages must maximize cognitive and academic proficiency. Programs using two languages can either use them separately or integrate them. Separation of languages may be by time, personnel, subject, and manner of delivery. Integration, on the other hand, is more a function of students' developing competencies; the students themselves determine whether one, the other, or both languages are used.

Separation of languages. Bilingual programs may devote a specific *time* to each language. In an "alternate use" model, languages are used on alternating days: Monday, primary language; Tuesday, English; Wednesday, primary language, and so on. In a "divided day" model, the morning may be devoted to the primary language and the afternoon to English. In both these models, academic instruction is occurring in both languages.

Languages can be separated by *teacher*. In a team teaching situation, one teacher may speak in English, the other in the primary language. When working with an aide, the teacher will use English and the aide the primary language. A caution in using this latter design is the association of the minority language with school personnel who do not have fully credentialed teaching status.

Bilingual instructional models also can divide language use by *subject*— primary language for mathematics, English for science. Again, for this model, school personnel need to be cognizant of which subjects are taught in which language. Models where the primary language is used only for language arts, music, and art, whereas English is used for science and mathematics, send a message about the status of the primary language.

Manner of delivery. The novice bilingual teacher may say everything twice, first in English and then in the primary language. This *concurrent translation* model has been found to be ineffective because students tune out when their subordinate language is spoken. Another approach is *preview/review*, in which the introduction and summary are given in one language and the presentation in the other. In situations where content area materials are not available in the minority language, preview/review has been found to be particularly useful (Lessow-Hurley, 1990).

Primary language use. Primary language instruction is defined as follows:

> [Primary language instruction is] the planned and systematic use of the primary language as both the source of and vehicle for instruction. It includes instruction focused on the development of the language itself (oral and literacy skills) through use of authentic written and oral literature and discourse as well as academic instruction through the primary language. (Sánchez, 1989, p. 2)

Primary language instruction permits students to transfer their life experiences into an understanding of the purposes of reading and writing. Students who have a well-developed conceptual base in their primary language can translate into English concepts and ideas that are firmly established rather than facing the far more difficult task of learning fundamental concepts in an unfamiliar language (Lessow-Hurley, 1990). Hearing and reading familiar songs, poems, folktales, and stories in the native language exposes students to literary language and various genres. Many teachers use self-expressive journals so that students have an authentic purpose for communicating (Hudelson, 1987). Once literacy is established in the native language, children can use these resources as they move into English reading and writing. With a firm base, they are willing to experiment in a new language by using what they already know to create their own English texts and to read English material written by others (Flores et al., 1985).

As students become more proficient in English, several factors help to determine which language they use. The primary factor is the students themselves. They are free to respond in whichever language is comfortable and appropriate to them. Teacher proficiency and material availability are other factors. In some cases, teachers may provide instruction in English while students, in their groups, talk and write in the home language. Code switching, the alternation between two languages, is accepted in this model; bilingual teachers and students may habitually alternate between the two languages that are used in their community (Valdés-Fallis, 1978). It is regarded as a developmental aspect in acquiring a second language and/or as a reflection of the community's language use. An excellent example of a fifth-grade bilingual class moving into English literacy while maintaining their first language is Hayes, Bahruth, and Kessler's *Literacy con Cariño* (1991).

Classroom Organization

Several forms of organization have been found useful in bilingual classrooms. Alternatives to teacher-directed instruction may increase the ability for children to learn language effectively.

Cooperative groups. Teaching in classrooms with language minority students involves different types of organizational structures. The teacher can no longer dispense information and expect learning to occur. One strategy teachers have successfully implemented for students who are learning English is cooperative grouping. Working cooperatively with native speakers of English increases students' opportunities to hear and produce English and to negotiate meaning with others. Students develop friendships with others of different linguistic backgrounds that stimulate language growth (Johns, 1992). Cohen's complex instruction (Cohen, Lotan, & Catanzarite, 1990) encourages equal access for all students in a cooperative group by assigning well-defined roles to each group member and insuring that these roles rotate frequently. In addition to encouraging academic learning and language proficiency, cooperative learning also helps children to learn classroom conventions and rituals and become an active part of the culture of the classroom. To be most effective, grouping needs to be flexible and heterogeneous in language, gender, ability, and interest.

Student-centered groups. Although cooperative grouping has been used for a number of years, certain formats encourage active student involvement and learning, whereas others continue to reinforce teacher-centered instruction. Cooperative Integrated Reading and Composition (CIRC) was originally developed to be used with monolingual English students and has been applied in a bilingual model (Calderón, Tinajero, & Hertz-Lazarowitz, 1992). The CIRC program consists of teacher-directed instruction in reading comprehension and "Treasure Hunt" activities based on worksheets provided by the teacher. Instructional materials in Spanish use basal reading programs.

A contrasting program was implemented in a school in South Texas with a large number of migrant children (Hayes et al., 1991). During their fifth-grade year, students were empowered to teach themselves—they talked and wrote about their lives outside the classroom, about what they were learning and the effect this learning had on their lives. Students were given choices and opportunities to express themselves using daily journals and class-made books. Writing conferences helped them evaluate their own writing and that of their classmates. A rich supply of stories and nonfiction books encouraged them to read.

Collaborative teaching. Teaching has traditionally been an isolating experience. When teachers have the opportunity to collaborate, however, they can share interests and experiences and build on each other's strengths for the benefit of their students. An example of teachers working together is found in the Holistic English Literacy Program (HELP) at Elderberry Elementary School in Ontario, California. Three teachers, one in second grade, one in a bilingual third grade, and one in fourth/fifth grade, worked together to organize the structure of the school day to accommodate the needs of their language minority students, to plan thematic units, and to support each other's areas of expertise (see Chapter 12 for a more complete description).

BILINGUAL EDUCATION AT THE MILLENNIUM

Since the first federally funded bilingual education programs in the late 1960s following the arrival of Cuban refugees, the students served have been primarily those with Spanish as a primary language. During the 1970s, the U.S. population grew by 11.6 percent overall, while the number of Hispanics increased by 61 percent and of Asian-Americans by 22.3 percent (Crawford, 1991). At present, only 1 percent of the U.S. population is considered to have limited English proficiency. Within Vietnamese and Hispanic groups, however, approximately 75 percent are considered LEPs (Sosa, 1992). Educators working with language minority students have come to realize that learning English is not the sole guarantor of achievement; educators must work to reduce the number of language minority students in special education, to increase the number identified for gifted and talented programs, and to raise the expectations of teachers for minority students. Bilingual funds have become increasingly available for developmental or maintenance bilingual programs.

Issues for the 1990s and Beyond

Bilingual educators continue to face numerous challenges in the 1990s and beyond. Some of these are as follows (Sosa, 1992):

- The need to integrate innovations (cooperative learning, etc.) into bilingual education
- The need to use testing toward instructional decision making rather than labeling students for compensatory programs
- The need to explore ways to avoid placing language minority students in programs that contribute to dropping out
- The need to increase the number of bilingual teachers
- The need to examine state policies that adversely affect LEP students (e.g., exit exams for graduation, remedial ESL classes)

The Reauthorization of Title VII of the ESEA: The Bilingual Education Act

Under the current Elementary and Secondary Education Act (ESEA), language minority students receive assistance under a number of federal assistance programs not funded under Title VII. Among these programs are Chapter 1 Migrant Education, Indian Education, Bilingual Vocational Training, Adult Education, Special Education, and Head Start (U.S. Department of Education, 1991, 1992a). The National Association for Bilingual Education (NABE) has recommended eliminating or amending the statutes that exclude limited-English-proficient students from general Chapter 1 services. Moreover, NABE recommends that Title VII be authorized for a minimum of ten years and that schoolwide grants be available for longer periods of time to develop exemplary programs that include the use of technology in the classroom for language minority students and that provide funding for bilingual teacher training (Lyons, 1993).

Educators who met in Washington in January 1992 explored the current state of Native American education. Among the outcomes of this conference was the following quote. The ideas contained therein go beyond the topic of Native American education only and might be taken as a theme for education in the next millennium.

> [E]ducation should have a "holistic approach focusing on all segments of Native communities and all aspects of being human (emotional, physical, spiritual, and intellectual)." (quoted in Reyhner, 1992, p. 7)

Chapter 7

Language and Content Area Assessment

A school is good when it moves away from factory-like processing procedures and toward more humanistic, individualized judgments.

The idea is to make evaluation a learning experience.

A school is good when its priorities are broadly conceived, rather than narrowly hierarchical.

A school is good when it does not use standardized tests, or uses them only with extreme caution and skepticism.

Testing should grow from what is taught, and what is taught should grow from who is taught. (Postman & Weingartner, 1973)

Reading tests do not test reading: They actually test similarity to the test writer. (Edelsky, 1991)

Assessment is a process for determining the current level of a learner's performance or knowledge. The results of the assessment are then used to modify or improve the learner's performance or knowledge. Ideally, a test informs educators about the strengths and needs of the language learner so that students are properly placed and appropriately instructed. In an English language development context, assessments can test language ability or content knowledge or both; in the process of testing these, one must take care that culture is not a hidden part of the test. In the model presented in Figure I-1, assessment has an impact on instruction, learning, and culture and is itself affected by culture.

Various evaluation methods have been used with language minority students. Some are required by government programs and legal mandates, and others, more informal, are devised by classroom teachers. Educators involved in assessment must be careful to ensure that tests are fair (free from cultural and linguistic bias) and valid (measuring what they purport to measure). Furthermore, tests must advance students' understanding and ability if they constitute a valid part of education. Tests should not be merely instruments of diagnosis for labeling and placing and designing remediation.

If testing is aligned with a curricular goal that emphasizes the production of well-formed English utterances over learner-centered communication, the learners may in fact relinquish control of the activity of learning English to the teacher and take no real responsibility for active intentional learning of the second language. Testing must therefore be an integral part of a learning environment that encourages students to seek meaning and use a second language to fulfill academic and personal goals.

PURPOSES OF ASSESSMENT

Assessment instruments can be used for a number of purposes: Proficiency tests determine a student's level of performance; diagnostic and placement tests provide information to place students in the appropriate level of academic or linguistic courses; achievement tests assess the student's previous learning; and competency tests assess whether or not a student may be promoted or advanced.

Proficiency Tests

Proficiency tests measure the test takers' overall ability in English, usually defined independently of any particular instructional program. These tests may help determine whether the test taker is ready for a job, or ready to proceed to a higher level of instruction. Proficiency tests are sometimes divided into subskills or modes of language, including speaking, listening, writing, reading, vocabulary, grammar, and sociolinguistic or strategic discourse competence. Within the last decade, tests have become much more assessments of communicative competence than measures of knowledge about discrete points of grammar or vocabulary.

Proficiency tests are poor tests of achievement because, by design, their content has little or no relationship to the content of an instructional program. They may also poorly diagnose what specific knowledge a student has or is lacking. Educators should be cautious about using proficiency tests to predict academic or vocational success, because language is only one element among many that contribute to success (Alderson, Krahnke, & Stansfield, 1987).

Diagnosis and Placement Tests

Diagnosis and placement tests are administered to determine specific aspects of a student's proficiency in a second language. Most tests that purport to be diagnostic tests are in reality tests of relative proficiency in various skills (Alderson et al., 1987). Placement tests, which may be the same as proficiency tests, determine the academic level or the grade level into which students need to be placed. These tests should contain the same types of skills that are taught in the instructional program and should not include unfamiliar tasks that may negatively affect a student's performance.

In addition to standardized placement tests, educators have other sources of information about students' language abilities with which to make placement decisions. Cheng (1987) offers the following:

- Observe students in multiple settings, such as classroom, home, and playground.
- With the help of a trained interpreter if necessary, obtain histories (medical, family, previous education, immigration experience, home languages).
- Interview current or previous classroom teachers for information about learning style and classroom behavior.
- Seek information from other school personnel (counselor, nurse), especially if they are capable of assessing the home language.
- Ask the student's parents to characterize a student's language and performance skills in the home and the community.

Educators who draw from a variety of information sources can see the students' needs in a broader context and thus design a language program to meet these needs.

Achievement Tests

An achievement test measures a student's success in learning specific instructional content whether language (knowledge about English) or another subject (mathematics, science). This test is given after instruction has taken place and should contain only material that was actually taught. The staff of the instructional program usually prepares such a test. The trend in achievement testing is away from testing samples of a student's storehouse of knowledge and toward testing a student's ability to think knowledgeably. For example, a beginning English language learner may be given clues to a treasure hunt to practice the vocabulary associated with the schoolroom (eraser, chalk, globe), and a teacher may observe the student's ability to collect all the relevant items in an informal assessment. A science achievement test might present students with a problem to solve and various materials to help them reach a solution. During the exercise, the students' language is less relevant than their ways of thinking.

Competency Tests

Many states feature minimum competency testing programs that are used to identify students who may be promoted or graduate. In some states, such as Florida, limited-English-proficient students in certain grades who have been in an ESL program for two or fewer years may be exempt from the state minimum competency testing program. Other states offer modifications in the testing such as extended time, a separate site, small group testing, or testing supervised by a familiar person (Evaluation Assistance Center—East, 1990). These provisions that modify or exempt testing for language minority students may allow instructional progress until students are ready for standardized testing.

METHODS OF ASSESSMENT

One of the major activities in U.S. education is the comparison of children with one another to assess academic growth. Test scores, classroom grades, and teacher observation and evaluation are common bases for determining student progress. The judgments resulting from this testing may affect students' present adjustment to school and their future academic and social success. The social and economic pressures from testing often overshadow the curriculum and the affective goals of schooling. Performance-based testing is a growing alternative to standardized testing, although standardized testing will probably persist because of the economic and political investment in this type of assessment. For classroom purposes, teacher observation and evaluation—supplemented by other sources of data—remain potent allies for students' academic progress. Students can play a role in the assessment process by evaluating their own language development, content knowledge, and strategies for learning (Pierce & O'Malley, 1992).

The Role of Assessment in the Integrated Curriculum

The use of an integrated curriculum promotes language and academic development for language minority students. Units of study in literature, math, science, and social studies may be combined into an interdisciplinary program in which students can use a variety of communication systems (language, art, music, drama) to pursue open-ended assignments. Students develop proficiency through activities such as silent reading, experiments, questioning, discussion, free writing, focused writing, and other integrated activities. Assessment is a natural part of this curriculum. Student outcomes are documented in a variety of ways—time capsules, surveys, creative works, posters, and so forth. Good records allow teachers to track individual progress and also reflect and store many observations about students' skills and interests. The *Whole Language Evaluation Book* (Goodman, Goodman, & Hood, 1989) details a wealth of evaluation and assessment formats that are consonant with a whole language approach to integrating the curriculum. An approach that uses assessment to capture the excitement of students' learning and communicate their abilities in a varied and positive way keeps the focus on learning rather than on testing.

Performance-Based Assessment

Performance-based testing is testing that corresponds directly to what is taught in the classroom. Performance-based testing procedures can easily be incorporated into classroom routines and learning activities. Methods for performance assessment can be divided into two main types: structured (e.g., tests, checklists, observations, rating scales, questionnaires, structured interviews) and unstructured (e.g., student work samples, journals, games, debates, story retelling, anecdotal reports, and behavioral notes).

Students may be assessed through structured means such as teacher-designed examinations that are intended to be scored quickly. Questionnaires and surveys can help teachers to learn about many students' skills and interests at once. An observation checklist allows teachers to circulate among students while they are working and monitor specific skills. The advantage of structured assessment is its speed and standard means of scoring.

Unstructured assessment, on the other hand, has been criticized for being time-consuming, labor-intensive, imprecise, and subjective even though much effort is put into developing acceptable concurrence among assessors (Maeroff, 1991). Despite these difficulties, unstructured assessments can furnish valuable information about students' abilities. One way currently being employed to keep students' records is in portfolios. Using a combination of formal and informal assessments provides a crosscheck of student capabilities (Navarrete, Wilde, Nelson, Martínez, & Hargett, 1990).

Classroom tests. Classroom tests may reflect functional or communicative goals, whether they require a set of unrelated phrases or answers from students or solicit answers embedded in a naturalistic sequence of discourse. Tests may be highly convergent (one right answer required) or may be open-ended, with many answers possible. By testing only outcomes of learning, these tests tend to divide knowledge into small pieces away from an applied context. On the other hand, more authentic tests of ability require students to have a repertoire of responses that call for judgment and skill in using language to meet challenges within the target culture. Such alternative assessments are being pioneered by projects like the California Learning Assessment System (CLAS) and the proposed Vermont Statewide Assessment System in Writing and Mathematics (Wiggins, 1989).

Portfolio assessment. Portfolio assessment is often used synonymously with the term *alternative assessment.* The purpose of portfolio assessment is to maintain a long-term record of students' progress, to provide a clear and understandable measure of student productivity instead of a single number, to offer opportunities for improved student self-image as a result of showing progress and accomplishment, to recognize different learning styles, and to provide an active role for students in self-assessment (Cudog, Castro, & Carrillo, 1991). Portfolios may include writing samples (compositions, letters, reports, drawings, dictation); student self-assessments; audio recordings (retellings, oral think-alouds); photographs and video recordings; semantic webs and concept maps; and/or teacher notes about students (Glaser & Brown, 1993).

The Fairfax (VA) County public schools maintain portfolios in the ESL program to record students' progress in reading, oral language, and writing. The reading assessment component begins with an initial reading assessment. Group and individual checklists document reading-related behaviors, and reading samples are recorded for inclusion in the folder. The oral assessment includes opportunities for students to invent a story, to listen/retell, and to produce spontaneous speech. The oral language is scored in communicative stages. The writing assessment component includes rough drafts as well as final copies. The content is scored on a developmental scale with separate scoring rubrics for grades 2–6 and secondary school levels. Other comprehensive ELD assessments are used by the English Language Center in three California school districts: the Hayward Unified School District, the San José High School District, and the San Diego City Schools' Hispanic Writing Project.

Standardized Tests

Standardized tests for second or foreign language teaching offer means for employing a common standard of proficiency or performance despite variations in local conditions or student abilities. For example, ESL curriculum in the United Kingdom uses a standard called the Graded Tests that advance students through various levels of ESL. These tests are produced by national examination boards and are used to determine ESL/EFL proficiency and readiness for entry into British universities. The Test of English as a Foreign Language (TOEFL), developed by the Educational Testing Service in Princeton, New Jersey, is a similar test used for nonnative speakers of English at eleventh grade or above. It is administered in more than 170 countries and areas for students wishing to study in universities and colleges in the United States. The benefits of standardized tests include speed in administration and convenience in scoring. They are also considered to be unbiased, although questions arise as to their impartiality.

Norm-referenced tests. These tests compare student scores against a population of students with which the test has been standardized or "normed." These scores may be expressed in a variety of forms such as *T*-scores, stanines, and *z*-scores. These measures compare each score with the average on the test. An example of a norm-referenced test is the Language Assessment Scales (LAS), a test designed to measure oral language skills in English and Spanish. This is a standardized test with mean scores and standard deviations based on various age groups. Students are given a LAS oral proficiency level from 1 to 5 depending on their total score on two levels of the test.

Criterion-referenced tests. These are used principally to find out how much of a clearly defined domain of language skills or materials students have learned. The focus is on how the students achieve in relation to the material, rather than to one another or to a national sample. A common example of a criterion-referenced test is a final examination for a language course. On this type of test, all students may score 100 percent if they have learned the material well. In an ELD program with many levels, students may be required to pass criterion-referenced tests to progress from one level to the next.

Teacher Observation and Evaluation

Teachers are in the best position to observe and evaluate students on an ongoing basis. Moreover, teachers are responsible for communicating students' progress to administrators, parents, and students themselves. Documenting student progress and diagnosing student needs are two major purposes of teacher evaluation. Much of this data can be obtained as teachers design tests and observe students as they learn.

Observation-based assessment. As students interact and communicate using language, an observant teacher can note individual differences. In addition to formal notes, teachers may record a cooperative or collaborative group working together; students telling a story, giving a report, or explaining information; or children using oral language in other ways. These observations of speaking and listening should extend across all areas of the curriculum and in all types of interactional situations. Observations may be formal (e.g., miscue analysis) or informal. They may be based on highly structured content or on divergent and creative activities. Multiple observations show student variety and progress (Crawford, 1993).

Teacher-made tests. Teacher-made tests are often the basis for classroom grading. Tests can assess skills in reading comprehension, oral fluency, grammatical accuracy, writing proficiency, and listening. Teacher-constructed tests may not be as reliable and valid as tests that have been standardized, but the ease of construction and administration and the relevance to classroom learning makes them popular. Because of their own past testing experiences and the nature of tests connected with texts or text series, teachers may have a tendency to devise "discrete-point" tests—those that ask students for specific items of grammar or vocabulary. However, Canale (in Cohen, 1991) believes that communicative functions can be used as proficiency-oriented achievement tests. He offers criteria for good communicative tests:

- Tests should put to use what is learned.
- The focus is on the message and function, not just on the form.
- There is group collaboration as well as individual work.
- Respondents are called on to resolve authentic problems in language use, as opposed to contrived linguist problems.
- Testing looks like learning.

Grading. A variety of approaches has been used to assign grades to language minority students. Teachers sometimes experience frustration stemming from making these nontraditional students fit into a traditional evaluation system. Some schools in which all classes are taught in sheltered English assign a *traditional A–F grade scale* in accordance with grade level expectations. Assignments are adjusted to meet the students' language levels. Students receive a separate grade in the subject areas of their ESL class and performance standards are not lowered in content classes. A *modified A–F grade scale* is used in schools where language minority students are congregated in one ESL class regardless of grade level. During their time in this class, students' work is assessed with an A–F grade based on achievement, effort, and behavior, with report card grades modified by a qualifier signifying work performed above, at, or below grade level. A third type of grade system is the *pass/fail grade scale* used by schools whose language minority students are integrated into the regular classroom. This scale avoids comparing the language minority student with English-proficient classmates ("From the Classroom," 1991).

Cautions about Testing

Tests are an influential part of the U.S. schooling system and are used in every classroom. When choosing standardized tests, teachers can consider the following guidelines (Worthen & Spandel, 1991) to help them determine the benefits and limitations of the test:

- Does the test correspond to the task that it measures?
- Does the score approximate the students' ability?
- How can the score be supplemented with other information?
- Does the test drive the curriculum?
- Is the test a fair sample of the students' skills and behaviors?
- Is the test being used unfairly to compare students and schools with one another?
- Are tests that involve minimum standards being used to make critical decisions regarding classification of students?

STATE MANDATES

Twenty-nine states have specific laws and provide procedural guidelines regarding identification procedures for language minority students. Many states also have procedures for redesignating students and for placing them in mainstream classes. Some states do not have state laws but do provide guidelines for the assessment of language minority students. Generally speaking, students are first evaluated; then, if identified as language minority, they are placed in suitable programs, if available. They are then periodically reevaluated for purposes of reclassification.

Identification Procedures for Language Minority Students

A variety of methods are used to identify language minority students needing services. The *home language survey*, a short form administered by school districts to determine the language spoken at home, is one of the most frequently used methods to identify language minority students. *Registration* and *enrollment* information collected from incoming students can be used to identify students with a home language other than English. Identification through *observation* is often done by a teacher or tutor who has informally observed a student using a language other than English. *Interviews* may provide opportunities to identify students, as may *referrals* made by teachers, counselors, parents, administrators, or community members (Cheung & Solomon, 1991).

Assessment for Placement

Once a student is identified, California requires assessment in the native language of the student within 90 days of enrollment. To be in compliance with this requirement, assessment must be done by staff with the language skills to communicate in the family's native language. Sometimes, however, assessment consists only of a conversational evaluation in English by an untrained person. Parents and students should be provided with orientation about the assessment and placement process and the expectation and services of the school system. Most important, the school staff needs to be trained, aware, and sensitive to the backgrounds and experiences of the student population.

Specific tests have been designed to help districts place language minority students. The Language Assessment Scales (LAS), grades 2–5 (LAS I) and grades 6 and up (LAS II) are designed to measure oral language skills in English or Spanish. Verbal and motor responses are compared with expected answers, and total correct answers are converted to weighted scores which convert to the LAS Oral Proficiency Level (1–5). The test is individually administered and takes 20 minutes for the long form, which assesses phonemic, lexical, and pragmatic language systems.

Another frequently used proficiency test is the Bilingual Syntax Measure (BSM) I, grades K–2 and BSM II, grades 3–12. This test is designed to measure oral proficiency in English and/or Spanish grammatical structures and language dominance. The BSM is a short, oral test that includes 25 questions in each language. Students are asked questions about seven colorful cartoon drawings. Items are scored immediately and the student is classified into one of several English levels (non-English-proficient—NEP; limited-English-proficient—LEP; fluent English-proficient— FEP).

The Basic Inventory of Natural Language (BINL) is designed to measure oral proficiency in English. Pictures are used to elicit natural speech, and spoken sentences are analyzed for fluency, average length of utterance, and level of syntactic complexity. Students are classified as non-English-speaking (NES), limited English-speaking (LES), fluent English-speaking (FES), and proficient English-speaking (PES). The test is individually administered and takes about 10 minutes.

The IDEA proficiency test is designed to measure oral language proficiency in English. As students point, name objects, complete sentences, and respond verbally, these responses are scored for accurate comprehension and production. Students are classified in one of six levels from A (most basic) to F (fluent). The test is individually administered and takes approximately 15 minutes.

Quick Start in English, another assessment test, uses a rating of ten levels of receptive and expressive language usage. As students move through the ten levels, they take competency tests to advance. Language in the Quick Start program is sequenced grammatically.

Even after administering these tests, appropriate academic placement may be difficult. First, the tests only measure language proficiency. They say nothing about a student's academic background. Students may be highly prepared in certain subject areas and very weak in others. They may be very strong academically but have poor English skills, or, conversely, excellent

English skills and few academic skills. Placement by age is also a problem. Students may need much more time in the system to learn English, but placement in an earlier grade may lead to social adjustment problems. Interested readers may wish to consult *Bridges: Promising Programs for the Education of Immigrant Children* (Olsen & Dowell, 1989), a publication of the California Tomorrow Immigrant Students Project, which describes several outstanding orientation and assessment programs.

Redesignation/Exit Procedures

Some states, such as California, permit school districts to establish reclassification criteria to determine when language minority students have attained the English language skills necessary to succeed in an English-only classroom. The reclassification process may utilize multiple criteria (California State Department of Education, 1984), including, but not limited to, all of the following:

- Teacher evaluation, including a review of the student's curricular mastery
- Objective assessment of language proficiency and reading and writing skills
- Parental opinion and consultation
- An empirically established range of performance in basic skills based on nonminority English-proficient students of the same grade and age

Some districts organize bilingual education advisory committees to ensure ethnic parent representation and participation in implementing redesignation criteria that are reliable, valid, and useful. Norm-referenced tests using national norms or district, regional, or state nonminority norms can be employed for purposes of reclassification, as can standardized criterion-referenced tests. States set various cutoff scores on language and achievement tests that are used as criteria for proficiency in the process of redesignation.

LIMITATIONS OF ASSESSMENT

Tests play a large role in placing and reclassifying ELD students. Often, pressure is applied for programs to redesignate students as fluent English-speaking in a short period of time. Tests may be used to place language minority students into mainstream programs before they are ready. Continuing support such as tutoring, follow-up assessment, and primary language help is often not available after reclassification.

Standardized tests, though designed to be fair, are not necessarily well suited as measures of language ability or achievement for language minority students. In fact, some have argued that the very use of tests is unfair because tests are used to deprive people of color of their place in society. As Sattler (1974) comments, "No test can be culture fair if the culture is not fair" (p. 34). The goal of tests notwithstanding, both the testing situation and the test content may be rife with difficulties and bias for language minority students.

Difficulties in the Testing Situation

The context in which a test is administered needs to be examined to understand how students may be affected. Factors within the context of testing such as anxiety, lack of experience with testing materials, time limitations, and rapport with the test administrator may cause difficulties for culturally and linguistically diverse students.

Anxiety. All students experience test anxiety, but this anxiety can be compounded if the test is alien to the students' cultural background and experiences. Certain test formats such as multiple-choice tests, cloze procedures, and think-aloud tasks may provoke higher levels of anxiety because students may fear these assessments inaccurately reflect their true proficiency in English (Oh, 1992; Scarcella, 1990). Allowing students to take practice exams may familiarize them with the test formats and reduce test anxiety.

Time limitations. These may cause anxiety in students who do not operate under the same conception of time as do European-Americans. Some students may need a time extension or should be given untimed tests.

Rapport. When testers and students do not share the same language or dialect, the success of the testing may be reduced. Students may not freely verbalize if they are shy or wary of the testing situation. Students who ostensibly share the primary language with the test administrator may not have in common certain dialectic features, with reduced understanding as a result. Rapport may also suffer if students are defensive about teachers' negative stereotypes or if students resent the testing situation itself.

Problematic Test Content

For the most part, language placement tests are well suited to assess language. Other tests, however, particularly achievement tests, may have translation problems or bias that affect the performance of language minority students.

Equivalent first and second language versions. Translating an English language achievement test into Spanish or vice versa to create equivalent vocabulary items may cause some lack of correspondence in the frequency of the items. For example, *belfry* in English is a much less frequently understood term than its Spanish counterpart, *campanario*. The translation of a test is a hybrid belonging to neither culture. Additionally, even the most obvious test items may be difficult or impossible if the items have not been experienced by the child in either language (Sattler, 1974).

Linguistic bias. This can take several forms. *Geographic bias* happens when test items feature terms used in particular geographic regions but which are not universally shared. *Dialectical bias* occurs when a student is tested using expressions relevant to certain dialect speakers that are not known to others. *Language-specific bias* is created when a test developed for use with one language is used with another language. For example, a test that measures a student's ability to use appropriate thanking behavior in English may demonstrate linguistic bias because the "thank-you" routines in another culture may occur under very different circumstances and require different behaviors. Instead of testing purely linguistic knowledge, such a test is actually biased toward those students whose first language has similar routines.

Cultural bias. Tests may be inappropriate not only because the language provides a dubious cue for students, but also because the content may represent overt or subtle bias. For the most part, overt bias and stereotypes are absent, but subtle bias persists. For example, a contemporary ESL series contains a picture of children on the cover whose depiction is stereotypic: The Mexican-appearing child wears sandals and serape, and the Chinese-appearing child wears a straw coolie hat. Another series features a Chinese child named "Ching-Ching," a type of name that in China is used only for pandas. Moreover, testing itself may be offensive. Native American children may not understand a culture in which mastery over nature takes the place of harmony with nature, science rather than mythology explains natural phenomena, and competing and climbing the ladder of success takes the place of cooperating and maintaining the ways of the status quo. These values of the dominant culture appearing in test items may be understood differently or not at all by language minority students.

Cultural content appearing in tests may provide difficulty for students without that cultural background. Many students never experience common European-American food items such as bacon; common sports in the United States may be unfamiliar; musical instruments may be mysterious to students; nursery rhymes and children's stories may refer to only one culture. Even mathematics, a domain that is supposedly language free, has been shown to cause difficulties because language proficiency plays a relatively more important role than previously suspected (Kintsch & Greeno, 1985).

Students may be naive about the process of testing and not recognize that these tests perform a gatekeeping function. Deyhle (1987) found that students at the Red Canyon School (a pseudonym) on the Navajo Reservation did not perform well on standardized tests largely because they did not attribute importance to the test process. Students in grade 2 became very excited when taking tests, but the test-taking behavior showed "inappropriate" shouting out and frequent sharing of answers among students. Older Navajo children showed quite different responses, far from the gamelike approach taken by younger students. The older students were well aware that failure on a test could lead to lack of promotion and failure to move on with their friends to the next grade. Their anxiety and apprehension were palpable as the students twisted their hair and fumbled their pencils often.

Interpretation of Test Results

One last caution in the assessment of English language learners is to understand the emphasis of the test: Is it on language proficiency or on content knowledge? When testing content, educators should select or devise tasks on which language minority students can achieve, regardless of their language proficiency. When scoring the test, teachers must evaluate students' responses to distinguish responses that are conceptually correct but may contain language problems from those that are conceptually incorrect.

TECHNICAL CONCEPTS

A good test has three qualities: validity, reliability, and practicality. A test must test what it purports to test (valid), be dependable and consistent (reliable), and applicable to the situation (practical).

Validity

A test is valid if it measures what it claims to be measuring. If a test measures the ability to read English, then it should test that ability. A test has *content* validity if it samples the content that it claims to test in some representative way. For example, if a decision is made that a reading test should include proficiency in reading for inference or reading for vocabulary, then a test of reading would include tests of inference and vocabulary. *Empirical* validity is a measure of how effectively a test relates to some other known measure. One kind of empirical validity is predictive: How well the test correlates with subsequent success or performance. A second type of empirical validity is concurrent, or correlating well with another measure used at the same time. Teachers often apply this concept of concurrent validity when they grade examinations. Intuitively, they expect the better students to receive better scores. This is a check for concurrent validity between the examination and the students' daily performance.

Reliability

A test is reliable if it yields predictably similar scores when it is taken again. Although many variables can affect a student's test score, such as error introduced by fatigue, hunger, or poor lighting, these variables usually do not introduce very large deviations in students' scores. A student who scores 90 percent on a teacher-made test probably has scored 45 on one half of the test and 45 on the other half, regardless whether the halves are divided by odd/even items or first/last sequence. These are common ways of checking for reliability.

Practicality

A test may be valid and reliable but may cost too much to administer either in time or in money. A highly usable test should be relatively easy to administer and score. An authentic testing situation is one in which the teacher uses test items that are a representative of actual tasks performed in the classroom or in the community at large. When a portfolio is kept to document student progress, issues of practicality still emerge. The portfolio should be easy to maintain, accessible to students, and scored with a rubric agreed on by teachers and students. In this way, authentic assessments stem directly from classroom activities, allow students to share in the process of evaluating their progress, and are valid and reliable in that they truly assess a student's classroom performance in a stable manner. Although authentic assessments have been criticized as subjective and anecdotal, the advantage of authentic assessment is that it is directly related to classroom performance and permits teachers to design and offer the extra mediation that students may need as determined by the assessment.

Regardless of how valid, reliable, and practical a test may be, if it serves only the teachers' and the institution's goals, the students' language progress may not be promoted. Testing must instead be an integral part of a learning environment that encourages students to seek meaning and use a second language to fulfill academic and personal goals.

Chapter 8

The Nature of Culture
and Cultures in Contact

Joe Suina (1985) tells of his impressions upon entering school at the age of six:

> ... unlike my grandmother, the teacher did not have pretty brown skin and a colorful dress. She wasn't plump and friendly. Her clothes were of one color and drab. Her pale and skinny form made me worry that she was very ill. . . . The teacher's odor took some getting used to also. Later I learned from the girls this smell was something she wore called perfume. The classroom . . . was terribly huge and smelled of medicine like the village clinic I feared so much. Those fluorescent light tubes made an eerie drone. Our confinement to rows of desks was another unnatural demand made on our active little bodies. . . . We all went home for lunch since we lived a short walk from the school. It took coaxing, and sometimes bribing, to get me to return and complete the remainder of the school day.

The narrative of this Pueblo youth illustrates two cultural systems in contact. Neither is right or wrong, good or bad, superior or inferior. Suina was experiencing a natural human reaction that occurs when a person moves into a new cultural situation—culture shock. He had grown up in an environment that had subtly, through every part of his life, taught him appropriate ways of behavior—for example, how people looked (their color, their size, their dress, their ways of interacting) and how space was structured (the size of rooms, the types of lighting, the arrangement of furniture). His culture had taught him what was important and valuable. The culture Suina grew up in totally enveloped him and gave him a way to understand life. It provided him with a frame of reference through which he could make sense of the world.

Culture is so pervasive that often people perceive other cultures as strange and foreign without realizing that their own culture may be equally mystifying to others. Schools, as institutions of learning and socialization, are representatives of a particular culture. Culture, though largely invisible, influences instruction, policy, and learning in schools (see Figure I-1). Members of the educational community accept the organization, teaching/ learning styles, and curriculum of the schools as natural and right. And the schools *are* natural and right for members of the community that created them. As children of nondominant cultures enter the schools, however, they may find the organization, teaching/learning styles, and curriculum to be alien, incomprehensible, and exclusionary.

As an initial step in learning about the complexity of culture and how the culture embodied within the school affects diverse students, the following sections examine the nature of culture and issues that occur when cultures come into contact. A knowledge of the deeper elements of culture— beyond superficial aspects such as food, clothing, holidays, and celebrations—can give teachers a crosscultural perspective that allows them to educate students to the greatest extent possible. These deeper elements include values, belief systems, family structures and child-rearing practices, language and non-verbal communication, expectations, gender roles, biases—all the fundamentals of life that affect learning.

THE NATURE OF CULTURE

Does a fish understand water? Do people understand their own culture? Teachers have a primary responsibility to help pass on cultural knowledge through the schooling process. Can teachers (masters of the culture of schooling) step outside this culture long enough to see how it operates and to understand its effects on culturally diverse students? A way to begin is to examine what culture is, how culture affects perception, how geography affects culture, what differences occur naturally within cultural groups, and how cultures provide congruence.

Definitions of Culture

The term *culture* is used in many ways. It can refer to activities such as art, drama, and ballet or items such as pop music, mass media entertainment, and comic books. It can be used for distinctive groups in society—adolescents and their culture. It can be used as a general term for a society—the "French culture." Such uses do not, however, define what a culture is. As a field of study, culture is conceptualized in various ways.

TABLE 8-1 Definitions of Culture

Definition	Source
The explicit and implicit patterns of behaviors, symbols and ideas that constitute the distinctive achievements of human groups.	Kroeber and Kluckhohn (1952)
That complex whole which includes knowledge, belief, art, morals, law, custom, and any other capabilities acquired by humans as members of society.	Tylor (in Pearson, 1974)
Discrete behaviors, traditions, habits, or customs that are shared and can be observed.	Spradley (1972)
The sum total of a way of life of a people; patterns experienced by individuals as normal ways of acting, feeling, and being.	Hall (1959)
A dynamic system of symbols and meanings that involves an ongoing, dialectic process where past experience influences meaning, which in turn affects future experience, which in turn affects subsequent meaning, and so on.	Robinson (1985)
Patterns for living . . . the individual's role in the un-ending kaleidoscope of life situations of every kind and the rules and models for attitude and conduct in them.	Brooks (1968)
The means by which a community communicates . . . a commonly agreed-upon set of meanings in interactions with one another.	Steele (1990)

The definitions in Table 8-1 have common factors but vary in emphasis. The important idea is that culture involves both observable behaviors and intangibles such as beliefs and values, rhythms, rules, and roles. Culture is the filter through which people see the world.

Too often, culture is incorporated into classroom activities in superficial ways—as a group of artifacts (baskets, masks, distinctive clothing), or celebrations of holidays (Cinco de Mayo, Martin Luther King, Jr., Day), or a laundry list of traits and facts (Asians are quiet; Hispanics are family-oriented; Arabs are Moslem). Teachers who have a deeper view of culture and cultural processes are able to use their understanding to move beyond the superficial and to recognize that people live in characteristic ways. They understand that the superficial (observable) manifestations of culture are but one aspect of the cultural web—the intricate pattern that weaves and binds a people together. Knowing that culture provides the lens through which people view the world, teachers can look at the "what" of a culture—the artifacts, celebrations, traits, and facts—and ask "why."

Perceptions of Culture

All cultures provide templates for the rituals of daily interaction: the way food is served, the way children are spoken to, the way people's needs are met. Some human needs are so fundamental that they are provided for in all cultures. Thus, all cultures share some universal characteristics. The manner in which these needs are met differs across cultures, and within a culture no two individuals view the world in exactly the same way. Each may exhibit very different personalities and behaviors and may vary in their beliefs and values. What their culture does for them is provide them with an internalized way to organize and interpret experience. The interpretation is individual.

Cultural universalism. All human beings create culture. Members of a particular culture tend to believe that their own ways are the best. Culture influences how and what people see, hear, and feel, and how people and events are evaluated. Each group responds in its own way to meet humanity's basic needs: food, shelter, clothing, family organization, religion, government, social organization, defense, arts and crafts, knowledge acquisition, and survival skills.

Cultural influences help unify a society by providing a common base of communication and common social customs. The patterns that dominate a society form the *macroculture* of that society. For example, in the United States a variety of cultures coexist, but the Anglo-European tradition has largely determined the social values and formal institutions. Individuals who grow up within a macroculture and never leave it may assume that many of its values are universal. When encountering cultures of radically different beliefs, they may be unable or unwilling to recognize that alternative beliefs and behaviors are legitimate.

Cultural relativism. The fact that each culture possesses its own particular traditions, values, and ideals means that the culture of a society provides judgments that make any action right or wrong for its members. Actions may only be judged in relation to the cultural setting in which they occur. This point of view has been called *cultural relativism*. Attempting to impose "international" standards on diverse peoples with different cultural traditions causes problems. This means that some cardinal values held by teachers in the United States are not cultural universals—for example, the value that academic activities should be based on competition or that children are expected to work on their own. Whole systems of instruction in the schools of the United States are based on these cultural values of competition and individualization (spelling contests, computer assisted instruction, independent study projects). Students who come from cooperative, group-conforming cultures, where it is permissible and even desirable to work together and where it is abhorrent to display knowledge individually, may find themselves negatively evaluated because of their different value system, not because of any academic shortcomings.

Physical Geography and Its Effects on Culture

A social group must develop the knowledge, ideas, and skills that it needs to survive in the kind of environment the group inhabits. The geographical environment or physical habitat challenges the group to adapt to or modify the world to meet its needs. When the Native Americans were the sole inhabitants of the North American continent, a wide variety of cultures existed, a necessary response to the variety in the environment. The Iroquois were a village people who lived surrounded by tall wooden palisades. The Chumash, in contrast, lived a leisurely seashore existence on the California coast, where fishing was plentiful and the climate moderate. Still a third group, the Plains Indians, were a nomadic people who followed the bison. Each group's culture was adapted for success in the physical environment.

Classrooms constitute physical environments. These environments have an associated culture. In a room in which the desks are in straight lines facing forward, participants are enculturated to listen as individuals and to respond when spoken to by the teacher. What a contrast this must be for a young Pueblo child whose learning takes place largely in the communal courtyards outside comfortable adobe dwellings and who is taught the traditional recipes by a mother or grandmother, or the secrets of tribal lore in an underground kiva by the men of the village. The physical environments in which learning takes place vary widely from one culture to another. Can we really say that the hard wooden desk and the inkwell were the best way to educate children in early America?

Intragroup Differences

Even among individuals from the same general cultural background, there are intragroup differences that affect their world view. In her study of students of Mexican descent, Matute-Bianchi (1991) described the differences between successful Mexican immigrant students and unsuccessful non-immigrant Chicano students at a high school in the California central coast area. A range of identities and behaviors were identified that were associated with varying patterns of school performance. Most of the students could be placed in five major categories: (1) recent Mexican immigrants, (2) Mexican-oriented, (3) Mexican-American, (4) Chicano, and (5) Cholo.

The recent immigrants had arrived within the last three to five years and still referred to Mexico as home. They dressed differently from the rest of the student body, and their clothing was considered unstylish by other groups. Most of these students were monolingual in Spanish, with varying levels of English proficiency. Within the group, students used various differences to distinguish among themselves (e.g., rural versus urban, upper class versus working class, *mestizo* versus *indio*).

The second group of students had lived most of their lives in the United States but still maintained a strong identity as Mexicanos. Their parents were Mexican-born, and there was often considerable interaction with family members still in Mexico. These students tended to be bilingual.

The Mexican-American students were almost always U.S.-born English speakers. Many were Mexican in last name only, were strongly acculturated, and did not manifest any overt cultural symbols. Often they did not speak Spanish well and preferred to use English.

The fourth group, the Chicanos, were usually the second generation of their family in the United States. They were among the most alienated Mexican-descent students in the school. They called themselves "homeboys" or "homegirls," in contrast to the academic achievers, whom they called "schoolboys" or "schoolgirls." They sometimes displayed an attitude of apathy toward or outright defiance of the school culture. Even though they declared a desire to do well in school, according to Matute-Bianchi's interviews, they frequently disrupted class or were absent.

The last group, Cholo, were frequently identified as gang members by other students. Even though some exhibited obvious stylistic cultural symbols (particular kinds of pants, shirts, shoes, and ways of walking), many were not necessarily gang-affiliated.

Each of these groups can be considered a *microculture* within the larger microculture of people of Mexican descent living within the United States.

In the above case, social identification and language usage, as well as dress, were the markers of the distinct microcultures. In some cases, generational experiences cause intragroup differences. The first generation of Japanese came to the United States starting about 1900 and were, for the most part, young men who became agricultural laborers or skilled craftsmen. They often referred to themselves as *issei* or first-generation immigrants to the United States. The industrious labor of this generation was often seen as a threat by European-Americans. These immigrants were often the target of discrimination and attempts at exclusion. This discrimination peaked after the attack on Pearl Harbor, when *issei* were divested of their property and removed to relocation camps. Their children, the *nisei* generation (born in the United States), bore the responsibility of reassimilating into the macroculture after World War II. This generation is often considered to have very low ethnic profile, perhaps as a response to the treatment given to their parents (Leathers, 1967).

Cultural Congruence

Cultures are more than the mere sum of their traits. There is a wholeness about cultures, an integration of the various responses to human needs. "A culture, like an individual, is a more or less consistent pattern of thought and action" (Benedict, 1934, p. 42). Cultures, Benedict goes on to say, have coherent organizations of behavior. Unfortunately, the organization, the pattern of a way of life, is often lost from view when people focus on exotic, external elements of other people's cultures.

In classrooms, cultural content takes two forms. The first form is the explicit teaching of culture. There is a danger here: If one studies the artifacts of another culture without examining the patterns of the culture, one might fail to understand that these patterns represent responses to the physical environment that prompted the need for those artifacts. Cultures cannot be understood only by assembling a collection of cultural artifacts. The second form of cultural content is implicit: the actual contact of cultures that occurs daily in U.S. schools. In this contact the congruence or lack thereof between mainstream and minority cultures has lasting effects on students. Students from families whose cultural values are similar to those of the European-American culture may be relatively advantaged in schools. For example, Japanese-Americans are often stereotyped as the model minority because Japanese cultural values toward schoolwork are similar to European-American values. The ethic of hard work, traditional to Japanese values, aims at individual honor. Coupled with a deferential, self-denying behavior in a variety of situations, these values are at once fundamentally Japanese and congruent with behaviors encouraged in the typical United States school (Bennett, 1990).

In contrast, African-American students often do not use work as a means of gaining individual honor but, rather, have been taught to seek assistance and help each other in work situations and to be individualistic and competitive in play activities. They learn at home that play involves projecting their personalities and calling attention to their individual attributes (Gay, 1975). Such actions are not generally accepted by the school culture, often leading to poor academic performance by African-American children.

People of many cultures have come to the United States. Today's schools have the responsibility to educate students from these diverse cultures. This education may be relatively easy for students whose values, beliefs, and behaviors are congruent with U.S. schooling. Other students may find the process excruciatingly painful. The teacher who can find a common ground with diverse students will promote their further education. Besides having an understanding of the nature of culture and its varied manifestations, the thoughtful teacher recognizes that the process of intercultural contact is often a bumpy road. The meeting of two cultures may include some cultural conflict, which will not disappear if it is ignored. Relationships between individuals or groups of differing cultures are built through commitment, a tolerance for diversity, and a willingness to communicate.

CULTURAL CONTACT

We cannot know all things about all cultures, but it is possible to understand what happens when cultures come into contact with one another and how this contact can affect schooling. When cultures meet, they affect one another: Cultures can be swallowed up *(assimilation)*; one culture may adapt to a second *(acculturation)*; both may adapt to each other *(accommodation)*; or they may coexist *(pluralism* or *biculturalism)*. When an individual comes in contact with another culture, there are characteristic responses, usually stages, an individual goes through in adapting to the new situation. Contact between cultures is often not a benign process. It may be fraught with issues of prejudice, discrimination, and misunderstandings. Means of mediation or resolution must be found to alleviate cultural conflict, particularly in classrooms.

Concepts of Cultural Contact

The 1980s witnessed an unprecedented flow of immigrants and refugees into the United States. Many of them were from countries in Central America undergoing revolution. An estimated 300,000 to 400,000 Salvadorans immigrated to the United States between 1979 and 1983; almost one million Guatemalans became refugees as a result of war in that country, many settling in the United States. After the bloody overthrow of Somoza's dictatorship, over 200,000 Nicaraguans left their country, 30,000 of whom settled in Miami. In southern California, so many immigrants from around the world have arrived that many school districts not only have students speaking three or more languages in a single classroom, but also have students who speak the same non-English language but who come from different cultures. School officials have found, for example, that many immigrants from Central America do not follow the same pattern of school performance as Mexican-American students. These demographic issues pose a number of questions about cultures in contact. Are there characteristic differences in the patterns of adaptation to schooling among individuals from various cultures? Can we understand how to increase the school success of all students by studying the process of cultural contact?

Cultures in general and individuals specifically respond in certain ways to contact with another culture. This contact can result in assimilation, deculturalization, accommodation, acculturation, pluralism, or biculturalism. Each of these concepts will be explored in relation to the classroom.

Assimilation. Assimilation is a process in which members of an ethnic group are absorbed into the dominant culture, losing their culture in the process (deculturalization). This is done without regard to the ramifications for ethnic community life or the cultural identity of individuals. For assimilation to be complete, there must be both cultural and structural assimilation (Gordon, 1964). *Cultural assimilation* is the process by which individuals adopt the behaviors, values, beliefs, and lifestyle of the dominant culture. In the U.S. context, there have been both individuals and groups who have so assimilated. *Structural assimilation* is participation in the social, political, and economic institutions and organizations of mainstream society. It is structural assimilation that has been problematic for many. Gordon (1964) found that only limited structural assimilation occurred for groups other than white Protestant immigrants from northern and western Europe.

Individuals may make a choice concerning their degree of cultural assimilation. However, the dominant society determines the extent of structural assimilation. These two related, but differing concepts have important consequences in classrooms. Teachers may be striving to have students assimilate (see the Point/Counterpoint on pp. 199–200), but may be blind to the fact that some of their students will not succeed because of attitudes and structures of the dominant society.

Acculturation. Acculturation means adapting effectively to the mainstream culture. This concept should be distinguished from *enculturation,* the process through which individuals learn the patterns of their own culture. To acculturate is to adapt to a second culture without necessarily giving up one's first culture. It is an additive process in which, while individuals adapt to the mainstream culture, their right to participate in their own heritage is preserved (Finnan, 1987). Some researchers have emphasized the importance of acculturation for success in school. For example, Schumann (1978a) claims that the greater the level of acculturation in a particular individual, the greater the second language learning will be for that individual.

Assimilation, not acculturation, was the aim of many immigrants who sought to become part of the "melting pot." More recently minority groups and their advocates have begun to assert that minority ethnic groups have a right, if not a responsibility, to maintain valued elements of their ethnic

---

Point/Counterpoint: What is the teacher's role in the instruction of culturally diverse students?

Schools have traditionally been society's melting pot, the place in which the children of immigrants are inculcated with the basics of U.S. culture and cultural values. Teachers were the front-line workers in the

(Continued)

struggle to enculturate newcomers. Is this the best role for teachers to play in the education of culturally diverse students?

Point: Teachers are "assimilators."

Teachers who see themselves as agents of assimilation tend to promote the melting pot as a model for their students. This entails the belief that nonmainstream students should change their cultural patterns to match those of the society at large, and should seek success in mainstream terms. Students whose beliefs and behaviors do not mirror those of successful mainstream students may be seen as lacking in ability, prior knowledge, motivation, or communication skills. In applying a single frame of reference to denote success, such teachers may not realize that standard measures of achievement and aptitude have traditionally been most appropriate for European-American, middle-class groups, as have instructional content and strategies. The past experiences, knowledge, and learning styles of ethnically different students may not be fully recognized and valued, either by the teacher or by mainstream peers. Lack of respect and esteem from teacher and peers may lead to feelings of rejection and lowered expectations, a recipe for reduced academic success (see Bennett, 1990).

Counterpoint: Teachers are "accommodators."

Teachers who can accommodate instruction to facilitate learning for nonmainstream students help to widen the doors of opportunity for classroom learning and academic success. When students feel respected by teachers for who they are, regardless of their cultural, ethnic, or socioeconomic background, they can maintain throughout their school years the natural excitement and love of learning that is characteristic of children just entering school. Some students respond better to cooperation than to competition; some are motivated by peer approval, external rewards, or the chance to perform before others. Whatever the background, prior knowledge, motivation, or communication skills each student brings, the teacher who has a variety of teaching techniques, activities, and themes can inspire positive learning within all students. Teachers may need to spend additional moments with nonmainstream students to teach those responses, behaviors, and language skills that are often assumed to be present in students from homes that represent mainstream, middle-class European-America. Flexibility (Ramirez, 1991) and the ability and desire to innovate, if necessary, to meet the learning needs of culturally diverse students is a characteristic of accommodating teachers. These teachers realize that nontraditional schooling may be a key to unlocking achievement in the nontraditional student.

cultures (Kopan, 1974). The pluralist position is that coexistence of multicultural traditions within a single society provides a variety of alternatives that enrich life in the United States.

Schools are the primary places in which children of various cultures learn about the mainstream culture. Sometimes culture is taught explicitly as a part of the ELD curriculum (Seelye, 1984). According to Cortés (1993):

> Acculturation . . . should be a primary goal of education. Schools have an obligation to help students acculturate because additive acculturation contributes to individual empowerment and expanded life choices. But schools should not seek subtractive assimilation, which can lead to personal and cultural disempowerment by eroding students' multicultural abilities to function effectively both within the mainstream and within their own ethnic milieus. School-fostered acculturation is empowering—"adducation." School-fostered assimilation is disempowering—"subtractucation." Although assimilation is acceptable, it should be regarded as a student's choice and not as something for the school to impose. In our increasingly multicultural society, even traditional additive acculturation is not the only acculturation goal. Education for the twenty-first century should embrace what I call "multiculturation," the blending of *multiple* and *acculturation*. (p. 4)

Accommodation. Accommodation is a two-way process: Members of the mainstream culture change in adapting to a minority culture, the members of which in turn accept some cultural change as they adapt to the mainstream. Thus accommodation is a mutual process; it is not only the minority that is asked to adapt. To make accommodation a viable alternative in schools, teachers need to demonstrate that they are receptive to learning from the diverse cultures in their midst, and they also need to teach majority students the value of "interethnic reciprocal learning" (Gibson, 1991b). Research has shown that immigrants from Mexico, El Salvador, Korea, Turkey, and India succeed in schools in the United States not because they assimilate but, rather, because they have strong home cultures and a positive sense of their ethnic identity. These cultures and identities are a resource that schools need to sustain and support.

Philips (1972) gives examples of ways in which non-Indian teachers can adapt schooling to accommodate the culture of Native American students.

> . . . conspicuous in Indian classes is the absence of the ubiquitous "show and tell" or "sharing," through which students learn to get up in front of the class, standing where the teacher stands, and presenting, as the teacher might, a monologue relating an experience or describing a treasured object that is supposed to be of interest to the rest of the class. When asked whether this activity was used in the classroom, one teacher explained that she had previously used it, but so few children ever

volunteered to "share" that she finally discontinued it. . . . While in non-Indian classes students are given opportunities to ask the teacher questions in front of the class, and do so, Indian students are given fewer opportunities for this because when they do have the opportunity, they don't use it. Rather, the teacher of Indians allows more periods in which she is available for individual students to approach her alone and ask their questions where no one else can hear them. (pp. 382–383)

Pluralism. Pluralism is the condition in which members of diverse cultural groups have equal opportunities for success, in which cultural similarities and differences are valued, and in which students are provided cultural alternatives (BEOutreach, 1993). But does pluralism endanger society, as cultural purists have charged, by heightening ethnic group identity, leading to separatism and intergroup antagonism? Although some separatism is unavoidable, in order for society to survive, all groups must conform to some set of common, necessary norms. A dynamic relationship between ethnic groups is inevitable. In a healthy society, these groups may sometimes clash in the process of coexistence, but the strength of the society is founded upon a basic willingness to work together to resolve conflicts. According to Bennett (1990), schools can evince *integrated pluralism* (actively trying to foster interaction among different groups) or *pluralistic coexistence* (different racial or ethnic groups informally resegregate). Integration creates the conditions for cultural pluralism. Merely mixing formerly isolated ethnic groups does not go far enough, because groups rapidly "unmix" and resegregate.

Biculturalism. Biculturalism is the state of being able to function successfully in two cultures. Everyone is to some extent bicultural. For example, the medical student who attends class in the morning and accompanies practitioners in hospital rounds in the afternoon dwells in two distinct cultures every day. Every pluralistic society (take, for example, life in New York City) contains individuals who become a part of more than one culture. At a minimum level, everyone who works outside the home functions daily in two cultures—personal (home) and professional (work). For some individuals, the distance between the cultures of work and home are almost indistinguishable, while for others the distance is great. For example, Native American children sent to Bureau of Indian Affairs boarding schools often experienced great difficulties in adjusting to the disparate cultures of home and school.

What is it like to be bicultural in the United States? Bicultural people are sometimes viewed with distrust. The suspicion toward Japanese-Americans during World War II, and the resulting internment is an example of this. Parents may also be threatened by their bicultural children. Appalachian families who moved to large cities to obtain work often pressured their children to maintain an agrarian, preindustrial lifestyle, a culture that is in many ways inconsistent with urban environments (Pasternak, 1994).

The process of becoming bicultural is not without stress, especially for students who are expected to internalize dissimilar, perhaps conflicting values. Darder (1991) defines biculturalism in the following manner:

> a process wherein individuals learn to function in two distinct sociocultural environments: their primary culture, and that of the dominant mainstream culture of the society in which they live. It represents the process by which bicultural human beings mediate between the dominant discourse of educational institutions and the realities they must face as members of subordinate cultures. More specifically the process of biculturation incorporates the different ways in which bicultural human beings respond to cultural conflicts and the daily struggle of racism and other forms of cultural invasion . . . and conditions of cultural subordination. (pp. 48–49)

Madrid (1991) describes the experience of having been raised in an isolated mountain village in New Mexico and ultimately becoming a member of the faculty at Dartmouth College. As he grew older and his schooling moved him into an increasingly European-American environment, the daily challenge of living in two worlds with conflicting values resulted in his internalizing and embracing his own complex consciousness.

Stages of Individual Cultural Contact

Experiencing a second culture causes emotional ups and downs. Reactions to a new culture vary, but there are distinct stages in the process of experiencing a different culture (Brown, 1987). The stages are characterized by typical emotions and behaviors beginning with elation or excitement, moving to anxiety or disorientation, and culminating in some degree of adjustment (see Levine & Adelman, 1982). Since classrooms are a culture in themselves, these same emotional stages can occur for all students. The intensity will vary depending on the degree of similarity between home and school culture, the individual child, and the teacher.

Euphoria. Euphoria may result from the excitement of experiencing new customs, foods, and sights. This may be a "honeymoon" period in which the newcomer is fascinated and stimulated by experiencing a new culture.

Culture shock. Culture shock may follow euphoria as cultural differences begin to intrude. The newcomer is increasingly aware of being different and may be disoriented by cultural cues that result in frustration. Deprivation of the familiar may cause a loss of self-esteem. Depression, anger, or withdrawal may result. The severity of this shock may vary as a function of the personality of the individual, the emotional support available, and the perceived or actual differences between the two cultures.

Adaptation. Adaptation to a new culture may take several months to several years. Some initial adjustment takes place when everyday activities such as housing and shopping are no longer a problem. Long-term adjustment may take several forms. Ideally, the newcomer accepts some degree of routine in the new culture with habits, customs, and characteristics borrowed from the host culture. This results in a feeling of comfort with friends and associates, and the newcomer feels capable of negotiating most new and different situations. On the other hand, individuals who do not adjust as well may feel lonely and frustrated. A loss of self-confidence may result. Certain aspects of the new culture may be actively rejected. Eventually, successful adaptation results in newcomers finding value and significance in the differences and similarities between cultures and in being able to actively express themselves and to create a full range of meaning in the situation.

In the classroom, students can be experiencing the same range of emotional and behavioral reactions to the school culture. Some students may show this as withdrawal, depression, or anger. Mental fatigue may result from continually straining to comprehend the new culture. Individuals from different cultural backgrounds learn differently, both in methods and in the time they need to integrate new learning. Individuals may need time to process personal and emotional as well as academic experiences. Great care must be taken that the teacher does not belittle or reject a student who has misunderstood or reacted in a way different from the teacher's expectation. Situations such as these only show the necessity for cultural understanding.

Dynamics of Prejudice

One factor that inhibits cultural adaptation is prejudice. Although prejudice can include favorable feelings, it is generally used in a negative sense. Allport (1954) defined ethnic prejudice as follows:

> Ethnic prejudice is an antipathy based upon a faulty and inflexible generalization. It may be felt or expressed. It may be directed toward a group as a whole, or toward an individual because he is a member of that group. (p. 10)

Prejudice takes various forms: excessive pride in one's own ethnic heritage, country, or culture so that others are viewed negatively; ethnocentrism where the world revolves around oneself and one's own culture; a prejudice against members of a certain racial group; and stereotypes that label all or most members of a group. All humans are prejudiced to some degree, but it is when people act on those prejudices that discriminatory practices and inequalities result.

Allport (1954) offers several explanations for the phenomenon of prejudice. First, an historical explanation suggests that people may become prejudiced as an outcome of the history of relations between groups of people; for example, European-Americans may be prejudiced against African-Americans because of the history of slavery. A sociocultural explanation is that the pressures of urban life have caused people to depersonalize and discriminate against minorities. A third explanation combines the historical and sociocultural approach to postulate that all groups discriminate against nonmembers, and that such discrimination is a part of the psychology of humans. Another explanation is that people learn prejudice from others around them. A psychodynamic explanation is that people are prejudiced because prejudice acts as a release from personal frustration. Yet another explanation is that prejudice is an outcome of people's perception of the world; some people view others as repulsive, annoying, or threatening. A last explanation is that certain ethnic minority traits are those that invite disapproval and hostility ("they're lazy—they don't want to work"). Members of cultures view the traits of other cultures in terms of their own values and perceived threats to these values.

A simpler, more global explanation for prejudice is that it is based on fear: fear of the unknown, fear of engulfment by foreigners, fear of contamination. Allport observes that much of the human tendency to separate into groups may be due to a need for ease. Eating, visiting, even mating are easier when they are done with one's own kind. People find congeniality and pride in distinct ethnic group identity. This impulse for separatism, however, may readily lead to misunderstanding of other groups.

A closer look at various forms of prejudice, such as racism and stereotyping, as well as resulting discriminatory practices, can lead to an understanding of these issues. Teachers can then be in a position to adopt educational methods that are most likely to reduce prejudice.

Racism. Racism is the view that a person's race determines psychological and cultural traits—and, moreover, that one race is superior to another. Racism is a process that categorizes people according to observable traits and then uses these to infer personality, behavioral, or mental traits. For example, the nineteenth-century justification for slavery was that African-Americans lacked initiative and were not as intelligent as European-Americans, and that therefore they had to be taken care of. Racism can also be cultural when one believes that the traditions, beliefs, language, artifacts, music, and art of other cultures are inferior. On the basis of such beliefs, racists justify discriminating against or scapegoating other groups. Weinberg (1990) points out that racism is "a system of privilege and penalty," in which people are rewarded or punished by simply belonging to a particular group regardless of their merits or faults. More important, goods and services as well as respect is distributed in accordance with such judgments of unequal worth.

Stereotypes. Stereotypes often result from racist beliefs. A stereotype is a preconceived and oversimplified generalization about a particular ethnic or religious group, race, or gender. The danger of stereotyping is that people are not considered as individuals but are categorized with all other members of a group (Anti-Defamation League of B'nai B'rith, 1986). One might believe that a racial group has a global trait (e.g., Asians are "overambitious overachievers"), and subsequently all Asians one meets are judged in this stereotypic way. Conversely, an individual may judge an entire group on the basis of an experience with a single individual. A stereotype may be favorable or unfavorable; but, whether it is positive or negative, the results are negative: The perspective of an entire group of people is distorted.

Racism and stereotyping are difficult to combat because this type of prejudice is irrational and illogical. Furthermore, many teachers feel that teaching about values and beliefs is not a part of the curriculum. They have been reluctant to address these subjects, as well as topics such as racism, prejudice, and discrimination. To work effectively with diverse student populations, however, teachers can open the dialogue and help students understand the effect that racist ideas and behaviors have on all people. Even students who voice racist beliefs or act in a prejudiced manner may not be deeply prejudiced and may benefit from an attempt to reduce ethnic group stereotypes. An ideal outcome of discussions of racial and cultural heritage would be that students would feel an ethnic pride in their own background without becoming ethnocentric and believing that their group was superior to others.

School curriculum can be used to help students be aware of the existence and impact of racism. Science and health teachers can debunk myths surrounding the concept of race. Content area teachers can help students develop skills in detecting bias. Positive interracial attitudes can be fostered whenever students have an opportunity to work together. Students and teachers alike must raise awareness of racism in the attempt to achieve racial equality and justice. Christine Bennett, in the book *Comprehensive Multicultural Education* (1990), offers a checklist (pp. 352–354) that students can use to recognize examples of racism. Such a list can be used as the springboard for discussion. Other antiracist activities and discussion topics include the following (from Bennett, 1990, p. 78):

- Recognize racist history and its impact on oppressors and victims.
- Understand the origins of racism and why people hold racial prejudices and stereotypes.
- Be able to identify racist images in the language and illustrations of books, films, television, news media, and advertising.

- Be able to identify current examples of racism in the immediate community and society as a whole.
- Identify specific ways of combating racism.
- Examine personal attitudes, experiences, and behaviors concerning racism.
- Become antiracist in personal behavior.

Institutional racism. Institutional racism consists of "those laws, customs, and practices which systematically reflect and produce racial inequalities in American society" (Jones, 1981). An individual may not personally be a racist but may work in an institution in which policies and practices effectively discriminate against a group of people as a class. Classroom teaching that aims at detecting and reducing racism may be a futile exercise when the institution itself—the school—promotes racism through its policies and practices. For example, many testing practices in schools are ethnocentric and racist because some students are stigmatized and labeled while others are not. The European-American culture represented in these tests makes it difficult for members of certain other racial and ethnic groups to identify with the test content. A second example of institutionalized racism is the shortage of minority group teachers in classrooms where children are predominately of minority background. Is this the fault of the European-American teacher who is employed in this classroom? Probably not. The nature of the institution of schooling itself has made it difficult for minorities to attain the education and certification needed for employment as a teacher.

Discrimination. Discrimination refers to actions that serve to limit the social, political, or economic opportunities of particular groups. Discriminatory practices tend to legitimize the unequal distribution of power and resources between groups defined by such factors as race, language, culture, gender, and/or social class. There may be no intent to discriminate on the part of an institution such as a school; however, interactions with minority students may reflect unquestioned assumptions about the abilities or participation of these students. Blatant discrimination, in which differential education for minorities is legally sanctioned, may be a thing of the past, but discrimination persists. De facto segregation continues; most students of color are still found in substandard schools. Students of color tend to receive a curriculum that is watered down and at a lower level than that which European-American students receive. Schools with a high percentage of minority enrollment tend to employ faculty who have less experience and academic preparation. Teachers who do not share the ethnic background of their students may not communicate well with their students or may tend to avoid interaction, including eye and physical contact (Ortiz, 1988). Teachers may communicate low expectations to minority students. The "hidden curriculum" of tracking and differential treatment results in schools that perpetuate the structural inequities of society. Thus, school becomes a continuation of the discrimination experienced by minorities in other institutions in society (Grant & Sleeter, 1986).

In the past, those in power often used physical force to exclude people and to discriminate. Those who did not go along were physically punished: Children were separated from their parents and their own group and were punished for speaking their language or adhering to their own cultural or ethnic customs. With the spread of literacy, there is a trend away from the use of physical force and toward the use of shame and guilt. The school plays a part in this process. The values, norms, and ideology of those in power are taught in the school. Skutnabb-Kangas (1981, 1993) calls this symbolic-structural violence. Direct punishment is replaced by self-punishment, and the group discriminated against internalizes the shame associated with rule breaking. The emotional and intellectual bonds of internalized injustice make the situation of minorities more difficult. Schooling, too often, helps to keep minority children powerless—socially, economically, politically—and perpetuates the powerlessness of parents.

School programs in which children are separated from their own group are examples of structural discrimination. Students are not taught enough of their own language and culture to be able to appreciate it and are made to feel ashamed of their parents and origins. The message is that the native language is only useful as a temporary instrument in learning the dominant language. Majority students, on the other hand, are seldom taught enough about the minority culture to achieve appreciation. Skutnabb-Kangas (1981) cites a variety of examples of how discrimination operates on a daily basis against minority students in Swedish and Norwegian schools.

> The headmaster said, "You have a name which is difficult for us Swedes to pronounce. Can't we change it? . . . And besides, perhaps some nasty person will make fun of your name." "Well, I suppose I'd better change it," I thought. (p. 316)

> I love my parents and I respect them but what they are and everything they know count for nothing. . . . Like lots of Turkish children here, they know lots about farming and farm animals, . . . but when is a Turkish child given the task at school of describing the cultivation of vines? (p. 317)

> Sometimes the teacher asks us to sit together in pairs and then no one wants to sit with me. Even when the teacher says someone has got to sit with me, still no one wants to. (p. 317)

> The longer all this went on, the more urgent and deep the pressure to conform. I began to avoid my brothers and sisters. . . . I refused to go shopping with my mother and when we had a Christmas party at school, I simply told my parents they weren't to come. (p. 318)

Strategies for Conflict Resolution

Students experiencing cultural conflict may meet racism and anti-immigration sentiments from others in their environment. Subtle incidents occur every day on campuses across the United States. Graffiti are the most visual evidence: Obscene wall messages foster hatred against ethnic, racial, and religious groups. Verbal abuse, threats, and physical violence, motivated by negative feelings and opinions, are all too common. The scope of these incidents together with the increasing involvement of young adults (see Bodinger-deUriarte, 1991) is a disturbing trend on today's campuses. In Los Angeles, a recent survey reported hate crimes in one-third of the county schools with the highest rates occurring at junior highs and middle schools. Schools are crucial to the resolution of hate crimes because the young are perpetrators and the schools are staging grounds. Policies, curriculum, and antiracism programs are needed to prevent and control hate crimes.

Even well-intended educators have found that censoring racially and ethnically incendiary speech is problematic (Siegel, 1993). The University of Wisconsin at Madison instituted a hate speech code on September 1, 1989, in an attempt to reduce the frequency of racist epithets and hate crimes on campus. The Wisconsin American Civil Liberties Union brought suit against the University of Wisconsin arguing that the speech codes were unconstitutional. Minority students on campus filed many claims charging students and student groups with incidences of hate speech. In the end, the university rescinded the speech code and, in its place, prohibited only epithets that "would tend to evoke an immediate violent response" (p. 46). The irony was that the hate speech code could not have prohibited or punished any of the series of racial hate incidents that led to its inception. U.S. courts have upheld the notion that U.S. citizens have the right to free speech, even speech that denigrates others. Rather than prohibiting public speech that exhibits racial or ethnic prejudice, schools must find ways to alter the school climate or work directly with individuals to increase interethnic harmony.

> I am sensitive to cultural barriers that exist among educators. These barriers are created by lack of communication between people coming from different backgrounds and cultures. We don't discuss cultural conflicts openly. We have learned that conflicts are negative and produce racial disharmony when, in fact, the opposite is true.—Latina elementary teacher.
>
> (The Institute for Education in Transformation, 1992)

In general, research suggests that substantive changes in attitudes, behaviors, and achievement occur only when the entire school environment changes to demonstrate a multicultural atmosphere. Parents are welcomed in the school; counselors, teachers, and other staff utilize culturally compatible practices; and programs are instituted that permit interactions among students of different backgrounds. Appropriate programs are needed to prepare the communities and schools that anticipate large numbers of minority students. Students must learn to understand cultures different from their own. A culturally receptive host school may preclude these minority students from internalizing negativity about their culture and customs. Cooperative learning groups and compensatory programs that allow interaction among students of diverse backgrounds usually result in fewer incidents of name calling and ethnic slurs as well as in improved academic achievement (Nieto, 1992).

Effective educational programs, according to Allport (1954), have the following characteristics:

- Lead to a sense of equality in social status.
- Occur in ordinary purposeful pursuits.
- Avoid artificiality.
- Enjoy the sanction of the community in which they occur.
- Involve participants who regard themselves as part of a team.

In contrast, those programs that teach about "group differences," involve exhortation or mere verbal learning, or are designed directly for "prejudice reduction" are usually not effective.

It is not easy for students to maintain pride in cultures that represent minority points of view if these cultures suffer low status in the majority culture. Students feel conflict in this pride if their culture is devalued. Many students face the burden of having either to deny or lose their culture if they want to succeed or to keep it and fail (Nieto, 1992). In many cases, bilingual programs are responsible for helping students to value their home language and culture. When the languages and cultures of students are highly evident in their schools and teachers refer to them explicitly, they gain status. Schools that convey the message that all cultures are of value—by displaying explicit welcome signs in many languages, by attempts to involve parents, by a deliberate curriculum of inclusion, and by using affirmative action to promote hiring of a diverse faculty—help to maintain an atmosphere that reduces interethnic conflict.

Should interethnic conflict occur, techniques exist for problem solving. Katz and Lawyer (1993), in their book *Conflict Resolution, Building Bridges*, offer means of understanding and resolving conflicts. Many authorities, particularly in schools, attempt to handle conflict by punitive and suppressive measures or, at the other extreme, by "counseling" individuals without administering consequences for irresponsible or inflammatory acts. By understanding the source of conflicts and teaching various parties to value productive dialogue that includes compromise, collaboration, and accommodation to diverse views, conflicts can be resolved in a manner that forges positive cooperation and communication.

There is much that teachers can do to resolve conflicts in the classroom. First, teachers can talk to students privately, encouraging the sharing of perceptions on volatile issues and communicating expectations that students will be able to resolve their differences. In this way, teachers can intervene in the early stages of conflicts to defuse the problem. If problems escalate to the point of confrontation, allowing students to vent feelings as a group and setting aside a brief period of verbal expression can provide an outlet for frustration. A teacher must resolve to be calm in the face of verbalized anger and hostility, and violence or personal attacks should not be tolerated. Educators for Social Responsibility (ESR) is an organization that brings teachers together to develop approaches to multicultural education, social issues, cooperative problem solving, and conflict resolution. For more information about this organization, contact ESR, N.Y.C., 475 Riverside Drive, Room 450, New York, NY 10115.

One should not assume that cultural contact entails cultural conflict. Perhaps the best way to prevent conflict is to include a variety of cultural content and make sure the school recognizes and values cultural diversity. If conflict does occur, however, there are means to prevent its escalation. Teachers should be aware of conflict resolution techniques before they are actually needed.

Let us revisit briefly Joe Suina, the Pueblo youth whose contact with school created cultural conflict for him. How could the school have been more accommodating? This chapter has emphasized the profound influence of culture on people's perceptions, feelings, and actions, and the variety of ways in which individuals experience contact with other cultures. Ideally, Suina's teacher would be a Pueblo Indian and would share his culture. Classrooms in a Pueblo school would resemble the home, with intimate spaces and furniture designed for student comfort. If these conditions are not feasible, a non-Pueblo teacher would accommodate to the ways of the students in the same way that students are expected to accommodate to the school. Actually, students of any culture would appreciate schools that were more comfortable and less institutional, wouldn't they?

Chapter 9

Cultural Diversity in the United States

Before I came to America I had dreams of life here. I thought about tall Anglos, big buildings, and houses with lawns. I was surprised when I arrived to see so many kinds of people—Black people, Asians. I found people from Korea and Cambodia and Mexico. In California I found not just America, I found the world.—Mexican immigrant student (Olsen, 1988)

They still come—a medical student from India who remains in Knoxville to set up a practice; a Danish *au pair* worker who meets a U.S. college student and extends her green card; a Vietnamese grandmother who follows her daughter who followed her teenage sons; a Salvadoran resistance fighter who seeks political asylum; a Mexican lawyer who sets up an import-export practice in Tijuana and San Diego; Romanian orphans brought to the United States through the Seventh Day Adventist adoption services; a Hong Kong capitalist who settles his family in San José while he commutes by jet to maintain his businesses. The immigration that has enriched the United States shows little sign of abating. Compared to the Mekong Delta, Iowa is empty. There is still plenty of room for more Americans.

Each successive wave of immigration has had unique characteristics, a special quality, and a distinct impact on U.S. society. Whether attracted to the United States or forced here from their native country, immigrants have brought with them cultural, political, religious, and economic values, along with multiple tongues and various skills. The laws and policies of the United States have, in turn, accepted, constrained, and rejected these people. For many, these laws exist to be circumvented. Whether legally or illegally residing in the United States, immigrants contribute material aspects of their culture (crafts, foods, technology) as well as nonmaterial aspects (family values, spiritual beliefs, medical practices). During the process of settlement, these immigrants require social services to help them adapt to their new environment.

The extent of immigration and the policies that shape it have been controversial issues since the founding of this country. This great experiment—the United States of America—has required the innovation, fabrication, and synthesis of whole new patterns of existence. Those who have participated in this great cultural amalgamation have been themselves transformed. This transformation has not ended and will not end in the foreseeable future. Not only do we need to live with it, but we also have the unique opportunity to enjoy and value it.

HISTORICAL PERSPECTIVES

The North American continent has hosted people from all over the world. Diverse ethnic groups have arrived on both coasts and have caused continuous intermingling and confrontation with indigenous populations and among themselves. In what was to become the United States, these contacts began when the English arrived in the original thirteen colonies and met the several cultures of the Native American Indians. The colonists imported Black slaves who brought with them the various cultures of Western Africa. Then, as settlers moved toward the interior, they encountered different native groups in the plains and pueblos. In the mid-nineteenth century, English-speaking Americans expanded into the Southwest, home to Native Americans as well as the Spanish-speaking heirs of land grants dating back to the sixteenth century. Finally, in the nineteenth and twentieth centuries, immigrant groups from all over the world poured into the United States, coming into contact with the descendants of all earlier groups.

From this contact came the expectation that these many cultures would merge into a homogeneous, shared national culture. The idea that the United States was a melting pot nation generated pressure on newcomers to conform in thought and behavior—or, if this were not possible, pressure for children of these newcomers to assimilate. For some, assimilation was easier than for others, and language, clothing, and other forms of distinction were easy to erase. For others, however, discarding traditions was not so easy. The Hassidic Jews, the Amish, the Hopi, the Navajo—those clinging to religious rites, lifestyles, or property without choosing to compromise—resisted assimilation pressures (Rubel & Kupferer, 1973). These groups and others have created a more modern metaphor, that of the salad bowl—a mix in which the individual ingredients are not melted but, rather, retain their flavor and texture. Another powerful metaphor is that of the kaleidoscope, in which the shifting patterns of culture, language, and race combine and recombine ceaselessly, yet are bound together by an idea: that the United States means diverse peoples held together through common ideals. The contributions of the ethnic cultures to the United States cannot be underestimated, yet the picture is not uniformly sunny. Dark and sordid episodes of conflict among, and discrimination against, various groups cloud the history of this nation. Minorities have systematically been denied opportunities and rights accorded the more privileged. Those groups that are least similar to the original Anglo-European immigrants have suffered exploitation and, in some cases, linguistic, racial, or cultural genocide. Despite the hardships that many have endured, ethnic groups in this country have become inseparable threads in the cultural tapestry of the United States.

Contributions

The North American continent had a myriad of indigenous cultures characterized by high levels of civilization before the European invasion began. These civilizations were obliterated, or they accommodated the arrival of new cultures through the creation of a hybrid New World. The result has been a broad mix of lifestyles and contributions of both artifacts and patterns that reflect life in contemporary North America. For the most part, European invaders attempted to replicate the life they had lived in the Old World, and those who were not a part of this main stream of culture had the choice of assimilating or leading a separate existence. Assimilation was never intended for everyone. Those who could not assimilate were largely left alone to carry on their linguistic and cultural traditions. Many contributions of nonmainstream peoples remained just beneath the surface of the American dream—in some cases, *too* far beneath to influence the main paths of culture. For example, the spiritual heritage of the Native Americans— the deep and abiding respect for nature—has scarcely the impact on the dominant culture that may be necessary for the survival of the flora and fauna of the continent.

In many ways, the indigenous civilizations of precolonial North America were more highly developed than European cultures. The cities and roads of the Mayan culture astounded the European conquerors. The agricultural systems featured advanced forms of irrigation with the cultivation of foods that were unknown to the old world. Some of these foods (potato, corn, peanuts, and other grains) were later to provide 60 percent of Europe's diet and were responsible for the greatest explosion of population since the Neolithic age (Feagin & Feagin, 1993). Other substances (chocolate, tobacco, coca) were to provide Europeans with exhilarating addictions in the centuries to come. Medicinal products from the Americas revolutionized the treatment of disease in Europe and still fascinate pharmacologists with as yet untapped treasures. The political systems of native peoples ranged from the religious theocracies in Mexico, sources for advanced astronomical and mathematical achievement unparalleled in the world of that day, to the democratic councils of the Algonquin, Iroquois, and other nations that were much admired by Franklin and Jefferson (Hardt, 1992).

African-American culture has evolved from an African base that survived despite harshly limiting circumstances: Slaves could bring little or none of the material aspects of African culture with them. The aspects that survived did so in the hearts and minds of those who were forcibly carried to the new world. The present-day legacies of the African past (Bennett, 1990) are evident not only in the dance, music, literature, and religion of the contemporary African-American, but also in the sheer power of the patterns of everyday life and language that were strong enough to survive despite centuries of oppression. Ironically, that genre of music most associated with the U.S.—jazz—is permeated with African-American influence. One could argue that the music of America would not exist in its current form without this influence. Even today, the endlessly mutating forms of African-American culture constitute an ongoing avant-garde (Criston, 1993), aspects of which are alternately embraced and denigrated by the wider society. Despite substantial discrimination, a long line of African-American writers, such as James Weldon Johnson, Claude McKay, Richard Wright, Ralph Ellison, James Baldwin, Imamu Baraka (Le Roi Jones), Maya Angelou, Toni Morrison, and Langston Hughes have enriched U.S. literature and have inspired a new generation of poets, writers, and rapsters. The religion of Black America has been a source of sustenance to African-Americans since the arrival of the first slaves and has played a major role in fomenting protest for social justice. The nonviolent civil disobedience movement from the mid-1950s to the 1970s had religious underpinnings with prominent minister-leaders such as the Reverend Martin Luther King, Jr.

African-Americans have made substantial contributions to science. In the years preceding 1900, more than 1,000 patents were awarded to African-American inventors, despite the fact that slaves were barred from applying for patents. For example, Jo Anderson, a slave in the Cyrus McCormick household, was the co-inventor of the McCormick reaper. A slave of Jefferson Davis, president of the Confederate States of America, invented a boat propeller but was unable to patent the device. In the twentieth century, major scientists were active in such fields as aviation, electrical, mechanical, and construction engineering, rocketry, and many others (Carlson, 1970). African-Americans who have contributed in social science and philosophy are W. E. B. DuBois, Marcus Garvey, Elijah Mohammed, Frederick Douglass, E. Franklin Frazier, Oliver C. Cox, and Malcolm X (Cherry, 1970).

The story of Ernest E. Just illustrates the difficulties faced by African-American scientists in their ascent to prominence. Just, a marine biologist, rose to become vice-president of the American Society of Zoologists, but was once refused admittance to Rockefeller Institute. Although Just authored over 60 scholarly papers and was a leading authority on egg fertilization, artificial parthenogenesis, and cell division, he was never appointed to a White university and became embittered by the lack of professional recognition and research funding. By contrast, George Washington Carver never aspired to take his place alongside White scientists in their well-equipped, well-financed research facilities but was content to work in his small laboratory in Tuskegee (Carlson, 1970).

Hispanic contributions have also been significant. Hispanic influence in North America predates the landing of the Pilgrims at Plymouth Rock. Hispanic settlers in the Southwest helped to lay the foundations for the agricultural, mining, and cattle industries on which early city and state economies were built (Hispanic Concerns Study Committee, 1987). This influence continues today. With the outpouring of Cubans during the 1960s, Miami was transformed from a sleepy beach town to a vibrant international and bicultural metropolis. New York and its environs contain more Puerto Ricans than the island of Puerto Rico. Los Angeles is now the second largest Latin American city in the world. Although Hispanics living in the United States can trace their roots to several different countries, a common denominator of Hispanic culture in the United States includes language, religious beliefs and practices, holidays, and life patterns. Values shared among Hispanics include the importance of interdependence and cooperation of the immediate and extended family and the importance of emotional relationships. Self-pride and individual worth tie the individual to the family. As the mainstream culture comes into more contact with the Hispanic culture, it is beginning to recognize the importance of these family values.

In politics, Hispanic Americans have influenced urban life and education. The political impetus behind bilingual education stems from the culmination of Cuban immigrant pressure in Florida and the Chicano power movement of the 1960s. A lasting contribution of this bilingual legislation may be current attempts to preserve the "small incidence" languages of Native Americans and Micronesia, linguistic resources that are endangered. Thus Hispanic leadership has helped to preserve cultural resources in unforeseen ways. In literature and the other arts, Hispanic Americans have made significant contributions. An impressive folk tradition of Spanish songs and ballads has maintained a musical current containing the history, joys, and sorrows of the Mexican-American, Puerto Rican, and Cuban experience. Spanish radio stations and newspapers have played a major role in sustaining the language and reinforcing the values of Spanish America. Spanish words have enriched the minds and tongues of North Americans. Fiction and poetry, in both languages, affirm the Hispanic heritage and identity. Puerto Rican and Mexican-American theater has dramatized the struggles for a voice. The public art of Mexico is a centuries-old tradition with the colorful *steles* of the Aztecs and Mayans vibrating through time and reappearing in the murals of the barrios and the public art of cities throughout the Southwest. Art, to the Hispanic, is a breath of culture, and artists, like intellectuals, are esteemed as the cultural leaders. The culinary contributions of Hispanics are legion, and include enchiladas from Mexico, black beans from Cuba, *mangú* from the Dominican Republic, and *pasteles* from Puerto Rico.

Contributions of the Pacific Rim peoples to the United States will be of increasing importance in the twenty-first century. The economic power of Asian capital stems not only from Japanese post–World War II efforts, but also from the Chinese diaspora that has provided capital for economic investment in much of Southeast Asia, Indonesia, Australia, and California. Although Chinese and Japanese immigration to western America was severely curtailed throughout the history of the United States, by sheer force of numbers and by the volume of the international trade, Asian economic and cultural influences on the United States have been consistent. The cultures of Asia, characterized by unparalleled continuity from ancient times to the present, have contributed to Western culture in innumerable ways. The U.S. fascination with Asian cultures has included the martial arts, Eastern spiritual philosophies, fireworks, acupuncture, and Oriental decor and gardening. One might venture that more people in the United States routinely visit Chinese restaurants than any other ethnic establishment. The chief stumbling block toward greater acceptance of Asian influences in the United States is the perceived linguistic barrier. The fact that more Asians speak English than the reverse closes the doors to Asian cultures for many Americans. Perhaps the current generation of high school students will begin to bridge this gap; Japanese is now taught in California secondary schools.

Exploitation

The contributions of minorities to the cultural mainstream have not consistently been valued. On the contrary, many peoples in the cultural mix have been exploited. Their labor, their art, their votes have been used and abused without adequate compensation.

From the beginning, the European settlers exploited others. Many indentured servants worked at low wages for years to repay their passage to the New World. Native Americans brought food to the starving Puritans and, in return, were eventually given blankets smeared with smallpox virus in a deliberate attempt to eradicate them. The fertile coastal plain of the eastern seaboard was the first land to be taken from its native inhabitants, and the westward movement features many a sordid tale of killing and robbery on the part of the European settlers (Eckert, 1992). On the west coast, the Spanish missionaries also colonized the natives with somewhat more pious motives and a similar result. The Hispanic settlers in the West were, in turn, exploited when European-Americans desired hegemony. Although superior firearms still carried the day, legal manipulations carried out in the English language systematically disenfranchised Hispanic settlers and caused them to lose their property and water rights on a vast scale. Chinese settlers who were permitted into the West during the nineteenth century found that their labor was valued only in the meanest way and the jobs available constituted "woman's work," such as laundry and cooking. And the story of exploitation of Africans brought to the New World is a tale of tears mixed with genocide and forced miscegenation.

In many cases, this exploitation continues to this day as the underclass of America, whether white, brown, or black, is inadequately paid and under-educated, without health benefits or adequate housing. Temporary jobs without benefits are the hallmark of the crueler, harsher world of the twenty-first century as economic and political forces polarize society.

The most difficult piece of the puzzle is the challenge of population growth. Creating jobs for a burgeoning population that will provide the financial means for the purchase of health care, education, housing, and an adequate diet is the issue. The growth of the population of the United States is so uneven, with European-Americans having the lowest birth and immigration rate, that the challenge can almost be redefined as that of providing adequate employment for minorities. Demographic pressures will not abate in the next century. The population in 2050 is projected to consist largely of Third World peoples. The challenge is evident. Wrongs from the past cannot be righted, but present and future citizens can avoid those wrongs by understanding exploitative measures and working to disable them.

DEMOGRAPHY

By the year 2000, the United States will have 260,000,000 people. One of every three of them will be either African-, Hispanic-, or Asian-American. This represents a dramatic change from the image of America throughout its history: In the past, when Americans have looked in the mirror, they have seen a largely European-American reflection. Immigration, together with differing birth rates among various populations, is responsible for this demographic shift. Along with the change in racial and ethnic composition has come a dramatic change in the languages spoken in the United States and the languages spoken in U.S. schools.

The changing demographics have impacted society in many ways. Whether this impact is seen as positive or negative depends on one's point of view; certainly the trends are mixed. Some economists have balanced the cost–benefit ratio for immigration and found that immigrants contribute considerably to the national economy by filling low-wage jobs that help keep domestic industry competitive, by spurring investment and job creation, by revitalizing once decaying communities, and by paying billions annually in taxes. Unfortunately the money generated from taxes that is paid to the federal government is not returned to those areas of the country most affected by immigration. Communities with large immigrant populations tend to spend local dollars in disproportionate amounts on schools, hospitals, and social services needed by new citizens (Shuit & McConnell, 1992).

The resultant stress on these services raises the level of ethnic and/or racial consciousness on the part of residents who may view newcomers negatively.

The Changing Face of America

Within two decades, the U.S. population will have shifted from a predominately European-American population to one that is substantially nonwhite, and for the next 40 years the trends show no signs of abating. In 1980, 74 percent of the population consisted of European-Americans; 14.5 percent African-American; 8 percent Hispanic; and 3 percent other (including Asians, Pacific Islanders, Native Americans and all others). In the year 2000, the profile will be changed with a decrease in the European-American population by 10 percent and an increase in other groups: 17 percent for Hispanics, 16 percent for African-Americans, and 3 percent for all others. In 2040, the projected ethnic composition of the United States will be 59 percent European-American; 12.4 percent African-American; 18 percent Hispanic; and 10.3 percent Asian, Pacific Islanders, Native Americans, and all others (González, 1990).

From these figures, it is clear that the increase in Hispanics plays a large role in the demographic shift. This group comprises several components. In 1989, 12.6 million U.S. Hispanics (62.6 percent) identified themselves as Mexican-American; 2.5 million (12.7 percent) as Central and South American; 2.3 million (11.6 percent) as Puerto Rican; 1.1 million (5.3 percent) as Cuban; and 1.6 million (7.8 percent) as other Hispanic origin. This population is largely urban. The ancestors of today's Hispanics, between the year 1542 and 1777, created 200 new cities throughout North and South America, and 92 percent of Hispanics still live in cities today. More than 21 U.S. cities had at least 100,000 Hispanic residents in 1990, with one-fourth of the U.S. Hispanic population found in eight cities (New York, Chicago, San Antonio, Houston, El Paso, Los Angeles, San Diego, and Miami). The Hispanic subgroups are found in distinct geographic areas, with Mexican-Americans in the Southwest, Puerto Ricans in the Northeast, and Cubans in Florida.

The U.S. Asian population in 1980 was 3.4 million; this grew to 6.9 million in 1990, a 100 percent increase. The population of Chinese-Americans has doubled, the number of Hmong people has increased by 1,600 percent, Cambodians and Bangladeshis by 800 percent, Pakistanis by over 400 percent, and Japanese-Americans by only 21 percent. Pacific Islander populations increased by 41 percent in the decade 1980–1990. Asian immigration is largely to the South and West. Of the 22 largest cities where "minorities" became "majorities," seven are in California (Long Beach, 31 percent to 50 percent minority; Ontario, 32 percent to 53 percent; San Jose, 35 percent to 50 percent; Fresno, 36 percent to 50 percent; Stockton, 41 percent to 56 percent; San Bernardino, 42 percent to 54 percent; and San Francisco, 46 percent to 53 percent) (Bovee, 1991).

In fact, California is experiencing the initial wave of immigration that will soon impact the entire United States. California is the nation's most racially diverse state with a greater percent of Asian and Latino residents than any other state and the second highest number of African-Americans and Native Americans of any state. The 1990 census reports that the 29.8 million people living in California listed themselves as 69 percent White (including Hispanic), 9.6 percent Asian, 7.4 percent Black, 0.8 percent Native American, and 13.2 percent other. The state's 2.8 million Asian population is ten times as large as that of any other state, with varied geographic distribution: Cambodians and Hmong in the Central Valley, and Chinese-Americans largely in urban areas such as San Francisco. The Latino population in California is 25.8 percent of the state's population, 7.7 million people (Fulwood, 1991). This population is expected to grow to 15 million in 2020, almost double the current level. Most of this population is concentrated in the southern part of the state.

The Impact of America's Changing Population

The changing demographics in the United States is a result of immigration as well as higher birth rates among minority populations than among European-Americans. The two minority groups—immigrants, and economically disadvantaged minorities within the country—face similar challenges. Both immigrants and indigenous minorities must adjust to the demands of modern technological societies and must redefine their cultural self-identity. Economic and educational achievement are not equally accessible to these minorities. A key difficulty for many minorities is that of poverty. Nearly 28 percent of African-American and 24 percent of Hispanic families fell below the poverty line in 1988, compared to 9.4 percent among non-Hispanic families (Vobejda, 1990). Poverty is associated with a host of other difficulties, such as underemployment, homelessness, educational deprivation, single-parent homes, and other types of family instability. However, not all poverty can be linked to these difficulties; some minorities continue in poverty because of social and political factors in the country at large, such as racism and discrimination.

Poverty hits minority children particularly hard: In 1983, 40 percent of all minority children lived in poverty. This poverty impacts the ability of the family to devote resources to educational effort. This situation, coupled with social and political factors that mitigate against minority children in schools, stack the deck against minority student success. Demographic trends ensure that this is will be a continuing problem in the United States. More than two-thirds (67.7 percent) of the Hispanic population is under 35 years of age, compared with a little more than half (53.2 percent) of the non-Hispanic population. Mean family size for Hispanic families is 3.75 persons, compared with 3.11 for non-Hispanics (National Education Association, 1991). The average Hispanic female is well within childbearing age, and Hispanic children constitute the largest growing school population. Thus, the educational achievement of Hispanic children is of particular concern.

The economy of the United States in the future will rest more on Asian and Hispanic workers than at present. As a consequence, the education of these populations will become increasingly important. A larger percentage of Asian-American students attend high school than of Hispanics. Nearly one-half of Chicanos and Puerto Ricans do not finish high school, and their dropout rate is three times higher than that of European-Americans. Mexican-American youth, in particular, are more likely to be enrolled two or more years below grade level than are other Hispanics or other minorities, and only 53.3 percent of Mexican-Americans graduate from high school. Seventeen percent of Mexican-Americans have less than a fifth-grade education (González, 1990). Among African-Americans and Hispanics, 43 percent drop out before graduating from high school in California (Highsmith, 1990).

Minorities now constitute the majority of public school students in fifteen of the country's largest school systems—for example, Miami, 71 percent; Philadelphia, 73 percent; Baltimore, 80 percent (Kellogg, 1988). Hispanic students, in particular, typically live in racially isolated neighborhoods and are more likely to attend segregated schools than are African-American students. Orum (1986) found that more than one-fourth of Hispanic students attended schools with minority enrollments of 90 to 100 percent. Minority children are overrepresented in compensatory programs in schools. Poor African-Americans are 3.5 times more likely to be identified as mentally retarded than their European-American counterparts and constitute 28 percent of total enrollment in special education, while they make up only 12 percent of public school enrollments (University of Texas at Austin, 1991).

The data on persons who have completed college show that European-Americans have a rate twice that of African-Americans and Native Americans, and three and one-half times that of Hispanics. The rate of Asians exceeds that of Whites (Sue & Padilla, 1986). The scarcity of enrollment in higher education affects the entry of minorities into the professions, and particularly into teaching. In 1986–1987, of the degrees conferred in education, 6 percent of B.A., 8 percent of M.A., and 8 percent of Ph.D. diplomas were awarded to African-American and Hispanic students. In 1991, the elementary and secondary teaching force was 3 to 5 percent minority. In 1989, of the 661,000 university and college professors, 4.6 percent were African-American and 3.1 percent were Hispanic (University of Texas at Austin, 1991). Minorities in scientific professions are even rarer. Hispanics make up 2.4 percent of college majors in engineering, 2.2 percent in biology, and 0.8 percent in the physical sciences. Only 1 percent ever attained a master's degree in biology, physics, or mathematics.

The conclusion is inescapable: The educational system of the United States has been fundamentally weak in serving the fastest growing school-age populations. At many high schools with large minority enrollments the attrition rate is close to 70 percent. Even among those who graduate, very few are eligible for college, and fewer still will obtain a bachelor's degree (Haycock & Navarro, 1988). Today's minority students are entering school with significantly different social and economic backgrounds from those of previous student populations, and thus require educators to modify their teaching approaches to ensure that these students have access to the American dream (Hyland, 1989).

Many minority students come to school with home languages other than English. According to the 1990 census, one American in seven, 32 million, speaks a language other than English at home. Seventeen million of these speak Spanish, the most used language in the nation after English. French, German, Italian, and Chinese follow with between one million and two million speakers each. More than three million Americans speak East Asian languages, double the number in 1980. Nearly one-third of these said they speak English poorly or not at all (Waggoner, 1992). The U.S. Department of Education estimates that, of the 40.5 million students in public and private schools, 2.3 million have limited English proficiency. The highest number, by far, is found in California, with over one million limited-English-proficient students in 1992, over one in five of the total California student population. The impact of these large numbers of students with English learning needs is felt in schools as personnel departments struggle to find enough bilingual teachers. The shortage of bilingual teachers and aides is forcing schools to adopt such alternative approaches as team teaching and cooperative learning to extend the thin bilingual services to reach a maximum number of students. Moreover, schools are faced with the challenge of helping mainstream teachers incorporate teaching techniques that meet the needs of English learners (Banks, 1989).

IMMIGRATION AND MIGRATION

The United States has historically been a nation of immigrants, but the nature and causes of immigration have changed over time. The earliest settlers to the east coast of North America came from England and Holland, Northern European seafaring nations, while those to the south and west came mainly from Spain. In the early eighteenth century, these settlers were joined by involuntary immigrants from Africa. Subsequent waves of immigrants came from Scotland, Ireland, and Germany, and later from central and eastern Europe. Immigration from the Pacific Rim countries was constrained by severe immigration restrictions until the last decades of the twentieth century. However, imperialistic policies of the United States, primarily the conquest of the Philippines, Puerto Rico, Hawaii, and the Pacific Islands, has caused large influxes of these populations throughout the twentieth century. The wars in Southeast Asia and Central America throughout the 1970s and 1980s led to increased immigration from these areas.

Immigrants have come to the United States for a variety of reasons. The earliest immigration was prompted by the desire for adventure and economic gain in a new world, combined with the desire to flee religious and political persecution. These factors provided both attractive forces ("pull") and expulsive forces ("push"). Later, U.S. foreign policy created connections with populations abroad that pulled certain groups to the United States. For example, the conquest of the Philippines at the turn of the century eventually resulted in large Philippine immigration to the United States. Immigration laws have responded to both push and pull factors throughout the nineteenth and twentieth centuries, at times curtailing immigration from specific regions and at other times allowing increased immigration. Both immigrants and natives of the United States have historically been restless populations. Much of the history of the United States consists of the migration of groups from one part of the country to another.

Causes of Immigration

Migration is an international phenomenon. Throughout the world, populations are dislocated by wars, famine, civil strife, economic changes, persecution, and other factors. The United States has been a magnet for immigrants seeking greater opportunity and economic stability. The social upheavals and overpopulation that characterized nineteenth-century Europe and Asia brought more than 14 million immigrants to the United States in the forty-year period between 1860 and 1900. Ninety years later, this phenomenon can be witnessed along the border between the United States and Mexico. Politics and religion as well as economics provide reasons for emigration. U.S. domestic and foreign policies affect the way in which groups of foreigners are accepted. Changes in immigration policy, such as amnesty, affect the number of immigrants who enter the country each year.

Economic factors in immigration. The great disparity in the standard of living attainable in the United States compared to that of many underdeveloped countries makes immigration attractive. Self-advancement is uppermost in the minds of many immigrants and acts as a strong incentive despite the economic exploitation often extended to immigrants (lower wages, exclusion from desirable jobs). Immigrants may bring with them specific unique skills. On the whole, however, the economy of the United States does not have an unlimited capacity to employ immigrants in specialized niches.

Immigration policy has corresponded with the cycles of boom and bust in the U.S. economy; the Chinese Exclusion Act in 1882 stopped immigration from China to America because of the concern that Chinese labor would flood the market and leave no jobs for Americans. The labor shortage in the western United States resulting from excluding the Chinese had the effect of welcoming Japanese immigrants who were good farm laborers. Later, during the Depression of the 1930s, with a vast labor surplus in the United States, the U.S. Congress severely restricted Philippine immigration, and policies were initiated to "repatriate" Mexicans back across the border. When World War II transformed the labor surplus of the 1930s into a severe worker shortage, the United States and Mexico established the Bracero Program, a bilateral agreement allowing Mexicans to cross the border and work on U.S. farms and railroads. The border was virtually left open during the war years (Wollenberg, 1989). Despite the economic attractiveness of the United States, however, most newcomers to this society experience a period of economic hardship.

Political factors in immigration. Political factors, such as repression, civil war, and change in government, create a "push" for emigration from foreign countries while political factors within the United States create a climate of acceptance for some political refugees and not for others. After the Vietnam War, many refugees were displaced in Southeast Asia: Some sense of responsibility for their plight caused the U.S. government to accept many of these people into the United States. For example, Cambodians who cooperated with the U.S. military immigrated to the United States in waves: first, a group including 6,300 Khmer in 1975; second, 10,000 Cambodians in 1979; third, 60,000 Cambodians between 1980 and 1982 (Gillett, 1989a). The decade of the 1980s was likewise one of political instability and civil war in many Central American countries, resulting in massive civilian casualties. In El Salvador, for example, 1,000 civilians were killed each month by death squads comprising both paramilitary right-wing groups and guerrillas. Such instabilities caused the displacement of 600,000 Salvadorans, who live as refugees outside their country (Gillett, 1989b). Through the Deferred Enforced Departure program of the U.S. government, nearly 200,000 Salvadoran immigrants have been given the right to live and work legally in the United States.

Other populations, such as Haitians claiming political persecution, have been turned away from U.S. borders. In a similar fashion, women fleeing from abusive husbands in male-dominated cultures have been refused immigration rights with the argument that these are personal rather than political issues. In the case of the Haitians, one might suspect that racial issues in the United States make it more difficult for them to immigrate. In the case of the abused women, women's rights activists argue that wife abuse is indeed a political issue. In both cases, however, it becomes clear that the issue of what constitutes political grounds for asylum is clouded by confounding factors.

In sum, people are pushed to the United States because of political instability or political policies unfavorable to them in their home countries.

Political conditions within the United States affect whether immigrants are accepted or denied.

U.S. foreign policy. As the United States grew as a capitalist nation, economic forces had a great influence on U.S. foreign policy. In the early growth of commercial capitalism from 1600 to 1865, the settlers were a source of labor; Africans were enslaved to provide plantation labor, and poor Europeans such as Irish Catholics were recruited abroad for low-wage jobs in transportation and construction. U.S. foreign policy supported unfettered international sea trade to ensure a steady source of imported labor. In the phase of industrial capitalism (1865–1920), U.S. treaties with Europe and intervention in European affairs (World War I) maintained the labor supply until the 1924 Immigration Act. U.S. imperialist policies in Asia (conquest of the Philippines and Hawaii) ensured a supply of raw materials and a home for U.S. military bases in the Pacific but immigration policy denied access to the United States for the majority of Asians. As U.S. capitalism advanced to multinationalist capitalism (1920–1990), U.S. foreign policy encouraged industries to employ cheap labor abroad. Immigration was restricted from Asia and Europe, and immigrants from Puerto Rico and Mexico fulfilled the domestic need for low-wage labor. The U.S. opposition to communist Cuba resulted in the acceptance of large numbers of Cuba's upper and middle classes in the 1960s. U.S. intervention in Asia caused an influx of Asian immigrants in the 1970s and 1980s. These foreign policies, largely driven by capitalism, have been closely connected with U.S. immigration policies.

Religious factors in immigration. Many of the early English settlers in North America came to the New World to found colonies in which they would be free to establish their form of religious domination. Later, Irish Catholics left Ireland in droves because their lands were taken by Protestants. Many eastern European Jews, forced to emigrate because of anti-Semitic pogroms in the nineteenth century, came to the United States in great numbers. Unfortunately, during the 1930s and 1940s, Jews persecuted by Nazism were not free to emigrate and were killed. Under the communist regime in the former USSR, Russian Jews were allowed to emigrate in small numbers and were accepted into the United States. For the most part, however, today's immigration policies permit refugees to be accepted for political rather than religious reasons.

Family unification. The risks associated with travel to the New World have made immigration a male-dominated activity since the early settlement of North America. In some cases, such as that of the Chinese in the nineteenth century, immigration laws permitted only young men to enter. Initial Japanese immigration, which was not restricted as severely as Chinese, involved predominantly young men between the ages of 20 and 40. Similarly, today's Mexican immigrant population consists largely of young men who have come to the United States to work and send money home. Once settled, these immigrants seek to bring family members. Family unification is a primary motivation for many applications to the U.S. Immigration and Naturalization Service (INS).

Another humanitarian ground for immigration is medical treatment in the United States. The INS reviews thousands of visa applications for medical care annually. Would-be visitors are required to prove that they can pay for the operation and a return ticket without entering the U.S. work force. Such visas have strict time constraints attached. Those who remain in the United States under temporary visas can enter the INS lottery for permanent status, a contest with 10,000,000 entries per year.

Migration

Americans have always been restless. Historically, crowding and the promise of greater economic freedom were reasons for moving west. The Gold Rush attracted, for the most part, English-speaking European-Americans from the eastern United States, but other minority groups and foreign immigrants were also drawn to the search for instant wealth. Miners from Mexico, Peru, and Chile increased California's Latino population; Greeks, Portuguese, Russians, Poles, Armenians, and Italians flocked to the San Francisco Bay area. During the Depression, many of these populations migrated once again to California's central valley to find work as farm laborers (Wollenberg, 1989). With the rise of cities, rural populations saw economic advancement in urban environments. Many African-Americans migrated to northern cities after World War I to escape prejudice and discrimination. Now, many immigrants are sponsored by special interest groups such as churches and civic organizations that invite them to reside in the local community. Once here, however, some groups find conditions too foreign to their former lives and eventually migrate to another part of the United States. For example, a group of Hmong families sponsored by Lutheran charities spent two years in the severe winter climate of the Minneapolis area before resettling in California. Hispanics, on the other hand, are migrating from cities in the Southwest, New York, and Miami toward destinations in the Midwest and middle South (Wilson, 1984).

Immigration Laws and Policies

Economic cycles in the United States have affected immigration policies, liberalizing them when workers were needed and restricting immigration when jobs were scarce. These restrictive immigration policies were often justified with overtly racist arguments. Asian immigration was targeted for specific quotas. The first Asian population that was specifically excluded was the Chinese (the Chinese Exclusion Act of 1882), but the growth of Japanese immigration as a result of this quota prompted Congress to extend the concept of Chinese exclusion to Japan (1908) and the rest of Asia. The immigration laws of the 1920s (the National Origins Acts of 1924 and 1929) banned most Asian immigration and established quotas that favored northwestern European immigrants. The quota system did not apply to Mexico and the rest of the Western Hemisphere, nor did the immigration laws affect the Philippines, which was a U.S. territory. In 1943, Congress symbolically ended the Asian exclusion policy by granting the United States' wartime ally, China, a token quota of 100 immigrants per year. The Philippines and Japan received similar tiny quotas after the war.

A great change in immigration policy came as a result of a comprehensive reform of the immigration law in 1965. Congress abolished the old quota system and set up a new preference system emphasizing family ties and occupation. The total annual limit of immigrants remains at 300,000 (170,000 from Africa, Asia, and Europe, and 130,000 from North and South America), but no single nation is to contribute more than 20,000 immigrants per year. The net effect of the new immigration policy was to give Asia equal status with Europe. For the first time also, there was an annual numerical limit on Mexican immigration. No accompanying effort was made to seal the Mexican border, however, and a growing percentage of Mexican immigrants became illegal or undocumented aliens (Wollenberg, 1989).

Legal status. Many immigrants are *documented*—legal residents who have entered the United States officially and live under the protection of legal immigration status. Some of these are officially designated *refugees* with transitional support services and assistance provided by the U.S. government. Most immigrants from Cambodia, Laos, Vietnam, and Thailand have been granted refugee status. *Undocumented* immigrants are residents without any documentation, who live in fear of being identified and deported. Many Central American immigrants are undocumented, and applications for refugee status or political asylum are seldom granted. Because these immigrants have come since 1986, they are not eligible for amnesty under the provisions of the 1986 immigration law.

Being in the United States illegally brings increased instability, fear, and insecurity to school-age children because they and their families are living without the protection, social services, and assistance available to most immigrants. With the passage of the Immigration Reform and Control Act, however, undocumented children are legally entitled to public education. Often they and their families are unclear about this right, and school staff and authorities sometimes worsen the situation by illegally asking for immigration papers when children are being registered (Olsen, 1988).

Resources available to immigrants. The California State Department of Education Bilingual Office publishes an *Annotated Directory of Resources for* *the Emergency Immigrant Education Program* (1988a). This directory provides names and contact information for professionals in the field of resettlement, refugee community leaders, social service professionals, psychologists, and educators who are involved in working with immigrant families. Also included is a list of readings and audiovisual materials about the needs and experiences of immigrant children.

How far have we come? The Puritans brought to New England a religion based on a monochromatic world view. They outlawed Christmas and disapproved of celebration. The United States of America has struggled with this severe cultural reductionism since its founding. As the beauty and celebratory spirit of many other world cultures have been imported to this continent, the people of the United States have opened up to accept the beauty and brilliant hues that immigrants have brought. As more and more diverse groups settle and resettle throughout the continent, customs and traditions mingle to create an ever-new mix. The salad bowl, the kaleidoscope—these are metaphors for diversity in taste, in pattern, and in lifestyle. The American portrait is still being painted, in ever brighter hues.

Chapter *10*

Manifestations of Culture: Learning about Students

> *"Teacher," Maria said to me as the students went out for recess. "Yes, Maria?" I smiled at this lively Venezuelan student and we launched into conversation. The contents of this talk are now lost from me, but not the actions. For as we talked, we slowly moved, she forward, me backward until I was jammed up against the chalkboard. And there I remained for the rest of the conversation, feeling more and more agitated. She was simply too close.*
>
> *This incident and thousands of others, which may be unpredictable, puzzling, uncomfortable, or even threatening, occur in situations in which cultural groups come into contact. Because I knew the differing cultural norms from which Maria and I were operating—the fact that the requirement for space between interlocutors is greater for me as a North American than for her as a South American—I did not ascribe any negative or aggressive tendencies to her. But knowing the norm did not lessen my anxiety. What it afforded me was the knowledge that we were behaving differently, and that such differences were normal for our respective groups. (K.W.)*

This knowledge about various cultural norms is critical in multicultural situations. Teachers should not expect that they will be fully knowledgeable about every cultural nuance, nor should they be; but there are general patterns of behavior within which all human societies operate. An understanding of the patterns will help teachers understand the worlds of their students and help guide students to an understanding of the cultural norms of school life. Culture influences every aspect of school life (see Figure I-1); as a domain of learning, culture can be a specific area of study within the curriculum.

This chapter first outlines those general areas of culture that teachers, in their role as educators, will find most useful. Techniques are then offered that can be used to learn about students' cultures. Teachers can in turn use this new knowledge about students' cultures to design appropriate classroom organizational procedures and can use culturally responsive teaching behaviors.

WHAT TEACHERS NEED TO LEARN ABOUT THEIR STUDENTS

Any learning that takes place is built on previous learning. Students have learned the basic patterns of living in the context of their families. They have learned to value some things and not others. They have learned the verbal and nonverbal behaviors appropriate for their gender and age and have observed their family members in various occupations and activities. The family has taught them about love, and relations between friends, kin, and community members. They have observed community members cooperating to learn in a variety of methods and modes. Their families have given them a feeling for music and art, have shown them what is beautiful and what is not. Finally, they have learned to use language in the context of their homes and communities. They have learned when questions can be asked and when silence is required. They have used language to learn to share feelings and knowledge and beliefs. Indeed, they are native speakers of the home language by the age of five, and can express their needs and delights.

The culture that students bring from the home is the foundation for their learning. Cultures must be valued; all cultures provide an adequate pattern of living for their members. Therefore, no children are "culturally deprived." Certain communities may exist in relative poverty; that is, they are not equipped with middle-class resources. Poverty, however, should not be equated with cultural deprivation. Every community's culture incorporates vast knowledge about successful living. Teachers can utilize this cultural knowledge to organize students' learning in schools.

In-depth background on the culture and history of all minority groups in the United States is clearly beyond the scope of this book. However, all cultures share general features. These features will be discussed here, along with ways in which insightful teachers can use this general knowledge in their classrooms. Teachers who need background on specific cultures may begin to obtain this information from sources such as the New Faces of Liberty Project, University of California, Berkeley (Jorgenson-Esmaili, 1988) or from the California State Department of Education's culturally specific handbooks, as well as through interviews, observations, and participation.

Values, Beliefs, and Practices

Values are "what people regard as good or bad, beautiful or ugly, clean or dirty . . . right or wrong, kind or cruel, just or unjust, and appropriate or inappropriate" (Lustig, 1988). Values come to the fore when cultures organize systems to govern their members and regulate and manage social life. Values are particularly important to people when they educate their young because education is a primary means of transmitting cultural knowledge. Parents in minority communities are often vitally interested in their children's education even though they may not be highly visible at school functions.

Values can not be seen, heard, or tasted but are manifest in social customs; in rituals and ceremonies, in vital areas of life such as health, religion, and law, and in ways of working and playing. All the influences that contribute to the cultural profile of the family and community affect the students' reaction to classroom practices. Students whose home culture is consistent with the beliefs and practices of the school are generally more successful in school. However, teachers concerned about advancing the success of all their students make every effort to understand that various cultures organize the general facets of individual and community behavior in radically different ways—ways that, on the surface, may not seem compatible to school practices and beliefs. To understand these differences is to be able to mediate for the students by helping them bridge relevant differences between the home and school cultures.

Social customs and mores. Social customs and mores dictate very different ways of living daily life. These customs are paced and structured by deep habits of using time and space. *Time* is organized in culturally specific ways:

> Adela, a Mexican-American first grade girl, arrived at school about twenty minutes late every day. Her teacher was at first irritated and gradually exasperated. In a parent conference, Adela's mother explained that braiding her daughter's hair each morning was an important time for the two of them to be together. This family time presented a value conflict with the school's time norm.

Other conflicts may arise when teachers demand abrupt endings to activities in which children are deeply engaged or when events are scheduled in a strict sequence. In fact, schools in the United States are often paced very strictly by clock time, whereas family life in various cultures is not regulated in the same manner. Some students may resent the imposition of an arbitrary beginning and ending to the natural flow of an activity. Moreover, teachers often equate speed of performance with intelligence, and standardized tests are often a test of rapidity. Many teachers find themselves in the role of "time mediator"—helping the class to adhere to the school's time schedule while working with individual students to help them meet their learning needs within the time allotted.

Within the dimension of time, teachers can consider these facets:

- How students have been taught to make use of their time
- How students deal with punctuality in their cultures
- What kinds of activities students perform quickly, and which they do not

Space is another aspect of cultural experience. Personal space varies: In some cultures individuals touch each other frequently and maintain high degrees of physical contact; in other cultures, touch and proximity cause feelings of tension and embarrassment. A cultural sense of space influences the rooms and buildings in which people feel comfortable. Large, cavernous classrooms may be overwhelming to students whose family activities are carried out in intimate spaces. The organization of the space in the classroom sends messages to students: how free they are to move about the classroom, how much of the classroom they "own," how the desks are arranged. Both the expectations of the students and the needs of the teacher can be negotiated to provide a classroom setting in which space is shared.

Teachers can be sensitive to the following aspects of space:

- What personal distance students use in interacting with other students and with adults
- How the culture determines the space allotted to boys and girls
- How the spatial organization of the home compares to that of the school

Once a teacher has recognized that time and space are culturally organized, then individual differences can be more easily accommodated. Other *symbolic systems*, however, may involve more subtle behaviors that have not been studied as thoroughly. These systems include overt indicators of meaning, such as dress and personal appearance. For example, a third-grade girl wearing makeup is communicating a message that some teachers may find inappropriate because, to the teacher, wearing makeup symbolizes premature sexuality. Other symbolic systems are intrinsic, such as beliefs about natural phenomena, luck and fate, vocational expectations, and so forth. For example, a new teacher noticed during a strong earthquake that the Mexican-American students seemed much less perturbed than did their European-American peers. In succeeding days, several of the European-American children were referred to the school counselor because of anxiety, but the Mexican-American children showed no signs of this anxiety. The principal attributed this difference to the Mexican-Americans' cultural belief that nature is powerful and that humans must accept this power. In contrast, European-American culture views nature as something to be conquered; when natural forces are greater than human control, anxiety results. Thus, behavior during earthquakes is a result of a symbolic system that is consonant with the culture.

Some facets to consider in understanding symbolic systems include:

- How dress differs for age, gender, and social class
- What clothing and accessories are considered acceptable
- What behavior is called for during natural phenomenon such as rain, lightning, thunder, earthquakes, and fire

Rites, rituals, and ceremonies. Each culture incorporates expectations of the proper means to carry out formal events. Formal events can be holidays and/or holy days in which particular ceremonies are incorporated. People celebrate births, marriages, and deaths with specific rites and rituals. Schools themselves have ceremonies. For example, the school culture of the United States mandates that assemblies begin with formal markers such as the Pledge of Allegiance, a flag salute, or a greeting from the principal. Rituals in some elementary classrooms in the United States are also relatively formal. For example, students must line up, come in quietly, take their seats, and wait for the teacher. Hmong students from Laos are accustomed to a different type of formality in the classroom. In Laos, when it is time for recess or lunch break, students rise and stand by their seats, waiting for permission to leave the room. When passing the teacher, students clasp their hands in front of their faces in a ritual of respect. Few students dare to raise their hands to ask questions when a teacher is lecturing (Bliatout, Downing, Lewis, & Yang, 1988).

Rituals are also involved in parent conferences. Greeting and welcome behaviors, for example, vary across cultures. The sensitive teacher understands how parents expect to be greeted and incorporates some of these behaviors in the exchange.

In considering how rituals affect the classroom, teachers should think about the following:

- What rituals students use to show respect
- What celebrations students observe and for what reason (political, seasonal, religious)
- How and where parents expect to be greeted when visiting the class room

Work and leisure systems. Cross-cultural variation in work and leisure activities is one of the most frequently discussed value differences. Many members of mainstream U.S. culture value work over play; that is, one's status is directly related to one's productivity, salary, or job description. Play is often used in ways that reinforce this status. For example, executives conduct business informally on the golf course, co-workers form bowling leagues, and alumni enjoy "tailgate" parties before attending football games. Young people, particularly those in the middle class, are trained to use specific tools of play, and their time is structured to attain skills (organized sports, music lessons). In contrast, other cultures do not afford children any structured time to play but, instead, expect children to engage in adult-type labor at work or in the home. In still other cultures, such as that of the Hopi Nation in Arizona, children's play time is relatively unstructured, and parents do not interfere with play. Cultures also vary in the typical work and play activities expected of girls and boys. All these values have obvious influence on the ways children work and play at school (Schultz & Theophano, 1987).

In work and play groups, the orientation may be *individual* or *group*. The United States is widely regarded as a society in which the individual is paramount. This individualism often pits students against one another for achievement. In Japan, by contrast, individuals compete fiercely for admission to prestigious universities, but accompanying this is a sense that one must establish oneself within a group. Competition in the Japanese classroom is not realized in the same way as in U.S. schools; being singled out for attention or praise by teachers may result in embarrassment (Furey, 1986). American Indian children who come from group-directed cultures may enjoy competing against one another in teams but not as individuals (Philips, 1972).

Teachers can learn about work and play, individual and group orientation by considering the following:

- What types of work students are expected to perform and at what age, in the home and the community
- The purpose of play
- Whether individual work is private or shared
- The extent to which students are expected to work together

Health and medicine. Health and medicine practices involve deep-seated beliefs because the stakes are high: life and death. Each culture has certain beliefs about sickness and health, beliefs that influence the interaction in health care settings. Students may have problems—war trauma, culture shock, poverty, addiction, family violence, crime—whose solutions must be culturally acceptable. When students come to school with health issues, teachers need to react in culturally compatible ways. Miscommunication and noncooperation can result when teachers and the family view health and disease differently (Witte, 1991). For example, health professionals in the schools who attempt to communicate the danger of AIDS often encounter virulent reactions prompted by parental taboos. Likewise, community health practices, such as the Cambodian tradition of coining (in which a coin is dipped in oil and then rubbed on a sick person's back, chest, and neck), can be misinterpreted by school officials who, seeing marks on the child, swiftly call Child Protective Services.

Teachers and other school personnel can use the following questions to help inform them of beliefs about health:

- Who or what causes illness and who or what is responsible for curing illness?
- What practices exist regarding personal hygiene?
- If a student were involved in an accident at school, would any of the common first aid practices be unacceptable? (Saville-Troike, 1978)

Institutional influences: Economic, legal, political, and religious. The institutions that support and govern family and community life have an influence on behavior and beliefs and, in turn, are constituted in accordance with these behaviors and beliefs. The economic institutions of the United States are largely dual: small business enterprises and large corporate/government agencies. Small businesses reward and channel the initiative to those who come to the United States with capital to invest, but generally pay low wages to low-skilled workers. Professional workers in the larger corporate and governmental agencies (education, utilities, medicine, law) must pay dues to enter, whether by passing elaborate licensing and examination processes or by achieving a close fit to the corporate culture. These institutions influence daily life in the United States by means of a complex web of law, custom, and regulation that provides the economic and legal infrastructure of the dominant culture. These institutions can be affected through formal political processes or via more informal means such as selective purchasing and retail participation (boycotts, consumption of ethnic products).

Interwoven into this rich cultural/economic/political/legal texture are religious beliefs and practices. In the United States, religious practices are heavily embedded but formally bounded: Witness the controversy over Christmas trees in schools, but the almost universal cultural and economic necessity for increased consumer spending at the close of the calendar year. Religious beliefs underlie other cultures even more fundamentally. Immigrants with Confucian religious and philosophical beliefs subscribe to values that mandate a highly ordered society and family through the maintenance of proper social relationships. In Islamic traditions, the Koran prescribes proper social relationships and roles for members of society. When immigrants with these religious beliefs encounter the largely secular U.S. institutions, the result may be that customs and cultural patterns are challenged, fade away, or cause conflict within the family (Chung, 1989). In many of the cultures in U.S. society, religion influences people's beliefs about authority and reactions to classroom behaviors such as questioning and creativity (Heath, 1983b).

Teachers may want to consider the following issues about institutional influences in the home and community culture:

- What jobs/income are available in the community and to whom?
- What role does the law play in community life, and what relationships exist with legal authorities (police, immigration officials)?

- Who dominates the political processes in the community?
- What aspects of religion should not be discussed in school, and what behavior should not be required?

Educational systems. Educational systems in the past were designed to pass on cultural knowledge and traditions, much the same learning that parents taught their children. However, in the increasingly complex and technologically changing society of the United States, schools have shifted their emphasis to teaching unforeseen kinds of content: "a change from a stable pattern of cultural transmission to the teaching of what the parents never knew" (Singleton, 1973, p. 279). This shift affects all students but is particularly troublesome for children whose parents teach them in different ways than the school does. Students come to school already steeped in the learning practices of their own family and community. They come with expectations about learning and generally expect that they will continue to learn in school. Many of the organizational and teaching practices of the school may not support the type of learning to which students are accustomed.

For immigrant children with previous schooling, experience in U.S. classrooms may engender severe conflicts. For example, Polynesian students coming from the South Pacific have experienced learning as a relatively passive activity. They expect teachers to give explicit instruction about what to learn and how to learn it, and homework to be checked daily with careful scrutiny. When these students arrive in the United States and encounter teachers who value creativity and student-centered learning, they may appear passive as they wait to be told what to do (Funaki & Burnett, 1993). Indochinese students expect to listen, watch, and imitate. They may be reluctant to ask questions or volunteer answers and may be embarrassed to ask for the teacher's help or reluctant to participate in individual demonstrations of a skill or project (Armour, Knudson, & Meeks, 1981). Teachers who can accommodate to these students' proclivities can gradually introduce student-centered practices while supporting an initial dependence on teacher directions.

Teachers who seek to understand the value of education within the community can examine the following questions:

- What methods for teaching and learning are used in the home (e.g., modeling and imitation, didactic stories and proverbs, direct verbal instruction)?
- What role does language play in learning and teaching?
- How are children expected to interact with teachers (observe only, ask questions, volunteer)?
- How many years are children expected to attend school?

Roles and Status

Cultures differ in the roles people play in society and the status that is accorded to these roles. For example, in the Vietnamese culture, profoundly influenced by Confucianism, authority figures are ranked in the following manner: The father ranks below the teacher, who ranks only below the king (Chung, 1989). Such a high status is not accorded to teachers in U.S. society, where, instead, medical doctors enjoy this type of prestige. Such factors as gender, social class, age, occupation, and educational level influence the manner in which status is accorded to various roles. Students' perceptions about the roles possible for them in their culture affect their school performance.

Gender. Gender is related to social roles in a similar way in many cultures. Anthropologists have found men to be in control of political and military matters in all known cultures. Young boys tend to be more physically and verbally aggressive and to seek dominance more than girls do. Traditionally, women have had the primary responsibility for child rearing, with associated tasks, manners, and responsibilities. Immigrants to the United States often come from cultures in which men and women have rigid and highly differentiated gender roles. The gender equality that is an ostensible goal in classrooms in the United States may be difficult for students of these cultures. For example, parents may spend much time correcting their sons' homework while ascribing little importance to their daughters' schoolwork.

To assess the roles played by males and females in various cultures, teachers may consider the following:

- What tasks are performed by boys, what tasks by girls?
- When, where, and how may girls and boys interact?
- What expectations do parents and students hold for boys' and girls' achievement, and how does this differ by subject?

Social class. Social class stratification differs across cultures. Cultures that are rigidly stratified, such as India's caste system, differ from cultures that are not as rigid or, in some cases, border on the anarchic, such as post-Communist Russia. The belief that education can enhance economic status is widespread in the dominant culture in the United States, but individuals in other cultures may not have similar beliefs. For example, immigrants to St. Croix from West Indian islands to the south (Antigua, Trinidad, St. Lucia, Nevis) appeared to view schooling as instrumental to their future success and were willing to work hard and abide by the rules. In contrast, young men born in St. Croix appeared to perceive education as an instrument of oppression and a threat to their identity. The native-born males believed that they could achieve prestigious government positions on the basis of their family connections, not through educational success (Gibson, 1991a).

In general, individuals and families in the upper socioeconomic status levels are able to exert power by sitting on college, university, and local school boards and, in this way, determining who receives benefits and rewards through schooling. However, middle-class values are those that are generally incorporated in the culture of schooling. The social class values that children learn in their homes largely influence not only their belief in schooling but also their routines and habits in the classroom.

Teachers can observe closely the following social class differences that may affect students' behavior:

- What type of home environment do students have—the amount and quality of material possessions, housing, consumer goods, and diet?
- What power do parents have to obtain information about the school or to influence educational choices?
- What resources are available in the home to augment school assignments?

Age. Age interacts with culture, socioeconomic status, gender, and other factors to influence an individual's behavior and attitudes. In Puerto Rico, for example, breakfast food varies depending on age: Children may eat creamed cereal, while adults drink strong coffee and eat bread. In contrast, in the United States, both adults and children eat cereal for breakfast. In various cultures, expectations about appropriate activities for children and the purpose for those activities differ. Middle-class European-Americans expect children to spend much of their time playing and attending school rather than performing tasks similar to those of adults. Cree Indian children, on the other hand, are expected from an early age to learn adult roles, including contributing food to the family. Cree Indian parents may criticize schools for involving children in tasks that are not related to their future participation in Cree society (Sindell, 1988).

Cultures also differ in their criteria for moving through the various (culturally defined) life cycle changes. An important stage in any culture is the move into adulthood, but the age at which this occurs and the criteria necessary for attaining adulthood vary according to what *adulthood* means in a particular culture. For example, in a culture in which the duty of the male adult is to show prowess in war, then entry into adulthood involves long-term preparation and is therefore delayed. In contrast, in cultures where adulthood includes the privilege of dancing in representation of masked gods, adulthood is awarded at a younger age (Benedict, 1934).

Teachers can begin to understand how age is a factor in students' interaction by considering the following:

- What activities and roles are expected of individuals at different life stages?

- What activities and behaviors are appropriate—or forbidden—for children of various ages?
- What criteria define the various stages or periods in the life cycle?

Occupation. Occupation, in the United States, very often determines income, which in turn is a chief determinant of prestige in the culture. Other cultures, however, may attribute prestige to those with inherited status or to those who have a religious function in the culture. Prestige is one factor in occupational choices. Other factors can include cultural acceptance of the occupation, educational requirements, gender, and attainability. Students thus may not see all occupations as desirable for them or even available to them and may have mixed views about the role education plays in their future occupation. Some cultural groups in the United States are engaged in a voluntary way of life that does not require public schooling (e.g., the Amish). Other groups may not be adequately rewarded in the United States for school success but expect to be rewarded elsewhere (e.g., children of diplomats and short-term residents who expect to return to their home country). Still another group may be involuntarily incorporated into the U.S. society and relegated to menial occupations and ways of life that do not reward and require school success (e.g., Chicanos in the Southwest). As a reaction they may not apply academic effort (Ogbu & Matute-Bianchi, 1986).

Teachers may wish to ask students their views of occupations and work. The following information may be relevant:

- What kinds of work are considered prestigious or desirable?
- What assumptions exist about the attainability of specific occupations?
- What role does education play in achieving occupational goals?

Educational level. Educational level, for many individuals, is a factor of the job desired, the importance parents ascribe to education, and the investment in education that the culture values. The son of blue-collar workers may not value a college education because his parents, who have not attained such an education, have nevertheless prospered. The daughter of a college professor may find her parent's work load too demanding and desire a less stressful occupation. The educational opportunity available in the United States may appeal to immigrants from other cultures who may not desire to have their children remain in the United States to establish occupations. For example, parents who are residents of Hong Kong will often sacrifice to send their children abroad to the United States, Great Britain, or Canada, but these parents are careful to maintain dual residences so that children can return to Hong Kong to carry on family business or tradition. For these parents, the educational level attainable in Western countries may serve solely an instrumental (goal attainment) function and not an affiliative (social-relation) purpose.

In working with diverse students, teachers will want to know:

- What educational level the student, family, and community desire for the student
- What degree of assimilation to the dominant culture (and to English) is expected and desired

Family Socialization: The Structure of Daily Life

The family unit is a complex web that influences and shapes the individual. Family relationships make up an intricate network of affiliations that contribute to the child's learning and adjustment. School socialization must build on, rather than replace, that of the family because the family has helped to create the child's personality and habits—in effect, helped develop identity itself. In the home, a child is named and thus learns about names and forms of address. The child is taken care of and thus learns how people are cared for. The child interacts with parents and thus learns roles for children and adults. The child is fed and thus learns what to enjoy and what to abhor.

Naming practices and **forms of address.** These practices differ across cultures. The custom in the United States is to have a first or given, a middle, and a last or family name. On lists, the first and last names are often reversed in order to organize or "alphabetize" the names. In Vietnam, names also consist of three parts, in the following order: family name, middle name, and given name. The names are always given in this order and cannot be reversed because doing so would denote a different person—Nguyên Van Hai is different from Hai Van Nguyên. Similarly, Puerto Ricans generally use three names: a given name, followed by the father's surname and then the mother's surname. If one last name must be used, it is generally the father's surname. Thus, Esther Reyes Mimosa can be listed as Esther Reyes. If the first name is composed of two given names (Hector Luis), both should be used. This person may have a brother who is Hector José; for either to be called simply Hector would be a loss of identity.

In addressing people, practices also vary considerably. Vietnamese are never known by their family names, but are always called by their given names. These given names can be preceded by a title—Mr., Mrs., or Dr. In contrast, Koreans can be addressed with Mr., Mrs., or Dr. before their family names. Teachers should avoid using given names when addressing adults, as these are used for addressing those who are younger, who are very close friends, or who are of lower status (California State Department of Education, 1992).

In many cultures, adults are referred to by their function rather than their name. In Hmong, *xib fwb* means "teacher," and Hmong children may use the English term "teacher" in the classroom rather than a title plus surname ("Mrs. Jasko"). Middle-class European-American teachers may consider this to be rude rather than realizing this is a cultural difference.

Educators often change and mispronounce the names of immigrants. A sensitive teacher strives not only to understand the use and order of names but also to pronounce them correctly.

Child-rearing practices. Child-rearing practices have wide implications for schools. Factors such as who takes care of children, how much supervision they receive, how much freedom they have, who speaks to them and how often, and what they are expected to do affect their behavior upon entering schools. Many of the misunderstandings that occur between teachers and students arise because of differing expectations about behavior, and these differing expectations stem from early, ingrained child-rearing practices. In Hmong society, for example, family values are placed above individual concerns. Children spend the majority of every day in close physical proximity to their parents. Parents carry and touch their children more than is common in Western cultures (Bliatout et al., 1988). Hmong children may expect the same type of treatment from their teachers, whereas teachers expect independence and self-initiation from the children. Similarly, students from Korean-American backgrounds may be accustomed to an authoritarian discipline style in the home. These parents often seek to influence their children's behavior by expecting reciprocity for the sacrifices made for them. Decision-making strategies reward conformity and obedience, and teachers are expected to reinforce this. An egalitarian classroom atmosphere may create conflicts for Korean-American students between the pressures they experience in their families and the school environment (California State Department of Education, 1992). Several excellent sources that describe child-rearing practices in various cultures are currently available from the California Department of Education. In addition, a rich description of child-rearing practices among Mexican immigrant families can be found in *Crossing Cultural Borders* (Delgado-Gaitan & Trueba, 1991).

Teachers cannot expect to know all aspects of child-rearing practices in their students' cultures. However, they can be sensitive to the fact that parents have goals and values for their children that they expect schools to honor. By listening to parents and community representatives and, in turn, being knowledgeable about school practices, teachers can work together with parents to provide rewarding schooling experiences for their students.

Parental involvement. Parental involvement in the school is influenced by cultural beliefs. The U.S. system was developed from small, relatively homogeneous local schools with considerable community and parental control. The pattern of community and parental involvement continues today with school boards, PTAs, and parent volunteers in the schools. This pattern is not universal outside the United States. For example, in traditional

Cambodia, village families who sent their children to schools in cities had no means of involving themselves in the school (Ouk, Huffman, & Lewis, 1988).

In cultures where teachers are accorded high status, parents may consider it improper to discuss educational matters or bring up issues that concern their children. Other factors that make parental involvement difficult are school procedures such as restrictive scheduling for parent conferences and notification to parents that siblings are not welcome at school for conferences and other events. These procedures tend to divide families and exclude parents. School staffs can involve the community by talking with parents and community liaisons to work out procedures that are compatible with cultural practices.

Food preferences. Food preferences are an important consideration in schools as the numbers of school-provided breakfasts and lunches increase. Further, as more courses in health and nutrition are mandated, teachers who are knowledgeable about students' dietary practices can incorporate their students' background knowledge into instruction. Besides knowing in general what foods are eaten, in what order, and how often, teachers will want to find out about students' favorite foods, taboo foods, and typical foods. A home visit is an excellent means for gaining knowledge about food habits and preferences. In some cultures, a visitor to a home can expect to be offered a refreshment, and refusing is a discourtesy (Armour, Knudson, & Meeks, 1981). Besides customs of what and when to eat, eating habits vary widely across cultures, and "good" manners at the table in some cultures are inappropriate or rude in others. For example, Indochinese consider burping, lip smacking, and soup slurping to be common behaviors during meals, even complimentary to hosts. Teachers who eat lunch with their students can use the opportunity to learn about students' habits, rather than blindly insisting on culturally specific table habits. If, however, a student's habits alienate peers, the teacher may need to discuss appropriate manners.

Humanities and the Arts

In many cultures, crafts performed at home such as food preparation, sewing and weaving, carpentry, home building and decoration, religious and ritual artistry for holy days, holidays, and entertaining are an important part of the culture that is transmitted within the home. Teachers can draw upon these when involving parents in classroom activities by inviting parents to demonstrate these arts and crafts. Parents are also an important means of access to the humanities, and visual and performing arts of the students' culture. Often, if immigrants are to gain an appreciation of the great works of art, architecture, music, and dance that have been achieved by their native culture, it is the classroom teacher who must provide this experience and awareness by drawing on the resources of the community and then sharing these with all the members of the classroom.

Learning Styles

Not only do the humanities provide a means of sharing cultural achievements and arousing pride on the part of students, but they also provide important alternative learning modalities. Humanities and other culturally based activities can engender cooperation among groups of students as they work together to produce visual arts or performances. Thematic units enriched by music, art, theater, and crafts can be means for teaching basic skills. Students respond positively to material when their preferred mode of learning is used for transmitting information and demonstrating knowledge.

Learning style can be defined as individual preferences for processing information. Information is perceived or gathered; it is stored or attached to the memory base; and it is then used for making decisions and taking action. Culture appears to influence each part of this process by providing a set of rules that guide the way individuals select strategies and approach learning (Shade & New, 1993). Learning styles can be thought of as perceptual styles (a preference for certain sensory modalities) and thinking styles (variations in the way opinions, beliefs, attitudes, and values are formed).

Thinking and learning are highly dependent on social interaction. This social interaction takes place within a complex cultural context, and children use the language, tools, and practices of their culture to learn concepts. In mathematics, for example, Japanese children use the abacus as a tool in mental calculation. It ultimately provides a framework around which they can decipher, conceptualize, and reason about quantitative information (Shade & New, 1993).

The culture determines what kind of thinking is important and what kind is devalued. Students who live in a farming community may have sensitive and subtle knowledge about weather patterns, knowledge that is essential to the economic survival of their family. This type of knowledge may predispose students to value learning in the classroom that helps them better understand natural processes like climate. These students may prefer kinesthetic learning activities that build on the same kind of learning that has made it possible for them to sense subtleties of weather. In a similar manner, Chicano children from traditional families who are encouraged to view themselves as an integral part of the family may prefer social learning activities. Ramirez (1988) describes this as a "field-sensitive" learning style, one that leads to a greater awareness of social cues. For more discussion of learning strategies and cognitive styles, see Chapter 2.

Learning modalities. Students can acquire knowledge via several distinct means: visualizing, viewing the written word, listening, and acting. These modalities are often combined in culturally specific ways. The Navajo child is often taught by first observing and listening, then taking over parts of the task in cooperation with and under the supervision of an adult. In this way, the child gradually learns all the requisite skills. Finally, the child tests himself or herself privately—failure is not seen by others, whereas success is brought back and shared. The use of speech in this learning process is minimal (Phillips, 1978). In contrast, acting and performing are the focus of learning for many African-American children. Children observe other individuals to determine appropriate behavior and to appreciate the performance of others. In this case, observing and listening culminates in an individual's performance before others (Heath, 1983b). Reading and writing may be primary learning modes for other cultures. Traditionally educated Asian students equate the printed page with learning and appear to need the reinforcement of reading and writing in order to learn. Observing students learning from one another in a natural, unstructured setting can inform teachers of students' preferred ways of learning. This knowledge can be transferred to the classroom teaching and learning situation.

Cooperation versus competition. Cultures also differ in their emphasis on cooperation over competition. Traditional U.S. classrooms mirror middle-class European-American values of competition: Students are isolated in individual seats set in rows, expected to "do their own work"; rewarded publicly through star charts, posted grades, and academic honors, and admonished to do their individual "best." In the Cree Indian culture, however, children are raised in a cooperative atmosphere, with siblings, parents, and other kin sharing food as well as labor (Sindell, 1988). In the Mexican-American culture, interdependence is a strength; one has a commitment to others, and all decisions are made together. Those who are successful have a responsibility to others to help them succeed. A classroom structured to maximize learning through cooperation can help students extend their cultural predilection for interdependence. This interdependence does not devalue the uniqueness of the individual. The Mexican culture values *individualismo,* the affirmation of one's intrinsic worth and uniqueness aside from any successful actions or grand position in society (de Unamuno, 1925). A workable synthesis of this individualism/interdependence would come from classroom activities in the classroom that are carried out as a group but that affirm the unique gifts of each individual student.

Use of Language

In learning a second language, students (and teachers) often focus on the form. Frequently ignored are the ways in which that second language is used. The culture that underlies each language prescribes distinct patterns and conventions about when, where, and how to use the language (see Labov, 1972). Heath (1983b) noted that children in "Trackton," an isolated African-American community in the South, were encouraged to use spontaneous verbal play, rich with metaphor, simile, and allusion. In contrast, the children of "Roadville," a lower-middle-class European-American community in the South, used language in more restricted ways, perhaps because of habits encouraged by a fundamentalist religious culture. Heath contrasts language usage in these two cultures: verbal and nonverbal communication (the said and the unsaid), the use of silence, discourse styles; the nature of questions, and the use of oral versus written genres.

Social functions. Using language to satisfy material needs, control the behavior of others, get along with others, express one's personality, find out about the world, create an imaginative world, or communicate information seems to be universal among languages. How these social functions are accomplished, however, varies greatly among cultures. For example, when accidentally bumping some one, Americans, Japanese, Koreans, and Filipinos would say "excuse me" or "pardon me." The Chinese, however, would give an apologetic look. Within a family, Hispanics often do not say "thank you" for acts of service, whereas European-American children are taught to say "thank you" for any such act, especially to a family member. Social functions provide the basis for the modern ESL curriculum (routines for apologizing, expressing disappointment, telling a story, asking for permission, giving opinions). Often, not only must the language routines be rehearsed, but the intent of the language must be explained because each culture has a unique way of using language to fulfill functions.

Verbal and nonverbal expression. Verbal and nonverbal means are used to communicate a language function. Educators are oriented toward verbal means of expression and are less likely to accord importance to the "silent language." However, more than 65 percent of the social meaning of a typical two-person exchange is carried by nonverbal cues (Birdwhistell, 1974). *Kinesic* behavior, including facial expressions, body movements, postures, and gestures, can enhance a message or constitute a message in itself. For example, a gesture such as the expressive Gallic shrug of the shoulders can communicate emotions (disillusionment, frustration, and disbelief) far beyond the capacity of verbal language. *Physical appearance* is an important dimension of the nonverbal code during initial encounters. *Paralanguage*—the nonverbal elements of the voice—is an important aspect of speech that can affirm or belie a verbal message. *Proxemics*, the communication of interpersonal distance, varies widely across cultures. Last, but not least, *olfactics*—the study of interpersonal communication via smell—may constitute a factor that is powerful yet often overlooked.

The role of silence. People throughout the world employ silence in communicating. Silence can in fact speak loudly and eloquently. The silence of a parent in front of a guilty child is more powerful than any ranting or raving. As with other language uses, however, silence differs dramatically across cultures. In the United States, silence is interpreted as expressing embarrassment, regret, obligation, criticism, or sorrow (Wayne in Ishii & Bruneau, 1991). In Asian cultures, silence is a token of respect, particularly in the presence of the elderly. Being quiet is a sign of respect for the wisdom and expertise of others. Silence can also be a marker of personal power. In Eastern cultures, women view their silent role as a symbol of control and self-respect. In many Native American cultures, silence is used to create and communicate rapport in ways that language cannot.

> Norman, a Paiute youth from Reno, Nevada, had an agonizing decision to make. At the age of 18, he had graduated from the Indian Youth Training Program in Tucson, Arizona, and was free to return home to live. Living at home would possibly jeopardize the hard-won habits of diligence and self-control that he had learned away from the home community, in which he had been arrested for juvenile delinquency. As the counselor in Norman's group home, I knew he could possibly benefit by talking over his decision. After school, I entered his room and sat on the chair by his bed, indicating that I was available to help him talk through his dilemma. One half hour of total silence elapsed. After thirty minutes he began to speak. Silence rather than language had achieved the rapport I sought. (L.D-R.)

In a research project that took place in several Ogala Sioux classrooms, a central factor was the withdrawal of the Sioux students. Teachers were faced with unexpectedly intense, sometimes embarrassingly long periods of silence. They cajoled, commanded, badgered, and pleaded with students, with an inevitable monosyllabic or nonverbal response. Yet outside the classroom children were noisy, bold, and insatiably curious. Closer observation revealed a student-developed and -controlled silence, a tactic on the part of whole groups of children to shut the teacher out and defend against the teacher-student learning exchange. The lack of verbal responses from students frustrated teachers. When teachers redefined the silence as an intercultural opportunity, they were able to create conditions of change. The solution? The teachers involved themselves in the daily life of the community and reduced the isolation of the school from the values of the community. They went so far as to locate classrooms in community buildings. In a differing context, students were more willing participants (Dumont, 1972).

The role and nature of questions. The role of silence in the language acquisition classroom may extend to intercultural differences in asking and answering questions. In middle-class European-American culture, children are exposed early on to their parents questioning. While taking a walk, for example, a mother will ask, "See the squirrel?" and, later, "Is that a squirrel? Where did that squirrel go?" It is obvious to both parent and child that the adult knows the answer to these questions. The questions are asked to stimulate conversation and to train children to focus attention and display knowledge. In the Inuit culture, on the other hand, adults do not question children or call their attention to objects and events in order to name them

(Crago, 1993). Responses to questioning differs across cultures. Students from non-Western cultures may be reluctant to attempt an answer to a question if they do not feel they can answer absolutely correctly. For Korean students, for example, to put forth a mistaken answer would be a personal embarrassment and a personal affront to the teacher (California State Department of Education, 1992). Students do not share the European-American value of answering questions to the best of their ability regardless of whether that "best" answer is absolutely correct or not, nor will students from many Eastern countries speak up when they do not understand or ask questions solely to demonstrate intelligence.

Discourse styles. Cultures may differ in ways that influence conversations: the way conversations open and close; the way people take turns; the way messages are repaired to make them understandable; and the way in which parts of the text are set aside. Those who have traveled to a foreign country recognize that a small interaction, such as answering the telephone, may have widely varying sequences across cultures. Sometimes callers may give immediate self-identification, sometimes not. Sometimes politeness is accorded the caller automatically; sometimes greetings are followed with "how are you" sequences. Deviations from these routines may be cause to terminate a conversation in the earliest stages. These differences in discourse are stressful for second language learners. Multiply this stress by the long hours children spend in school, and it is no wonder that non-English-speaking children may feel subjected to prolonged pressure.

Discourse in the classroom can be organized in ways that involve children positively, in ways that are culturally compatible. A group of Hawaiian children, with the help of an encouraging and participating adult, produced group discourse that was co-narrated, complex, lively, imaginative, and well connected. Group work featured twenty-minute discussions of text in which teacher and students mutually participated in overlapping, volunteered speech and in joint narration (Au & Jordan, 1981). In contrast, Navajo children in a discussion group patterned their discourse after the adults of their culture. Each Navajo student spoke for an extended period with a fully expressed statement, and other students waited courteously until a clear end was communicated. Then another took a similar turn. Ideas were developed at greater length and were often individualistic. There might be little articulation with the ideas of previous speakers. In both communities, children tended to connect discourse with peers rather than the teacher functioning as a central "switchboard." If the teacher acted as a central director, students might respond with silence and eventual resentfulness (Tharp, 1989a).

Oral versus written language. Orality is the foundation of languages. Written expression is a later development. In fact, of the three thousand reported languages in use, only 78 have a written literature (Edmonson, 1971).

Research has suggested that acquiring literacy involves more than learning to read and write. Thinking patterns, perception, cultural values, communication style, and social organization can be affected by literacy (Goody, 1968; Ong, 1982; Scribner & Cole, 1978). In studying oral societies, researchers have noted that in the structure and content of messages, words are integrally related to deeds and events. Interpersonal messages tend to be narrative, situational, oriented toward activity, and lacking in detail. In contrast, the style of literacy is conceptual rather than situational. Words are separate from the social context of deeds and events, and ideas can be extracted from narratives. Oral narrative tends to focus on critical incidents in which character and deed are highlighted, and details about time, date, and place that are often critical in written narration are not integral elements.

In an oral society, learning takes place in groups because narration must have an audience. This contrasts a literate society in which reading and writing can be solitary experiences. Separation from the group appears to be one of the burdens of literacy. In an oral society, much reliance is placed on memory as this is the principal means of preserving practices and traditions. Basically, "you know what you can recall" (Ong, 1982, p. 33). Activities in an oral society are learned by doing, and those who learn by reading often are unable to achieve the level of performance attained by apprenticeship learning.

Hmong immigrants in the United States demonstrate the comparative disadvantage of an individual from an oral culture when expected to perform in a literate environment. When registering children in school, Hmong parents are required to know such details as children's birthdates, ages, and immunization dates—facts that are not normally maintained by these families—whereas the knowledge that they have about their children's abilities, strengths, and skills is never tapped. In the abstract, categorical world of school, detached from situation and nature, Hmong individuals may become frustrated. The very concept of independent study is alien to this culture because learning had always occurred in community groups. Learning in groups of strangers and doing homework, a solitary endeavor, may run counter to traditional group practices and may distance children from their families. As Hmong children become literate and engage in independent study, parents may become disturbed over the loss of centrality and power in their children's lives. This may produce family tension (Shuter, 1991).

Children from nonindustrial societies may begin school in the United States with what have been labeled "dual handicaps" if they have not been exposed to written texts. Several Southeast Asian hill tribes, including the Hmong, have had almost no exposure to written materials and rarely, if ever, have had someone else read to them. These students have little experience in the difference between written and spoken language (Niyekawa, 1982). Students from literate cultures whose alphabet radically differs from the Roman alphabet may experience delays in acquiring written English. Some writing systems represent a direct sound–symbol correspondence;

Khmer, for example, is far more regular and phonetic than the English writing system. Other writing systems, such as Korean and Japanese, which incorporate Chinese ideographs, have an even more indirect sound–symbol correspondence than does English. Vietnamese students have an advantage over Cambodian, Laotian, and Chinese students in studying English, because Vietnamese writing uses the Roman alphabet with the addition of diacritical marks to represent different tonal values. The California State Department of Education handbooks (*Handbook for Teaching Korean-American Students, Handbook for Teaching Khmer-Speaking Students, The American Indian: Yesterday, Today, and Tomorrow, A Handbook for Educators,* and others) provide valuable insights into educating students from cultures with a non-Roman alphabet or with a strong oral tradition.

Understanding in general how culture affects education can enable teachers to adapt instruction to bridge the home–school gap for language minority students. Teachers need to pursue specific information about the cultures of their students by means of two distinct learning routes. One approach is to research the students' cultures through reading, viewing films, and using other media that present cultural information. A second approach is to interact directly with students' cultures by attending community meetings, making home visits, getting to know parents or spokespersons in the community, and inviting such people to the classroom. Recent techniques borrowed from anthropology can be used to investigate culture more closely.

HOW TEACHERS CAN LEARN
ABOUT THEIR STUDENTS

Schools are organized to expect certain processes: ways of thinking, communicating, and participating. When children possess the repertoires on which school depends, they are predisposed to succeed in the school environment. When cultures provide a different set of social and psychological practices, teachers and students may become mutually frustrated. Teachers who understand the culture of their students can introduce changes in the classroom to make practices more compatible with students' styles. The study of culture is important because this information can help to understand how groups of students are similar in their reaction to schooling. The need to educate individual students does not decline in importance but, rather is heightened through a deeper understanding of individuals within their cultural context. With this cultural knowledge, classroom routines can be organized to encourage more effective learning, and information about the students' cultures can be incorporated into the content of instruction.

One method, ethnographic study, has proved useful in learning about the ways that students' cultural experiences in the home and community compare with the culture of the schools. Ethnography can show how cultural assumptions and values shape interaction and can cause crosscultural miscommunication. These cultural assumptions and values can lead to differing attitudes and approaches toward the learning situation. Ethnography is an inquiry process that seeks to provide cultural explanations for behavior and attitudes. Culture is described from the insider's point of view, as the classroom teacher becomes not only an observer of the students' cultures but also an active participant (Erickson, 1977; Mehan, 1981; Robinson, 1985). Techniques that encourage this active participation are interviews, home visits, and participation in community events. Parents and community members, as well as students, become sources for the gradual growth of understanding on the part of the teacher.

Techniques

Ethnography involves gathering data in order to understand two distinct cultures: first, the culture of the students' communities and, second, the culture of the classroom. Some techniques can be employed specifically for understanding the home and community environment: participation in community life, interviews with community members, and visits to the home. Other techniques are appropriate for understanding the school culture: observations in a variety of classrooms, observations by visitors in one's own classroom; audio- and videotapes of classroom interaction; and interviews with other teachers and administrators.

Observations. Observations must be carried out, ideally, with the perspective that one is seeing the culture for the first time from the point of view of a complete outsider. Nunan (1993) calls this the use of an "estrangement device"—for example, pretending one is an alien from Mars and watching without preconceived ideas. Of course, when observing interactions and behaviors in another culture, one always uses the frame of reference supplied by one's own culture. When observing a religious ceremony in a local church, for example, one would feel a sense of strangeness and discomfort in not knowing quite how to react in comparison with behavior in one's own church. This is the essence of observation/participation. The differences in the culture of the observer and the observed become part of the data. When inviting a colleague to one's own classroom to make observations, the mutual culture of instruction provides a shared focus that may, unfortunately, incorporate the biases and values of this culture. It is hard to observe one's own culture!

Observers need to be descriptive and objective and make explicit their own attitudes and values in order to overcome hidden sources of bias. This requires training. However, the classroom teacher can begin to observe and participate in the students' culture, making field notes after participating and perhaps summing up the insights gained in an ongoing diary that can be shared with colleagues in shared inquiry. Such observation can document children's use of language within the community, etiquettes of speaking, listening, writing, greeting, getting or giving information, values, and aspirations, norms of communication—in short, data about the categories of culture described in this chapter. When analyzing the culture of the classroom, one might look at classroom management and routines; affective factors (students' attitudes toward activities, teachers' attitudes toward students); classroom talk in general; and nonverbal behaviors and communication. In addition to the raw data of behavior, the thoughts and intentions of the participants can also be documented. Interviews with participants add further insight into the observed behavior.

Interviews. Interviews can be divided into two types: structured and unstructured. Structured interviews have a set of questions predetermined to gain specific kinds of information. Unstructured interviews are more like conversations in that they can range over a wide variety of topics, many of which the interviewer would not necessarily have anticipated. As an outsider learning about a new culture, the classroom teacher would be better served initially with an unstructured interview, beginning with general questions and being guided in follow-up questions by the interviewee's responses. The result of the initial interview may, in turn, provide a structure for learning more about the culture during a second interview or conversation. A very readable book about ethnography and interviewing is Michael Agar's *The Professional Stranger: An Informal Introduction to Ethnography* (1980).

Home visits. Home visits are one of the best ways teachers can learn what is familiar and important to their students. The home visit can be a "social call" or a brief report on the student's progress that enhances rapport with students and parents. Scheduling an appointment ahead of time is a courtesy that some cultures may require and provides a means for one to ascertain if home visits are welcome. Dress should be professional. The visit should be short (20 to 30 minutes) and the conversation positive, especially about the student's schoolwork. Viewing the child in the context of the home provides a look at the parent–child interaction, the resources of the home, and the child's role in the family. One teacher announces to the class at the beginning of the year that she is available on Friday nights to be invited to dinner. Knowing in advance that their invitation is welcomed, parents and children are proud to act as hosts.

Sources

As literate individuals, teachers can use printed materials, books, and magazines to learn about other cultures. However, the richest source of information is local—the life of the community. Students, parents, and community members can provide insights about values, attitudes, and habits.

Students. Students generally provide teachers with their initial contact with other cultures. Through observations, one-on-one interaction, and group participatory processes, teachers gain understanding about various individuals and their cultural repertoire. Teachers who are good listeners offer students time for shared conversations by lingering after school or opening the classroom during lunchtime. Teachers may find it useful to ask students to map their own neighborhood. This is a source of knowledge from the students' perspectives about the boundaries of the neighborhood and surrounding areas.

Parents. Parents can be sources of information in much the same way as their children. Rather than one or two formal conferences, PTA open house events, and gala performances, the school may encourage parent participation by opening the library once a week after school. This offers a predictable time in which parents and teachers may casually meet and chat. Parents can also be the source for information that can form the basis for classroom writing. Using the Language Experience Approach, teachers can ask students to interview their parents about common topics such as work, interests, and family history. In this way, students and parents together can supply knowledge about community life. Although it may be more difficult to involve working parents, the work that they perform can be a source about the knowledge and expertise in the community.

Community members. Community members are an equally rich source of cultural knowledge. Much can be learned about a community by walking or driving through it, stopping to make a purchase in local stores and markets. One teacher who was hesitant about visiting a particular area in a large city arranged to walk through the neighborhood with a doctor whose office was located there. Other teachers may ask older students to act as "tour guides." During these visits, the people of the neighborhood can be sources of knowledge about housing, places where children and teenagers play, places where adults gather, and sources of food, furniture, and services.

Through community representatives, teachers can begin to know about important living patterns of a community. A respected elder can provide information about the family and which members constitute a family. A community leader may be able to contrast the community political system with the city or state system. A religious leader can explain the importance of religion in community life. Teachers can attend local ceremonies and activities to learn more about community dynamics.

HOW TEACHERS CAN USE WHAT THEY LEARN ABOUT THEIR STUDENTS (CULTURALLY RESPONSIVE PEDAGOGY)

The selection of a particular teaching method reflects cultural values more than it argues for the superiority of the method. Cultures succeed in educating those they choose to educate, and whom they choose to educate also reflects a cultural bias. . . . [N]othing about the educational process is absolute. Every component reflects a cultural choice, conscious or unconscious, about whom to educate, how, when, in what subjects, for what purpose, and in what manner. (Andersen & Powell, 1988, pp. 210–211)

Culture is embedded in the life of the school. Teachers are cultural transmitters. The way they teach is a product of their own culture and the way that their culture taught them to learn. For some children, the culture of the school may be so different from the culture of the home that they have difficulty learning in the context and manner provided by the school. However, it is not enough simply to explain children's differential school success as a cultural mismatch between home and school. What happens in a classroom can be influenced by teachers whose behavior and values bridge any gap between home and school for the benefit of the students.

Teachers who understand students' cultures can design instruction to meet children's learning needs. They invite students to learn by welcoming them, making them feel that they belong, and presenting learning as a task at which they can succeed. Barriers are often erected between students of culturally diverse communities and the school because teachers and students do not share the same perceptions of what is acceptable behavior and what is relevant learning. Teaching styles, interaction patterns, classroom organization, curriculum, and involvement with parents and the community are factors that are within the teacher's power to adapt. The result is culturally compatible teaching.

Teaching Styles (Cultural Orientation)

Becoming an active member of a classroom learning community requires specific cultural knowledge and the ability to use that knowledge appropriately in specific contexts. Students from a nonmainstream culture are acquiring a second culture in school. The contrast between the patterns acquired at home and those demanded by the school may create behavioral conflicts that require selective change and adjustment (Trueba, 1989). The new values are embedded in the organization of school activities and their reward system. The way teachers are taught to teach is a reflection of the expectations of U.S. culture. Teachers raised in a mainstream culture have elements of that culture embedded in their personal teaching approach. Some of these elements may need to be modified to meet the needs of students from other cultures. As a beginning step, teachers can examine six teaching styles that have been identified by Fischer and Fischer (1979).

1. *Task-oriented* teachers demand specific performance from students. They may wish students to be independent of the social environment when working. Such an orientation may be more compatible with students who have field-independent learning styles. Students from cultures that are more field-sensitive may prefer to perform tasks in groups.

2. Teachers who *plan cooperatively* with students may find that students from some cultures are more comfortable taking responsibility for their own learning than are others.

3. Teachers who are *emotionally exciting* rather than relatively subdued may find that some students respond to this sense of excitement, whereas others may be overstimulated and unable to complete tasks.

4. A *child-centered* teacher often structures learning activities in which students can pursue their own interests. Students from cultures that center around adults and their needs may find the child-centered orientation mystifying.

5. *Subject-centered* teachers focus on "covering" the curriculum. Often this curriculum has been designed by others, and the teacher feels little ownership of the content other than an obligation to complete it. Students from diverse cultural backgrounds may find some aspects of the curriculum more relevant than others. The teacher may have to make decisions to emphasize some parts of the curriculum and deemphasize others.

6. The *learning-centered* teacher has equal concern for the students and for the subject to be learned. The focus is on the individual student's ability. The learning-centered teacher may be more successful than the overtly child-centered or subject-centered teacher when cultural learning patterns are taken into consideration.

Even in monocultural classrooms, the teacher's style is more in accordance with some students than with others. Flexibility becomes a key in reaching more students. In a multicultural classroom, this flexibility is even more crucial. With knowledge of various teaching styles, teachers can examine their own style, observe students' reactions to that style, ask questions about a teacher's expected role and style in the community, and modify their style as necessary (see the examples of the teachers of Warm Springs Indian children in Chapter 2).

Teacher–Student Interactions

The teacher–student relationship is culturally mandated in general ways, although individual relationships vary. The patterns of interaction that characterize a class are related to cultural attitudes toward the teacher. These attitudes may derive from parent–child relationships or from values transmitted by the parent toward teachers and schooling. Some students who have immigrated from other countries may have brought with them very different teacher–student interactions. For example, in some cultures, learning takes place in an absolutely quiet classroom where the teacher is in complete control and authority is never questioned. In other cultures, students talk among themselves and move freely about the classroom, readily criticizing teachers if they feel they are wrong. Attitudes toward authority, teacher–student relationships, and teacher expectation of student achievement vary widely. Yet the heart of the educational process is in the interaction between teacher and student. This determines the quality of education the student receives.

Power and authority are invested in and expected from teachers, and teachers expect respect from students. Respect is communicated verbally and nonverbally and is vulnerable to cultural misunderstanding. In the United States, respect is shown to teachers by looking at them, but in some cultures looking at the teacher is a sign of disrespect. Moreover, students are expected to raise their hands in North American classrooms if they wish to ask or answer a question. Vietnamese culture, on the other hand, does not have a way for students to signal a desire to talk to a teacher; students speak only after the teacher has spoken to them (Andersen & Powell, 1991). In general, one must not conclude that a particular behavior is disrespectful; it may be that the child has learned different customs for communicating with those in authority.

Teacher–student relationships also show cultural influences. In some parts of the world, it is acceptable to call a teacher by the first name indicating that relations between teachers and students are warm, close, and informal. Others may need an explicit communication of warmth and friendliness, and still others may be wary of a teacher's motives and take a long time to share a feeling of rapport. The role of teachers in multicultural classrooms is to make explicit their understandings of the teacher–student relationship, to elicit from students their respective expectations, and to build a mutually satisfying classroom community.

The manner in which a teacher interacts with students does more than communicate a cultural tie: *Teachers' expectations for student achievement* are also a feature of student-teacher interactions. Students of whom much is expected are given more frequent cues and prompts to respond, are asked more and harder questions, are given a longer time to respond, are encouraged to provide more elaborate answers, and are interrupted less often (Good & Brophy, 1984). Teachers tend to be encouraging toward students for whom they have high expectations. They smile at these students more often and show greater warmth through nonverbal responses such as leaning toward the students and nodding their head as students speak (Woolfolk & Brooks, 1985). Some teachers expect more from Asian-Americans than from other minorities because of the "model minority" myth. Acting toward students on the basis of these stereotypes is a form of racism, which is detrimental to all.

Classroom Organization

The typical organization of U.S. classrooms is that of a teacher-leader who gives assignments or demonstrates to the students, who act as audience. Teacher presentations are usually followed by some form of individual study. Learning is then assessed through recitation, quizzes, or some other performance. Small group work, individual projects, or paired learning require distinct participation structures, ways of behaving and speaking. Learning appropriate behaviors in these settings may require explicit cultural adaptation. Many students new to U.S. classrooms have never before taken part in group problem solving, story retelling, or class discussion. Such activities entail social as well as linguistic challenges. Teachers can help students by providing clear instructions and ample models, by calling on more self-confident students first, and by assigning self-conscious students minor roles at first in order not to embarrass them.

The explicit cultural knowledge needed to function well in a classroom is evident when students first encounter school, in preschool or kindergarten. Heath (1983b) describes children from two distinct communities as they play in preschool. Children from one community were able to comply with teachers' rules for various activity centers (block building, reading, playing with puzzles). They had learned in their homes to play only certain kinds of games in certain areas and to put their toys away when finished. Children from a different community did not confine toys to specific areas but, instead, were creative and improvised new and flexible functions for the toys, often mixing items from different parts of the room. A puzzle piece that looked like a shovel, for example, was taken outside to the sandbox. The preschool teacher, in despair, could only remind them, "Put the puzzle pieces back where they belong." As Heath points out:

[These] children . . . were accustomed to playing with toys outdoors almost all of the time and they insisted on taking the school's "indoor toys" outside; at home, almost all their toys stayed outside, under the porch, or wherever they were left when play ended. Moreover, at home, they were accustomed to using toys for purposes they created, not necessarily those which the toy manufacturer had envisioned. (p. 275)

Thus, the cultural difference in the home created differences in the school that teachers used to validate their perceptions about which students were better behaved and which students were more academically capable than others.

Curriculum

Many aspects of the school curriculum are highly abstract and contain themes and activities for which many minority students have little referent. Some teachers, rather than finding ways in which students can become familiar with academically challenging content, are quick to devise alternative activities of lower academic worth. Research on Alaska Native Education suggest a number of abuses perpetrated in the name of "being sensitive to children's cultural backgrounds." Teachers often exempt Alaska Native students from standards applicable to other students. For example, they assign an essay on "Coming to the City from the Village" as a substitute for a research paper. They justify the lack of challenging courses with comments such as, "Well, they are going home to live in their village. What do they need algebra for anyway?" Too many lessons are created featuring stereotypic content (kayaks and caribou) that demonstrate a shallow cultural relevance (Kleinfeld, 1988).

Teachers who lack a solid foundation of cultural knowledge are often guilty of trivializing the cultural content of the curriculum. The sole cultural reference may be to holidays or food, or they may have "ethnic" bulletin boards only during certain times of the year (Black History Month). Books about children of color are read only on special occasions and units about different cultures are taught once and never mentioned again. People from cultures outside the United States are only shown in "traditional" dress and rural settings or, if they are people of color, are always shown as poor. Native Americans are always represented as from the past. Moreover, students' cultures are misrepresented if pictures and books about Mexico, for example, are used to teach about Mexican-Americans or books about Africa are used to teach about African-Americans (Derman-Sparks & Anti-Bias Curriculum Task Force, 1988). The following checklist can help teachers assess the extent to which ethnic, linguistic, and gender biases exist in the curriculum.

- What groups are represented in texts, discussion, and bulletin board displays? Are certain groups invisible?
- Are the roles of minorities and women presented in a separate manner from other content—isolated or treated as a distinct topic?
- Are minorities (and women) treated in a positive, diversified manner or stereotyped into traditional or rigid roles?
- Are the problems faced by minorities presented in a realistic fashion, with a problem-solving orientation?
- Is the language used in the materials inclusive, or are biased terms used such as masculine forms (mankind, mailman)?
- Does the curriculum foster appreciation of cultural diversity?
- Are experiences and activities, other than those common to middle class/ European-American culture, included?

For further resources on eliminating bias and including a multiethnic perspective, see Sadker and Sadker's *Sex Equity Handbook for Schools* (1982) and *Guide for Multicultural Education, Content and Context* (California State Department of Education, 1977).

Parental Involvement in Cultural Mediation

Parent and community involvement supports, encourages, and provides opportunities for parents and educators to work together in educating students. Parents need to become involved in different settings and different levels of the educational process. Parents help teachers to establish a genuine respect for their children and the strengths they bring to the classroom. Parents can work with their own children at home or serve on school committees. Collaborative involvement in school restructuring includes parent and community members who help to set goals and allocate resources.

Parents play an important role as "brokers" or go-betweens who can mediate between the school and home to solve cultural problems and create effective home–school relations (Arvizu, 1992). One Chinese-American parent successfully intervened in a school situation to the benefit of her daughter and her classmates:

> After my daughter was teased by her peers because of her Chinese name, I gave a presentation to her class on the origin of Chinese names, the naming of children in China, and Chinese calligraphy. My daughter has had no more problems about her name. What is more, she no longer complains about her unusual name, and she is proud of her cultural heritage. (Yao, 1988)

It is important that parents not be used in a compensatory manner or given the message that they need to work to bring students "up" to the level of an idealized norm. This approach often makes parents feel that they are the cause of their children's failure in school. Attributing students' lack of success to parental failure does not recognize that the school itself may be the culprit by failing to meet students' needs.

Whether parents are willing to come to school is largely dependent on their attitude toward school, a result in part of the parents' own school experiences. This attitude is also a result of the extent to which they are made welcome to the schools. "Invitational barriers" can exclude parents as well as students. On the other hand, teachers who are willing to reach out to parents and actively solicit information from them about their children and their hopes for their children's schooling are rewarded with a richer understanding of students' potential. Ways to involve parents, as mentioned in Chapter 6 and in earlier parts of this chapter, include the following:

- Establish an explicit open-door policy so parents will know they are welcome.
- Send written information home about classroom assignments and goals, and encourage parents to reply.
- Call parents periodically when things are going well and let them know when they can call.
- Suggest specific ways parents can help in assignments.
- Get to know the community by visiting the community, letting parents know when you are available to visit homes or talk at some other location.
- Arrange several parent conferences a year and let parents talk about their child's achievement.
- Solicit parents' views on education by a simple questionnaire, telephone interviews, or student–parent interviews. (Banks, 1993).

Teachers can play an important role in helping communities preserve primary languages in the home. Parents and older siblings can be encouraged to work with preschool and school-age children in a variety of activities. Rather than recommending that parents speak English more at home (speaking broken English may severely limit the quality and quantity of verbal interaction between parents and children), teachers can encourage parents to verbalize with children in ways that build underlying cognitive skills. They can sit with the child and look at a book, pointing to pictures and asking questions; they can read a few lines and let the child fill in the rest; or let the child retell a familiar story. Children can listen to adults discuss something or observe reading and writing in the primary language. Schools can assist communities with implementing literacy or cultural classes or producing a community primary language newspaper. The school can also educate students and parents on the benefits of learning the home language of the parents and can find ways to make dual-language proficiency a means of gaining prestige at school (Ouk, Huffman, & Lewis, 1988).

The best way to understand culture is to use direct personal observation of social behavior to construct an image of that culture from the perspective of the members of that culture. This understanding can then be used to organize classroom activities in ways that are comfortable for the members of that culture and that promote learning. In a multicultural classroom, there may be no single best way. A variety of activities—ones that appeal to different students in turn—may be the most effective approach. The observation cycle continues as teachers watch students to see *which* approaches meet *whose* needs. The key for the teacher is to be sensitive, flexible, and open.

Chapter 11

The Role of Teachers in Language Planning and Policy

The teacher had a new student who came from Ethiopia and spoke no English. She could not speak the student's language... but rather than allowing him to languish, she chose to allow him to teach the class enough of his native language so that they could all communicate a little bit.... The children got excited about discovering a new language. This led to the teacher doing a unit on Africa complete with a wall-size relief mural of the entire continent. The end result was that the Ethiopian student was treated as a valued part of the class. He was able to contribute the richness of his culture while learning about his new home. (Freeman & Freeman, 1992b)

Teachers have a significant influence over the daily life of students in their classroom. They can actively create a climate of warmth and acceptance for language minority children, supporting the home language while fostering the growth of a second language. Conversely, they can allow policies of the school to benefit only the language majority students by accepting the exclusive use of the dominant language, and permitting majority language students to gain through the social and cultural reward system at the expense of those students who speak minority languages. This day-to-day influence and reaction of teachers amounts to a language policy.

Language policies determine the organization and management of schooling (see Figure I-1). Such factors as class size, allocation of classrooms, availability of primary language instruction, availability of support services for English learners, and funds for curricular materials are determined by policies that are made by decisions at the federal, state, local, or school level. The question of who makes policy and who influences policy is important. Can teachers influence language policy and planning on a scale larger than their single classroom—on a schoolwide level, on a districtwide level, on the level of a community as a whole, on a statewide or national basis? Or are decisions of language planning and policy too remote from the daily life of classrooms for teachers to be influential?

Language planning has been defined by Rubin (1976) as "the study of solutions to language problems by authorized government organizations" (p. 403). Robinson (1988) echoes the idea that language planning is a governmental activity. "Language planning is official, government-level activity concerning the selection and promotion of a unified administrative language or languages. It represents a coherent effort by individuals, groups, or organizations to influence language use or development" (p. 1). The central idea of language planning is that actions and decisions are deliberate: The term *language planning* suggests "an organized pursuit of solutions to language problems typically at the national level" (Fishman, 1973, pp. 23–24). An example of a government language decision is the Voting Rights Act of 1975, which mandates that bilingual ballots be provided in areas in which over 5 percent of the population is non-English-speaking. In many countries of the world, such decisions regarding native languages are top down, stemming from the highest levels of government. In the United States, language decisions are made at many levels, depending on the jurisdiction of the government agencies involved. Therefore, it is important to examine language planning and policy decisions at many levels.

Planning and policies can be formal and official or informal, such as efforts exerted to create and manipulate attitudes toward languages and language variations (Corson, 1990). Both formal and informal policies have an impact on second language teaching. Like it or not, teachers work under conditions that are highly affected by social and political conditions. Language planning is performed on a daily basis by classroom teachers. Ideally, such daily decisions are performed within a context of support for exemplary instructional practices. If this is not the case, classroom teachers' efforts are undermined or undone by other forces.

Teachers *can* influence language planning and policy, and those who are experts on the education of language minority students *should* be influential. If teachers do not influence planning and policy, decisions will be made by others: by the force of popular opinion, by politicians, by bureaucrats, by demagogues. Teacher influence will not be felt, however, by wishing or hoping. Teachers need to examine closely the possibilities that exist for influence on policy and planning, and then work hard to make this influence a reality. This influence can be wielded in different ways in various social and political arenas.

PLANNING AND POLICY IN THE CLASSROOM

Language diversity can be seen as a *problem,* as a *right,* or as a *resource* (Ruiz, 1984). The view that dual language proficiency is a problem that must be remedied is, at best, socially and economically shortsighted and, at worst, the foundation for linguistic genocide (defined by Skutnabb-Kangas, 1993, as "systematic extermination of a minority language"). The position that language diversity is a right has been the basis for the court cases and congressional mandates that have created bilingual education; however, these movements have probably been successful because of the emphasis on transitional efforts, with bilingual education seen as a right that expires when a student makes the shift into English.

The idea that language diversity is a resource—particularly economic, but also social and personal—is a difficult proposition for many North Americans. They share a common belief that this rich continent has infinite natural resources, and investing in human cultural and linguistic resources is not essential. The persistent trade deficit incurred by the United States has been caused in large part because people in other countries use English to market goods successfully in the United States, whereas North Americans, for the most part, are not fluent in two or more languages and cannot reciprocate. Instead of a successful dual language educational system, many schools in the United States allow a young child's primary language to wither and die and then fail to create foreign language proficiency within a three-year high school program. Dual language proficiency has become the privilege of the elite, who can afford private tutors and foreign travel. Too often, the working class maintains conversational proficiency in the primary language but does not attain a high level of cognitive/academic proficiency either in the primary language or in English. A policy that promotes dual language proficiency as a local, state, or national resource begins in the classroom, with teachers who carefully plan and carry out equitable, empowering educational practices.

Educational Equity

Equitable educational practices require discipline and vigilant self-observation on the part of the classroom teacher (Tollefson, 1991). Practicing gender, socioeconomic, racial, and cultural equity requires that males and females from minority and majority races and cultures, whether rich or poor, receive equal opportunity to participate, such as being given equally difficult questions to answer during class discussion, along with adequate verbal and nonverbal support. Cultural equity requires teachers to accept students' personalization of instruction; to use multicultural examples to illustrate points of instruction; to listen carefully to the stories and voices of the students from various cultures; and to tie together home and school for the benefit of the students. Issues of socioeconomic equity arise, for example, when assignments for at-home projects are evaluated more highly when they incorporate a wealth of resources that some families can provide and others cannot. Teachers must endeavor to extend the rich, close relationship of mentor and protégé to all students. Referrals to special education, on the one hand, and to gifted or enriched instruction, on the other, should not favor or target students of one gender, race, or culture unfairly. (If school site or district criteria result in de facto lack of equity in these areas, teachers may need to ask for a review of the criteria.) Practicing "everyday equity" ensures the possibility of equal opportunity for all. The following class-room policies promote inclusion for students:

- Teachers value the experiences of culturally different children.
- The primary language is seen as a worthy subject for instruction and as a means by which students can acquire knowledge.
- Classroom strategies guarantee boys and girls equal access to the teacher's attention.

The Social Environment

Students come to school for social as well as academic reasons. In observing instruction, students who are socially successful, for a variety of reasons, are often assigned a "halo effect" that makes them also appear more academically successful (Lotan & Benton, 1989). Cohen has demonstrated that an equitable social environment is furthered when cooperative grouping explicitly treats the status differences among students in the classroom (Cohen, DeAvila, Navarrete, & Lotan, 1988; Cohen, Lotan, & Catanzarite, 1990).

School practices in noncurricular areas, such as discipline, and in extra-curricular activities, such as school clubs, should be nondiscriminatory. These activities provide ways in which the school climate can foster or retard students' multicultural competence (Bennett, 1986). If the school climate is accepting of the linguistic and cultural identities of students, these identities will develop in ways that are consonant with an academic environment. If not, a resistance culture may develop that rejects schooling, with outcomes such as high dropout rates and high incidences of school vandalism. The formal and the hidden curriculum of a school need to be consistent with one another so that they support diversity and achievement. The social climate of the school can be one of acceptance for all students in the following ways:

- Culturally and linguistically diverse students are grouped heterogeneously.
- Children and staff learn about the cultural practices of the families represented in the school.

- Students can win prestige positions in extracurricular activities regardless of their ethnic or cultural background.
- Dress codes do not discriminate against some subcultures while allowing others to dress as they wish.
- School staff (e.g., office personnel) are equally courteous to all students and visitors.

The Policies Embodied in Teachers' Plans

Teachers can be explicit about issues of equity and multicultural inclusion in planning yearly units and daily lessons. Teachers are responsible for obtaining materials that are nonbiased and promote positive role models from a variety of ethnic groups, and for designing and planning instruction that makes success possible for all students. This responsibility cannot be transferred to other decision-making bodies. Materials are readily available that describe multicultural education (see Bennett, 1990; Harris, 1992; Nieto, 1992); it is each teacher's responsibility to make these approaches real for students. Teachers can plan for culturally and linguistically fair instruction in the following ways:

- Students' interests and backgrounds are taken into consideration when planning instruction.
- Materials depict individuals of both genders and of various races and cultures in ways that suggest success.
- Materials for bilingual and multicultural instruction receive an equitable share of budgeted resources.
- Daily plans include adequate time for development of primary language skills.

POLICY AT THE SCHOOL LEVEL

Demonstrating outstanding instruction is a teacher's greatest contribution at the school site. Positive outcomes in the classroom are evident throughout the school as students of exemplary teachers provide leadership, goodwill, and academic models for other students. Teachers can play explicit roles in school site decision making, whether or not restructuring efforts have encouraged this.

Collaboration with Colleagues

Schools can benefit greatly when teachers work together. Sharing resources, working together to plan instruction, and teaching with each other add insights and vitality to a job that is often isolating. However, not all teachers at a school seek collaboration. Those teachers who choose to work together should do so, while others may wish to work alone. Regardless, it is vital that personal relations be established and maintained with all colleagues at a school site to ensure that the staff not be polarized along lines of cultural, linguistic, or philosophical differences. Decisions that are often made collaboratively are the following:

- Extra duty assignments are adjusted for teachers who must translate letters sent home to parents or develop primary language materials.
- Assistance is available for teachers whose classes are affected by students who may be making a transition out of primary language instruction.
- Primary language materials and other materials are freely shared among professional staff.
- Primary language instructors are socially integrated with the mainstream staff.

School-Site Leadership

School authorities, particularly principals, can support ELD and bilingual instruction in many ways. Often, principals are the leading advocates for funding increases at the district level. Principals can work with teachers to configure classes and class sizes to the benefit of the language minority students. Appointing a lead or mentor teacher can help new teachers to adjust to and meet the needs of language minority students. Lead teachers may be able to develop professional presentations that showcase student abilities or program features. Districtwide principals' meetings or school board meetings may be venues where these presentations can be seen and heard. By communicating to others about students' abilities as well as innovative program structures for language minority students, principals begin to develop a climate of acceptance for linguistic and cultural diversity. This can be accomplished in the following ways:

- Grading policies are monitored to ensure that all students have equal opportunity to receive high grades.
- Staff members with expertise in English language development or primary language instruction are given time to be of assistance to other teachers.
- Teachers with English language development or primary language assignments are given an equal share of mentoring and supervisory assistance.
- Leaders in the school set an example of respect and encouragement for diverse language abilities and cultures within the school.

The Academic Ambiance of the School

Schools that are noted for academic excellence attract community attention because of the success of their students and alumni. Academic competitions outside of schools are one way in which certain schools garner academic laurels and gain the reputation for an academic ambiance. Although spelling bees are traditional competitive events, too often these promote decontextualized skills. Academic decathlons, by contrast, are team efforts in which dedicated teachers can involve students from many ability levels. The better examples of this type of competition tend to promote problem solving rather than simple recall skills. Competitions that require inventive thinking are also available, and the fact that these are less language-dependent may be more attractive to English learners. Schools can foster an academic ambiance in a variety of ways:

- Teachers who sponsor academically oriented extracurricular activities are given extra pay as are athletic coaches.
- Funds are available for students to travel to intellectual competitions.
- Individuals from diverse cultural and linguistic backgrounds are actively solicited for teams that compete for academic awards.
- Some intellectual activities such as contests are held in the primary language.

Involving Parents

Encouraging parents to participate in school activities is vital. The extra step of sending parents letters, reports, and notices in their home language helps to build rapport and extend a welcome to the school. These language policies constitute the daily message that home languages are important and valued. Parents can receive the message that they are valued in many ways:

- Representative parent committees can advise and consent on practices that involve culturally and linguistically diverse students.
- Parents can use the school library to check out books with their children.
- School facilities can be made available for meetings of community groups.

POLICY IN LOCAL SCHOOL DISTRICTS

The policies of the local school districts are shaped by the values of the community. This may create frustration for teachers who feel that educational decisions are not in the hands of educators. On the other hand, teachers who take responsibility for helping to shape the community's beliefs and values may find that their leadership as teachers is very welcome.

Professional Growth and Service

Serving on district curriculum adoption committees is a way in which teachers can share and contribute their expertise. Teacher-led presentations to other teachers, staff, or community members are also important contributions. Many opportunities exist for such service. Service clubs such as Rotary and Kiwanis provide opportunities for speakers: What better way to reach the business leaders of the community with current information about multicultural and linguistic issues? These activities deliver the message that teachers are knowledgeable and interested in the community at large. Consider the following ideas for teacher involvement:

- Teachers' opinions are consulted for materials purchased by school district and community libraries.
- Teachers perform staff training for others.
- Teachers can participate in leadership training for language minority student programs.

The School Board

Teachers are very much aware that school policies are determined by the beliefs of school board members as well as by legal precedents set by state and federal court decisions. Part of the advocacy position suggested by Cazden (1986) is the need for teachers of language minority students to espouse and support ESL and bilingual programs before local boards. Federal regulations for schools receiving Title VII (Office of Bilingual Education and Minority Languages Affairs, U.S. Department of Education) funds mandate that school districts organize and maintain parent advisory groups at the school site level. Such parent groups can be effective in marshaling support for programs designed for language minority groups. School board policies can be influenced in positive ways:

- Policy committees can place policies before the school board in a timely manner, with clear, concise, well-researched presentations.
- Frequent attendance at school board meetings sends the message that the meetings are monitored by friends of language minority issues.

COMMUNITY SUPPORT FOR LANGUAGE MINORITY STUDENTS

A supportive community offers a home for linguistic and cultural diversity. This support takes many forms: affirming variety in neighbors' lifestyles, patronizing minority businesses, fundraising for college scholarships for language minority students, and providing community services that are user-friendly for all.

The Public Forum

Communities accept other languages being spoken in the community if there is little fear of economic or political encroachment by immigrants. The following case study illustrates one community's reaction to linguistic diversity:

> Monterey Park, a California community with a large number of Chinese immigrants, was designated an all-American city because of its apparent racial harmony. The Fall 1986 edition of the community activities publication featured articles on the Monterey Park golf course, senior citizens' center, and other local services and included a page written in Chinese to summarize the contents of the issue. Even as this issue was in press, however, a city council meeting in June of that year passed resolutions endorsing legislation to make English the official language of the United States (Roy, 1990). Dicker (1992) describes the following incident. Barry Hatch, a Monterey Park city council member and supporter of the state proposal making English the official language, led a fight to halt the use of public funds for the purchase of Chinese language books for the city's library. Viewing these books as solely benefiting the Chinese community overlooks the fact that the Chinese population has as much right to be supported by the government as any other group. Furthermore, such a view does not recognize the possibility that English-speaking Americans studying Chinese might benefit from these books. In this case, the linguistic chauvinism of a community leader determined local language policy in a de facto manner.

Policies of community agencies such as the library can be influenced by the following teacher-led activities:

- Librarians can file teachers' lesson plans in the library and make specific materials accessible to students.
- Bilingual teachers can justify to librarians the need for primary language materials.
- Schools can encourage parents to make better use of community resources such as libraries.

Community Organizations

Service organizations are often run by community leaders who set the tone for the community and who are a source of employment for workers. Business leaders sometimes have strong ideas about education. They usually enjoy dialogue with professional educators and seek to be updated on current beliefs and practices. It is in this dialogue that professional educators need to present the foundation for current pedagogy. The leaders of community organizations want to help schools to improve so that their children and their workers will be productive. Obtaining this help is easier when requests are concrete and the justification is strong.

Opposing Everyday Racism

In the teachers' lounge, at the post office, and at social gatherings, people express opinions about others' behavior. Often these opinions serve to test the waters, to find out who else holds similar opinions. Remarks that are derogatory to individuals on the basis of race, language, or culture do not further liberty and justice for all. One minority teacher responded to such comments by widening her eyes and saying, "Why, it surprises me to hear a person like you express that kind of opinion." In this way she affirms the person while refusing to accept the derogatory sentiment. Letters to the editor of the local paper are sometimes sources of misinformation or expressed prejudice. Literate people need to protest to the editor of newspapers that publish overtly racist letters and should write letters to rebut such opinions. Teachers and other staff members can oppose racism in several ways:

- Teachers can refuse to use materials that contain derogatory images toward certain races and cultures.
- Majority group members can promote the appreciation of minority cultures.
- The school can feature minority languages and cultures in school shows, written communications, and displays.

STATE COMMISSIONS AND PROFESSIONAL ORGANIZATIONS

Outside the immediate community, a larger community awaits. Statewide commissions organized by the office of the governor or state boards of education are opportunities for teachers to be involved in writing statewide curricula, adopting textbooks, and serving on advisory boards. Professional organizations at the state and national level have state counterparts. Joining TESOL (Teachers of English to Speakers of Other Languages) or NABE (National Association for Bilingual Education) puts educators in contact with language development specialists nationally and internationally. TESOL and NABE publications carry news from state affiliates, and newsletters from the state organizations carry news of local associations. If there is no local organization, why not start one?

The Voice of the Expert

Attending district or regional professional conferences is a beginning step toward developing one's own expertise on linguistic and cultural issues and teaching practices. Successful teachers may be able to join with colleagues to develop school-level or district-level presentations about some area of instruction. Reading articles in professional magazines and journals helps to develop particular expertise, as does advanced university coursework. Some journals and publishers solicit publications from teachers. This is one way to share successful classroom practices.

Professional Leadership Roles

A career is developed over a lifetime. Expertise in particular areas continues to grow along with teaching experience. One can envision a more just and equitable society thirty years from now as today's new teachers reap the harvest of the support for linguistic and cultural diversity that they have promoted. Who acts as a leader in the teaching profession is a direct function of who has the energy to devote to policy issues outside the classroom. Those who are willing to take responsibility within professional organizations by serving on committees, drafting proposals, attending meetings, calling members, stuffing envelopes, and other activities are those who can be called on to serve in leadership positions. It is particularly important for mentors and other experienced teachers to invite beginning teachers to professional meetings so the organizations can benefit from fresh energy. In this way, new teachers can form relationships with peers outside their school site.

Legislation and Public Opinion

State and national legislators are responsive to popular opinion as expressed by letters of support and phone calls on controversial issues. Bilingual education and language issues often arouse strong emotions, perhaps because language itself is so closely connected to the soul of a person or because language policies affect the criteria set for success in the employment vital to economic survival and success in the United States (Heath, 1983a). It is important for legislators to hear from professionals in the field to balance the effect of those who perceive that language and cultural diversity as a threat. The debate that takes place within a legislature brings to public attention the issues involved in any complex area of public life, and allows a public forum for criticizing government policies (Jewell, 1976). The strong backing of professional organizations supports legislators who have the courage to promote dual language education. Public policy can be supported in the following ways:

- Organizations can send subscriptions to professional magazines to legislative libraries.
- Teachers and parents can organize letter-writing campaigns and visit legislators personally to convey interest in language minority issues.

INFLUENCING FEDERAL POLICIES

In countries where more than one language is spoken, rarely do these languages share an equal social status. Speakers of the dominant language are those who make social policy, including language policy. These policies can range from support for the subordinate language, through benign neglect, to overt language suppression. Decisions are primarily made on political and economic grounds and reflect the values of those in political power (Bratt Paulston, 1992). In general, language situations within a country are symptoms of social and cultural conditions. In the history of the United States, decisions about subordinate languages were sometimes supportive; early schooling in German for German immigrants was common, and a number of states, beginning with Wisconsin in 1854, passed laws prohibiting school authorities from interfering with German or any foreign language in the public schools. The hysteria that swept the country at the onset of World War I resulted in aggressive policy decisions to eradicate non-English languages from the public schools. The approximately 9 million German-Americans who had been striving to support German schools, newspapers, and religious and community organizations met a backlash of anti-German feelings as German was barred not just from many private and public schools but also from public meetings, telephone conversations, and the streets (Hakuta, 1986). Japanese-language schools were closed down during World War II, and Hispanics were commonly punished for using Spanish in the schools until the 1960s. This pendulum swing from support to suppression defines the extremes of U.S. second language policy. In times of plenty, the attitude toward immigrant languages has been benign neglect. Americans tend to rely on social pressure to enforce the English-only dominance of society. In times of stress, explicit attempts are made to suppress other languages. The current English-only movement (see Chapter 6) is just such an attempt.

English-only groups are particularly incensed by state services in foreign languages, such as drivers' tests, welfare applications, school notices, and state university financial aid forms (Crawford, 1992). Bilingual education funds are the particular target of their lobbying efforts. The success of this movement in California is particularly ironic because Spanish was widely used in early California, and the first California state constitution was written in both English and Spanish (Roy, 1990). Language planning and policy has been influenced by economic and social climates ranging from supportive to repressive; on the whole, teachers have traditionally made little effort to exert any influence within the sphere of these forces. Teachers, however, particularly through their professional organizations, have an increasingly important role to play in public debate.

Federal Funds for Innovation

The grant funds available to school districts through the Office of Bilingual Education and Minority Languages Affairs (Title VII) can provide leverage to create better schooling opportunities for language minority students. Teachers can work with district grant specialists to write successful grant proposals in categories such as Transitional Bilingual Education, Developmental Bilingual Education, Short-Term Training, Academic Excellence, and other categories open to school district applications. One does not have to teach in a bilingual classroom to initiate grant proposals.

It is important, however, to use the grant programs to increase the long-term capacity of the school district to deliver services to language minority children, so that programs do not wither and die when federal funds are no longer available. Notices about competitions for funds and special programs are usually available from state and county offices of education. Individuals who have competed successfully for such funds may be willing to offer workshops for others to increase the general expertise in such areas.

Federal Legislation

Programs such as Title VII originate in Congress. Periodically, such programs must be reauthorized and legislation introduced that continues or modifies them. At such intervals, public opinion plays a large role in determining the continuation of programs that benefit language minority students. When bills are introduced that commit federal funds on a large scale to minorities, conservative forces within Congress often target these programs for extinction. At these times, lobbying efforts are needed to communicate the demand for these programs. Cards and letters to congressional representatives may be requested by professional organizations. This is a chance for teachers to use the literacy they advocate.

At the national level, there is also a strong movement toward the establishment of national educational standards in various content areas. These standards would be used as benchmarks of achievement. With this terminology comes the underlying assumption that some kind of testing would be instituted. Although some educators promise that exciting and innovative means could be used to display exemplary student work (see Sizer & Rogers, 1993), others warn that these standards would prove to be unfair to language minority students (Garcia, 1993). The argument is that national assessments would be problematic because there is no guarantee that these assessments would take place in the student's language. Those students who are in transitional and/or dual language programs may be penalized. Moreover, the fact that assessments are being developed in discreet knowledge domains (mathematics, science, and English-language arts) tends to disregard current pedagogy which emphasizes the importance of instruction that is integrated across subject matter domains. Thus, the national standards would represent a throwback to the separation of content areas, a process that is particularly harmful to the acquisition of a second language. It is important to hear the voices of teachers in the debate about national standards.

The National Spirit

A national spirit is created in part by individuals who voice their opinions freely. A national magazine, for example, offers a platform to writers whose opinions can be influential. These magazines are responsive to consumer forces. Writing letters to national magazines on a regular basis helps editors sense the opinions of their readers. Teachers need to exercise their writing skills frequently and at length in order to participate in national arguments that are rehearsed in the media.

Controversial actions and media figures also shape the national spirit. When demagogues arise who voice reactionary or incendiary viewpoints, the population at large must take steps to defuse their voices. Letters to national networks voicing an opposition and distaste for antiminority or racist viewpoints, for example, are necessary in order that these media do not glorify controversial figures and give them undue voice. The United States operates on a system of checks and balances. Those who oppose racism or bigotry must speak up and must speak as loudly as the voices of separation and intolerance. Often, teachers of language minority students must become advocates for their concerns until the voices of the minority community become skilled enough to speak for themselves and powerful enough to be heard. Teachers who share the culture and language of the minority community have a natural function as community leaders.

CONCLUSIONS

In a nation consisting of 260 million people, the majority of whom share English as the language of daily interchange, the language skills and rights of minorities are a fragile resource. In times of economic hardship, the majority often turns on the minorities, looking for scapegoats. In times of exterior threats, such as in the national crisis of a world war, differences are forgotten and the efforts of all citizens, including minorities, are needed to achieve victory. Unfortunately, too often in the past, the call for national unity has resulted in segregation, repression, or expulsion of minority groups.

Social and political forces on a national scale may seem overwhelming. Indeed, as much as individualism is a part of the national mythology of the United States, the individual is important only when backed by hundreds of thousands of supporters or hundreds of thousands of dollars. To attain national influence, teachers need to achieve the leadership of large professional organizations and use this leadership wisely to effect constructive change in the education of language minority children. This constructive change is possible at every level, from the national to the local, by the use of appropriate professional activities.

At the level of the classroom, language planning and policy mean creating an educational and social climate that makes school a place where all students are comfortable, where all students meet success in learning. The days are past when the failure of large numbers of language minority students could be blamed on the students' personal shortcomings or supposed deficiencies in family backgrounds. When students fail to learn, schools and teachers have failed.

If teachers are willing to step outside the confines of the classroom to help students be successful, then it is time to learn how to influence policy on a larger scale. The belief that teachers have no role in language planning and language politics is a denial of professional responsibility, an abdication of authority. A teacher who believes in the potential for success of language minority students is in a strong position to fight for the recognition of their rights and the allocation of resources that make educational success possible.

Chapter *12*

<hr>

Theory and Practice: Elementary and Secondary Programs and Issues

The U.S. school system is constantly being challenged. The influx of immigrants from nations across the world is not new. At present, the schools of the United States are a microcosm of the world, opening their doors to students with diverse ethnic, racial, and linguistic backgrounds. The task of educating these students is at once daunting and exhilarating. To point out possibilities in working with language minority students, this final chapter will describe how elementary and secondary faculty grapple with cultural, linguistic, and academic issues in program design and management. First, a case study is presented of a teacher whose instruction meets the needs of multicultural and multilingual students. This is followed by a description of an evolving elementary program that has been especially tailored to meet the needs of English learners. Next, a case study is presented in the form of a conversation in a faculty lounge at a high school to illustrate a variety of opinions about educating language minority students. This is followed by a discussion of the challenges peculiar to secondary programs.

HELP: A HOLISTIC ENGLISH LITERACY PROGRAM FOR MULTILINGUAL ELEMENTARY CLASSROOMS

(with Monica Ford)

The underlying assumptions, pedagogical practices, and cultural and linguistic understandings discussed in this book have been effectively put into practice in a number of schools and classrooms across the United States. The following scenario and description highlight a program being implemented at Elderberry School in Ontario, California (Ford, 1992; Weed & Johns, 1992).

A Second-Grade Multiethnic/Multilingual Class: A Case Study

The ethnic makeup of the 31 children in Monica Ford's second-grade classroom was not unusual for an urban southern California school: 1 Vietnamese child labeled LEP (limited-English proficient); 2 African-Americans; 8 Hispanics whose language proficiency has been designated with labels—1 NEP (non-English proficient), 4 LEP, and 3 FEP (fluent-English proficient); 8 Hispanics who are native speakers of English; and 12 European-Americans. Monica, a third-year teacher, had participated in an excellent teacher education program but was struggling with the demands of a linguistically diverse student classroom population. What was unusual was that Monica did not regard linguistic diversity as an insurmountable problem to be left to experts. She believes that all children can learn, and that a sound, integrated curricular program is beneficial for all. In order to learn, *all* children must be immersed in a language-rich environment. They must be provided daily with experiences that give them opportunities to express themselves and to interact with others. This is important for all students, but particularly crucial for language minority children. The fastest way for them to learn, according to Monica, is to use language. Thus, all children are involved daily in "reading the room" (reading the charts, poems, posters, songs posted around the room), silent reading, listening to stories on tapes, taking turns reading and listening to others read, reading with the teacher, writing in their journals, and writing stories based on their literature books.

Monica and two other teachers worked throughout the year to develop a thematic, integrated curriculum. They chose a theme for each month, selected resources, worked on lesson outlines, and planned guest speakers and field trips. Through the integrated curriculum, a variety of experiences built on each other and helped the children achieve one of the teachers' goals—for children to have confidence in their language ability. To accomplish this goal, the children in Monica's room read and wrote every single day and were actively involved in all the language processes. Monica spent much of her time observing, pulling students individually for specific needs, pairing and grouping those who would benefit from working together, and prodding, pushing, and cajoling.

In October, the theme was "Weather." One of the literature books included with the district-adopted basal text was *Cloudy with a Chance of Meatballs* by Judi Barrett. A few days before the children were to begin working with the text, Monica read the story aloud to them. They then brainstormed all the items they could think of under the title "Foods." Monica copied their ideas onto a large blue "plate" she had cut from butcher paper. This plate was posted and became incorporated into the daily "reading-the-room" (environmental reading) activity. All students were thus exposed to the words and concepts on a *continuing* basis and many asked to add words to the chart.

Instead of working directly with the book first, a task that could have been daunting for many beginning second-grade students, Monica instead helped the students produce their own books following the *Cloudy* storyline. Since this was the first book-writing activity, she provided frame sentences that incorporated the main episodes from the story and the spelling words designated in the basal text. The students copied the sentences from sentence strips in a pocket chart, added their own words or those found on the poster, and illustrated their books. Their books consisted of the title and four pages:

Cloudy with a Chance of _____

1 Once in Chewandswallow it rained only _____.

2 Awful things were beginning to happen. On Friday there was a hurricane of _____.

3 There was a storm of _____ that nearly shut down the school. (A phrase that the children particularly enjoyed!)

4 To escape they made rafts of _____ and sailed away.

These books were then used during the reading portion of the program. Activities included read-arounds where groups of children read their respective versions to each other, buddy reading where two children took turns reading their own stories, silent reading, and book exchanges where children read the others' versions. The original book, with copies for all students, was also available for reading, comparing, and discussing.

In this initial book-making, reading activity, the teacher provided a means for all children to feel successful. They all had practice in listening to a story, using that story as a model for one of their own, and reading their own and the original story. They had produced a product that was meaningful to them, that could help all students develop skill in reading, and that allowed them to work at their own level. This particular activity, using frame sentences, has often been aimed at beginning readers and has not always been transferred for use with language minority students in regular classrooms. It should be apparent how the practice in hearing and rehearing, writing and illustrating, and reading and rereading can be of particular benefit to these students.

The next book to be read was *The Cloud Book* by Tomie de Paola. A poem, "What does a cloud feel like," was also introduced, and again the students brainstormed, this time on words relating to how something feels. These words were then transferred onto a large cloud that was also hung in the classroom and became part of the daily "reading-around-the-room." The children made large, puffy clouds (of butcher paper stuffed with newspaper) that were hung from the ceiling over their group tables. They studied kinds of clouds and they made cloud books. Cotton was formed into various cloud types on each page of dark blue construction paper These were then labeled with chalk. More books were then available to read, share, discuss, and add to the growing classroom collection.

A final writing activity came after the children had heard, chanted, and beat the rhythm of patterned poems about nature. They used descriptive words from the cloud poster they had previously brainstormed or their own words, and wrote their own poems. Because these poems were to be "published," the children were involved in the complete writing process, including writing a rough draft, sharing, peer editing, and writing a final draft. The final draft was written on light blue raindrops, which were then hung below the hanging clouds.

As Monica pointed out, she was still following the prescribed program of her school, using the basal readers and accompanying books, using the designated spelling words, and involving the students in writing. The difference was in the way she organized her program, allowing all the children to meet with success. The poems shown in Figure 12-1 are illustrative of those produced in her class. Samples of both "average" native-English speakers and language minority students are included. Can you tell which are the language minority students'?

The products of all the children in the class show the usual range that can be found in a class of 31 children. The ESL children are able to produce work of the same high quality as the native-English-speaking. The activities are such that the children not only feel success but they *show* their successes by publishing their work. An important component of this classroom for the language minority students is that language is available to them on a continuing basis. They are not introduced to a new word or concept one day and moved on to something different the next. They are surrounded in an atmosphere of sounds and the sounds they hear one day are visually available to them from that moment on. There is continuous sharing of work so that the children are exposed not only to "teacher talk" but to that of their fellow students as well.

The HELP Program

The classroom atmosphere and activities shared in the preceding section highlight what one teacher can accomplish in working with a linguistically and ethnically mixed group of students. By the following year, however, the student population at Elderberry School where Monica is a teacher had

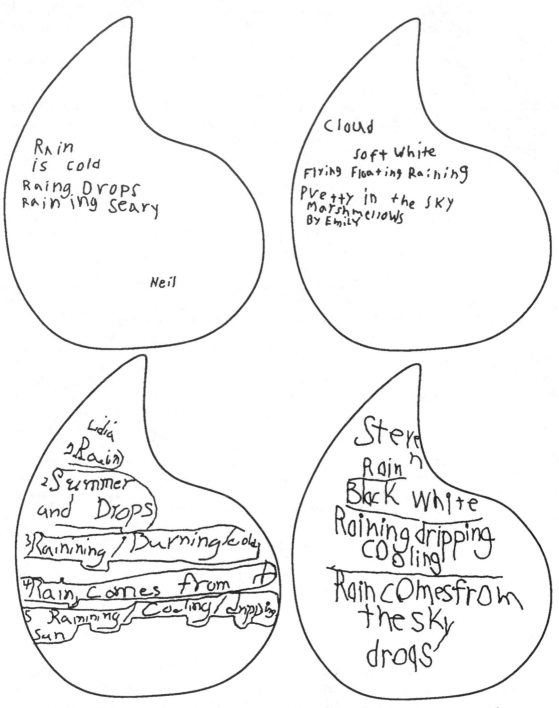

The examples on the left were done by LEP students.

FIGURE 12-1   Limited-English and Native English-Speaking Children's Poems.

become increasingly diverse. Many students traveled to Elderberry School from another part of town on buses. Of the 659 students in grades 1 through 6, approximately 70 percent came from diverse, multicultural backgrounds. These increasing numbers posed challenges for the school as a whole and for the bilingual program in particular. There were only two Spanish-speaking bilingual teachers for the large number of children whose primary language was Spanish, but no teacher or aide for those with other primary languages. Few teachers had expertise in working with language minority students. The situation came to a head when the principal pointed out that a young Armenian boy was doing quite well in his bilingual first-grade class. He was in fact becoming bilingual—in Armenian and Spanish!

The question became "How can *the school as a whole* meet the needs of all its students?" The challenges identified by the school included a large and increasingly diverse population of students whose age, needs, and English literacy ranged widely; a lack of qualified staff to address primary languages and English language development; a lack of adequate or appropriate role models in bilingual classrooms; and isolation and segregation of children from their peers. As a first step, the principal and staff established a Language Development Council to look into various models and curriculum designs on which to base a new program.

After evaluation of program options, student population, staff, and resources (the only funding source was the district's existing bilingual budget), no single existing program design was found to fit the school's needs. Therefore, the staff took a variety of components from several programs, and, using the Continuity Model (Weed & Díaz-Rico; see Appendix A) as a framework, developed a new model based on a whole language philosophy. HELP (Holistic English Literacy Program) was born.

The program is designed to address the language, academic, and social needs of Elderberry's multilingual students who are acquiring English as another language. It uses specially designed English language instruction, curriculum, and materials to help language minority students develop English language proficiency. A key tenet of this whole language–based program is that no one becomes literate without personal involvement with literacy. All children come to school with language and experience. To facilitate their second language acquisition and to ensure a meaningful education, HELP begins by finding out the ways in which children are already readers and writers. Their life experiences and culture are incorporated into daily routines, and the curriculum is negotiated with the students.

In the initial year (1991–1992), five classrooms were reconfigured to include only non-English- and limited English-speaking students. Three teachers—Monica (second grade), Irma (fourth/fifth grade), and Liza (bilingual third grade)—collaborated to implement the program across several grade levels. In addition, two first-grade teachers worked together following the program's stated goals. The following description recounts the evolution of the program based on the experiences of the three cross-grade teachers.

HELPing teachers. One of the challenges at the school was to overcome the deficit myths about language minority students. Priority was given to teacher education with the aim of increasing sensitivity and appreciation for multicultural students. This benefited all staff, but not all were interested in participating in a newly designed program. Interested teachers attended summer training in preparation for additional certification that allowed them to provide ESL and academic instruction to language minority students. This training provided a common base of knowledge and increased multicultural awareness among participating teachers. It also enabled them to express goals and concerns for the children in the program more effectively with one another.

On an ongoing basis, the HELP team uses weekly meetings to share in thematic planning, referring to state guidelines and the Ontario/Montclair School District's master curriculum to ensure that grade level requirements are being met. As a collaborating team of teachers, they provide each other with suggestions and feedback on ideas and strategies. They share solutions to problems and, together, discuss students' progress, evaluate program goals, and form objectives such as those listed in Table 12-1. Overall, the teachers believe they have become better teachers by being part of a collaborating team. They share equally in their responsibility to the students. From their several perspectives, they gain a better view of students' individual strengths and needs and are able to plan more effectively for meaningful instruction. Together, they learn from their students and from each other. As part of a team, the sense of isolation has been alleviated.

HELPing students. The teachers decided to group children across the range of grade levels (2 through 5) and stages of English language proficiency. Such grouping took advantage of cross-age and peer tutoring situations and made class sizes more equitable. Initially, the groups were divided by stages of English language acquisition (Krashen & Terrell, 1983), but it soon was apparent that more heterogeneous groups were needed in order to have successful collaboration among the children.

Groups of children rotate through a daily schedule that takes them to each teacher's classroom. On Mondays, Thursdays, and Fridays, the children follow the same schedule. On Wednesdays, participating teachers share a preparation period in the morning that allows for program and thematic planning. During this time, the children participate in physical education along with children from mainstream classes under the direction of a specialized physical education teacher. By grouping students and having them rotate among the classrooms, the teachers are able to capitalize on each one's area of interest and expertise. About 100 students are able to flow through Liza Syndergaard's primary language classroom four out of five days a week. During their time in Liza's classroom, children are engaged in the same types of literacy experiences found in any whole language classroom. The only difference lies in the language used by the teacher (Spanish). Liza uses

TABLE 12-1   HELP Teacher Objectives

HELP teachers will continually strive to do the following:

- Create a curriculum that is meaningful and child-centered.
- Create an environment where the social nature of language is respected and provided for.
- Establish use of cooperative and flexible learning groups.
- Provide for all levels of English language proficiency and learning styles.
- Provide adequate amounts of comprehensible input.
- Develop language across all areas of the curriculum.
- Plan thematic cycles that span the curriculum and are built from student interests and background experiences.
- Use quality literature containing positive multicultural perspectives and images to provide the basis for instruction.
- Make available to children materials that enhance literacy.
- Provide many opportunities for children to progress naturally in literacy, ensuring ample time is given to uninterrupted reading and writing.
- Integrate use of technology that enhances literacy.
- Use authentic assessment that focuses on children's strengths.
- Accept close approximations and children's oral and written miscues, providing guidance as children progress toward conventions.
- Accept music, literature, drama, and art as expressions and valid interpretations of meaning and understanding.
- Keep evaluation in perspective, and use information gained to plan for future instruction.

theme cycling (Edelsky, Altwerger, & Flores, 1991) as a means of pursuing lines of inquiry that are based on children's interests and questions. Because themes are common among the classes, misinterpretations or lack of understanding of content presented in other classrooms can be explored and clarified. Rotating Spanish-speaking children through Liza's class has benefited more children than was previously possible, without overwhelming her with an extremely large class size.

Grouping also makes it possible for more children to make use of the technology available at the school. Irma Reitz uses her expertise to teach children how to use multimedia (audio and video equipment, including VCRs, video disc players, video cameras, and related computer software) and computers as tools for authoring and publishing. These provide children with comprehensible input in the form of information that they can readily access. As part of the integrated curriculum that spans HELP classrooms, multimedia and computers are invaluable tools.

In Monica's classroom, the authoring cycle serves as a curricular frame (Harste, Short, & Burke, 1988). Aspects of this were described in the case study at the beginning of the chapter.

The teachers found that they had to let go of the idea that one specific group of children "belonged" to them for the entire day. The result has been that the children feel that all the participating teachers "belong" to them. To facilitate children seeing teachers as a team, everyone meets together for about fifteen to twenty minutes each morning for oral language activities that include chants, songs, and poems. The safety in very large numbers gets everyone involved and is always fun. As they interact and relate to a wider range of both children and adults during the school day, children in the program have truly become less isolated.

HELPing parents. Parents play an integral role in HELP. HELP teachers have found most parents to be very willing to help at home and to be extremely concerned about their children's success at school. A major obstacle has been that they did not know *how* to help. Quarterly meetings are held with parents in which they receive program information, participate actively in developing goals for the program, and discuss schoolwide issues and options. These meetings are in addition to regularly scheduled Back-to-School Night, Open House, and parent–teacher conferences. They are scheduled at times suggested by the parents. Liza is present at meetings to interpret for Spanish-speaking parents; other interpreters, many who are parents themselves, also volunteer to help out.

Parents are also actively involved in a home reading program with their children. They are encouraged to read to and with their children in their home language. The teachers emphasize the importance of children becoming literate in two languages, and encourage parents to be their child's best access to their native language. Parents fill out weekly logs of their child's home reading and return it to school each Friday.

Parents are also asked to volunteer in the classroom. For many different reasons, this often is not possible. Many who do not live near Elderberry lack transportation; others work during school hours; or have younger children to care for. For these parents, a program of recording stories was initiated. A tape and recorder are sent home, and the parents choose what they would like to record. They return the tape and loan the book from which they have read. Another option they often use is retelling favorite stories, which they then write down and illustrate with the help of their children. At school, these are placed in the listening center and made available to all children. Children take great pride in sharing with others what they and their parents have contributed. This has added access to primary language by children with diverse languages. It has also proved to be one of the greatest ways of encouraging home literacy events. The parents often express their pride in being able to contribute to their child's education in a very meaningful way.

Weekly homework notices are sent home to inform parents of requirements for their children. Songs and poetry introduced in the classroom are sent home to read and practice and make up a great deal of the homework, which includes daily home reading. Parents are also kept abreast of classroom happenings through the students' publication of a monthly newsletter. Parents enjoy seeing their child's published work in the newsletter and encourage them to work toward this goal. In many ways, parents have proven to be the program's greatest assets.

Conclusion. During the 1991–1992 academic year, Elderberry School implemented the Holistic English Literacy Program. The program's first year (described here) focused on students in grades 2 through 5. The challenges still exist that the school faced when the program began. The number of students acquiring English as a second language continues to increase. Although some teachers continue to teach in traditional ways, others are interested in adopting classroom techniques that increase success for language minority students. In the second year (1992–1993), the program expanded to include grades 1 through 6. Some of the students from the first year were placed in mainstream classes, and a mainstream teacher's class was integrated into the HELP rotation. This integration facilitated further interaction among students—language minority students worked with native-English students on academic projects and native-English students began learning Spanish from the bilingual teacher. In the third year, further expansion with other mainstream classes (along the lines proposed in the Continuity Model) is planned.

With HELP, teachers have found support through collaborative team teaching. Flexible grouping of children across classrooms has helped to alleviate children's sense of isolation while engaging them in meaningful literacy experiences. Parents have found that they are valuable to the school community. Overall, children are experiencing success in acquiring English through their active engagement with literacy.

SECONDARY EDUCATION: EQUITY AND QUALITY ISSUES FOR LANGUAGE MINORITY STUDENTS

by Rosalie Giacchino-Baker

The challenges faced by elementary schools in planning and implementing programs appropriate to meet the needs of diverse student populations are compounded at the secondary level. The passage of eight years or more increases the expectations for linguistic and academic proficiency in all students, yet the preparation that language minority students bring to the secondary school can vary immensely. The task of providing appropriate programs for such a wide range of students is formidable. The following conversation among high school teachers illustrates typical attitudes on the part of educators whose schools are rapidly changing in demographics. The subsequent presentation of issues puts into perspective the needs of secondary schools.

Overheard in a Teachers' Lounge: A Case Study[1]

"Can we talk about something else? I'm about ready to get sick talking about ESL students. Let's talk about Christmas or anything."

The lights were twinkling on the Christmas tree in the third-floor teachers' lounge. Looking relaxed in the high-ceilinged, sun-filled room, seven instructors sat on couches and chairs around the coffee table. The lunch period had begun, and the smell of microwave popcorn filled the air as the group ate their lunches. Barbara Vasquez had just left to duplicate handouts for her sixth-period Spanish class and for her friend Nancy Henry's sheltered math class.

The teachers had formed friendships as well as uneasy truces during short lunchtime breaks spent discussing personal plans, complaining about administrators, and occasionally comparing notes on individual students.

Dan Terrell, the biology teacher, walked in late. He was greeted by Sam Lopez, the outspoken history teacher, who yelled, "What's the matter? Can't you tell those wetbacks to get lost so you can eat some lunch? We haven't seen you in here for a while."

Conversation continued with only slight glances toward Dorothy Martin, the ESL teacher, who spent countless hours counseling recent immigrants at Capital High. Dorothy shot a disapproving look at Sam and chose to continue her discussion with Bob Tyler, a substitute teacher. This was Bob's second week at Capital High. He had been hired on an emergency teaching credential that allowed him to teach the Level III English-as-a-Second-Language class even though he had only just begun the teacher education program at a local university. Dorothy had shared her materials with him after he had confided to her that his degree in English and a few weeks of teaching at a private school had left him feeling very inadequate with ESL students.

This day, Dorothy was giving Bob some background on Capital High. Others in the group also found themselves listening. "When Capital High

---

[1]The scene from the teacher's lounge is a synthesis of dialogues that took place during an eighteen-month study on the campus of a southern California high school identified by the pseudonym Capital High, as presented in Giacchino-Baker (1992). All of the teachers speak in their own voices, under different names. Only two, Sam Lopez and Chris Richardson, are composites of several instructors on the staff.

School's campus was built as a community college in 1911, people were really proud of the wood-paneled library and administration building. The town welcomed the college as a sign of its growth and maturity. When the campus became a high school in the 'thirties, it still felt like a college campus because of all the different departmental buildings and the athletic facilities."

"This place is huge," interrupted Bob.

"You said it," said Sam. "Over sixty-five acres—and all the shaded grassy areas and cement benches offer great places for gangs to get together and plan how to outsmart teachers. With buildings scattered all over the place, there's no way anyone can patrol this place."

Dan Terrell took one look at Dorothy's face and decided to act as intermediary, "Not all students in this school are gang members, Sam. You know that."

"We all know that," agreed Chris Richardson, another English teacher. "Capital High has gotten a lot of bad publicity lately. Not that many of our students are directly involved, but they sure have suffered from the tensions from gang activity in this area. I'm tired of seeing the cops on campus."

"Who isn't?" said Dorothy. "I'm especially worried about recent immigrants who are natural targets for the gangs. Many Mexican-Americans won't have anything to do with the recent immigrants. They call them *nopaleros*, cactus eaters, or *mojados*, wetbacks. The new kids are offered helping hands by the gang members who demand unquestioning obedience in return. I haven't met a single newcomer who hasn't been approached at least once to join a gang.

"Most of Capital High's students can't afford to live in the big homes near this school," Dorothy continued. "Those areas to the east and south of campus are a step up from the barrios of Los Angeles, but the gangs have discovered this low-income housing, too. Only a few of my students' families can afford the new housing that's springing up outside of town."

Turning to Bob, Dorothy continued, "Student populations at Capital High have really changed over the years. Like all schools in our district, it is experiencing a steady increase in language minority students. About half of our students have Spanish surnames. European-Americans form less than 40 percent of the student body, with African-Americans accounting for about 8 percent and Asians about 3 percent of our students. We aren't teaching the same kind of kids we taught in the past."

"Yeah," quipped Sam. "Think of everything we could be doing if our staff wasn't kept busy processing students who keep moving to find jobs, to live with different relatives, or to move back to Mexico."

"Why do you always blame the students, Sam?" Dorothy rejoined. "When was the last time you talked to students to get their side of the story? No one at this school keeps track of students who leave school before graduation or even where students attend school—if they're lucky enough to graduate."

"I talk to the students every day," Sam started to say as Barbara Vasquez walked back in the room with her pile of handouts in one hand and an apple in the other. Barbara listened carefully, expecting to disagree with him as she usually did.   "As I was saying," continued Sam, "these kids aren't going to make it unless they learn to speak English. In my class I tell them I don't want to hear any Spanish, even among themselves. Students have complained, but I tell them that they have to get with English speakers to make it. Some of my students have gone to Cal State, but only by cutting themselves off from Spanish and trying hard in English."

By this time, Barbara could stand it no more. She almost choked on her bite of apple as she said, "Students talk to me, too, Sam. They talk to me in Spanish because that's the only way they can tell me what's really in their hearts. They tell me how they can't understand why some of their Mexican teachers don't let them ask questions in Spanish. They're not talking about their ESL classes where the teachers help them understand and speak English. They're talking about history and economics classes which they are thrown into without academic background or English language skills. My Spanish classes are the only ones that are offered at this school for native speakers of Spanish. These kids have questions that could easily be answered through cooperative learning groups where they could help each other in Spanish. They are having trouble with basic concepts, Sam. Once they understand the concepts in Spanish, you only have to help them get the English labels."

All eyes turned to Sam, who had started to interrupt: "Some of these kids speak English better than we do. They don't even belong in my sheltered history class. We're spoonfeeding them, Barbara. Nobody helped me when I came here from Mexico. I made it."

"I couldn't agree more," said Chris, who teaches both remedial and honors English classes. "I don't know which of my students came from ESL classes, and it wouldn't make any difference if I did. They have to learn the same stuff anyway. I teach the same way if they're ESL students or not."

"But it's not working," Barbara exploded. "Only about 75 percent of Latinos graduate from high school. I think kids don't make it because of work responsibilities and a lack of support by teachers and counselors. Quiet ones, especially girls, get overlooked. I was lucky to be identified as bright, and teachers nurtured me. Others aren't so lucky. Expectations have to be high for all students. They need to be treated like individuals. So many of them are really bright. They can't help it if they weren't well educated in Mexico. If we tell them they can do it, they will succeed."

"The system sets up barriers for them at every turn," added Dorothy. "How can teachers run around trying to help students navigate through a biased system? Why are schedules so inflexible? I've had it with the tracking system at this school! We constantly isolate LEP students. They are stuck in classes by themselves or with low-achieving students. Why are my ESL kids always put into remedial classes?"

Chris and Dorothy had been friends for years, but they usually avoided talking about language minority students. Chris could not let Dorothy's statements go unchallenged. "Get off your bandwagon, Dorothy. My tax dollars are being spent to pay for illegal immigrants to crowd our classes so that nobody can learn. They're never going to graduate anyway. They can't speak English."

Dorothy countered, "Kids in this school are placed in classes based on their English proficiency, not on their academic interests or backgrounds. We have made it impossible for ESL students to get courses they need to graduate, much less go to college."

"These kids aren't going to four-year colleges. Kids in this school generally just don't make it," said Sam with a knowing smirk.

"Let's back up a minute to what you were saying about placements. I've been wondering what was happening in my Basic Math classes," said Nancy Henry, who had been listening carefully. "A lot of my kids don't belong in there. Gabriel and Claudio were telling me the other day that they were studying algebra when they left Mexico. No wonder they look bored when we add decimals. I should try to get some of those kids out of there and into algebra, but we don't have a teacher who'll teach it in Spanish or as a sheltered class. Staying in my class doesn't do anything for their self-esteem."

"That's the problem," said Dorothy. "They start to see themselves as others see them. Other people think they're slow, so they start to doubt their own abilities. In the process, they're falling farther and farther behind academically. Adriana came to see me the other day. I just found out that she didn't get rescued from the remedial English class. She is now convinced that she can't do any better. She told me that her class was very easy, that they hardly did anything. She doesn't read books; she does workbook exercises! "

Dan Terrell, the sheltered science teacher, cleared his throat and seemed to phrase his thoughts carefully. "The work my ESL students do is every bit as challenging as what the native English speakers do. I spend a lot of time doing demonstrations and developing vocabulary. I use picture files, specimens, and laser disk materials, anything that will make them understand what I'm saying. They show me they understand through activities like making model DNA or doing dissections. They can help each other in Spanish during these activities. We use the regular text. I chose it because it has good supporting graphic organizers and illustrations that support the scientific vocabulary. I just wish I had had more time to prepare audiovisual and hands-on materials. It takes careful planning. But really, it's just good teaching."

"Textbooks and materials are a big issue," agreed Dorothy. "My ESL kids often bring their books from other classes for me to help them. Most of them are much too difficult for them to read. Take José, for example. He was placed in a sheltered U.S. history class because he is seventeen years old. He hadn't studied English during seven years of schooling in Mexico. When discussing his work in U.S. history class, José admitted that he understands almost nothing in the book. How can José be expected to read about and analyze the difference between the Federalist and anti-Federalist systems of government in English when he is still unable to fill out basic forms in our language?"

"My biggest problem is that I can only get one set of the books we're reading in English for all of my classes," chimed in Chris. "Some kids take longer to read, but I can't let them take books home. They'll just have to learn to read under time pressure."

"Eventually, yes, but they are just starting to do academic stuff in English. They can't do everything at once. Even with our tight budgets I made sure my kids have biology books they can read at home," added Dan Terrell.

"I still say it would be easier for the beginners to take science, history, and other academic subjects in Spanish," said Barbara.

"Of course, you would," said Chris, who glanced at her watch, noting that the bell would ring in about five minutes. "Can we talk about something else? I'm about ready to get sick talking about ESL students. Let's talk about Christmas or anything."

For the next five minutes, they only talked about Christmas.

Issues for Limited-English-Proficient Students: The Bottom Line

Many high schools in the United States are not "user-friendly," equitable, or efficient places of learning for language minority students. Only recently have researchers begun to focus on why dropout rates for adolescent LEP students are so high. The findings of five studies (Berman et al., 1992; Giacchino-Baker, 1992; Lucas, Henze, & Donato, 1990; Sobul, 1984; Tikunoff et al., 1991) present similar conclusions about the severity of the problems and the desperate need for reforms.

Secondary schools have been identified as the weakest links in our educational systems. Studies within the past decade (Boyer, 1983; Goodlad, 1984; Kozol, 1992; Sizer, 1984, 1992; Welsh, 1986) have focused on problems that include general confusion over the roles of secondary education, coursework that is irrelevant to students' lives, class scheduling that fragments learning; ineffectiveness of traditional teaching methods, large class sizes, overt or covert tracking systems, inequitable distribution of resources, and authoritarian administrative structures that inhibit shared governance and interdisciplinary teaching and communication. All these conditions compound the challenges that language minority students have to face in becoming literate in a second language while meeting graduation requirements and preparing for postsecondary vocational and/or academic success.

Minicucci and Olsen's 1992 study of secondary school LEP students pinpointed several problems. First, there is a *lack of appropriate theoretical and operational models of second language acquisition for older students.* Teenage LEP students walk through high school doors with an alarm clock ticking loudly. They race against a five- to seven-year clock (Cummins, 1981a; Krashen, Long, & Scarcella, 1979) to develop cognitive academic language proficiency (CALP) in English and meet graduation requirements before they are forced by law to leave the public school system. If they have already spent time in effective U.S. elementary and/or middle schools, they stand the greatest chance of graduating from high school and achieving the cognitive benefits of additive bilingualism before they are nineteen. Other potentially successful students include those who have been educated in their home countries and who enter a high school program that allows them to take coursework in their primary language while developing proficiency in English. Unfortunately, many LEP students in high schools lack literacy skills in their first language and the educational backgrounds equivalent to their U.S. peers. They may be unable to catch up academically in programs that do not provide strong English language development and coursework in primary languages.

The second major problem area is a *lack of access to the core curriculum*. When language minority students enter a high school, they are usually placed in classes on the basis of language proficiency rather than previous academic background. Once in the remedial ESL classes, students often are not permitted to schedule higher level academic courses. On the other hand, students may be placed in academic courses that are taught in English, classes that they are not able to understand. Some high schools depend on sheltered classes to meet the needs of LEP students, regardless of English proficiency or previous academic background. Sheltered content classes are most effective for LEP students who have already achieved an intermediate level of fluency in English. For non-English-speaking students, classes in their primary languages allow them direct access to the core curriculum. In the survey by Minicucci and Olsen (1992a), only 6 of the 27 surveyed high schools gave LEP students full access to the core curriculum.

The third type of problem related to LEP students in secondary schools is a *critical shortage of secondary teachers, counselors, and administrators with appropriate linguistic and cultural education and experiences.* Many teachers have not been given appropriate preservice or inservice education about second language acquisition processes or the challenges faced by linguistically and culturally diverse students. Language minority students struggle without appropriate counseling and instruction. The result may be that high schools shuffle students from one office and classroom to another. LEP students look in vain for information they can understand and role models with whom they can identify.

The fourth type of problem has been identified as a *scarcity of appropriate textbooks and materials*. Most LEP students are placed in academic classes where English textbooks are too difficult for them to read. Very few of them have access to materials in their primary language or to academically challenging texts in English that have been adapted to their reading levels. These LEP students face page after page of dense text with few supporting graphic organizers or illustrations. Students often cannot take these books from the classroom, a limitation that reduces the time available for them to read their assignments.

Inaccurate and inefficient assessment and reclassification procedures are the fifth problem. Language minority students are often hastily assessed. Content area teachers are seldom informed of these students' language proficiency level in either their native language or English. Reassessment procedures also vary; often, however, once students have been designated LEP, few are reclassified as FEP and gain access to the mainstream curriculum.

The sixth problem in secondary schools, and perhaps the most difficult to resolve, is that of *departmentalized structures and scheduling complexities.* Most schools lack flexibility in scheduling. All students must take classes in similar sequences. In the case of LEP students, schools do not provide options for those with different linguistic and/or academic backgrounds.

Recommendations for Improvement

Berman et al. (1992) make several recommendations for secondary school reform that will improve schooling for language minority students.

- Develop principles and practices for effective education of LEP students at the secondary level.
- Disseminate information about how to adapt education for a variety of different demographic populations.
- Include information on cultural and linguistic diversity into teaching credential programs.
- Develop a set of assessment measures that enables teachers to diagnose the needs of language minority students.
- Increase funding for materials, programs, and services for secondary-level language minority students.

On the basis of research at six secondary schools in California and Arizona that successfully promoted the achievement of their Latino students, Lucas, Henze, and Donato (1990) found eight characteristics that led to success. These characteristics create opportunities for language minority students.

- Value is placed on the students' languages and cultures.
- High expectations of language minority students are made concrete.
- School leaders make the education of language minority students a priority.
- Staff development is explicitly designed to help teachers and other staff members serve language minority students more effectively.

- A variety of courses and programs for language minority students are offered.
- A counseling program gives special attention to language minority students.
- Parents of language minority students are encouraged to become involved in their children's education.
- School staff members share a strong commitment to empowering language minority students through education.

Reforming the secondary schools in the United States is a process that involves a change in attitude and skills on the part of teachers, staff, and administrators. The same principles that promote academic success at the elementary level also apply to secondary schools. However, elementary schools and secondary schools differ in one respect: Secondary students are closer to the end of their school career and the community at large exerts pressure on the schools to produce results. Teachers may feel that their power to create a difference for language minority students is more limited at the secondary level, but this may be a misconception. See Díaz-Rico (1993) for an example of positive change that took place in a middle school. Teachers who are skilled in techniques that promote crosscultural, language, and academic development can make a difference in the education of language minority students.

Literacy, in addition to the ability to raise a voice and be heard, is the foundation for participation in a democratic society. Teachers who work in English language development help students to acquire English in an environment of respect for the primary language. Students who have acquired English fluency are more powerful participants in the social, political, and economic realms of their nation and the world. Even more powerful are those who have preserved a home language during the process of acquiring English. And most powerful yet are those students who maintain their cultural values as they accommodate to life in the United States. They are important ambassadors for a key U.S. value: the ability to accept and accommodate the diverse peoples of this nation. With one foot in the native or immigrant culture and the other foot planted firmly in U.S. mainstream culture, these students are in a position to enrich their families, their schools, their neighborhoods, and their communities, as well as themselves.

Appendix *A*

The Continuity Model for English Language Development

K. Weed and L. Díaz-Rico

Basic Principles

The Continuity Model for English Language Development provides a teacher/class configuration that promotes uninterrupted student progress. The model is based on several key English language development principles. First, students understand English more readily when they receive instruction in a meaningful, comprehensible manner. Second, students' cognitive development is accelerated when they receive quality instruction in language that they can understand. Third, students learn to speak and understand English more rapidly when they participate in cooperative, meaningful activities with language-heterogeneous peer groups.

Classroom Configuration

Explanation of the configuration (Figure A-1). Students are placed in one of three classroom configurations: Non-English-speaking (NES) students are in one class; limited-English proficient (LEP) and monolingual English-only (EO) students are grouped together in another class; fluent English proficient (FEP) and monolingual English-only students are grouped in a third class. Students stay in their respective classes for literature and language arts instruction. During science and social studies, students are regrouped across linguistic abilities. Students work cooperatively so that those

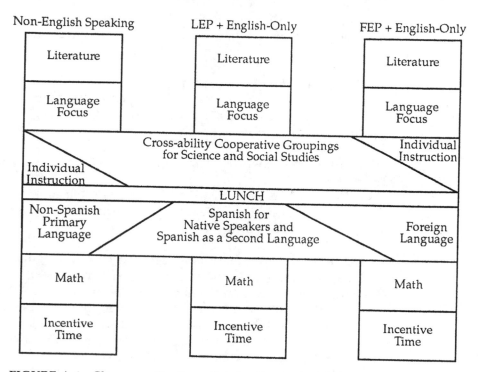

FIGURE A-1   Classroom Configuration for Continuity Model

with lesser English ability are able to work with more proficient peers. Teachers work and plan cooperatively with one other (linked) class. Individual instruction during this period aids those who need highly structured learning or who develop projects needing additional attention. During the afternoon, students are involved in native speaker/foreign language classes. A particularly strong feature of the program is the opportunity for English-only students to experience learning in a second language. Parents and community volunteers are invited to help with the primary languages that are not spoken by any of the school staff. Students again return to their homeroom for instruction in mathematics. Incentive time is provided at the end of the day for continuing work on projects, for creative activities, and/or for homework under the guidance of a tutor or peer.

Goals and Assumptions

Meaningful student-centered curriculum. Within the scope and sequence of the designated learning curriculum, students are given opportunities to choose topics of interest. Assessment of learning is carried out within the context of instruction. Teachers strive to articulate concepts to individuals in ways that they can best assimilate. Students are encouraged to *produce* as well as *consume* knowledge.

Clear goals and objectives for language development. Milestones of language achievement are clearly delineated for students and teachers. The staff continually records and reports students' language progress. Parents are involved in celebrating achievement.

Thinking skills, writing, and concept formation focus. The language modalities on which maximum focus is placed are thinking skill development, writing, and concept formation. Reading, spelling, and oral language skills are not assessed independently of the cognitive and expressive content of communication, which is considered primary.

Commitment to primary language and foreign language development. Language development occurs best in an environment in which students and staff alike are committed to acquiring bilingual skills, those students and staff members who are not dual language speakers work hard to acquire a second language, and the school staff extends language awareness to the community by promoting communication both in the home language and in English. Educational materials are available in many home languages, and bilingual communication with parents is promoted using translators.

Teachers linked for cooperative planning. Because students are grouped for cooperative learning and peer language stimulation across classes, teachers need to cooperate for planning, lesson development, and evaluation. Thematic units, materials, and resources can be shared between or among cooperating teachers.

Strong identification between student and assigned teacher. While students are grouped for cooperative learning and peer language stimulation across classes, no teacher is responsible for more than 45 students during the year, and no class contains more than 30 students at one time.

Daily peer language stimulation across ability levels. Cooperative groups in content extension areas such as science and social studies encourage heterogeneous language grouping across proficiency levels. Teachers are responsible for creating heterogeneous groups and teaching cooperative learning skills.

Availability of individual attention for extra mediation and enrichment. Students who need additional time and attention to absorb instructional materials or closer adult mediation can be placed in smaller groups with volunteer teachers while other children work cooperatively with more independence. Small group instruction can also be made available for students whose projects are more sophisticated and who need expert collaboration to locate resources or explain challenging concepts.

Opportunity for students to do supervised homework in school. Many students whose home environment is not conducive to homework completion may benefit from instructional time set aside for supervised homework completion at the end of each day. This encourages an atmosphere of serious study at the end of each day. Those students who have demonstrated homework completion may use this time to identify resources or carry out sustained silent reading.

Supervised homework opportunity: Minimum of 15 minutes of reading and math. Parents need to be informed of a constant requirement for homework. Reading with parents may take place in the home language or in English and is documented with a sheet to be filled out each evening and submitted on Friday. Math homework is predictable and reviewed daily. It may be skills-based or creatively formatted, but it requires parents' signature upon completion. In this way, parents can be informed about and involved with their child's math progress.

Bibliography

Ada, A. (1989, Summer). Los libros mágicos. *California Tomorrow,* pp. 42–44.

Adamson, H. (1993). *Academic competence.* New York: Longman.

Addison, A. (1988, November). Comprehensible textbooks in science for the nonnative English-speaker: Evidence from discourse analysis. *The CATESOL Journal, 1*(1), 49–66.

Af Trampe, P. (1994). Monitor theory: Application and ethics. In R. Barasch & C. James (Eds.). *Beyond the monitor model.* Boston: Heinle and Heinle.

Agar, M. (1980). *The professional stranger: An informal introduction to ethnography.* Orlando, FL: Academic Press.

Alderson, J., Krahnke, K., & Stansfield, C. (Eds.). (1987). *Reviews of English language proficiency tests.* Washington, DC: Teachers of English to Speakers of Other Languages.

Allen, E., & Valette, R. (1977). *Classroom techniques. Foreign languages and English as a second language.* San Diego, CA: Harcourt Brace Jovanovich.

Allport, G. (1954). *The nature of prejudice.* Garden City, NY: Doubleday Anchor.

American Association for the Advancement of Science (AAAS). (1989). *Science for all Americans.* Washington, DC: Author.

Amery, H. (1979). *The first thousand words: A picture word book.* London: Usborne Publishing.

Amery, H., & Milá, R. (1979). *The first thousand words in Spanish.* London: Usborne Publishing.

Andersen, J., & Powell, R. (1988). Cultural influences on educational processes. In L. Samovar & R. Porter (Eds.). *Intercultural communication: A reader,* 5th ed. Belmont, CA: Wadsworth.

Andersen, J., & Powell, R. (1991). Intercultural communication and the classroom. In L. Samovar & R. Porter (Eds.), *Intercultural communication: A reader,* 6th ed. Belmont, CA: Wadsworth.

Anti-Defamation League of B'nai B'rith. (1986). *A world of difference.* New York: Author.

Armour, M., Knudson, P., & Meeks, J. (1981). *The Indochinese: New Americans.* Provo, UT: Brigham Young University Language Research Center.

Arvizu, S. (1992). Home–school linkages: A cross-cultural approach to parent participation. In M. Saravia-Shore & S. Arvizu (Eds.), *Cross-cultural literacy: Ethnographies of communication in multiethnic classrooms.* New York: Garland.

Asher, J. (1982). *Learning another language through actions: The complete teachers' guidebook.* Los Gatos, CA: Sky Oaks.

Asher, J., & Garcia, R. (1969). The optimal age to learn a foreign language. *Modern Language Journal, 8:* 334–341.

Association for Supervision and Curriculum Development (ASCD). (1987). *Building an indivisible nation: Bilingual education in context.* Alexandria, VA: Author.

Au, K., & Jordan, C. (1981). Teaching reading to Hawaiian children: Finding a culturally appropriate solution. In H. Trueba, G. Guthrie, & K. Au (Eds.), *Culture and the bilingual classroom: Studies in classroom ethnography.* Rowley, MA: Newbury House.

Baker, C. (1993). *Foundations of bilingual education and bilingualism.* Clevedon, England: Multilingual Matters.

Baker, K. (1987). Comment on Willig's "A meta analysis of selected studies of bilingual education." *Review of Educational Research, 57*(3), 351–362.

Banks, C. (1993). Parents and teachers: Partners in school reform. In J. Banks & C. Banks (Eds.). *Multicultural education: Issues and perspectives.* Boston: Allyn and Bacon.

Banks, S. (1989, November 21). Schools are frustrated by bilingual class demands. *Los Angeles Times,* pp. A1, A24.

Barnitz, J. (1985). *Reading development of nonnative speakers of English.* Center for Applied Linguistics. Orlando, FL: Harcourt Brace Jovanovich.

Barrett, J. (1978). *Cloudy with a chance of meatballs.* New York: Scholastic Books.

Benedict, R. (1934). *Patterns of culture.* New York: New American Library.

Bennett, C. (1986). *Comprehensive multicultural education: Theory and practice.* Boston: Allyn and Bacon.

Bennett, C. (1990). *Comprehensive multicultural education: Theory and practice,* 2nd ed. Boston: Allyn and Bacon.

BEOutreach (1993, March). *A glossary for diversity,* 4(1), 2.

Berman, P., Chambers, J., Gandara, P., McLaughlin, B, Minicucci, C., Nelson, B., Olsen, L., & Parrish, T. (1992). *Meeting the challenge of language diversity. An evaluation of programs for pupils with limited proficiency in English.* Berkeley, CA: BW Associates.

Bilingual Education Office. (1987). *Guide for bilingual education advisory committees.* Sacramento: California State Department of Education.

Birdwhistell, R. (1974). The language of the body: The natural environment of words. In A. Silverstein (Ed.), *Human communication: Theoretical explorations.* Hillsdale, NJ: Lawrence Erlbaum.

Bliatout, B., Downing, B., Lewis, J., & Yang, D. (1988). *Handbook for teaching Hmong-speaking students.* Folsom, CA: Folsom Cordova Unified School District, Southeast Asia Community Resource Center.

Blot, D., & Davidson, D. (1988). *Put it in writing.* New York: Newbury House.

Bodinger-deUriarte, C. (1991, December). The rise of hate crime on school campuses. *Research Bulletin, Phi Delta Kappa,* No 10.

Bolinger, D., & Sears, D. (1981). *Aspects of language,* 3rd ed. New York: Harcourt Brace Jovanovich.

Bosnos, D. (1991). Mathing: A whole language process. In Y. Goodman, W. Hood, & K. Goodman, (Eds.), *Organizing for whole language.* Portsmouth, NH: Heinemann.

Bovee, T. (1991, September 18). San Bernardino, Ontario gain ethnic majorities. *San Bernardino County Sun,* p. A8.

Boyer, E. (1983). *High school: A report on secondary education in America.* New York: Harper & Row.

Bransford, J., & Baca, L. (1984). Bilingual special education: Issues in policy development and implementation. In L. Baca & H. Cervantes (Eds.). *The bilingual special education interface.* St. Louis, MO: Times Mirror/Mosby.

Bratt Paulston, C. (1992). *Sociolinguistic perspectives on bilingual education.* Clevedon, England: Multilingual Matters.

Breen, M., & Candlin, C. (1979). The essentials of a communicative curriculum in language teaching. *Applied Linguistics, 1*(2), 99–104.

Brinton, D., Snow, M., & Wesche, M. (1989). *Content-based second language instruction.* New York: Newbury House.

Brooks, N. (1968). *Language and language learning: Theory and practice.* New York: Harcourt Brace Jovanovich.

Brown, D. (1987). *Principles of language learning and teaching,* 2nd ed. Englewood Cliffs, NJ: Prentice-Hall.

Brown, G., & Yule, G. (1983). *Discourse analysis.*

Cambridge, England: Cambridge University Press.

Brown, R. (1973). *A first language: The early stages.* Cambridge, MA: Harvard University Press.

Bunting, E. (1988). *How many days to America?* New York: Clarion.

Bye, M. (1975). *Reading in math and cognitive development.* Unpublished manuscript. (ERIC Document Reproduction Service No. ED 124 926).

Caine, R., & Caine, G. (1991). *Making connections.* Alexandria, VA: Association for Supervision and Curriculum Development.

Calderón, M., Tinajero, J., & Hertz-Lazarowitz, R. (1992, Spring). Adapting cooperative integrated reading and composition to meet the needs of bilingual students. *Journal of Educational Issues of Language Minority Students, 10,* Special Issue, 79–106.

California State Department of Education. (1977). *Guide for multicultural education, content and context.* Sacramento: Author.

California State Department of Education. (1984) *Individual learning programs for limited-English-proficient students.* Sacramento: Author.

California State Department of Education. (1985). *Model curriculum standards: Grades 9–12.* Sacramento: Author.

California State Department of Education. (1987). *Guide for bilingual education advisory committees.* Sacramento: Author.

California State Department of Education. (1988a). *Annotated directory of resources for the emergency immigrant education program.* Sacramento: Author.

California State Department of Education. (1988b). *Recommended readings in literature, kindergarten through grade eight.* Sacramento: Author.

California State Department of Education. (1989). *Foreign language framework.* Sacramento, CA.

California State Department of Education. (1990). *Recommended readings in literature, Kindergarten through grade eight, Addendum.* Sacramento: Author.

California State Department of Education. (1992). *Handbook for teaching Korean-American students.* Sacramento: Author.

Canale, M. (1983). From communicative competence to communicative language pedagogy. In J. Richards & R. Schmidt (Eds.), *Language and communication.* New York: Longman.

Carlson, L. (1970). The Negro in science. In J. Roucek & T. Kiernan (Eds.), *The Negro impact on western civilization.* New York: Philosophical Library.

Cartagena, J. (1991). English only in the 1980s: A product of myths, phobias, and bias. In S. Benesch (Ed.), *ESL in America: Myths and possibilities.* Portsmouth, NH: Boynton/Cook.

Casteñada v. *Pickard,* 648 F.2d 989 (5th Cir. 1981).

Cazden, C. (1986). ESL teachers as language advocates for children. In P. Rigg & V. Allen (Eds.), *When they don't all speak English.* Urbana, IL: National Council of Teachers of English.

Cazden, C. (1988). *Classroom discourse.* Portsmouth, NH: Heinemann.

Cazden, C., & Leggett, E. (1981). Culturally responsive education: Recommendations for achieving Lau remedies II. In H. Trueba, G. Guthrie, & K. Au (Eds.), *Culture and the bilingual classroom.* Rowley, MA: Newbury House.

Celce-Murcia, M. (Ed.). (1991). *Teaching English as a second or foreign language,* 2nd ed. New York: Newbury House.

Celce-Murcia, M., & Goodwin, J. (1991). Teaching pronunciation. In M. Celce-Murcia (Ed.), *Teaching English as a second or foreign language,* 2nd ed. New York: Newbury House.

Chamot, A., & O' Malley, J. (1987). The cognitive academic language learning approach: A bridge to the mainstream. *TESOL Quarterly, 21*(2), June, 227–249.

Chamot, A., & O' Malley, J. (1989). The cognitive academic language learning approach. In P. Rigg and V. Allen, (Eds.), *When they don't all speak English.* Urbana, IL: National Council of Teachers of English.

Charles, C. (1983). *Elementary classroom management.* New York: Longman.

Cheng, L. (1987). English communicative competence of language minority children: Assessment and treatment of language "impaired" preschoolers. In H. Trueba (Ed.), *Success or failure? Learning and the language minority student.* Boston, MA: Heinle and Heinle.

Cherry, F. (1970). Black American contributions to western civilization in philosophy and social science. In J. Roucek & T. Kiernan (Eds.), *The Negro impact on western civilization.* New York: Philosophical Library.

Chesterfield, R., & Chesterfield, K. (1985). Natural order in children's use of second language learning strategies. *Applied Linguistics, 6,* 45–59.

Cheung, O., & Solomon, L. (1991). *Summary of state practices concerning the assessment of and the data collection about limited English proficient (LEP) students.* Washington, DC: Council of Chief State School Officers.

Chomsky, N. (1959). Review of B. F. Skinner, "Verbal Behavior." *Language, 35,* 26–58.

Chung, H. (1989). *Working with Vietnamese high school students.* (Available from New Faces of Liberty/SFSC, P.O. Box 5646, San Francisco, CA 94101.)

Claire, E. (1990). *This is me.* San Francisco: Alta Book Company.

Clark, R., Moran, P., & Burrows, A. (1991). *The ESL miscellany: A treasury of cultural and linguistic information,* 2nd ed. Brattleboro, VT: Pro Lingua Associates.

Cochran, C. (1989, Summer). *Strategies for involving LEP students in the all-English-medium classroom: A cooperative learning approach.* Washington, DC: National Clearinghouse for Bilingual Education.

Cohen, A. (1991). Second language testing. In M. Celce-Murcia (Ed.), *Teaching English as a second or foreign language,* 2nd ed. New York: Newbury House.

Cohen, E., DeAvila, E., Navarrete, C., & Lotan, R. (1988). *Finding out/descubrimiento implementation manual.* Stanford, CA: Stanford University Program for Complex Instruction.

Cohen, E., Lotan, R., & Catanzarite, L. (1990). Treating status problems in the cooperative classroom. In S. Sharon (Ed.), *Cooperative learning: Theory and research.* New York: Praeger.

Cohen, R. (1969). Conceptual styles, cultural conflict, and nonverbal tests of intelligence. *American Anthropologist, 71,* 828–856.

College Composition and Communication. (1974). *Students' rights of language.* Urbana, IL: National Council of Teachers of English.

Collie, J., & Slater, S. (1987). *Literature in the language classroom.* Cambridge: Cambridge University Press.

Collier, V. (1987). Age and rate of acquisition of second language for academic purposes. *TESOL Quarterly, 21*(4), 617–641.

Corder, S. (1978). Language-learner language. In J. Richards (Ed.), *Understanding second and foreign language learning: Issues and approaches.* Rowley, MA: Newbury House.

Corson, D. (1990). *Language policy across the curriculum.* Clevedon, England: Multilingual Matters.

Cortés, C. (1993). Acculturation, assimilation, and "adducation." *BEOutreach, 4*(1), 3–5.

Crago, M. (1993). Communicative interaction and second language acquisition: An Inuit example. *TESOL Quarterly 26*(3), 487–506.

Crandall, J. (Ed.). (1987). *ESL through content-area instruction: Mathematics, science, social studies.* Englewood Cliffs, NJ: Regents/Prentice-Hall.

Crandall, J., Dale, T., Rhodes, N., & Spanos, G. (1987). *English skills for algebra.* Englewood Cliffs, NJ: Regemts-Prentice-Hall.

Crawford, J. (1991) *Bilingual education: History, politics, theory, and practice,* 2nd ed. Los Angeles: Bilingual Educational Services.

Crawford, J. (1992). *Hold your tongue: Bilingualism and the politics of "English only."* Reading, MA: Addison-Wesley.

Crawford, L. (1993). *Language and literacy learning in multicultural classrooms.* Boston: Allyn and Bacon.

Criston, L. (1993, May 23). Has he stepped out of the shadow? *Los Angeles Times Calendar,* pp. 6, 70, 72.

Crookall, D., & Oxford, R. (1991). Dealing with anxiety: Some practical activities for language learners and teacher trainees. In E. Horwitz & D. Young (Eds.), *Language anxiety: From theory and research to classroom implications.* Englewood Cliffs, NJ: Prentice Hall.

Cudog, W., Castro, E., & Carillo, V. (1991). *Authentic portfolio assessment: Evaluating students' performance in a whole language curriculum.* Paper presented at the California Association for Bilingual Education Annual Conference, Anaheim.

Cummins, J. (1976). The influence of bilingualism on cognitive growth: A synthesis of research findings and explanatory hypothesis. *Working papers on bilingualism, 9,* 1–43.

Cummins, J. (1979a). Cognitive/academic language proficiency, linguistic interdependence, the optimum age question and some other matters. *Working papers on bilingualism 19,* 121–129.

Cummins, J. (1979b). Linguistic interdependence and the educational development of bilingual children. *Review of Educational Research, 49(2),* 222–251.

Cummins, J. (1980). The cross-lingual dimensions of language proficiency: Implications for bilingual education and the optimal age issue. *TESOL Quarterly, 14(2),* 175–187.

Cummins, J. (1981a). Age on arrival and immigrant second language learning in Canada: A reassessment. *Applied Linguistics 2(2),* 132–149.

Cummins, J. (1981b). The role of primary language development in promoting educational success for language minority students. In *Schooling and language minority students: A theoretical framework.* Sacramento: California State Department of Education.

Cummins, J. (1982, February). Tests, achievement, and bilingual students. *Focus,* No. 9. Wheaton, MD: National Clearinghouse for Bilingual Education.

Cummins, J. (1984). *Bilingualism and special education: Issues in assessment and pedagogy.* San Diego: College-Hill.

Cummins, J. (1986, February). Empowering minority students: A framework for intervention. *Harvard Educational Review, 56(1),* 18–36.

Cummins, J. (1989). *Empowering minority students.* Sacramento, CA: California Association for Bilingual Education.

Cummins, J. (1990). Reflections on "empowerment." *California Association for Bilingual Education Newsletter, 12(3),* 7, 11.

Curran, C. (1982). Community language learning. In R. Blair (Ed.), *Innovative approaches to language teaching.* Rowley, MA: Newbury House.

Dale, T., & Cuevas, G. (1987). Integrating language and mathematics learning. In J. Crandall (Ed.), *ESL through content-area instruction: Mathematics, science, social studies.* Englewood Cliffs, NJ: Regents/Prentice Hall.

Dale, T., & Cuevas, G. (1992). Integrating mathematics and language learning. In P. Richard-Amato & M. Snow (Eds.), *The multicultural classroom.* White Plains, NY: Longman.

Darder, A. (1991). *Culture and power in the classroom.* New York: Bergen and Garvey.

De Ávila, E., Duncan, S., & Navarrete, C. (1992). *Finding out/descubrimiento.* Compton, CA: Santillana.

Delgado-Gaitan, C., & Trueba, H. (1991). *Crossing cultural borders: Education for immigrant families in America.* London: Falmer Press.

dePaola, T. (1975). *The cloud book.* New York: Holiday House.

Derman-Sparks, L., & Anti-Bias Curriculum Task Force. (1988). *Anti-bias curriculum: Tools for empowering young children.* Washington, DC: National Association for the Education of Young Children.

deUnamuno, M. (1925). *Essays and soliloquies.* New York: Knopf.

Deyhle, D. (1987). Learning failure: Tests as gatekeepers and the culturally different child. In H. Trueba, (Ed.), *Success or failure? Learning and the language minority student.* Boston: Heinle and Heinle.

Díaz, R. (1983). Thought and two languages: The impact of bilingualism on cognitive development. *Review of Research in Education, 10,* 23–34.

Díaz-Rico, L. (1991). Increasing oral English in the university classroom: Strengthening the voice of the multinational student. *Fine Points.* California State University, San Bernardino: Office of Faculty Development.

Díaz-Rico, L. (1993). From monocultural to multicultural teaching in an inner-city middle school. In A. Woolfolk (Ed.), *Readings and cases in educational psychology.* Boston: Allyn and Bacon.

Dicker, S. (1992). Societal views of bilingualism and language learning. *TESOL: Applied Linguistics Interest Section Newsletter, 14(1),* 1, 4.

Dobbs, J. (1992). Music as multicultural education. In P. Richard-Amato & M. Snow (Eds.),

The multicultural classroom. White Plains, NY: Longman.

Doggett, G. (1986). *Eight approaches to language teaching.* Washington, DC: Center for Applied Linguistics/ERIC Clearinghouse on Languages and Linguistics.

Doheny, K. (1993, January 19). Something catchy? *Los Angeles Times,* p. E2.

Doyle, W. (1983). Academic work. *Review of Educational Research, 53,* 287–312.

Dulay, H., Burt, M., & Krashen, S. (1982). *Language two.* New York: Oxford University Press.

Dumont, R. (1972). Learning English and how to be silent: Studies in Sioux and Cherokee classrooms. In C. Cazden, V. John, & D. Hymes (Eds.), *Functions of language in the classroom.* New York: Teachers College Press.

Duncan, S., & DeAvila, E. (1979). Bilingualism and cognition: Some recent findings. *NABE Journal, 4*(1), 15–50.

Dunlop, I. (1994). The true and the new. In R. Barasch & C. James (Eds.), *Beyond the monitor model.* Boston: Heine and Heine.

Dwyer, J. (1991). Talking in class. In J. Dwyer (Ed.), *"A sea of talk."* Portsmouth, NH: Heinemann.

Eakin, S. (1985). Vital signs. *American Journal of Semiotics 3,* 1–17.

Early, M. (1990). Enabling first and second language learners in the classroom. *Language Arts, 67* (October), 567–574.

Eckert, A. (1992). *Sorrow in our heart.* New York: Bantam.

Edelsky, C. (1991). *With literacy and justice for all: Rethinking the social in language and education.* London: Falmer Press.

Edelsky, C., Altwerger, B., & Flores, B. (1991). *Whole language: What's the difference?* Portsmouth, NH: Heinemann.

Edmonson, M. (1971). *Lore: An introduction to the science of fiction.* New York: Holt, Rinehart and Winston.

Eisner, E. (1985). *The educational imagination,* 2nd ed. New York: Macmillan.

Ellis, R. (1986). *Understanding second language acquisition.* Oxford: Oxford University Press.

Ellis, R. (1988). *Classroom second language development.* New York: Prentice-Hall.

Ellis, R. (1994). Variability and the natural order hypothesis. In R. Barasch & C. James (Eds.), *Beyond the monitor model.* Boston, MA: Heinle and Heinle.

Enright, D., & McCloskey, M. (1988). *Integrating English: Developing English language and literacy in the multilingual classroom.* Reading, MA: Addison-Wesley.

Erickson, F. (1977). Some approaches to inquiry in school-community ethnography. *Anthropology and Education Quarterly, 8*(2), 58–69.

Erickson, F., & Mohatt, G. (1982). Cultural organization of participant structures in two classrooms of Indian students. In G. Spindler (Ed.), *Doing the ethnography of schooling: Educational anthropology in action.* New York: Holt, Rinehart and Winston.

Escalante, J., & Dirman, J. (1990). The Jaime Escalante math program. *Journal of Negro Education, 59*(3), 407–423.

Evaluation Assistance Center–East. (1990, November). *State minimum competency testing practices.* Washington, DC: Georgetown University.

Feagin, J., & Feagin, C. (1993). *Racial and ethnic relations,* 4th ed. Englewood Cliffs, NJ: Prentice-Hall.

Farnan, N., & Fearn, L. (1991). *Developing writers: Process, craft, collaboration.* San Diego, CA: San Diego State University Developmental Writing Institute.

Ferguson, C. (1975). Toward a characterization of English foreigner talk. *Anthropological Linguistics, 17*(1), 1–14.

Fields, C. (1988, May–June). The Hispanic pipeline. *Change, 20*(3), 20–27.

Finnan, C. (1987). The influence of the ethnic community on the adjustment of Vietnamese refugees. In G. Spindler & L. Spindler (Eds.), *Interpretive ethnography of education: At home and abroad.* Hillsdale, NJ: Lawrence Erlbaum Associates.

Fischer, B., & Fischer, L. (1979, January). Styles in teaching and learning. *Educational Leadership, 36*(4), 245–251.

Fishman, J. (1973). Language modernization and planning in comparison with other types of national modernization and planning. *Language in Society, 2*(1), 23–42.

Flores, B., Garcia, E., Gonzalez, S., Hidalgo, G., Kaczmarek, K., & Romero, T. (1985). *Bilingual instructional strategies*. Chandler, AZ: Exito.

Flores, B., Tefft Cousin, P., & Díaz, E. (1991). Transforming deficit myths about learning language and culture. *Language Arts, 68,* 369-379.

Ford, M. (1992). *HELP: A holistic English literacy program for multiethnic elementary classrooms*. Unpublished master's project, California State University, San Bernardino.

Fox, B. (1987). *Discourse structure and anaphora*. Cambridge, England: Cambridge University Press.

Freeman, D., & Freeman, Y. (1992a). Is whole language teaching compatible with content-based instruction? *The CATESOL Journal* 5(1), 103-105.

Freeman, Y., & Freeman, D. (1992b). *Whole language for second language learners*. Portsmouth, NH: Heinemann.

Friedlander, M. (1991, Fall). *The newcomer program: Helping immigrant students succeed in U.S. schools*. Washington, DC: National Clearinghouse for Bilingual Education.

Fries, C. (1945). *Teaching and learning English as a foreign language*. Ann Arbor: University of Michigan.

From the Classroom. (1991). *Teachers seek a fair and meaningful assessment process to measure LEP students' progress*. Fountain Valley, CA: Teacher Designed Learning. 2(1) 1, 3.

Fromkin, V., & Rodman, R. (1983). *An introduction to language,* 3rd ed. New York: Holt, Rinehart and Winston.

Fulwood, S. III. (1991, June 13). California is most racially diverse state. *Los Angeles Times,* pp. A3, A30.

Fulwood, S. III. (1992, January 9). Segregation of Latino students increases. *Los Angeles Times,* p. A14.

Funaki, I., & Burnett, K. (1993). *When educational systems collide: Teaching and learning with Polynesian students*. Paper presented at the Association of Teacher Educators Annual Conference, Los Angeles.

Furey, P. (1986). A framework for cross-cultural analysis of teaching methods. In P. Byrd (Ed.), *Teaching across cultures in the university ESL program*. Washington, DC: National Association of Foreign Student Advisors.

Gadda, G., Peitzman, F., & Walsh, W. (1988). *Teaching analytical writing*. Los Angeles: UCLA Publishing.

Galambos, S., & Goldin-Meadow, S. (1990). The effects of learning two languages on metalinguistic development. *Cognition, 34,* 1–56.

Galvan, A., Macias, R., Magallan, R., & Orum, L. (1986). *Are English language amendments in the national interest? An analysis of proposals to establish English as the official language of the United States*. Claremont, CA: The Tomás Rivera Center.

Garcia, E. (1993, Winter). Linguistic diversity and national standards. *Focus on Diversity* 3(1), 1–2. University of California, Santa Cruz: Bilingual Research Group.

Gardner, R., & Lambert, W. (1972). *Attitudes and motivation in second language learning*. Rowley, MA: Newbury House.

Gatbonton, E., & Segalowitz, N. (1988). Creative automatization: Principles for promoting fluency within a communicative framework. *TESOL Quarterly, 22*(3), 473–492.

Gattegno, C. (1982). Much language and little vocabulary. In R. Blair (Ed.), *Innovative approaches to language teaching*. Rowley, MA: Newbury House.

Gay, G. (1975, October). Cultural differences important in education of Black children. *Momentum,* pp. 30–32.

Genesee, F. (1984). The social-psychological significance of bilingual code switching for children. *Applied Psycholinguistics, 5*(1), 3–20.

Giacchino-Baker, R. (1992). *Recent Mexican immigrant students' opinions of their use and acquisition of English as a second language in an "English-only" American high school: A qualitative study*. Unpublished doctoral dissertation, Claremont Graduate School, Claremont, CA.

Gibson, M. (1987). Punjabi immigrants in an American high school. In G. Spindler & L. Spindler (Eds.), *Interpretive ethnography of education: At home and abroad*. Hillsdale, NJ: Lawrence Erlbaum Associates.

Gibson, M. (1991a). Ethnicity, gender and social class: The school adaptation patterns of West

Indian youths. In M. Gibson & J. Ogbu (Eds.), *Minority status and schooling. A comparative study of immigrant and involuntary minorities.* New York: Garland.

Gibson, M. (1991b). Minorities and schooling: Some implications. In M. Gibson & J. Ogbu (Eds.), *Minority status and schooling. A comparative study of immigrant and involuntary minorities.* New York: Garland.

Gillett, P. (1989a). *Cambodian refugees: An introduction to their history and culture.* (Available from New Faces of Liberty/SFSC, P.O. Box 5646, San Francisco, CA 94101.)

Gillett, P. (1989b). *El Salvador: A country in crisis.* (Available from New Faces of Liberty/SFSC, P.O. Box 5646, San Francisco, CA 94101.)

Ginsburg, H. (1986). The myth of the deprived child: New thoughts on poor children. In U. Neisser (Ed.), *The school achievement of minority children: New perspectives.* Hillsdale, NJ: Lawrence Erlbaum Associates.

Giroux, H. (1983). Theories of reproduction and resistance in the new sociology of education: A critical appraisal. *Harvard Educational Review, 53,* 257–293.

Glaser, S., & Brown, C. (1993). *Portfolios and beyond: Collaborative assessment in reading and writing.* Norwood, MA: Christopher-Gordon.

Glick, E. (1988, August 8). English-only: New handicap in world trade. *Los Angeles Times.*

Golebiowska, A. (1987). *Getting students to talk.* Hertfordshire, England: Prentice-Hall International.

Gomez v. Illinois State Board of Education, 811 F. 2d 1030 (7th Cir. 1987).

Gonzalez, R. (1990). When minority becomes majority: The changing face of English classrooms. *English Journal, 79*(1), 16–23.

Good, T., & Brophy, J. (1984). *Looking in classrooms,* 3rd ed. New York: Harper & Row.

Goodlad, J. (1984). *A place called school: Prospects for the future.* New York: McGraw-Hill.

Goodman, K. (1986). *What's whole in whole language.* Portsmouth, NH: Heinemann.

Goodman, K., Bird, L., & Goodman, Y. (Eds.). (1991). *The whole language catalog.* Santa Rosa, CA: American School.

Goodman, K., Goodman, Y., & Hood, W. (1989).

The whole language evaluation book. Portsmouth, NH: Heinemann.

Goodman, Y., & Burke, C. (1980). *Reading strategies: Focus on comprehension.* New York: Holt, Rinehart and Winston.

Goodman, Y., Hood, W. J., & Goodman, K. (Eds.). (1991). *Organizing for whole language.* Portsmouth, NH: Heinemann.

Goody, J. (1968). *Literacy in traditional societies.* Cambridge, England: Cambridge University Press.

Gordon, M. (1964). *Assimilation in American life.* New York: Oxford University Press.

Grabe, W., & Kaplan, R. (1990). Writing in a second language: Contrastive rhetoric. In D. Johnson & D. Roen (Eds.), *Richness in writing: Empowering ESL students.* New York: Longman.

Graham, C. (1978a). *Jazz chants.* New York: Oxford University Press.

Graham, C. (1978b). *Jazz chants for children.* New York: Oxford University Press.

Graham, C. (1986). *Small talk.* New York: Oxford University Press.

Graham, C. (1988). *Jazz chant fairy tales.* New York: Oxford University Press.

Grant, C., & Sleeter, C. (1986). *After the school bell rings.* Philadelphia: Falmer.

Graves, D. (1983). *Writing: Teachers and children at work.* Portsmouth, NH: Heinemann.

Greenbaum, S., & Quirk, R. (1990). *A student's grammar of the English language.* Harlow, England: Longman.

Greene, M. (1986). Landscapes on meaning. *Language Arts, 63,* 776–784.

Guiora, A., Beit-Hallami, B., Brannon, R., Dull, C., & Schovel, T. (1972). The effects of experimentally induced changes in ego states on pronunciation ability in second language: An exploratory study. *Comprehensive Psychiatry, 13,* 421–428.

Gunderson, L. (1991). *ESL literacy instruction: A guidebook to theory and practice.* Englewood Cliffs, NJ: Regent-Prentice-Hall.

Hakuta, K. (1986). *Mirror of language.* New York: Basic Books.

Hall, E. (1959). *The silent language.* New York: Anchor Books.

Halliday, M. (1975). *Learning how to mean: Explorations in the development of language.* London, England: Edward Arnold.

Halliday, M. (1978). *Language as a social semiotic.* Baltimore, MD: University Park Press.

Halliday, M., & Hasan, R. (1976). *Cohesion in English.* London, England: Longman.

Hardt, U. (1992, Spring). Teaching multicultural understanding. *Oregon English Journal 14*(1), 3–5.

Harel, Y. (1992). Teacher talk in the cooperative learning classroom. In C. Kessler (Ed.), *Cooperative language learning.* Englewood Cliffs, NJ: Prentice-Hall.

Harkness, S. (1971). Cultural variation in mother's language. *Word, 27,* 495–498.

Harris, V. (1992). *Teaching multicultural literature in grades K–8.* Norwood, MA: Christopher-Gordon.

Harste, J., Short, K., & Burke, C. (1988). *Creating classrooms for authors.* Portsmouth, NH: Heinemann.

Hart, L. (1975). *How the brain works: A new understanding of human learning, emotion, and thinking.* New York: Basic Books.

Hart, L. (1983). *Human brain, human learning.* New York: Longman.

Hatch, E. (1978). *Second language acquisition: A book of readings.* Rowley, MA: Newbury House.

Hatch, E. (1979). "Apply with caution." *Studies in Second Language Acquisition, 2,* 123–143.

Hatch, E. (1992). *Discourse and language education.* Cambridge, England: Cambridge University Press.

Haycock, K., & Navarro, M. (1988). *Unfinished business: Fulfilling our children's promise.* (Available from The Achievement Council, 1016 Castro Street, Oakland, CA 94607.)

Hayes, C., Bahruth, R., & Kessler, C. (1991). *Literacy con cariño.* Portsmouth, NH: Heinemann.

Hazen, R., & Trefly, J. (1991). Science literacy: The enemy is us. *Science, 251,* 266–267.

Heald-Taylor, G. (1986). *Whole language strategies for ESL students.* San Diego, CA: Dormac.

Heath, S. (1983a). Language policies. *Society, 20*(4), 56–63.

Heath, S. (1983b). *Ways with words.* Cambridge: Cambridge University Press.

Hernandez, R. (1993, November 9). Use of terms "Anglo" and "Hispanic" is justifiable. *San Bernardino County Sun,* p. A9.

Hernández-Chávez, E. (1984). The inadequacy of English immersion as an educational approach for language minority students. *Studies on immersion education: A collection for U.S. educators.* Sacramento: California State Department of Education.

Highsmith, J. (1990, March 15). Educating the new immigrants. *CSU Academic Senator, 19*(3), 3.

Hispanic Concerns Study Committee. (1987). *Hispanic Concerns Study Committee Report.* (Available from National Education Association, 1201 Sixteenth Street, N.W., Washington, DC 20036.)

Holt, D., Chips, B., & Wallace, D. (1992, Summer). *Cooperative learning in the secondary school: Maximizing language acquisition, academic development, and social development.* Washington, DC: National Clearinghouse for Bilingual Education.

Hornsby, D. (1991). *Understanding whole language.* Workshop presentation, Riverside, California.

Horwitz, E., Horwitz, M., & Cope, J. (1991). Foreign language classroom anxiety. In E. Horwitz & D. Young (Eds.), *Language anxiety: From theory and research to classroom implications.* Englewood Cliffs, NJ: Prentice-Hall.

Hudelson, S. (1986). ESL children's writing: What we've learned, what we're learning. In P. Rigg & D. Enright (Eds.) *Children and ESL: Integrating perspectives.* Washington, DC: Teachers of English to Speakers of Other Languages.

Hudelson, S. (1987). The role of native language literacy. *Language Arts, 64*(8), 827–841.

Hudelson, S. (1989). Teaching English through content-area activities. In P. Rigg & V. Allen (Eds.), *When they don't all speak English.* Urbana, IL: National Council of Teachers of English.

Human touch: Instructor tailors grading. (1993, June 28). *San Bernardino County Sun,* p. B1.

Huynh, D. (n.d.). *What's your name? A study in cultural differences.* Oakland: Multifunctional Resource Center, Northern California and Southwest Center for Educational Equity.

Hyland, C. (1989, Summer). What we know about the fastest growing minority population:

Hispanic Americans. *Educational Horizons, 67*(4), 131–135.

Hymes, D. (1961). The ethnography of speaking. In T. Gladwin & W. Sturtevant (Eds.), *Anthropology and human behavior*. Washington, DC: Anthropological Society of Washington.

Hymes, D. (1972). On communicative competence. In J. Pride & J. Holmes (Eds.), *Sociolinguistics*. Harmondsworth, UK: Penguin Books.

Idaho Migrant Council v. *Board of Education,* 647 F. 2d 69 (9th Cir. 1981).

Institute for Education in Transformation. (1992). *Voices from the inside: A report on schooling from inside the classroom*. (Available from The Institute for Education in Transformation at the Claremont Graduate School, 121 East Tenth Street, Claremont, CA 91711-6160.)

Ishii, S., & Bruneau, T. (1991). Silence and silences in cross-cultural perspective: Japan and the United States. In L. Samovar & R. Porter (Eds.), *Intercultural communication: A reader,* 6th ed. Belmont, CA: Wadsworth.

Jewell, M. (1976). Formal institutional studies and language. In W. O'Barr & J. O'Barr (Eds.), *Language and politics*. The Hague: Mouton.

Johns, K. (1992). Mainstreaming language minority students through cooperative grouping. *The Journal of Educational Issues of Language Minority Students, 11,* 221–231.

Johnston, J., & Johnston, M. (1990). *Content points*. Reading, MA: Addison-Wesley.

Jones, J. (1981). The concept of racism and its changing reality. In B. Bowser & R. Hunt (Eds.), *Impacts of racism on White Americans*. Beverly Hills, CA: Sage.

Joos, M. (1967). *The five clocks*. New York: Harcourt, Brace and World.

Jorgensen-Esmaili, K. (1988). *New faces of liberty: A curriculum for teaching about today's refugees and immigrants*. (Available from New Faces of Liberty/SFSC, P.O. Box 5646, San Francisco, CA 94101.)

Jussim, L. (1986). Self-fullfilling prophecies: A theoretical and integrative review. *Psychological Review, 93*(4), 429–445.

Kagan, S. (1986). Cooperative learning and sociocultural factors in schooling. In Bilingual Education Office. *Beyond language: Social and cultural factors in schooling language minority students*. Los Angeles: Evaluation, Dissemination and Assessment Center, California State University, Los Angeles.

Kagan, S. (1989). *Cooperative learning: Resources for teachers*. San Juan Capistrano, CA: Resources for Teachers.

Kaplan, R. (1967). Contrastive rhetoric and the teaching of composition. *TESOL Quarterly, 1*(4), 10–16.

Katz, N., & Lawyer, J. (1993). *Conflict resolution: Building bridges*. Thousand Oaks, CA: Corwin Press.

Kellogg, J. (1988, November). Forces of change. *Phi Delta Kappan, 70*(3), 199–204.

Kelly, C. (1991, September). Migrant program teaches Hmong students to read in their native language. *BEOutreach, 2*(2), 4.

Kessler, C., and Quinn, M. (1980). Positive effects of bilingualism on science problem-solving abilities. In J. Alatis (Ed.), *Current issues in bilingual education*. Washington, DC: Georgetown University Press.

Kessler, C., & Quinn, M. (1987). ESL and science learning. In J. Crandall (Ed.), *ESL through content-area instruction: Mathematics, science, social studies*. Englewood Cliffs, NJ: Regents/Prentice-Hall.

Kessler, C., Quinn, M., & Fathman, A. (1992). Science and cooperative learning for LEP students. In C. Kessler (Ed.), *Cooperative language learning*. Englewood Cliffs, NJ: Regents-Prentice-Hall.

Keyes v. *School District #1,* Denver, Colorado, 576 F. Supp. 1503 (D. Colo. 1983).

Kinsella, K. (1992). How can we move from comprehensible input to active learning strategies in content-based instruction? *The CATESOL Journal,* April, 5(1), 127–132.

Kintsch, W., & Greeno, J. (1985). Understanding and solving word arithmetic problems. *Psychological Review, 92*(I), 109–129.

Kitao, S. (1989). *Reading, schema theory and second language learners*. Tokyo: Eichosha Shinsha.

Kitzhaber, A., Sloat, C., Kilba, E., Love, G., Aly, L., & Snyder, J. (1970). Language/Rhetoric VI. In A. Kitzhaber (Ed.), *The Oregon curriculum: A sequential program in English*. New York: Holt, Rinehart and Winston.

Kleinfeld, J. (1988, June). Letter to the editor. *Harvard Education Letter, 4*(3).

Koch, A., & Terrell, T. (1991). Affective reactions of foreign language students to natural approach activities and teaching techniques. In E. Horwitz & D. Young (Eds.), *Language anxiety: From theory and research to classroom implications.* Englewood Cliffs, NJ: Prentice Hall.

Kopan, A. (1974). Melting pot: Myth or reality? In E. Epps (Ed.), *Cultural pluralism.* Berkeley, CA: McCutchan.

Kozol, J. (1992). *Savage inequalities. Children in America's schools.* New York: Crown.

Krashen, S. (1980). The theoretical and practical relevance of simple codes in second language acquisition. In R. Scarcella & S. Krashen (Eds.), *Research in second language acquisition.* Rowley, MA: Newbury House.

Krashen, S. (1981a). Bilingual education and second language acquisition theory. In *Schooling and language minority students: A theoretical framework.* Los Angeles: Evaluation, Dissemination and Assessment Center, California State University, Los Angeles.

Krashen, S. (1981b). *Second language acquisition and second language learning.* Oxford: Pergamon Press.

Krashen, S. (1982). *Principles and practice in second language acquisition.* Oxford: Pergamon Press.

Krashen, S. (1985). *The input hypothesis: Issues and implications.* New York: Longman.

Krashen, S. (1991, Spring). *Bilingual education: A focus on current research.* Washington, DC: National Clearinghouse for Bilingual Education.

Krashen, S. & Biber, D. (1988). *On course: Bilingual education's success in California.* Sacramento: California Association for Bilingual Education.

Krashen, S., Long, M., & Scarcella, R. (1979). Age, rate, and eventual attainment in second language acquisition. *TESOL Quarterly, 13*(4), 573–582.

Krashen, S., & Terrell, T. (1983). *The natural approach: Language acquisition in the classroom.* Oxford: Pergamon Press.

Kroeber, A., & Kluckhohn, C. (1952). *Culture: A critical review of concepts and definition, 47*(1).

Cambridge, MA: Peabody Museum of American Archaeology and Ethnology, Harvard University.

Kroll, B. (1991). Teaching writing in the ESL context. In M. Celce-Murcia (Ed.), *Teaching English as a second or foreign language,* 2nd ed. New York: Newbury House.

Labov, W. (1969). *The study of nonstandard English.* Urbana, IL: National Council of Teachers of English.

Labov, W. (1972). *Sociolinguistic patterns.* Philadelphia: University of Pennsylvania Press.

Lambert, W. (1984). An overview of issues in immersion education. In California Department of Education, *Studies on immersion education.* Sacramento.

Larimer, R., & Vaughn, S. (1993). *Real conversations.* Boston: Heinle and Heinle.

Larsen-Freeman, D. (1985). State of the art on input in second language acquisition. In S. Gass & C. Madden (Eds.), *Input in second language acquisition.* Cambridge, MA: Newbury House.

Larsen-Freeman, D., & Long, M. (1991). *Introduction to second language acquisition research.* London: Longman.

Lau v. Nichols, 414 U.S. 563 (1974).

Law, B., & Eckes, M. (1990). *The more-than-just-surviving handbook.* Winnipeg, Canada: Peguis.

Leathers, N. (1967). *The Japanese in America.* Minneapolis, MN: Lerner Publications.

LeCompte, M. (1981). The Procrustean bed: Public schools, management systems, and minority students. In H. Trueba, G. Guthrie, & K. Au (Eds.), *Culture and the bilingual classroom: Studies in classroom ethnography.* Rowley, MA: Newbury House.

Leki, I. (1990). Potential problems with peer responding in ESL writing classes. *The CATESOL Journal, 3,* 5–19.

Leki, I. (1992). *Understanding ESL writers.* Portsmouth, NH: Heinemann.

Lenneberg, E. (1967). *Biological foundations of language.* New York: Wiley.

Lessow-Hurley, J. (1990). *The foundations of dual language instruction.* White Plains, NY: Longman.

Levine, D., & Adelman, M. (1982). *Beyond lan-*

guage: Intercultural communication for English as a second language. Englewood Cliffs, NJ: Prentice-Hall.

Lotan, R., & Benton, J. (1989). Finding out about complex instruction: Teaching math and science in heterogeneous classrooms. In N. Davidson, (Ed.), *Cooperative learning in mathematics: A handbook for teachers.* Menlo Park, CA: Addison-Wesley.

Lozanov, G. (1982). Suggestology and suggestopedia. In R. Blair (Ed.), *Innovative approaches to language teaching.* Rowley, MA: Newbury House.

Lucas, T. (1991). Individual variation in students' engagement in classroom personal journal writing. *The CATESOL Journal,* 4(1), 7–39.

Lucas, T., Henze, R., & Donato, R. (1990). Promoting the success of Latino language-minority students: An exploratory study of six high schools. *Harvard Educational Review,* 60(3), 315–340.

Lustig, M. (1988). Value differences in intercultural communication. In L. Samovar & R. Porter (Eds.), *Intercultural communication: A reader,* 5th ed. Belmont, CA: Wadsworth.

Lyons, J. (1993). NABE makes recommendations for federal elementary and secondary education programs. *NABE News,* 16(3), 1, 20, 21.

Macnamara, J. (1973). The cognitive strategies of language learning. In J. Oller & J. Richards (Eds.), *Focus on the learner.* Rowley, MA: Newbury House.

Madrid, A. (1991). Diversity and its discontents. In L. Samovar & R. Porter (Eds.), *Intercultural communication: A reader,* 6th ed. Belmont, CA: Wadsworth.

Maeroff, G. (1991, December). Assessing alternative assessment. *Phi Delta Kappan,* 73(4), 272–281.

Malavé, L. (1991). Conceptual framework to design a programme intervention for culturally and linguistically different handicapped students. In L. Malavé & G. Duquette (Eds.), *Language, culture and cognition.* Clevedon, England: Multilingual Matters.

Martel, M. (1991, September). Project OCEAN focuses on marine science. *BEOutreach,* 2(2), 4.

Martin, C. (1981). *Games, contests and relays.* Boston: American Press.

Marton, W. (1994). The antipedagogical aspects of Krashen's theory of second language acquisition. In R. Barasch & C. James (Eds.), *Beyond the monitor model.* Boston: Heinle and Heinle.

Matute-Bianchi, M. (1991). Situational ethnicity and patterns of school performance among immigrant and nonimmigrant Mexican-descent students. In M. Gibson & J. Ogbu (Eds.), *Minority status and schooling.* New York: Garland.

McCrum, R., Cran, W., & MacNeil, R. (1986). *The story of English.* New York: Elisabeth Sifton Books.

McDermott, R., & Gospodinoff, K. (1981). Social contexts for ethnic borders and school failure. In H. Trueba, G. Guthrie, & K. Au (Eds.). *Culture and the bilingual classroom: Studies in classroom ethnography.* Rowley, MA: Newbury House.

McLaughlin, B. (1987). *Theories of second-language learning.* London: Arnold.

McLaughlin, B. (1990). "Conscious" versus "unconscious" learning. *TESOL Quarterly,* 24(4), 617–634.

McLaughlin, B. (1992). *Myths and misconceptions about second language learning: What every teacher needs to unlearn.* Santa Cruz, CA: National Center for Research on Cultural Diversity and Second Language Learning.

Mehan, H. (1981). Ethnography of bilingual education. In H. Trueba, G. Guthrie, & K. Au (Eds.). *Culture and the bilingual classroom: Studies in classroom ethnography.* Rowley, MA: Newbury House.

Meyer v. *Nebraska,* 262 U.S. 390 (1923).

Milk, R. (1985). The changing role of ESL in bilingual education. *TESOL Quarterly,* 19(4), 657–672.

Miller, G. (1985). Nonverbal communication. In V. Clark, P. Eschholz, & A. Rosa (Eds.), *Language: Introductory readings,* 4th ed. New York: St. Martin's Press.

Minicucci, C., & Olsen, L. (1992a). *Meeting the challenge of language diversity* Vol. 5. Berkeley, CA: BW Associates.

Minicucci, C., & Olsen, L. (1992b, Spring). *Programs for secondary limited English proficient students: A California study.* Washington, DC:

National Clearinghouse for Bilingual Education.

Moll, L., & Díaz, E. (1987). Change as the goal of educational research. *Anthropology and Education Quarterly, 18*(4), 330–311.

Morley, J. (1991a). Listening comprehension in second/foreign language instruction. In M. Celce-Murcia (Ed.), *Teaching English as a second or foreign language,* 2nd ed. New York: Newbury House.

Morley, J. (1991b). The pronunciation component in teaching English to speakers of other languages. *TESOL Quarterly, 25*(3), 481–520.

Moskowitz, G. (1978). *Caring and sharing in the foreign language class.* Cambridge, MA: Newbury House.

Murphy, J. (1991). Oral communication in TESOL: Integrating speaking, listening, and pronunciaion. *TESOL Quarterly, 25*(1), 51–76.

Murray, B. (1989). Talking when English is a foreign language. In J. Dwyer (Ed.), *"A sea of talk."* Portsmouth, NH: Heinemann.

Nash, P. (1991). ESL and the myth of the model minority. In S. Benesch (Ed.), *ESL in America.* Portsmouth, NH: Boynton/Cook.

National Council of La Raza. (1986). *The education of Hispanics: Status and implications.* Washington, DC: Office of Research, Advocacy and Legislation.

National Council of Teachers of Mathematics. (1989). *Curriculum and evaluation standards for school mathematics.* Reston, VA: Author.

National Education Association. (1991, December). *Focus on Hispanics: Ethnic report.* (Available from Human and Civil Rights, 1201 16th Street, N.W., Washington, DC 20036.)

Navarrete, C., Wilde, J., Nelson, C., Martínez, R., & Hargett, G. (1990, Summer). *Informal assessment in educational evaluation: Implications for bilingual education programs.* Washington, DC: National Clearinghouse for Bilingual Education.

Newman, J. (Ed.). (1985). *Whole language: Theory in use.* Portsmouth, NH: Heinemann.

Nieto, S. (1992). *Affirming diversity.* New York: Longman.

Nieves-Squires, S. (1991). *Hispanic women: Making their presence on campus less tenuous.* (Available from the Association of American Colleges, 1818 R Street, N.W., Washington, DC 20009.)

Niyekawa, A. (1982). Biliteracy acquisition and its sociocultural effects. In M. Chu-Chang, (Ed.), *Asian and Pacific-American perspectives in bilingual education.* New York: Teachers College Press.

Nummela, R., & Rosengren, T. (1986). What's happening in students' brains may redefine teaching. *Educational Leadership, 43*(8), 49–53.

Nunan, D. (1991). *Language teaching methodology: A textbook for teachers.* New York: Prentice-Hall.

Nunan, D. (1993, April). *Exploring perceptions of the teaching process.* Symposium chaired by L. Henrichsen, Twenty-seventh Annual Teachers of English to Speakers of Other Languages Convention, Atlanta, GA.

Ochs, E. (1982). Talking to children in Western Samoa. *Language in Society, 11,* 77–104.

Office for Civil Rights. (1976). Office for Civil Rights guidelines: Task force findings specifying remedies available for eliminating past educational practices ruled unlawful under *Lau v. Nichols.* In J. Alatis & K. Twaddell (Eds.), *English as a second language in bilingual education.* Washington, DC: Teachers of English to Speakers of Other Languages.

Ogbu, J. (1978). *Minority education and caste: The American system in cross-cultural perspective.* New York: Academic Press.

Ogbu, J., & Matute-Bianchi, M. (1986). Understanding sociocultural factors: Knowledge, identity, and school adjustment. In Bilingual Education Office, *Beyond language: Social and cultural factors in schooling language minority students.* Los Angeles, CA: Evaluation, Dissemination and Assessment Center, California State University, Los Angeles.

Oh, J. (1992). The effects of L2 reading assessment methods on anxiety level. *TESOL Quarterly, 26*(1), 172–176.

Olsen, L. (1988). *Crossing the schoolhouse border: Immigrant students and the California public schools.* San Francisco: California Tomorrow.

Olsen, L., & Dowell, C. (1989). *Bridges: Promising programs for the education of immigrant children.* San Francisco: California Tomorrow.

Olsen, R. (1992a). Community connections. *California Association for Bilingual Education Newsletter, 14*(5), 9.

Olsen, R. (1992b). Cooperative learning and social studies. In C. Kessler (Ed.), *Cooperative language learning.* Englewood Cliffs, NJ: Regents/Prentice-Hall.

O'Malley, J., Chamot, A., Stewner-Manzanares, G., Kupper, L., & Russo, R. (1985a). Learning strategies used by beginning and intermediate ESL students. *Language Learning, 35*(1), 21–40.

O'Malley, J., Chamot, A., Stewner-Manzanares, G., Kupper, L., & Russo, R. (1985b). Learning strategy applications with students of English as a second language. *TESOL Quarterly, 19*(3), 557–584.

Omaggio, A. (1986). *Teaching language in context.* Boston: Heinle and Heinle.

O'Neil, J. (1990). Link between style, culture proves divisive. *Educational Leadership, 48*(2), 8.

Ong, W. (1982). *Orality and literacy.* London: Methuen.

Ortiz, F. (1988). Hispanic-American children's experiences in classrooms: A comparison between Hispanic and non-Hispanic children. In L. Weis (Ed.), *Class, race, and gender in American education.* Albany: State University of New York Press.

Orum, L. (1986). *The education of Hispanics: Status and implications.* Washington, DC: National Council of La Raza.

Ouk, M., Huffman, F., & Lewis, J. (1988). *Handbook for teaching Khmer-speaking students.* Sacramento, CA: Spilman Printing.

Oxford, R. (1990). *Language learning strategies.* New York: Newbury House.

Oyama, S. (1976). A sensitive period for the acquisition of nonnative phonological system. *Journal of Psycholinguistic Research, 5,* 261–284.

Page, R. (1991). *Lower-track classrooms: A curricular and cultural perspective.* New York: Teachers College.

Pappas, C., Kiefer, B., & Levstik, L. (1990). *An integrated language perspective in the elementary school.* White Plains, NY: Longman.

Pasternak, J. (1994, March 29). Bias blights life outside Appalachia. *Los Angeles Times,* pp. A1, A16.

Payan, R. (1984). Language assessment for bilingual exceptional children. In L. Baca & H. Cervantes (Eds.), *The bilingual special education interface.* St. Louis, MO: Times Mirror/Mosby.

Peal, E., & Lambert, W. (1962). The relation of bilingualism to intelligence. *Psychological Monographs, 76*(546), 1–23.

Pearson, R. (1974). *Introduction to anthropology.* New York: Holt, Rinehart and Winston.

Peck, S. (1992, April). How can thematic ESL units be used in the elementary classroom? *The CATESOL Journal, 5*(1), 133–138.

Peitzman, F. (1989). The enabling and responsive teacher: Coaching the ESL writer. In Teachers of the California Writing Project, *From literacy to literature: Reading and writing for the language minority student.* Los Angeles: UCLA Publishing.

Peñalosa, F. (1980). *Chicano sociolinguistics, a brief introduction.* Rowley, MA: Newbury House.

Pennington, M., & Richards, J. (1986). Pronunciation revisited. *TESOL Quarterly, 20*(2), 207–223.

Pérez, B., & Torres-Guzman, M. (1992). *Learning in two worlds.* New York: Longman.

Philips, S. (1972). Participant structures and communicative competence: Warm Springs children in community and classroom. In C. Cazden, V. John, & D. Hymes (Eds.), *Functions of language in the classroom.* New York: Teachers College Press.

Phillips, J. (1978). College of, by and for Navajo Indians. *Chronicle of Higher Education, 15,* 10–12.

Pierce, L., & O'Malley, J. (1992, Spring). *Performance and portfolio assessment for language minority students.* Washington, DC: National Clearinghouse for Bilingual Education.

Policy Analysis Center of the National Council of La Raza. (1990, August). *Hispanic education: A statistical portrait, 1990.* Washington, DC: National Council of La Raza.

Pooley, R. (1977). The definition and determination of "correct" English. In G. Goshgariian (Ed.), *Exploring language.* Boston: Little, Brown.

Porter, R. (1990). *Forked tongue: The politics of bilingual education.* New York: Basic Books.

Postman, N., & Weingartner, C. (1973). *How to recognize a good school*. Bloomington, IN: Phi Delta Kappan Educational Foundation.

Quinn, M., & Molloy, M. (1992). "I learned to talk mathematics": Using cooperative groups with college minority students. In C. Kessler (Ed.), *Cooperative language learning*. Englewood Cliffs, NJ: Prentice-Hall.

Ramírez, J. (1992, Winter/Spring). Executive summary, final report: Longitudinal study of structured English immersion strategy, early-exit and late-exit transitional bilingual education programs for language-minority children. *Bilingual Research Journal, 16*(1,2), 1–62.

Ramirez, M. III. (1988). Cognitive styles and cultural democracy in action. In J. Wurzel, (Ed.), *Toward multiculturalism: A reader in multicultural education*. Yarmouth, ME: Intercultural Press.

Ramirez, M. III. (1991). *Psychotherapy and counseling with minorities*. New York: Pergamon Press.

Ramirez, M., & Castañeda, A. (1974). *Cultural democracy, bicognitive development and education*. New York: Academic Press.

Reyhner, J. (1992). American Indian bilingual education: The White House conference on Indian education and the tribal college movement. *NABE News, 15*(7), 7, 18.

Richard-Amato, P. (1988). *Making it happen*. White Plains, NY: Longman.

Richard-Amato, P., & Snow, M. (1992). Strategies for content-area teachers. In P. Richard-Amato & M. Snow (Eds.), *The multicultural classroom*. White Plains, NY: Longman.

Richards, J. (1978). *Understanding second and foreign language learning*. Rowley, MA: Newbury House.

Rigg, P. (1989). Language experience approach: Reading naturally. In P. Rigg & V. Allen (Eds.), *When they don't all speak English*. Urbana, IL: National Council of Teachers of English.

Rigg, P. (1991). Whole language in TESOL. *TESOL Quarterly, 25*(3), 521–542.

Rist, R. (1970). Student social class and teacher expectations: The self-fulfilling prophecy in ghetto education. *Harvard Educational Review, 40*(3), 70–110.

Rios v. Read. 75 Civ. 296 (U.S. District Ct Ed NY, 1977).

Rivers, W., & Temperley, M. (1978). *A practical guide to the teaching of English as a second or foreign language*. New York: Oxford University Press.

Roberts, P. (1985). Speech communities. In V. Clark, P. Eschholz, & A. Rosa (Eds.), *Language: Introductory readings*, 4th ed. New York: St. Martin's Press.

Robinson, D. (1988, December). *Language policy and planning*. Washington, DC: Center for Applied Linguistics/ERIC Clearinghouse on Languages and Linguistics.

Robinson, G. (1985). *Crosscultural understanding*. New York: Pergamon Institute of English.

Rodriguez, R., Prieto, A., & Rueda, R. (1984). Issues in bilingual/multicultural special education. *Journal of the National Association for Bilingual Education, 8*(3), 55–65.

Romero, M. (1991). *Integrating English language development with content-area instruction*. Paper presented at American Educational Research Association Annual Meeting, Chicago.

Rooks, G. (1990). *Can't stop talking*. New York: Newbury House.

Ross, S. (1993, March 3). Study: Latinos getting short end of the executive stick. *San Bernardino County Sun*, p. B8.

Roy, A. (1990). The English only movement. In P. Eschholz, A. Rosa, & V. Clark (Eds.), *Language awareness*, 5th ed. New York: St. Martin's.

Rubel, A., & Kupferer, H. (1973). The myth of the melting pot. In T. Weaver (Ed.), *To see ourselves: Anthropology and modern social issues*. Glenview, IL: Scott, Foresman.

Rubin, J. (1976). Language and politics from a sociolinguistic point of view. In W. O'Barr & J. O'Barr (Eds.), *Language and politics*. The Hague: Mouton.

Rueda, R. (1987). Social and communicative aspects of language proficiency in low-achieving language minority students. In H. Trueba (Ed.), *Success or failure? Learning and the language minority student*. New York: Newbury House.

Ruiz, R. (1984). Orientations in language planning. *NABE Journal, 8*(2), 15–34.

Rumelhart, D. (1977). Toward an interactive

model of reading. In S. Dornic (Ed.), *Attention and performance.* New York: Academic Press.

Rumelhart, D. (1980). Schemata: The building blocks of cognition. In R. Spiro, B. Bruce, & W. Brewer (Eds.), *Theoretical issues in reading comprehension.* Hillsdale, NJ: Lawrence Erlbaum Associates.

Rutherford, W. (1987). *Second language grammar: Learning and teaching.* Harlow, England: Longman.

Sadker, D., & Sadker, M. (1982). *Sex equity handbook for schools.* New York: Longman.

Samway, K. (1992, Spring). *Writers' workshop and children acquiring English as a non-native language.* Washington, DC: National Clearinghouse for Bilingual Education.

Sánchez, F. (1989). *What is primary language instruction?* Hayward, CA: Alameda County Office of Education.

Santillana Publishing Company & San Diego Unified School District. (1992). *Bridge to communication,* rev. ed. Compton, CA: Santillana.

Sasser, L. (1992). Teaching literature to language minority students. In. P. Richard-Amato & M. Snow (Eds.), *The multicultural classroom.* White Plains, NY: Longman.

Sattler, J. (1974). *Assessment of children's intelligence.* Philadelphia: W. B. Saunders.

Saville-Troike, M. (1976). *Foundations for teaching English as a second language: Theory and method for multicultural education.* Englewood Cliffs, NJ: Prentice-Hall.

Saville-Troike, M. (1978). *A guide to culture in the classroom.* Rosslyn, VA: National Clearinghouse for Bilingual Education.

Scafe, M., & Kontas, G. (1982). Classroom implications of culturally defined organizational patterns in speeches by Native Americans. In F. Barkin, E. Brandt, & J. Orstein-Galicia (Eds.), *Bilingualism and language contact: Spanish, English, and Native American languages.* New York: Teachers College Press.

Scarcella, R. (1990). *Teaching language minority students in the multicultural classroom.* Englewood Cliffs, NJ: Prentice-Hall.

Schrega, M. (1991). *Content connection activity book.* Compton, CA: Santillana.

Schultz, J., & Theophano, J. (1987). Saving place

and marking time: Some aspects of the social lives of three-year-old children. In H. Trueba (Ed.), *Success or failure?* Cambridge, MA: Newbury House Publishers.

Schuman, J. (1992). Multicultural art projects. In P. Richard-Amato & M. Snow (Eds.), *The multicultural classroom.* White Plains, NY: Longman.

Schumann, J. (1978a). The acculturation model for second-language acquisition. In R. Gringas (Ed.), *Second language acquisition and foreign language teaching.* Washington, DC: Center for Applied Linguistics.

Schumann, J. (1978b). Social and psychological factors in second language acquisition. In J. Richards (Ed.), *Understanding second and foreign language learning: Issues and approaches.* Rowley, MA: Newbury House.

Schunk, D. (1991). Self-efficacy and academic motivation. *Educational Psychologist, 26,* 207–232.

Scovel, T. (1991). The effect of affect on foreign language learning: A review of the anxiety research. In E. Horwitz & D. Young (Eds.), *Language anxiety: From theory and research to classroom implications.* Englewood Cliffs, NJ: Prentice Hall.

Scribner, S., & Cole, M. (1978). Literacy without schooling: Testing for intellectual effects. *Harvard Educational Review, 48,* 448–461.

Searfoss, L. (1989). Integrated language arts: Is it whole language? *The California Reader,* May–June.

Searfoss, L., Smith, C., & Bean, T. (1981). An integrated language strategy for second language learners. *TESOL Quarterly, 15,* 383–389.

Seelye, H. (1984). *Teaching culture.* Lincolnwood, IL: National Textbook Company.

Selinker, L. (1972). Interlanguage. *IRAL, 10*(3), 209–231.

Selinker, L. (1991). Along the way: Interlanguage systems in second language acquisition. In L. Malavé & G. Duquette (Eds.), *Language, culture and cognition.* Clevedon, England: Multilingual Lingual Matters.

Serna v. Portales Municipal Schools, 499 F. 2d 1147 (10th Cir. 1974).

Shade, B. and New, C.(1993). Cultural influences

on learning: Teaching implications. In J. Banks & C. Banks (Eds.), *Multicultural education: Issues and perspectives.* Boston: Allyn and Bacon.

Shannon, S. (1994). Introduction. In R. Barasch and C. James (Eds.). *Beyond the monitor model.* Boston: Heinle and Heinle.

Short, D. (1991, Fall). *Integrating language and content instruction: Strategies and techniques.* Washington, DC: National Clearinghouse for Bilingual Education.

Shuit, D., & McConnell, P. (1992, January 6). Calculating the impact of California's immigrants. *Los Angeles Times,* pp. A1, A19.

Shukoor, A. (1991). What does being bilingual mean to my family and me? *NABE Conference Program.* Washington, DC: National Association for Bilingual Education.

Shuter, R. (1991). The Hmong of Laos: Orality, communication, and acculturation. In L. Samovar & R. Porter (Eds.), *Intercultural communication: A reader,* 6th ed. Belmont, CA: Wadsworth.

Siegel, B. (1993, March 28). Fighting words. *Los Angeles Times Magazine,* pp. 14–16, 18, 20, 44, 46, 48.

Simmons, J. (1989). The writing process for ESL students. In Teachers of the California Writing Project. *From literacy to literature: Reading and writing for the language-minority student.* Los Angeles: UCLA Center for Academic Interinstitutional Programs.

Sindell, P. (1988). Some discontinuities in the enculturation of Mistassini Cree children. In J. Wurzel (Ed.), *Toward multiculturalism.* Yarmouth, ME: Intercultural Press.

Singleton, J. (1973). Schooling: Coping with education in a modern society. In T. Weaver (Ed.), *To see ourselves: Anthropology and modern social issues.* Glenview, IL: Scott, Foresman.

Sizer, T. (1984). *Horace's compromise: The dilemma of the American high school.* Boston: Houghton Mifflin.

Sizer, T. (1992). *Horace's school: Redesigning the American high school.* Boston: Houghton Mifflin.

Sizer, T., & Rogers, B. (1993, February). Designing standards: Achieving the delicate balance. *Educational Leadership, 50*(3), 25–26.

Skinner, B. (1957). *Verbal behavior.* New York: Appleton, Century, Crofts.

Skutnabb-Kangas, T. (1981). *Bilingualism or not: The education of minorities.* (L. Malmberg & D. Crane, Trans.) Clevedon, England: Multilingual Matters.

Skutnabb-Kangas, T. (1981, February 3). *Linguistic genocide and bilingual education.* Paper presented at the California Association for Bilingual Education, Anaheim, California.

Slavin, R. (1991). A synthesis of research on cooperative learning. *Educational Leadership, 48,* 71–82.

Sloan, S. (1991). *The complete ESL/EFL cooperative and communicative activity book.* Lincolnwood, IL: National Textbook Company.

Smallwood, B. (1991). *The literature connection: A read-aloud guide for multicultural classrooms.* Reading, MA: Addison-Wesley.

Snow, C., & Hoefnagel-Hoehle, M. (1978). The critical period for language acquisition: Evidence from second language learning. *Child Development, 49,* 1114–1118.

Sobul, D. (1984). *Bilingual policy and practice: Loose coupling among curriculum levels.* Unpublished doctoral dissertation, University of California, Los Angeles.

Sobul, D. (1994, February). *Strategies to meet the goals of SDAIE.* Presentation at California Association for Bilingual Education, San Jose.

Sosa, A. (1992). Bilingual education—Heading into the 1990s. *Journal of Educational Issues of Language Minority Students, 10* (Special Issue), 203–216.

Spradley, J. (1972). Foundations of cultural knowledge. In J. Spradley (Ed.), *Culture and cognition.* San Francisco: Chandler.

Steele, R. (1990). Culture in the foreign language classroom. *ERIC/CLL News Bulletin.* Washington Center for Applied Linguistics, *14*(1), 1, 4, 5, 12.

Stephens, M. (1993, January 17). Pop goes the world. *Los Angeles Times Magazine,* pp. 22–26, 34.

Suarez-Orozco, M. (1987). Towards a psychosocial understanding of Hispanic adaptation to American schooling. In H. Trueba (Ed.), *Success or failure? Learning and the language minority student.* Boston: Heinle and Heinle.

Sue, S., & Padilla, A. (1986). Ethnic minority issues in the United States: Challenges for the educational system. In Bilingual Education Office, *Beyond language: Social and cultural factors in schooling language minority students.* Los Angeles: Evaluation, Dissemination and Assessment Center, California State University, Los Angeles.

Suina, J. (1985). . . . And then I went to school. *New Mexico Journal of Reading, 5*(2).

Suzuki, B. (1989, November–December). Asian Americans as the "model minority." *Change, 21,* 12–19.

Tarone, E. (1981). Some thoughts on the notion of communication strategy. *TESOL Quarterly, 15*(3), 285–295.

Taylor, B. (1983). Teaching ESL: Incorporating a communicative, student-centered component. *TESOL Quarterly, 17*(1), 69–77.

Terrell, T. (1981). The natural approach in bilingual education. In *Schooling and language minority students: A theoretical framework.* Los Angeles: Evaluation, Dissemination and Assessment Center, California State University, Los Angeles.

Terrell, T. (1982). Teaching comprehension skills in the natural approach. *CATESOL Occasional Papers, 8,* 1–6.

Tharp, R. (1989a). Culturally compatible education: A formula for designing effective classrooms. In H. Trueba, G. Spindler, & L. Spindler (Eds.), *What do anthropologists have to say about dropouts?* New York: Falmer Press.

Tharp, R. (1989b, February). Psychocultural variables and constants: Effects on teaching and learning in schools. *American Psychologist, 44*(2), 349–359.

Thomas, E., & Robinson, H. (1972). *Improving reading in every class: A source book for teachers.* Boston: Allyn and Bacon.

Thonis, E. (1981). Reading instruction for language minority students. In *Schooling and language minority students: A theoretical framework.* Los Angeles: Evaluation, Dissemination and Assessment Center, California State University, Los Angeles.

Tikunoff, W., Ward, B., Romero, M., Lucas, T., Katz, A., Van Broekhuisen, L., & Castaneda, L. (1991, April). *Addressing the instructional needs of the limited English proficient student: Results of the exemplary SAIP descriptive study.* Symposium conducted at the American Educational Research Association, Chicago.

Tollefson, J. (1991). *Planning language, planning inequality.* London: Longman.

Torbert, M., & Schneider, L. (1992). Using low organized games in multicultural physical education. In P. Richard-Amato & M. Snow (Eds.), *The multicultural classroom.* White Plains, NY: Longman.

Trueba, H. (1989). *Raising silent voices.* Boston: Heinle and Heinle.

Trueba, H., Cheng, L., & Ima, K. (1993). *Myth or reality: Adaptive strategies of Asian Americans in California.* Washington, DC: Falmer Press.

Trueba, H., Moll, L., & Díaz. S. (1982). *Improving the functional writing of bilingual secondary school students.* (Final Report, NIE 400-81-0023). Washington, DC: National Institute of Education.

United States Commission on Civil Rights. (1978, August). *Social indicators of equality for minorities and women.* Report of the U.S. Commission on Civil Rights, Washington, DC.

United States Department of Education. (1991). *The condition of bilingual education in the nation.* A report to the Congress and the president. Washington, DC.

United States Department of Education, (1992a). *The condition of bilingual education in the nation.* A report from the secretary of education to the president and the Congress, Washington, DC.

United States Department of Education, (1992b). *The condition of education in the nation.* A report from the secretary of education to the president and the Congress, Washington, DC.

University of Texas at Austin. (1991, Spring). Individuals with Disabilities Education Act challenges educators to improve the education of minority students with disabilities. *Bilingual Special Education Perspective 10,* 1–6.

Valdés-Fallis, G. (1978). *Code switching and the classroom teacher.* Washington, DC: Center for Applied Linguistics.

Vobejda, B. (1990, June 8). Census: Hispanics more likely to live in poverty. *Washington Post,* p. A10.

Vygotsky, L. (1978). *Mind in society*. Cambridge, MA: Harvard University Press.

Waggoner, D. (Ed.). (1992). *Numbers and Needs*, 2(5). Washington, DC: Author.

Walz, J. (1982). *Error correction techniques for the FL classroom*. Washington, DC: Center for Applied Linguistics.

Waters, W. (1987). *Constructivist theory into practice in a secondary linguistic minority classroom: Shared teacher and student responsibility for learning*. Unpublished paper, Claremont Graduate School.

Watson, D., Northcutt, L., & Rydell, L. (1989, February). Teaching bilingual students successfully. *Educational Leadership, 46*(5), 59–61.

Weed, K. (1989). *Oral tradition in a literate society*. Unpublished manuscript.

Weed, K., & Johns, K. (1992). *First and second language learners together in the language arts*. Manuscript submitted for publication.

Wegrzecka-Monkiewicz, E. (1992, April). How can content-based instruction be implemented at the high school level? *The CATESOL Journal, 5*(1), 139-144.

Weinberg, M. (1990). *Racism in the United States: A comprehensive classified bibliography*. New York: Greenwood Press.

Weinstein-Shr, G. (1992). *Stories to tell our children*. Boston: Heinle and Heinle.

Welsh, P. (1986). *Tales out of school. A teacher's candid account from the front lines of the American high school today*. New York: Viking Penguin.

Whisler, N., & Williams, J. (1990). *Literature and cooperative learning*. Sacramento, CA: Literature Co-op.

Wiggins, G. (1989, April). Teaching to the (authentic) test. *Educational Leadership, 46*(6), 41–47.

Williams, M. (1981). Observations in Pittsburgh ghetto schools. *Anthropology and Education Quarterly, 12*(3), 211–220.

Williams, J. D., & Snipper, G. C. (1990). *Literacy and bilingualism*. White Plains, NY: Longman.

Willig, A. (1985). A meta-analysis of selected studies on the effectiveness of bilingual education. *Review of Educational Research, 55*(3), 269–317.

Wilson, W. (1984). The urban underclass. In L. Dunbar (Ed.). *Minority report*. New York: Pantheon Books.

Witte, K. (1991). The role of culture in health and disease. In L. Samovar & R. Porter (Eds.). *Intercultural communication: A reader*, 6th ed. Belmont, CA: Wadsworth.

Wittrock, M. (1978). The cognitive movement in instruction. *Educational Psychologist, 13*, 15–30.

Wolfram, W. (1991). *Dialects and American English*. Englewood Cliffs, NJ: Prentice-Hall.

Wollenberg, C. (1989). *The new immigrants and California's multiethnic heritage*. (Available from New Faces of Liberty/SFSC, P.O. Box 5646, San Francisco, CA 94101.)

Wong-Fillmore, L. (1980). Learning a second language: Chinese children in the American classroom. In J. Alatis (Ed.), *Georgetown University round table on languages and linguistics 1980: Current issues in bilingual education*. Washington, DC: Georgetown University Press.

Wong-Fillmore, L. (1985). When does teacher talk work as input? In S. Gass and C. Madden (Eds.), *Input for second language acquisition*. Cambridge, MA: Newbury House.

Wong-Fillmore, L. (with L. Meyer). (1990). The classroom as a social setting for language learning. Oakland, CA: Celebrating diversity conference.

Woolfolk, A. (1990). *Educational psychology*. Englewood Cliffs, NJ: Prentice-Hall.

Woolfolk, A., & Brooks, D. (1985). The influence of teachers' nonverbal behaviors on students' perceptions and performance. *Elementary School Journal, 85*, 514–528.

Worthen, B., & Spandel, V. (1991). Putting the standardized test debate in perspective. *Educational Leadership, 48*(5), 65–69.

Yao, E. (1988). Working effectively with Asian immigrant parents. *Phi Delta Kappan, 70*(3), 223–225.

Yep, L. (1975). *Dragonwings*. New York: Harper & Row.

Yorio, C. (1980). The teacher's attitude toward the student's output in the second language classroom. *CATESOL Occasional Papers*, California Association of Teachers of English to Speakers of Other Languages, November 1–8.

Zelman, N. (1986). *Conversational inspirations for ESL*. Brattleboro, VT: Pro Lingua Associates.

Author Index

317

Subject Index